AT WAR
WITH THE
WIND

★ ★ ★ ★ ★ ★ ★ ★ ★ ★ ★

**The Epic Struggle with Japan's
World War II Suicide Bombers**

DAVID SEARS

CITADEL PRESS
Kensington Publishing Corp.
www.kensingtonbooks.com

CITADEL PRESS BOOKS are published by

Kensington Publishing Corp.
119 West 40th Street
New York, NY 10018

All Kensington titles, imprints, and distributed lines are available at special quantity discounts for bulk purchases for sales promotions, premiums, fund-raising, educational, or institutional use. Special book excerpts or customized printings can also be created to fit specific needs. For details, write or phone the office of the Kensington special sales manager: Kensington Publishing Corp., 119 West 40th Street, New York, NY 10018, attn: Special Sales Department; phone 1-800-221-2647.

First trade paperback printing: November 2009

10 9 8 7 6 5 4 3 2 1

Printed in the United States of America

Library of Congress Control Number: 2008929361

ISBN-13: 978-0-8065-2894-6
ISBN-10: 0-8065-2894-X

To Stan, Lucy and Larry

★ Contents ★

AT WAR WITH THE WIND

★ ★ ★ ★ ★

Portents: *Cole* and *Lindsey*

A great trial in your youth made you different—made all of us different from what we could have been without it.

—Oliver Wendell Holmes

On 12 October 2000 the *Cole* (DDG-67), a U.S. Navy 8,600-ton cruise-missile-firing destroyer, entered the Yemeni port city of Aden for a routine fuel stop. The Republic of Yemen, a Persian Gulf state, had the reputation of being a safe haven for terrorists. Yemen's troubled history included ties to Saddam Hussein's Iraq.

Cole completed mooring in the harbor at 0930 local time and refueling began an hour later. Sailors wielding automatic weapons were posted as sentries on *Cole*'s decks, but rules of engagement were precise and strict: no firing unless directly fired upon or unless permission had been obtained from the ship's skipper or a duty officer. The rules would be of little use in what followed.

At 1118 a small skiff suddenly approached the *Cole*'s port side. As the skiff drew alongside, its passengers smiled and waved at watching crewmen. Then, just as suddenly, the boat exploded, blasting a jagged 40-by-40-foot hole at the ship's waterline. The explosion mangled *Cole*'s engineering and crew mess spaces and set off fires and flooding. It was evening before *Cole*'s crew had the damage under control. Seventeen sailors were killed and 39 were injured in the blast. Many corpses lay snared in mazes of twisted steel and wire.

It took nine days for work crews of divers, metal cutters, welders, and medical corpsmen to recover the 17 sailors' bodies. New plates welded to interior bulkheads created a watertight dike around the hull puncture, and millions of gallons of seawater flooding the lower decks were pumped out. Seventeen days later the patched-up *Cole* limped away from Aden harbor guided by four Yemeni harbor tugs.

As the ship cast off, its crew lined up at the bow and stern to salute a giant Stars and Stripes fluttering stiffly from the mast, raised from half-mast after the mourning period for the sailors who were killed. Along with "The Star-Spangled Banner," the recorded tunes blasted from the destroyer's loudspeakers included "America the Beautiful," "Anchors Aweigh," the Marine Hymn, and the choice of the *Cole*'s enlisted crew, a Kid Rock rap titled "American Bad Ass." The defiant posturing of its lyric ("The chosen one / I'm the living proof / With the gift of gab / From the city of truth") was probably lost on most Yemenis within hearing range.

Once *Cole* was in open water, the harbor tugs passed control to the USS *Catawba* (ATA-210), a Navy deep-sea tug. *Catawba* then towed *Cole* 25 miles farther to a rendezvous with the chartered Norwegian salvage ship *Blue Marlin*. The next morning at first light, the Navy began the thirty-six-hour process of raising *Cole* onto *Blue Marlin*'s deck.

It was a slow-moving, but remarkable, show—one usually reserved for hoisting massive oil-drilling rigs in and out of the Persian Gulf and the North Sea. The salvage vessel pumped water into its ballast tanks, slid under the *Cole*, and then raised itself and the *Cole* by pumping the ballast water out again. When it was over, the *Cole* sat inert like a beached whale athwart *Blue Marlin*'s stadium-size midsection. The wound to her flank was still gaping and raw, but *Cole* was ready for the five-week, six-thousand-mile voyage home.

On 28 April 1945, nearly fifty-five years and six months before *Cole*'s labored departure from Aden, the Navy warship *Lindsey* (DD-771/DM-32) left another distant anchorage, this one ringed by a group of mountainous islands collectively called the Kerama Retto. Kerama Retto lies fifteen miles west of the southern tip of Okinawa, the main island in the Northern Pacific's Ryukyu chain, then and now sovereign Japanese territory.

Kerama Kaikyo, the strait separating the largest island in the Kerama Retto from five smaller islands to the west, can accommodate seventy-five ships in deepwater anchorages with good holding ground.

Equally important, both the north and south entrances to the one-and-a-half mile strait are narrow enough to protect against the lashing of Pacific typhoons and, in time of war, the intrusion of hostile shipping.

Since late March 1945, when U.S. forces had captured the islands of the Kerama Retto and moved in ships and personnel, the roadstead had buzzed with activity—the arrival, unloading, and departure of cargo ships and oilers and the reprovisioning, refueling, and rearming of hundreds of warships and small craft. Work crews labored without interruption, even though Japanese soldiers were still at large hiding in the islands' rugged terrain. But by the second week in April, the work associated with ship arrivals took on a new, more sobering and burdensome form.

Ships, often in tow, crawled into Kerama Kaikyo trailing wakes of leaking fuel oil and debris. Many sailors standing at railings to gawk at the battered newcomers arrive had themselves been passengers in earlier processions. Still, the sailors would often gaze dumbstruck at the conditions of new arrivals—drunken lists; flattened bows and fantails; punctured hulls; crumpled deckhouses; severed gun mounts, masts and stacks.

Once a new arrival anchored or moored, a cleared topside space might be lined with what, at a distance, could be mistaken for rows of seabags, mattresses, or sacks of laundry or mail. They were actually shrouds, usually fashioned from canvas, and the watching sailors knew that counting them gave a rough tally of that ship's dead. But only a rough count—remains of more than one sailor might be mistakenly combined in one bundle or unavoidably spread among several. And then, of course, there could still be bodies trapped below and others lost forever in the sea. It was both hard to look—and hard to look away. In the next days the bodies would be either carted ashore for interment or, if arrangements could be made with a more seaworthy ship in the roadstead, carried out of the strait for burial at sea. Before these ceremonies another object would be inserted in each canvas shroud. Most often it would be a gun projectile or shell casing, although sometimes a body might be laid atop the metal frame of a bunk. Whatever object was used had to be weighty enough to ensure that the shroud and its contents went all the way to the ocean floor.

Lindsey and *Cole,* although they'd been built half a century apart, nevertheless shared the same lineage. They were both U.S. Navy destroyers, although, shortly after its construction, *Lindsey* had been specially equipped for the dangerous work of laying coastal mines (a mission it never fulfilled). Each was—by the standards of its time—a fast, highly maneuverable, versatile, and lethal warship. *Lindsey,* however, at 2,200 tons, was barely a quarter the size of *Cole*, and her main armament cannons had nowhere near the punch or technical sophistication of *Cole*'s weaponry.

Lindsey had been towed stern first and lifeless into Kerama Kaikyo at twilight on 12 April 1945. During her relatively short time at anchor in the roadstead and then in dry dock, she was a startling example—though not the only one—of just how much punishment a warship could absorb and still remain afloat. The roadstead where *Lindsey* and other ships like her were gathered was fast becoming known as the Bone Yard.

It was hard to imagine and no easier to describe the appalling damage *Lindsey*—and her crew—had suffered. If the damage decades later to *Cole* could be compared to a shotgun blast at close range, the damage to *Lindsey* was more like a decapitation. *Lindsey* essentially had no bow. In the detached, autopsy-like narrative of her captain's official damage report, an explosion or series of explosions "blew off the bow from frame 30 forward from main deck to keel."

There was little of *Lindsey* left forward of her bridge and superstructure. What remained ("the main deck from frame 30 aft to frame 52 was blown upward at an angle of fifty degrees") was a cross-sectional slice of contorted steel beams, shards of steel plate, crumpled piping, and tangled wire. It was as if someone had opened *Lindsey*'s bow like a can of soup, pealed back the lid, and discarded the rest of the can—and its contents—while keeping the rim from which the top had been separated. *Lindsey*'s dismemberment had taken the lives of 57 sailors (roughly a fifth of her crew) and gravely or seriously wounded 61 others.*

---

*Conditions at the time often yielded different casualty figures for individual ships. For consistency, casualty figures used in this book are with few exceptions drawn from Morison, *Leyte, Liberation of the Philippines,* and *Victory in the Pacific.* Morison's figures are derived from ship's action reports at the time with occasional footnoted updates. Casualty figures are used in an effort to portray the scope of the events I describe and are not individual accountings for each ship. I anticipate with regret that certain casualty figures reported here will conflict with other—sometimes more accurate, sometimes less accurate—sources.

Lindsey's misery had plummeted from the sky in mid-afternoon in the form of two aircraft piloted by men intent on exchanging their lives for the destruction of a ship whose name they probably never knew.

One aircraft, colliding on the starboard side at the forward base of *Lindsey*'s superstructure, smashed into cooking and living spaces and burst into flames. Some aircraft remains catapulted onto a superstructure deck just forward of *Lindsey*'s bridge.

Pete Petersen, a third class petty officer stationed as a gunner on one of the ship's starboard side light machine guns, was standing on that deck when the plane crashed and watched in horror as his gun loader and six or seven other men nearby were mowed down by shrapnel. Reflexively, Petersen fled to *Lindsey*'s port side, only to see a second plane flying straight toward him.

The crash by the first plane caused considerable damage and resulting flames threatened more, but up to this point, there were no explosions. Those were the work of the plane that Petersen saw. This plane crashed too with the bomb strapped to its undercarriage flying on until it pierced the thin skin of *Lindsey*'s port side bow.

This second aircraft was the cocked hammer and its bomb the pulled trigger for an explosive cataclysm; the fuel was volatile smokeless gun powder packed in brass shell canisters in *Lindsey*'s forward ready ammunition room. The eruption lifted *Lindsey* up before dropping her nearly bowless to the sea. The bow-mounted No. 1 gun and its housing—five tons of armored steel—catapulted up and back to land on the ship's bridge, the gun's barrel pointing skyward.

The crewmen from *Lindsey*'s No. 2 gun mount—the turret just forward and below the bridge—were among the few survivors on stations forward of the bridge. Walter Gau, a shell loader, along with the rest of the dazed and confused gun crew, had been poised to jump out of the mount's port side hatch—a leap that would have landed them square in the path of the second plane. Instead, they left the mount to starboard and scrambled over and around the flaming carcass of the first aircraft on their way to relative safety. Nonetheless, virtually all of them sustained serious burns.

Still, No. 2's gun crew had been remarkably lucky and none more so than Paul LaRochelle. The usual battle station for LaRochelle, a carpenter's mate, was with *Lindsey*'s forward-most damage control party. On this morning, though, his station had been switched to No. 2 mount. LaRochelle's replacement, a sailor who doubled as *Lindsey*'s barber, lost his life along with the rest of the damage control party, all of them trapped belowdecks when the plane struck. Fate, blessed, or just lucky—LaRochelle would never know which word best described his continued life.

Miraculously, Petersen survived as well, though he, too, never knew how. When he awoke he was on the main deck, other wounded men lying around him, his head swathed in bandages, and an IV hooked up to his arm.

Had *Lindsey*'s skipper T. E. Chambers not instinctively screamed "All back full!" following the second collision and explosion—and had those still alive in the engineering spaces not responded—the pressure of onrushing water would likely have collapsed the ship's exposed forward interior bulkheads and sent her straight to the bottom.

As it was, seawater splashing mast high doused the largest fires started by the first collision, and the living worked furiously to restore power and communications and to keep the ship afloat. Other ships came alongside to assist; one ship provided antiaircraft cover while another sent over a medical officer to replace *Lindsey*'s own severely wounded doctor. By late afternoon fires were out, bulkheads shored, and *Lindsey* was in tow; by nightfall she'd completed the twenty-mile, stern-first trip to Kerama Retto, and another ship had come alongside to remove the dead and wounded.

Lindsey spent sixteen days in Kerama Retto. The worst of those days were the first ones, when the sad, nauseating work of picking through the ruins to extract bodies and pieces of the dead had to be done. One sailor volunteered to be lowered by rope into the ruins of the forward magazine where the dismembered remains of eight sailors were eventually found and removed.

When *Lindsey* left the Kerama Retto, she was again under tow—and again traveling stern first—one of a convoy of mangled ships (called a ghost fleet by sailors who traveled in it) slowly and clumsily making the journey a thousand miles southeast to Guam. Gau, LaRochelle, Peterson, and others of *Lindsey*'s 61 wounded (most of them burn victims) were laid up on a hospital ship traveling with the barely ambulatory convoy.

* * *

In the wake of the Ghost Fleet (and others like it to follow), Kerama Kaikyo remained packed with broken ships. By mid-April 1945 a system was beginning to be put in place; priority for repairs went to ships that could be quickly patched and sent back out.

The reasoning made sense, but it also meant crews of some of the most severely damaged ships idled long months in the stew of wreckage and carnage. One such ship, the *Leutze* (DD-481), that had lost its fantail (and thus its propulsion and steering) lingered three months before getting into drydock. During the wait, *Leutze* became a dispensary and temporary morgue for several new arrivals. *Leutze* crewmen, themselves just beginning to cope with the deaths of shipmates, were assigned to work details for gathering and bagging the remains of men from the decks and spaces of other ships.

Meanwhile, *Lindsey* was hauled the first leg of her return voyage—a slow rewind of the bounding journey ship and crew had taken west to the war. The work crews who labored over *Lindsey* in the roadstead and floating dry dock of Kerama Kaikyo could do little more than trim the mangled remains and reinforce the ship's forward bulkheads. Crews on Guam did better—fashioning and fitting a steel prosthetic "snowplow" bow. When their work was complete, *Lindsey* in profile resembled a sort of nautical centaur—a truncated trawler prow coupled to a warship's sleek superstructure, midsection and stern. With power and some propulsion restored, *Lindsey* set out for home.

The ship traveled bow first, just barely making headway, stopping briefly in Pearl Harbor and then San Pedro, California, before transiting the Panama Canal and arriving in Norfolk, Virginia, for final repairs on 15 August—the date marking the Pacific War's end. At each of these stops, *Lindsey*'s approach and docking attracted stares of wonder, disbelief, and dread.

For men in the skeleton crew who sailed back with *Lindsey,* the arrival in Norfolk was the signal to begin their thirty-day survivor leaves and reunions with their families. Some, but not all, of *Lindsey*'s wounded crewmen were already back in the States, scattered in hospitals, burn centers, and rehabilitation facilities across the country where more reunions occurred. For the families of the dead and missing, the ship's return was one more event in the long, fitful process of grieving and closure.

Late in May, the father of Robert V. Halabi, a *Lindsey* sailor whose battle station was on the same gun as Petersen, received a letter from *Lindsey*'s skipper dated 12 May 1945 addressed from the Fleet Post Office, San Francisco. "Dear Mr. Halabi," it began. "As Commanding Officer of the USS *Lindsey,* it was my sad duty to notify the Navy Department of the death of your son, Robert."

The letter continued for a page. It included some personal information about Halabi's son—a sincere but awkward effort to distinguish Robert Halabi by a ship's captain who likely did not know him well and who was responsible for writing fifty-six other such wrenching letters to next of kin. The letter concluded above Chambers' signature: "Needless to say, those of us who were spared will go back into the battle with a greater determination than ever to end this war and make sure of the ideals that your son gave his life for."

Erin Hayles of Water Valley, Mississippi, wife of Raymond S. Hayles, one of *Lindsey*'s fire room engineers, very likely received a similar letter from Commander Chambers at about the same time. On 3 April 1945, Erin had sent an airmail letter to her husband in care of the Fleet Post Office, San Francisco. The unopened letter was eventually returned; its address was crossed out and replaced with a "return to sender" stamp. The letter's return most likely followed a War Department telegram notifying Erin that her husband Raymond had been killed aboard *Lindsey.* The returned letter might have preceded or might have followed Chambers' condolence letter.

It was likely Erin, now widowed and the mother of three children, had all three messages in hand when, in late September or early October 1945, she received a letter from the wife of one of Raymond's shipmates. The letter began, "Erin, you probably know the *Lindsey* is now at Norfolk, Va., for repairs. My husband came home on a thirty-day leave, and he was telling me about Raymond." Her husband and Ray were close friends, and each had promised the other to contact family should one of them die and the other survive. But, she continued, "[A]fter it really happened . . . he just couldn't ever seem to get the nerve to write you. It was instantly & he was buried on Okinawa with four others."

* * *

The gut shot to *Cole* was soon overshadowed by gaping wounds to the Navy's pride (the *Cole* had been proudly named in honor of Marine Sergeant Darrell S. Cole, a machine gunner killed in action on Iwo Jima in 1945). The damage to the mighty ship had come at the hands of a couple young extremists in a tiny boat. The incident and its implications were probed in inquiries and hearings by admirals and congressional committees. The investigations ultimately revealed the explosive-laden craft had been piloted by two al-Qaeda-trained suicide bombers. It was, in fact, a full-fledged al-Qaeda operation supervised directly by Osama Bin Ladin who chose the target and location of the attack, selected the suicide operatives, and provided the money needed to purchase explosives and equipment.

Back in Afghanistan, Bin Ladin, expecting U.S. military retaliation, immediately fled into the desert. Even when Bin Laden eventually returned to his headquarters in Kandahar, his anticipation lingered; he began rotating among five to six safe houses, spending no more than one night at each location before moving to the next.

When it was clear that the United States would not be launching a retaliatory strike, Bin Ladin was surprised and frustrated. In fact, he complained about it frequently. According to one source, Bin Ladin wanted the United States to attack, and if it did not, he would launch something bigger. The bloody attack on the *Cole* proved to be a key event in a chain of ever larger and more globe shaking events leading to 9/11.

Invoking the powers of hindsight, participants in the inquires and hearings wondered aloud why those responsible hadn't seen the portents and clues pointing to the *Cole* attack and hadn't taken the preventive measures to avoid it. By 2000 it was a familiar ritual both to those who asked the questions and to those who faced the questioning and rebuke. And it was a ritual that repeated, in much escalated form, less than a year later.

In an age of instant global communication, news, photos, commentary, and furor about the *Cole* spread quickly. By contrast, until the very day *Lindsey* entered the Kerama Kaikyo, the release of news about her fate and the similar fate of other Navy ships was firmly embargoed by wartime censors. It was only on 12 April 1945 that sanctioned accounts began to filter out—though most of the early accounts competed poorly for newspaper and broadcast space with other war events and the wrenching news of Franklin Roosevelt's death.

When the stories finally reached the eyes and ears of people on the home front, attacks such as the one on *Lindsey* had been occurring daily for nearly seven months, to the bafflement of Navy leaders and the utter dread of sailors throughout the Southwest and Central Pacific. They knew what was happening—they'd witnessed its manifestations in a brutal series of island land battles where the Japanese fought beyond the bitter end. But they didn't know why it was happening or how it fit into what they understood to be a war's rules of engagement.

By and large their leaders also didn't know how to counter the phenomenon—and whether the burgeoning armada of the U.S. Navy's Pacific Fleet could ultimately outlast the grinding attrition. Shipboard sailors confronted a more basic misery: would they and their shipmates somehow outlive these relentless—and many thought personal—assaults to make it home in one living piece?

This is a story about pride, determination, and desperation. It is about a time when America's mighty wartime fleet, after all but obliterating Japan's formidable seagoing fighting capability, suddenly confronted a stunning new "backs-against-the-wall" paradigm for modern warfare: organized offensive suicide.

This is the story of the confrontation, what became a war within a war—literally thousands of furious and violent tactical engagements pitting sky against sea, men determined to die against men determined to live.

Finally, this is a story about portents; in this case the consequences of recognizing, heeding, and acting on portents. Decisions and actions during the course of the war presaged the war with the wind. The war with the wind led inevitably to the most fateful decision in the history of global conflict.

Before it takes to sea and sky, the story begins on land—in a ferocious war for beachheads.

★ Part One ★

THE WAR OF BEACHHEADS

★ Chapter 1 ★

The Alligator and the Bull

When things get tough, they send for the sons of bitches.
—Chief of Naval Operations Ernest J. King

Easter Fools' Day

On Easter Sunday morning, 1 April 1945, the American invasion of Okinawa—the inevitable climax to the U.S. Central Pacific campaign against the Imperial Japanese Empire—was poised to begin.

The choice of day must have unsettled many devout Christians among the hundreds of thousands of sailors, Marines, and GIs aboard the 1,300 ships assembled in Hagushi Roadstead. This would undoubtedly be a day for death not resurrection. However, to battle-hardened cynics—an interfaith group well represented among those same men— the coincidence of Easter, April Fools' Day, and an island assault made exquisite sense.

To the planners of this amphibious invasion—code name Operation Iceberg—1 April had stopped being Easter, April Fools' Day, or even Sunday. Instead, it was L (for Love)-Day, a date certain toward which their efforts, expectations, and fears had been pointing since preparations first began in October 1944.

Everything about L-Day's scheduling, approach, arrival, and outcome was part of a complex web of circumstances, contingencies, and events—some natural, some man-made, some minute, some massive, some within its planners' reckoning, and others well beyond reckoning.

This web included a number of details:

- The weather, a loose term encompassing winds, storms, sea currents, phases of the moon, tides, and all the other uncontrollable, often unpredictable, and occasionally gargantuan works of God and nature in the Central Pacific
- The progress—or bitter delay—of simultaneous battle campaigns being pressed elsewhere in the Pacific or amid Europe's charred remains
- The accuracy (always suspect) of intelligence estimates and reconnaissance photos detailing the strength and disposition of Japanese defenders
- The availability of ships needed to transport and service Iceberg logistics
- The availability of other ships to chase submarines, clear coastal minefields, launch forays by underwater demolition teams (UDTs) (see glossary for acronyms), add firepower to preinvasion bombardment, and do other chores either to project or to protect Iceberg
- The availability and capabilities of bomber and fighter aircraft to dominate the skies over Okinawa and the one hundred or more Japanese-held airfields within striking distance
- The inventories of fuel, ammunition, medicine, and food supplies essential to sustain Iceberg
- The compilation and controlled distribution of plan documents bulging with command chains, charts, timetables, routing orders, codes, call signs, ship and unit designations, communications circuits, and other details to govern Iceberg
- The readiness (above all) of the six troop divisions (the Marines' 1st and 2nd; the Army's 7th, 27th, 77th and 96th) whose skill, blood, and sacrifice would doubtless be required in full measure to take and hold Iceberg's objectives.

That all of Iceberg's moving pieces, interdependencies, and numbing details could be mastered by one mind seemed improbable. That they could be devised, organized, written, mobilized, and moved to completion largely through the sheer force of that same mind seemed inconceivable. But there actually was such a mind, and on the morning of L-Day, its proprietor, Vice Admiral Richmond Kelly Turner of the U.S. Navy, paced the deck of his flagship USS *Eldorado* (AGC-11).

Eldorado was an amphibious assault command ship, a special class of vessel designed to be the control and communication hub for invasion task forces such as this. *Eldorado* had begun life as a Maritime Commission ship. Even after her conversion for U.S. Navy use, *Eldorado*'s exterior still retained the boxy look of a merchant vessel, except that her rigging bristled conspicuously with a forest of antennas.

Inside, *Eldorado* was crowded with military brass and buzzing with nonstop activity. Her interior spaces housed the staffs for both the amphibious forces commander—Richmond Kelly Turner—and for Iceberg's landing force commander, an Army general with a colorful lineage and an equally colorful name: Simon Bolivar Buckner, Jr. *Eldorado*'s advanced radar and communication capabilities and well-equipped Combat Information Center (CIC) also made *Eldorado* the nerve center in Iceberg's air defense arrangements.

Finally, *Eldorado* was equipped with extensive radio broadcast facilities and served as headquarters for a bustling contingent of war correspondents. Some, like 35-year-old *Time* reporter Robert Sherrod, were old hands in the Pacific, having witnessed the war there since its earliest and most dismal days. Others were newly transplanted from Europe to the Pacific where, finally, the American newspaper and radio public seemed to be shifting its attention. One of these newer arrivals was *New Yorker* writer John Lardner (son of the famed sports journalist and short story writer Ring Lardner). Another was no less than Ernie Pyle, the roving Scripps Howard correspondent whose coverage of GIs in Europe had earned him the 1944 Pulitzer Prize and endeared him to enlisted servicemen everywhere.

Pyle, 45, was such a legend that he'd become part of the story for fellow correspondents, photographers, broadcasters, and even historians. "A frail little man, a gentle soul who hated war" was the impression of Samuel Eliot Morison, the Harvard historian on hand to chronicle America's ocean wars. Pyle was there, Morison observed, "owing to his sense of duty to tell the American people about the war with Japan and the way the ordinary soldier and sailor felt."

Iceberg was to be the penultimate act in the drama of war with

Japan—the final act, already in the early stages of planning, would be the invasion of Japan's home islands. The drama that had been unfolding ever since America took the offensive in the Pacific two-and-a-half years before. Considered in such terms, Turner was a combination producer, author, director, and stage manager. And the stage before him on this cool, humid, slightly overcast morning was just now emerging behind layered curtains of mist and smoke.

In its entirety, Okinawa is a large, elongated island, stretching some sixty miles north to south. Morison, who, after covering so many Pacific island invasions, had nearly run out of inventive ways to describe these island targets, likened Okinawa's shape to "a comic-strip dog with an elongated neck and an overgrown jowl."

Except for a pinched waist (to Morison, the "dog's neck") with flat terrain just two miles wide (either side bounded by a deepwater bay—on the west open to the East China Sea, on the east to the Pacific Ocean), a spine of steep, rugged limestone hills dominated Okinawa's terrain. Not all the island was bleak. In the south, the island sloped up gently from the beach. Umbrella-topped pine trees, plots of terraced farmland, and small stands of forest softened the austerity of the hills; and squares of rice paddies and sugarcane fields checkered its coastal plains. But days of preinvasion shore bombardment and air strikes had chewed up or flattened much of the scenery once visible through the binoculars and gun sights of the invasion fleet.

The limestone hills were themselves the summits of a summit. Okinawa is actually a sunken volcano peak, one in a chain of 140 or so other sunken peaks, whose collective formal Japanese name is the *Nansei Shoto*, or Southwestern Islands. The chain's more familiar name is the Ryukyus; roughly translated it means "bubbles on the water." The equivalent Chinese pronunciation of Ryukyu is Loochoo, the inspiration for what eventually became known to American veterans of the struggle for Okinawa as the "Great Loochoo."

The island, like most other Central Pacific islands, is entirely girdled by sharp coral reefs, 250- to 500-yard-wide barriers barely concealed by water at high tide, obstacles for landing craft trying to cross them, perils for any deep-bottom vessels that dared come close to shore. The Okinawa tides produced treacherous swells that surged at the reef line and broke onto its small, narrow beaches. Those beaches offered few good exits for the crowds of invasion troops whose lives and fortunes would soon depend on getting off the beaches quickly.

While beach exits were a concern, three other features of Okinawa, each related, crowded Turner's apprehensions. First was its sheer size—five hundred square miles. Although Southwest Pacific commanders—notably General Douglas MacArthur—now had experience in campaigns to capture and occupy large islands such as New Guinea and Leyte and Luzon in the Philippines, Turner was more practiced in planning and taking tiny, flat coral atolls. More land to conquer required more time to conquer, and more time to conquer in turn meant that large and vulnerable parts of the U.S. invasion armada would have to stay near Okinawa to support the troops ashore.

A second and more unsettling aspect was the Great Loochoo's proximity, not only to Japan, but as well to Formosa (present-day Taiwan) and Eastern China, two parts of Japan's shrinking empire still firmly in its grip. Okinawa lay roughly equidistant from Japan to its north, China to its west, and Formosa to its southwest. The short distance—an average of 330 miles—put the invasion fleet and its troops within easy striking distance by land-based Japanese aircraft. In contrast was the long distance the Americans had come. San Francisco was 6,200 miles due east. Of more immediate consequence, Okinawa lay fully 1,200 miles from Saipan or Ulithi, the Allies' nearest secure supply centers. Turner's forces, in other words, were operating within Japan's aerial sights while simultaneously crawling far out on the narrowing limbs of communications and logistics so vital to Iceberg's success.

The third concern, Okinawa's civilian population, went with size and proximity. The Ryukyus' total civilian census was just over 800,000, more than half of them inhabiting Okinawa. The island's civilians were both dispersed and concentrated. People living in the rugged and remote north, mainly subsistence farmers, peasants, and fishermen, were widely scattered; in the south, however, density was 2,700 people per square mile, three times the wartime population density of the U.S. state of Rhode Island.

Invading armies almost never respect the fragile lives, modest possessions, and meager hopes of civilian populations who happen to be in their way. By effort, luck, or both, most civilians may be spared their lives and their worldly possessions; but their commerce, families, and communities, along with any tranquility they may once have enjoyed, are invariably disrupted and very often destroyed.

In the worst of worlds, civilians become targets of intention—and this often seemed so when the Japanese or their Axis partner, the Germans, were the invaders. But even when the invaders were welcomed as liberators—as were the Americans returning to the Philippines—big civilian populations usually impeded the invaders' work. They wandered into firefights; or, as refugees, they clogged lines of advance; or, if they feared traveling during the day and chose to travel instead at night, they could be mistaken—and frequently were—for enemy infiltrators by rattled, trigger-happy sentries.

All these problems, Turner realized, were likely to befall the Okinawans. But there was one more. Although Japan treated this slice of its empire with condescension bordering on disdain, Okinawans were nonetheless Japanese citizens. Who knew for certain how they would react to the American presence? Would they be armed? Would they obstruct or resist? And in the worst case, would their men, and perhaps even their women and children, become a mobilized, fanatical auxiliary to the seventy thousand or so Japanese troops estimated to be dug in on Okinawa?

Terrible Turner

Turner was not particularly gracious or patient to those around him. He was more apt to pace, scowl, and bark orders than stand above the fray. For some early morning calls to Generals Quarter (GQ: ship's battle stations)—though never on invasion day itself—he was apt to show up hatless, decked out in an old bathrobe and slippers.

He lacked the flair or physical presence to be sized up as a leader for the ages—indeed Turner was widely rumored to operate in a drunken haze by late morning. Yet he embodied, in his own distinctive way, the faults and graces and the failures and triumphs of America's come-from-behind struggle with the Imperial Japanese Empire for victory in the Pacific War.

Turner, the son of a Portland, Oregon, union printer, was a bookish 1908 U.S. Naval Academy graduate with flair—if it could be called that—for order, organization, and mastery of voluminous details. On L-Day, thirty-seven years following his "Trade School" graduation and just two months shy of his 60th birthday, Turner had aged into a grousing (perhaps hungover) eminence with a close-cropped balding head, jug ears anchoring steel-rimmed glasses, and a perpetually furrowed expression. Turner's demeanor and expression were perhaps the gatekeepers of his singular abilities: Turner happened to know more about amphibious warfare and to be more successful in waging it than any man before him or since.

Iceberg was Turner's seventh major amphibious invasion in the Pacific. Japanese opponents, who had seen his operational genius poke through barrier after barrier in their ring of island defenses (and had seen the distinctive patch his amphibious sailors wore), begrudgingly called Turner "the Alligator," and put him front and center in their pantheon of loathing. A few days after the Marine landings on Iwo Jima two months before, a Japanese radio broadcast honored Turner with a particularly damning endorsement: "This man Turner shall not return home alive; he mustn't and won't; this is one of the many things we can do to rest at ease the many souls of those who have paid the supreme sacrifice."

Before an Iceberg preinvasion briefing began, several admirals buttonedholed *Time* reporter Sherrod to give him the measure of Turner: "One of the admirals said, 'They can replace me, and they can replace you,' and, turning to a third officer, 'somebody could fill your shoes, but there's nobody else who can do Kelly Turner's job.' "

Turner's "job" since the summer of 1942 was to plan, prepare, and execute ever more mammoth, complex, and logistics-defying seaborne invasions: hundreds of thousands of Marines, GIs, and sailors riding hundreds of ships embarked hundreds and sometimes thousands of ocean miles from forward staging areas (vast, yet portable floating bases, seemingly built overnight, only to be as quickly dismantled and moved forward) to the shores of Japanese island strongholds. In the last 16 months—since he'd first been assigned to the Central Pacific—Turner's foul-tempered genius had propelled American forces across 3,500 miles of Japanese-defended ocean and islands.

Amphibious warfare was an interest Turner took up when he was past 50 and commanding little more than a classroom at the Naval War College. It was also a departure from what thus far had been a ticket-punching career, blending assignments on battleships, cruisers, and destroyers and even training in aviation—the obligatory experiences needed for advancement to flag rank.

Amphibious warfare was not then a field promising new career vistas for a middle-aged naval officer. U.S. battle traditions included few examples of landing troops in the face of enemy fire and none since the Civil War. The abysmal failure of British landings at Gallipoli during World War I had discouraged all major powers—except Japan—from concentrating on amphibious warfare. Battles would be won on land or at sea, but not on beachheads.

Turner brought prodigious powers of assimilation to his new area of interest. He seemed to know everything in detail and was ready to lecture anybody; he coupled this encyclopedic knowledge with visionary strategic thinking, tenacity, and nonstop energy. Turner was often criticized for his failure to delegate authority to subordinates. It was a failure that only deepened as he climbed in rank and his staff expanded. For Turner it was like asking a dog to delegate a bone.

Another of Turner's shortcomings, unfortunately, was a seemingly boundless appetite for interservice conflict. If his age and his fascination with amphibious warfare seemed to limit Turner's horizons, the feeding of this appetite for conflict nearly cost Turner his career.

When war began, Turner was a rear admiral directing the Navy's War Plans Division in Washington, DC. Before Turner's arrival, War Plans was a backwater and he came in like a typhoon, rousing its once indolent staff and driving them to exhaustion. His method was flood them with "to do" items—dozens of items daily—scribbled down and torn from a green memo pad that was always with him. He got into everything, was always looking for more to do, and demanded everything be done his way.

Turner had seen Japan's might and militancy firsthand in 1939 when, after the Washington, DC, death of Japanese Ambassador Hirosi Saito, from tuberculosis, he commanded cruiser *Astoria* (CA-34) on a goodwill mission to bring Saito's ashes home. Turner returned from Japan convinced war in the Pacific was inevitable and, when it came, should be a bigger priority than Europe. But Turner's unyielding stance and, probably worse, his nonstop evangelizing, ultimately put him at odds with nearly all his peers and superiors on the Joint Army-Navy Board.

Turner's arguments with Army brass were legend—they nicknamed him "Terrible Turner"—and they eventually cost him his job. With Turner's Army bridges burned, and nearly at a loss for a suitable high-level assignment free from the nuances and humilities of interservice diplomacy, Chief of Naval Operations Ernest J. King finally assigned Turner to command the amphibious forces and transports for the upcoming assault on Guadalcanal in the Solomon Islands, America's first offensive foray in the Pacific.

King admired Turner for his tireless capabilities and shared his opinions about the importance of winning in the Pacific. King also understood Turner's personality only too well. His own ill-tempered reputation outdistanced Turner's and certainly had greater impact. With the possible exception of Britain's Field Marshal Bernard Law Montgomery, King was—at least among those on the Allied side—the most despised military leader of World War II. "Admiral Adamant's" circles of dislike were personal and domestic as well as global and political—King was a hard and belligerent drinker (another propensity shared with Turner), and he reserved his charms for a succession of subordinate officers' wives. One appraisal of King, attributed to various sources but almost certainly apocryphal, was that King actually possessed an even temper—mad at everyone and all the time. No less an observer than Franklin Roosevelt summarized King as "a man who shaves with a blowtorch."

King's civilian bosses tended to indulge King's blind spots and shortcomings because he had shown himself indispensable to rebuilding the fortunes of a navy grown top-heavy and languorous between wars. King had wiped out the obstacles blocking advancement for its most vigorous leaders, including both the irascible Turner and the courtly, even-tempered Admiral Chester W. Nimitz, whom King had the foresight to place in overall charge of Navy forces in the Pacific.

Despite his epic shortcomings, King was focused and single-minded and able to hold together, orchestrate, and meld the jumbled pieces of his naval kingdom. King minced no words about his value: "When things get tough they send for the sons of bitches." Secretary of the Navy Frank Knox eventually gave King a Tiffany-made miniature silver blowtorch gratefully inscribed with Roosevelt's words.

The 'Canal

Putting Terrible Turner into such a key role for the Guadalcanal assault—code name Operation Watchtower—was evidence to some of just how precarious a venture Watchtower would be. Guadalcanal, part of the sprawling nine hundred square mile Solomons chain, two elongated strands of Southwest Pacific islands separated by a broad navigable interior channel, seemed of little strategic interest either to Japan or to the Allies. In fact, Guadalcanal's existence was scarcely known to Japan's army high command—even though, in the months to come twenty-five thousand of the Imperial Japanese Army's (IJA) finest soldiers would die there. The Imperial Japanese Navy (IJN) administered matters in the Solomons. A seaplane base had already been built on nearby Tulagi. Now, the IJN decided to build a new airfield along the northern coast of Guadalcanal.

Seeing an opening to channel resources to the Pacific front, King pushed originally for the capture of Tulagi and its seaplane base as a quick, low-risk, first-land offensive against the Japanese. Plans for Watchtower's modest objective were well underway when intelligence operatives spotted the new airfield under construction. Because the Solomons jut directly into the vital sea and communication lanes between the U.S. West Coast and Australia and New Zealand, the airfield's location posed a direct threat to the Allied lifeline as well as to Australia's northeast coastal cities. When new intelligence reports showed the project nearing completion, Watchtower went into high gear and its scope expanded. While the Allies had lost many "Asiatic" possessions and were resigned to losing more, it was unthinkable that a "White" bastion fall to a "Yellow" enemy.

But now, as plans for Watchtower accelerated, the sense of desperation was also tempered by emerging confidence. In April 1942, barely four months after Japan's devastating attack on Pearl Harbor, U.S. carrier-based Army Air Force bombers led by Lieutenant Colonel Jimmy Doolittle, a 45-year-old former stunt pilot recalled to active duty, staged a bold raid on Tokyo. While Doolittle's bombers inflicted little physical damage, their psychic impact was enormous. "Today," Vice Admiral Matome Ugaki of Japan (chief of staff to Admiral Iso-roku Yamamoto, head of Japan's Combine Fleet) conceded in his diary, "the victory belonged to the enemy." The raid set in motion a chain of events ending with a huge U.S. victory in midsummer.

Stung by the audacity of a bombing raid on its sacred homeland (and clueless as to where the American air strike had originated), Yamamoto resolved to plug the gaps in the Northern Pacific defensive perimeter. The IJN lunged to capture Midway, the northernmost island in the Hawaiian chain while simultaneously trying to engage and obliterate the U.S. Navy's fledgling carrier task force. The gamble failed—cryptologists had broken Japan's most secure code, enabling U.S. strategists to spring a trap. In a breathless reversal of fate spanning barely minutes, U.S. Navy carrier-based aircraft delivered blows that sunk four Japanese carriers. Although it hardly seemed so at the time, the highwater mark in Japan's binge of conquest had passed.

Despite the Midway victory, not all of King's flag-level staff shared King and Turner's commitment to Watchtower's success. Vice Admiral Robert L. Ghormley, selected by King to be overall campaign commander, was convinced the situation in the Solomons was hopeless. And so was Vice Admiral Frank Jack Fletcher, who'd been chosen as Ghormley's on-scene task force commander. Fletcher had already lost two precious aircraft carriers, first *Lexington* (CV-2) during the Battle of the Coral Sea and then *Yorktown* (CV-5) at Midway, and had little taste for risking more in vain pursuit of a small piece of malarial real estate. He set a tight time limit for precious carrier-based air cover support during the invasion.

By the time Watchtower's small invasion fleet of eighty-two ships and seventeen thousand Marines assaulted on Tulagi and Guadalcanal on 7 August 1942, the operation was more fittingly, if privately, called Shoestring. But the landings caught Japan by surprise, and the Marines at first met only light resistance. Marines quickly secured Tulagi and the nearly completed airfield on Guadalcanal. Then the Japanese rebounded, putting up fierce counterattacks by sea, air, and land. The

Marines were pinched into a narrow river-bracketed beachhead perimeter along the 'Canal's northern shore.

From the start, U.S. troop casualties on Guadalcanal were appalling (more than 1,000 Marines and 500 GIs were to lose their lives there). But so, in their way, were U.S. Navy losses. On the evening of the landings, four American and Australian cruisers (including *Astoria)* were sunk and another crippled in a bold nighttime hit-and-run foray by a Japanese navy task force. One thousand sailors were killed, drowned, or eaten by sharks; Skylark Channel, the waters formed by the triangle of Guadalcanal, Tulagi, and tiny Savo Island, soon became known as Iron Bottom Sound.

Terrible Turner, who so far had been circumspect in his objections to Watchtower's skimpy resources and lack of air cover, held his tongue no longer. Howling that he'd been left "bare arse" by the withdrawal of Fletcher's carriers, Turner reluctantly but quickly withdrew his supply ships and most of the escorts. But the blame fell to the entire Navy—the Marines on Guadalcanal were left barely hanging on, starved for reinforcements, food, and ammunition. After the battle ended, some bitter 'Canal veterans devised a sardonic "campaign medal" that showed an arm bearing admiral's stripes dropping a hot potato into the hands of a kneeling Marine. The motto read "Faciat Georgius" (Let George do it). The message was bitter, lasting, and hard to reverse as the war continued: the chickenshit Navy had bugged out on the troops ashore.

Somehow, though, the Marines managed to hang on. While food and medicine were in constant shortage—the average teenaged leatherneck lost twenty-five pounds and most suffered in some degree from malaria, influenza, and dysentery throughout the campaign—some needs were met by a handful of expendable U.S. Navy destroyers slipping at night through the Japanese cordon with supplies of drummed gasoline, ammunition, and food.

As they clung to their perimeter, the Marines gained chilling perspective on the ferocity and tenacity of their enemy. As a scare tactic, the Japanese placed the severed heads of dead Marines on pikes visible from the perimeter. At one point Marine ground commander

Alexander "Archie" Vandegrift shared his own impressions in a letter to the Marine Commandant in Washington: "General, I have never heard or read of this kind of fighting. These people refuse to surrender. The wounded wait until men come up to examine them . . . and blow themselves up and the other fellow to death with a hand grenade." The Marines, having been savagely introduced to *bushido*, "the way of the warrior," for the most part set a reciprocal course for their own combat behavior toward the Japanese: no prisoners, no quarter asked, and none given.

The Bull

In October, resupply to Guadalcanal began to step up. Twenty-five hundred GI reinforcements and a mountain of stores made it ashore. Perhaps more important was the October replacement of theater commander Ghormley with 60-year-old Vice Admiral William Halsey. Temperamentally, the stocky, restive, and bushy-eyebrowed Halsey was more in Turner's mold. New Jersey-born, Halsey was nautical to his core, a descendant of a seafaring line. His great-great-grandfather had been a whaling captain out of Sag Harbor, New York, and lore held that an early-eighteenth-century forebearer had been a privateer, perhaps even a buccaneer. His father had attended the U.S. Naval Academy, and "Willie" Halsey followed in his footsteps to graduate in 1904. To his Annapolis classmates, Halsey looked "like a figurehead of Neptune."

During World War I, Halsey had been captain of a destroyer escorting convoys across the frigid, U-boat-filled North Atlantic. Between wars, Halsey pleaded his way into navy flight school and earned his wings in company with men barely half his age. As the War in the Pacific approached, Halsey had parlayed this credential into becoming a carrier task group commander. Good fortune found Halsey's task group away from Pearl (it was ferrying aircraft to a doomed Wake Island), and he returned to lead the first, albeit symbolic, offensive thrusts in the Pacific—February 1942 air raids on the Marshall and Gilbert Islands and Doolittle's April raid.

* * *

Halsey arrived in the South Pacific expecting to head a task force. Instead he took over all South Pacific naval operations and a decimated fleet seemingly unable to control the sea surrounding Guadalcanal. "Jesus Christ and General Jackson!" had been Halsey's first quotable reaction to the news that he would relieve his old friend Ghormley (they'd played together on the same Annapolis football team). Though the darkness on Guadalcanal did not lift immediately, Halsey delivered a new sense of grit and confidence to his forces. His contempt for the enemy was profanely racist, emphatic, and unbounded. When he'd first seen the destruction in Pearl Harbor, Halsey vowed that "Before we're through with 'em, the Japanese language will be spoken only in hell." "Kill Japs, Kill Japs, Kill More Japs!" became a hallmark South Pacific slogan; plastered on buildings and docks throughout Halsey's command; it was also the closing sentiment to most Halsey correspondence.

In November, U.S. Navy surface and air forces decimated a massive Japanese resupply effort, sinking 17 Japanese ships and killing or drowning 8,000 Japanese soldiers. It was the death knell to a branch of the infamous "Tokyo Express," an audacious nighttime supply chain of IJN destroyers and small transports that for months had poured tons of supplies and thousands of troop reinforcements into Guadalcanal, and the balance finally tipped in America's favor. By February 1943 the last beleaguered and emaciated remnants of Japan's land forces had quietly withdrawn. The 'Canal became a Navy-Marine triumph of mythic proportions—although its embittered veterans would forever memorialize it as "that fucking island."

Success at Midway and now Guadalcanal added some substance to the posture the Allies were taking against the Axis powers. In December 1941, during a radio speech after Pearl Harbor, President Roosevelt insisted that the United States could "accept no result save victory, final and complete." Then, in February 1943, during a strategy conference at Casablanca, Roosevelt and Churchill agreed to issue a public statement that the Allies were "resolved to pursue the war to the bitter end." Although this pronouncement was primarily a show of resolve in the face of lingering setbacks in Europe and an effort to bolster the resolve of the Soviet Union's Stalin, its import was global. Though it threatened to stiffen the war resolve of Germany and deepen the demonstrated implacability of Japan, the United States and its Allies would accept nothing short of unconditional surrender as the terms for ending the war.

Halsey's performance at Guadalcanal would prove to be his shining hour. It gave him a reputation and a nickname—"Bull"—that would resonate for both frontline troops and home front admirers. When asked what ship or unit they were attached to, many Pacific sailors (at any one time Halsey's task force organization commanded hundreds of thousands of sailors and airmen) would simply boast "I'm with Halsey." A woman approaching Halsey in the receiving line at a stateside ceremony swore afterward that she'd felt as if she were "touching the hand of God."

The figurehead of Neptune had by then become the most famous man in the U.S. Navy. Halsey was grounded and plain spoken enough not to put much stock in the adulation, and he preferred that his colleagues call him Bill, not Bull. Still, the hoopla would come to haunt him as his actions and judgments in the months ahead chipped away at the public relations facade.

For Terrible Turner by contrast, the 'Canal would be a low point—and a punishing lesson. The four cruisers lost on the night of the invasion had been part of Turner's command and thus his responsibility. The removal of Watchtower's transports—as sensible a move as it was following the destruction of the screening cruisers—lessened his reputation in the eyes of the Marines. Though King, Turner's boss and mentor, let him off the hook in his official reports ("We were surprised because we lacked experience"), Turner had little choice but to begin the uphill climb to redemption. He would keep plugging and learning.

After Guadalcanal was finally secured, Turner set up shop ashore. Calling on his remarkable powers of assimilation, Turner processed Watchtower's missteps and began formulating plans for the next beachheads. Unfortunately, those next operations—landings in the Russell and New Georgia island groups—did little to revive Turner's reputation. Operations offshore proved costly; a cruiser, a destroyer, and even

Turner's flagship *McCawley* (APA-4) were lost to the better weaponry and tactics of the IJN. Meanwhile, problems ashore during the assault on New Georgia prompted Turner to relieve an Army division commander. This move further strained his already miserable relationship with the Army—and there would be more such moves to follow.

By then the winds of strategy were changing. Navy brass had concluded the remote South Pacific was not the most efficient path of advancement against the Japanese, a conclusion likely influenced by the resurgence of the force of nature General Douglas MacArthur of the Army was proving himself to be.

Holed up in Australia since his escape from the Philippines, MacArthur had assembled a patchwork force of American GIs, Australians, and New Zealanders and somehow beaten back a Japanese offense on the southern tip of New Guinea. Much of the fighting on New Guinea had coincided with the fighting on Guadalcanal. New Guinea's terrain of mountains and jungles had been just as daunting, and the combat had been just as brutal. But the twin (though hardly coordinated) efforts paid off, splitting the attentions and resources of the Japanese and ultimately forcing them to quit Guadalcanal.

Gaining this toehold promised little more than a long, difficult road ahead. But the road would be almost exclusively MacArthur's in what was carved out as the Southwest Pacific Theater. Following the road would return him to the Philippines, as he'd brazenly promised. Accordingly, in August 1943, a year after the landings on Guadalcanal, Turner was called to Pearl Harbor and given command of the Central Pacific Amphibious Force.

Turner's redemption thus lay to the north, with planned stops in a new set of exotic island groups—the Gilberts, the Marshalls, the Marianas, the Bonins, and Ryukyus. To reach them and take them, Turner would require—and get—unprecedented resources in ships, troops, and shepherding airpower. And it was during these campaigns that Terrible Turner began his unique collaboration with U.S. Marine general Holland "Howlin' Mad" Smith, his counterpart and kindred spirit.

★ Chapter 2 ★

Dark Waters

The son of a bitch doesn't regret this half as much as I do!
—Lieutenant Commander Harry F. Bauer,
Commanding Officer USS *Gregory* (APD-3)

Full-Dress Armada

On Sunday morning 7 December 1941, Milton Mapou, then just 20 but already a two-year U.S. Navy veteran, was about to sit down to breakfast in the crew mess on *Detroit* (CL-8), an aging light cruiser moored near Ford Island, part of Hawaii's huge Pearl Harbor naval complex. With half of *Detroit*'s crew on shore liberty, Sunday was Mapou's duty day, though it promised to be a leisurely one, blessed with the balmy tropical weather so different from the bitter Ohio winters Mapou grew up with. But then the quiet of the morning suddenly erupted with the drone of aircraft followed by the muffled thump of explosions and the turmoil of stampeding crewmen. Leaving his breakfast untouched, Mapou bounded topside in time to see a Japanese plane—he would forever remember the prominent red "meatball" insignia against a deep green fuselage—launch a torpedo that just cleared *Detroit*'s bow to crash and explode into Ford Island.

Two adjacent ships, sister cruiser *Raleigh* (CL-7) and *Utah* (AG-16), an ancient battleship converted for antiaircraft training, were soon struck by torpedoes from the next wave of attackers (*Utah* would capsize with an unknown number of her crew trapped inside, while damaged *Raleigh* came through with only a few wounded). Meanwhile, sturdy *Detroit*, manned by her skeleton crew, was able to get underway and out to sea. Battling strafing passes en route, *Detroit*'s adrenaline-fueled gunners somehow managed to knock down several Japanese aircraft.

Jim Gilbert, a young officer assigned to destroyer *Macdonough* (DD-351), was playing cards at the home of *Macdonough*'s executive officer (XO) when the first wave of attackers hit. The two men commandeered a station wagon and reached their ship as the second wave came in. *Macdonough*'s guns shot down one plane and the ship was underway that afternoon.

By the time the aerial attacks on Pearl Harbor ended three hours later, Japanese bombs and torpedoes had reduced a good portion of America's Pacific fleet to sunken or burning ruins. Four U.S. battleships settled, capsized, or disintegrated in the shallows of Battleship Row. Fourteen more ships were lost in the deeper waters of Pearl Harbor's East Loch or mauled at the piers, moorages, and dry docks of Southeast Loch.

Yet, while it seemed at first impossible to look beyond the personal tragedy of the day's losses—nearly 2,500 Americans dead and more than 2,000 of them sailors, a toll eclipsing combined U.S. Navy deaths in World War I and the Spanish-American War—the destruction actually proved to be less than first feared. For one thing, Japan had taken a big bite out of a small apple. The prewar U.S. Navy was a shadow of what it had once been and would need to become. In gross ship tonnage, it was already smaller than the IJN, which had skirted arms limitations treaties and furtively doubled in size and fully modernized after the Great War.

Worse for Japan, considering all the planning and preparation, its superbly skilled carrier-based bomber and torpedo plane pilots had taken the wrong bite: sinking aging, outmoded battleships while, for now at least, the U.S. Navy's aircraft carriers—centerpieces of America's new Pacific Fleet—roamed untouched in open waters.

Still, to scan the horizon of ships present off the southwest beaches of Okinawa on L-Day, little more than three years later, was to marvel at what had emerged from the ashes.

First, at the sheer number of ships, 1,300 in all—a "full-dress armada" in the estimation of *The New Yorker*'s John Lardner. And this did not count the hundreds of other ships in the East China Sea and Pacific, not visible, but still performing missions essential to Iceberg:

- The fast carriers (and their equally fast escort ships) protecting the invasion's western flank, churning through the East China Sea to launch air strikes both on island bastions that might still pose a threat and on Japan itself.
- Army Air Force (AAF) B-29 Superfortress and B-24 Liberator strategic bombers launching long-range strikes against Honshu, Formosa, and coastal China.
- U.S. submarines guarding the exits to Japan's Inland Sea that were alert to movement of any IJN ships that dared emerge.
- Tankers and supply ships sailing from the sprawling mobile storehouse and repair facility at Ulithi to make running, mid-ocean deliveries of fuel and "bombs, beans, and bullets." Even the British, anticipating war's end in Europe and mindful of their postwar colonial interests in Southeast Asia, were represented by a task group of two Royal Navy battleships, five cruisers, and eleven destroyers bombarding islands north of Formosa.

Pearl Harbor veterans such as Mapou had every reason to be amazed by the power of the new ships added to the fleet (including his own ship, destroyer *Pringle* [DD-477]) and the resiliency of the old ships once seemingly left for dead at Pearl Harbor, but now literally, almost miraculously, resurrected.

Second, that the hastily assembled gun crews on the Mapou's aging *Detroit* were able to shoot down attacking Japanese aircraft during the first hours of the war. Once Mapou gathered his own senses that morning, he raced forward to his battle station in the gunhouse of the ship's bow-mounted main battery cannons. Though they were *Detroit*'s most potent weapons, the 6-inch guns never got off a shot as the ship withstood the marauding aircraft.* In Navy argot the 6-inchers were "single-purpose" weapons incapable of elevating high

---

*Naval cannon barrels are measured in two dimensions. The 6-inch dimension here refers to the diameter of the gun's barrel at the muzzle (its bore). The second dimension is the length of rifled gun barrel, measured as a multiple of the bore diameter. A "5-inch-38" refers to a cannon with a 5-inch bore and a rifled barrel that is 190 inches (5 × 38) long.

enough or tracking fast enough for effective antiaircraft use. The ship's smaller 3-inch guns were more nimble but also single purpose; they couldn't be elevated more than thirty-eight degrees. For antiaircraft protection, *Detroit* pretty much depended on short range, small-caliber machine guns. To be knocked down, an aerial attacker had to cooperate by coming in low and close, as the Japanese torpedo planes this day did, pretty much with impunity.

Though *Detroit* was offstage for L-Day, she was still very much afloat, serving as the flagship for a fast carrier replenishment group operating in the East China Sea. Still, from his topside GQ station aboard *Pringle,* Mapou might have been able to spot several other Pearl Harbor veterans in the vast armada, ships that were prime targets that earlier Sunday morning, including *Maryland* (BB-46), *Tennessee* (BB-43), and *West Virginia* (BB-48).

If Maxie Bennett had spotted *West Virginia,* it would have been like seeing a ghost, and a scarcely recognizable one. Kentucky-born Bennett, 26, was now a petty officer gunner's mate aboard destroyer *Heywood L. Edwards* (DD-663), but on 7 December Maxie and his two younger brothers, Lacey and Harry, were all young deck seamen on the huge ship with the diminutive nickname *Wee Vee.*

West Virginia was one of the worst casualties on Battleship Row. After taking nine torpedo hits, she had settled to the harbor bottom, fortunately on an even keel but so full of hull punctures, twisted debris, muck, and water that it took Pearl Harbor salvage crews (including the three brothers) over six months to refloat her. Once they did, dry dock crews made the grisly discovery of seventy corpses trapped in the lower-level compartments; in one of these spaces, a calendar was found with dates scratched off all the way through 23 December 1941.

In July 1944, when *West Virginia* finally emerged from a two-year overhaul at Puget Sound Naval Shipyard, she had a new look. *West Virginia*'s most prominent feature, two towering skeletal "cage" masts used for visual gunfire spotting, were gone, supplanted by less conspicuous but much more effective state-of-the-art radar equipment (then a top secret technology harnessed and made practical by American and British scientists precious steps ahead of the Axis powers) capable of tracking both surface and air contacts at great distances. *West Virginia* was still armed with huge 16-inch main battery guns (eight of them in four heavily armored gun housings: two housings forward and two aft). But, heeding Pearl Harbor's costly lesson that sea warfare was now about detecting and shooting down marauding aircraft, *West Virginia*'s outmoded single-purpose secondary guns were gone, replaced by 5-inch, dual-purpose guns augmented by a bristling arsenal of new rapid-fire antiaircraft guns.

West Virginia also had a new job to complement her new look. In 1941, ships like *West Virginia,* with a top (flank) speed of 21 knots, were already considered slow. Newly constructed ships, including the fleet carriers and the latest generation of battlewagons and cruisers, routinely achieved flank speeds in the 30-knot-plus range. *West Virginia* and her aging sisters simply couldn't keep up with these ships— and no amount of overhaul could much speed them up. However, the war of beachheads supplied an alternative and nearly ideal mission: as heavyweight floating artillery platforms for shore bombardment.

The costly landing on the Tarawa beachhead had betrayed a weakness in U.S. ordinance and tactics. Preinvasion bombardment and air strikes simply lacked enough punch to penetrate thick Japanese bunker, blockhouse, and cave defenses. The battlewagons' 14- and 16-inch guns, which could deliver high-explosive and armor-piercing payloads of a ton or more, were a potent solution in a combat setting where high speed and maneuverability mattered little.

Tin Cans

A third point of wonder was the unparalleled variety of ship types gathered under the same sky. Iceberg's fleet easily dwarfed the paltry task force cobbled together for Operation Watchtower in August 1942, not just in number, but in staggering diversity and versatility. It was as though the U.S. fleet had undergone both a relentless Darwinian-type evolution and an exponential population surge, although the cumulative span of this seagoing "survival of the fittest" was weeks, months, and a scant few years instead of eons or even generations.

The makeshift composition of Watchtower's eighty-two ships was just one reason the name Operation Shoestring stuck, but a compelling one. Many Shoestring ships were ill adapted to the unique demands of amphibious warfare. Virtually none had been explicitly designed for the Pacific war of beachheads. Those that survived to continue in service had since undergone overhauls, and many were converted to support once unanticipated, but now pressing, needs. *Crescent City* (APA-21), for example, had been a Shoestring troop transport. She'd now been reconfigured and stood ready as a makeshift hospital ship for evacuating battle casualties.

Vice Admiral Kelly Turner's flagship *Eldorado,* with its elaborate communications capabilities, was one more example of how the war of beachheads had diversified the shape and functionality of U.S. Navy ships. Though *Eldorado* was a conversion of a newly launched freighter, a host of other ships and craft had been built from the keel up just for amphibious assault. Interspersed among the more conventionally designed warships, transports, and freighters, these craft resembled breeds of uncertain lineage—ungainly, scrappy, and purposeful mongrels. Their designations—many, especially the amphibious craft, had letters and numbers without the inspirational lilt of human, patriotic, or geographical names—only reinforced this impression.

Perhaps the armada's swiftest and most spirited conventional ships were its destroyers. When shifting stations or being dispatched to new assignments, the destroyers seemed to move like penned-in greyhounds or newly bridled colts, as if they were trying to shake off the constraints of being so close to shore.

Destroyers—DD was the shorthand—were hardly a new type of ship. They'd originated in the nineteenth century as "torpedo boat destroyers" designed to counteract small high-speed attack boats armed with deadly and revolutionary new weapons: self-propelled, high-explosive surface torpedoes, first employed with devastating effect in 1891 during an obscure Chilean insurgency. Within a few years, however, the distinctions between cat and mouse blurred—in speed, maneuverability, and armament. The decision to equip torpedo boat destroyers with their own torpedoes all but eliminated the hunter/hunted distinction. Both ship types became known simply as destroyers.

To carrier, battleship, and cruiser sailors, destroyers (and their smaller siblings, destroyer escorts, called DEs) soon became known as "tin cans"—and for good reason. The destroyers were compact, nimble, light, and fast (the DEs, used primarily to hunt submarines, were even lighter, though less well armed and a little slower), but they also carried little armor protection; a well-placed high-caliber projectile or torpedo could easily rip one apart. Despite, or perhaps because of this vulnerability, destroyer crewmen firmly embraced their reputation as tin can sailors. The name conveyed a sense of scrappy, risk-embracing élan. As well, it inspired among these sailors the sort of independent-minded, self-sufficient, and authority-evading behavior not often possible in the more rigid, spit-and-polish worlds of battleships like *West Virginia* and cruisers like *Detroit*.

Destroyers always seemed to be part of any fleet operation because they filled so many roles. In addition to protecting aircraft carrier groups from submarine threats, the destroyers served as plane guards, positioned close astern of the aircraft carriers during launches and landings to retrieve pilots whose aircraft crashed or ditched. (Every destroyer sailor took this role personally and competitively. The standard exchange rate for returning a soaked but living pilot or air crewman to his carrier was ten gallons of ice cream.) Destroyers also escorted supply convoys and, like battleships and cruisers, became offshore artillery platforms before, during, and after amphibious landings.

Citizen Sailors

The tin cans were temporary ships with simple, uniform designs whose useful lives usually did not long outlast the war. And while each had a nucleus of experienced crewmen (like Milton Mapou on *Pringle* and Maxie Bennett on *Heywood L. Edwards*), wartime destroyers were mostly manned by temporary sailors—reserve seamen and freshly schooled petty officers. Though prewar Navy enlisted veterans were not rarities, their numbers had been swamped by hundreds of thousands of new young recruits, lacking sea legs (and sea sense) but often better trained and more technically proficient than Navy regulars.

The same was true for ship's officers. Between wars, Navy wardrooms were almost the exclusive province of Naval Academy graduates, but this began to change as the drumbeats of war intensified. P. A. (Tony) Lilly, a 1941 Naval Academy graduate noticed one of the first harbingers of the change when he arrived at Pearl Harbor for his inaugural seagoing assignment aboard destroyer *Stack* (DD-408). Lilly's scheduled summer graduation had been moved up to February—already a harbinger of the coming war—so he joined *Stack* in the spring, one of a crop of nine recently assigned junior officers. Eight of the nine were Trade School like Lilly, but the ninth was not and seemed out of step, almost from a different planet. He was a civilian college graduate who had been trotted through a quick course on becoming a navy officer—among the first of a tidal wave of fresh-faced "90-day wonders."

One feature of the Navy ranks that remained constant was its whiteness. Though perhaps more refined about it than the other World War II service arms, the Navy's racial segregation was nevertheless implacable. There were blacks and Asians (mostly of Philippine extraction) sprinkled within ranks. These men shared the same decks, passageways, and compartments as white sailors, but they were invariably consigned to a few service rates such as steward, commissary man, and mess cook.*

When Robert M. Morgenthau, a 90-day wonder and son of longtime U.S. Treasury Secretary Henry Morgenthau, Jr., was assigned as XO to destroyer *Lansdale* (DD-426) following tours on two other destroyers, he was both surprised and impressed that *Lansdale*'s skipper had assigned black commissary men to ship gun crews. Despite these occasional exceptions, the racial status quo largely held for enlisted sailors—and held even more firmly for officers. In that sense the case of Navy Commander Gordon P. Chung-Hoon, skipper of *Sigsbee* (DD-502) bordered on the astounding.

Chung-Hoon hadn't come from nowhere. His Hawaiian lineage was impeccable, and his father had been a former treasurer for the Territory of Hawaii, a pedigree that, given the times, likely influenced his Naval Academy appointment. Still, Chung-Hoon quickly made his own mark at the competitive and race-conscious Annapolis, becoming the Navy football team's triple-threat halfback and barefoot punter. That Chung-Hoon had, since graduation, been promoted four times

---

*The exception to this was the destroyer escort USS *Mason* (DE-529), commissioned on 20 March 1944. *Mason,* reputed to be the first Navy ship with a predominantly African American crew (but with a white skipper), served convoy duty in the Atlantic and also operated in the Mediterranean Sea before war's end.

and given command of a combat ship in the Pacific spoke volumes about his ability and tenacity.

If not for this war, most citizen sailors and 90-day wonders would never have gone to sea or been directly in harm's way. Now, as L-Day loomed, even many of those wartime recruits were experienced beyond their years, some to the point of crushing fatigue.

Sailors like Brooklyn-born Larry Finn on destroyer *Bennett* (DD-473) had ridden their ships since construction and commissioning. Finn, 19, by now a yeoman 2nd class with upward of two years' sea-going experience (what sailors called actuals) had already seen action on the "Dirty B" in eight South and Central Pacific battle campaigns including the Solomons, Bougainville, Rabaul, Saipan, Guam, Palau, and Iwo Jima. *Bennett* had been on the "giving" end of most of this action; her closest call was a hit by an airborne torpedo off Iwo Jima. The fish—luckily a dud—clanked *Bennett*'s bow causing minor damage that at first went unnoticed. Still, Finn and his shipmates wondered, just how long could such luck hold?

Compounding the risks of war were the cramped, leaky, exhausting, and nauseating conditions of shipboard life. Destroyers were not designed for crew comfort. On some of the older tin cans, enlisted crewmen's beds still consisted of canvas hammocks suspended from overheads (ceilings) and walls (bulkheads). The metal-framed canvas bunks in newer destroyers were not much better—stacked three high in narrow, low-overhead compartments with barely enough clearance for a sailor to roll over. Berthing compartments were crammed with asbestos-sheathed piping and wiring and dotted with watertight hatches giving access to machinery spaces. The constant clamor of noise and humanity passing through these "living" spaces made sleep a challenge, even under the best of circumstances. In an era that paid virtually no heed to ethnic (or racial) sensitivity, the residents called them "Guinea Pullmans."

Destroyers rode rough, pitching and rolling even in calm seas and tossing so violently in rough seas that the routine positions and functions of life—standing, sitting, walking, eating, sleeping, bathing, excreting—turned perilous and exhausting. This was especially so for older, prewar destroyers whose original designs had been undone by adding more and heavier gun mounts, antennas, transmitters, and other advanced equipment. The idea was to improve their combat capabilities, but what once had been trim ships were now top-heavy and less seaworthy.

Fatigue itself was built into the very fabric of ship schedules. The combination of duty watches (in rotating stints of two, four, or six hours) spaced around ship's maintenance, training, drills, and work parties made for uninterrupted sleep intervals that rarely exceeded two to four hours. The final unavoidable layer of activity was GQ. GQ in actual battle circumstances was one thing. But GQ was most often precautionary; the obscured visibility at dawn and dusk made these hours ideal times for Japanese attackers, so morning and evening calls to GQ were mandatory. It was no wonder that most sailors—despite the urges of youth—longed first and most for the tranquility of uninterrupted sleep.

Still, many seasoned ship veterans by now had learned how to adapt their lives to the landscape, routines, and boundaries of a seabound wartime life. Though no one could expect much privacy or personal freedom in the cramped quarters and working spaces of a combat ship, most somehow carved out a piece of life that was theirs and not the Navy's. For some it was the companionship of kindred souls, men who worked in the same division or gang or, if they didn't, might share a common background or geography.

Indiana native John Vaught, a fireman on destroyer *Bache* (DD-470), immersed himself in a small community of Hoosiers. Vaught, just turned 18, was one of fourteen brothers who all were or would be serving in the military. He had quit high school in 1944 to join the Navy and went to boot camp at Great Lakes with five other Indianans, all of them now on the *Bache*. The six Hoosier boys had a habit of convening on the fantail when assignments and watch schedules permitted. There they would trade shipboard stories and memories of home; one boy played guitar and accompanied the others as they sang familiar songs.

Still other sailors found space in contemplative moments of reading, drawing, or writing. Letter writing—and receiving—was a near universal obsession, but some also captured their thoughts in journals and diaries.

Diaries were a risky matter. Navy and shipboard regulations usually

forbid them—as they did having a camera to take personal photos—
for the legitimate concern that the writings might somehow fall into
enemy hands. Nevertheless, more than a few (and by no means just tin
can sailors) who were inclined and capable took the chance, suspecting
that they were playing at least a small part in world-changing events
and that, if they survived this time, someone later might appreciate
having a personal account of it.

Some wrote furtively, jotting cryptic notes on scraps of paper. As often as not the papers would be lost or discarded, but not always. Leon
Wolper, a shipfitter on destroyer *Richard P. Leary* (DD-664) systematically marked the stations of *Leary*'s journey toward Okinawa in a little
book of dates and places:

November 21st, went back to Manus . . . December 15th we left
Manus . . . Arrived in Palau on December 18th . . . Left January 1st,
1945 . . . Arrived Lingayen Gulf, Luzon, January the 6th . . . The
9th day was D-Day on Lingayen Gulf . . . Left on the 22nd of January and arrived in Ulithi in the Carolines on January 22nd . . . Left
February the 10th . . . Arrived in Saipan on February the 12th, and
left on the 14th . . . Arrived off Iwo Jima on the 16th . . . D-Day was
on the 19th . . . Left Iwo Jima on March the 1st . . . Arrived back in
Ulithi on March the 4th . . . Left Ulithi on the 21st of March. Arrived off Okinawa on the 25th of March.

It was no surprise crewmen whose shipboard duties already included
writing and record keeping—its junior officers, of course, but also its
quartermasters, radiomen, signalmen, and yeoman—were among the
most avid diarists. These men were also among the best informed: they
routinely received, decoded, filed, distributed, encoded, and transmitted information about the ship, its whereabouts, and its imminent activities. Sailors like Wolper knew where *Richard P. Leary* had been,
but not necessarily where she was going. Inside information about the
future made compelling, if speculative, fodder for journal entries.

Dwight Donnewald, a radioman petty officer on destroyer minesweeper *Ellyson* (DD-454/DMS-19) was diligent with a journal he'd
kept during virtually all his time aboard *Ellyson* both in the European
and Pacific Theaters. Some entries were short and a few dates passed

without remark, but usually there were entries that conveyed—in a concise mix of the mundane and the historic—that Donnewald was not just being swept along in the tide of history, but was actually swimming with it. On 18 March 1945, for example, Donnewald's entry marked *Ellyson*'s imminent departure for Okinawa: "Sent Mom Bulova watch. Anchored in Ulithi. Getting underway tomorrow for the big push. Sent Mary $35.00. Got mail."

Orvill Raines, 26, a yeoman on destroyer *Howorth* (DD-592) used his job and its prerogatives to express himself at unusual length and with unusual candor. Yeoman like Finn on *Bennett* and Raines on *Howorth* were the secretaries and administrators of ships' business, affording them unusual access and discretion when it came to the flow of information. Raines' background—he'd been a reporter for the *Dallas Morning News*—inevitably steered him to becoming a yeoman. On board *Howorth,* his watch and GQ stations were on the bridge where he could see and learn more than most other crewmen—including its officers—could. During the day Raines worked in the ship's office where he had the time, tools, and chance to write every day. The results were long, single-spaced typed letters to his wife Ray Ellen. The letters were also relatively unfettered. Ship's officers were responsible for censoring outgoing personal mail, often screening the letters of sailors whose personal lives and circumstances they might hardly know. In Raines' case, though, the censoring was minimal. The letters were reviewed by his division officer, and the only information excised (though not always) concerned *Howorth*'s specific location and the loss of other ships.

Anticipating censorship, cautious sailors self-censored, keeping their letters brief and withholding the core of true thoughts and feelings. By contrast, Raines' letters to Ray Ellen were models of self-expression and personal revelation. They displayed the range of emotions—hope, discouragement, optimism, fatalism—kaleidoscoping through the minds of multitudes of sailors so seemingly close to war's end yet so desperately far from safety and home.

Several days before L-Day Raines wrote: "Do you know that every time I learn about another operation, the first thing I think of is 'Boy that's dangerous as hell.' The second thing is you. Darling, I'm sure I'm not a coward. I realize that I get scared. It's my opinion that it does a little good to be afraid sometimes. (And honest, Baby, I'm not boasting.) But I sincerely believe I'm not afraid of dying. Naturally, I don't want to and it troubles me at times but really, deep down, my fear is not getting back to you."

Virtually every Navy ship experienced nuisance levels of gambling, larceny, and petty misdemeanors, the by-product of testosterone-drunk young men accommodating—but not entirely caving in to—military discipline. The results were usually more inventive and sanity preserving than nasty—in fact, the tighter the efforts to control it, the more it was likely to flare.

While a lot of this larcenous behavior involved snatching food, as much or more involved the distillation and consumption of forbidden spirits. On tin cans at least, the illicit beverage of choice was some variant of "torpedo juice," a concoction of citrus juice (usually filched during all-hand provision details before it reached ship's stores) and the high-proof, near lethal alcohol used to fuel the ship's torpedoes.

Not every sailor joined in these escapades, but nearly all at least appreciated that they were happening. The incidents made great scuttlebutt (gossip) and were living proof that military rank and shipboard discipline could still be subverted, challenged, or occasionally disregarded.

Appreciated most were the true artisans, veteran sailors who weren't so much pranksters or thieves as they were inventive and offhand naturals at practicing chicanery, at using concealment, and at making a difficult, often tedious, life just a tad better for themselves and their shipboard pals. These experts brewed torpedo juice in ingenious little stills; they snatched freshly baked bread loaves or pies; and they skimmed contraband from any valuable stores or supplies that came aboard ship.

One of the resident artisans on destroyer *Bache* was 24-year-old Roland O'Dette, a fireman assigned to the forward engine room. O'Dette was a true connoisseur of contraband: especially vegetables (for a soup he prepared), pies, and coffee. O'Dette also swiped whole chickens, suspending their carcasses from the engine room piping to tenderize them before cooking. But O'Dette's supreme achievement was a bathtub he'd rigged up, making use of the compartment's ready access to hot and cold freshwater plumbing. The tub was a unique luxury; it provided some bathing privacy and an alternative to saltwater showers. Of course, the tub also doubled as a still and a vat for cooking.

For every war-weary sailor like Finn, Mapou, and Bennett, there were sailors on the other side of the ledger: young boots and fresh graduates of fleet training schools eager to get in before the war—and history—passed them by. Electrician's Mate Third Class Bill Wyatt, a West Philadelphia native, was just one of these. Wyatt's parents had refused him permission to join the Navy, so when he came of age on his 18th birthday, Wyatt promptly enlisted. After boot camp Wyatt was sent to Purdue University for several months' training in electrical engineering. At the end of this training, he volunteered for submarine duty, only to find out he would be sent for still more months of training on gyroscopes. As 1945 began, Wyatt felt his chance for getting to sea and into the war slipping away; he applied for a transfer, and within the week was on the way to the West Coast where destroyer *Daly* (DD-519) was completing overhaul.

The war also seemed to be getting away from Brooklyn-born Jim Villiers. Villiers had also joined the Navy at 18, but that was in 1942. Since leaving boot camp, Villiers had been sent to one stateside shore billet after another, usually to do torpedo repair and overhaul work. By early 1944, when he reached destroyer *Cooper* (DD-695), then under construction in Kearny, New Jersey, Villiers was a torpedoman 2nd class, yet had never been to sea. As *Cooper* neared commissioning and and shakedown time, the ship's chief torpedoman, who experienced a few dustups with Villiers, wanted to get Villiers out of his hair by sending him to yet another advanced school. Since the school was open only to second class petty officers, Villiers went AWOL briefly, hoping punishment would cost him a stripe and keep him on the *Cooper*. Sent to Captain's Mast when he returned, Villiers explained his thinking to *Cooper*'s skipper who decided Villiers could keep both his stripe and his billet.

Yet another case was Fred Mitchell, an 18-year-old from Meadville, a farming community near Pittsburgh, who was a radar striker on the new destroyer *Drexler* (DD-741). Mitchell was a high school freshman at the time of Pearl Harbor and knew he'd be going into the service as soon as he graduated three years later.

To ready himself, Mitchell joined a cadet training program in his high school and soon was swept up in the heady prospect of becoming an Army aviation cadet. Mitchell's plans appalled his mother, a native of Austria, and she refused to sign the papers clearing him to begin aviation training. In the end Mitchell persuaded her to let him join the Navy, using the lever of his father's youthful service in the Czarist Russian merchant marine (Mitchell's original surname was Mihilov). His father, meanwhile, stood clear of the mother-son dispute. He knew Fred was afraid of heights and would never get far in aviation. Before Fred enlisted, his father also hinted that life at sea wasn't apt to be as glamorous as his son might think.

New recruit Don Roller, a 19-year-old signalman striker had begun his shipboard life on board *Cowell* (DD-547) in July 1944 when he joined her in Eniwetok, just weeks out of boot camp. Roller was assigned as a lowly deck seaman, as were most boot sailors sent to the fleet, but he was soon plucked from that drudgery. His deliverance came in an intra-ship baseball game on Eniwetok pitting *Cowell*'s left-arm rates (the deck and engineering gangs) and right-arm rates (technical specialists on the bridge, in communications, radar, radio, and signaling). The right-arm rates (the nerds of their day) were chronically short of good ballplayers, so Roller, who excelled in high school baseball and would pitch briefly in the Boston Braves farm system after the war, was drafted. He promptly clobbered two home runs to clinch the game for the right-arm rates. Next day *Cowell*'s chief signalman arranged for Roller to join the signal gang.

Even for the citizen sailors, the Navy was the first, though skewed, exposure to the notions of skills, careers, and family—things to consider beyond the next payday or shore leave. Given Depression-era realities, many had already done tedious, low-paying, often back-breaking work during or since their school years. Some had quit school early to earn some money or to escape poverty-plagued homes. However, for a typical young enlisted sailor enmeshed in his teenage years and his sense of invulnerability (and now being fed, housed, and clothed at government expense), it was simply too early to be giving thought to much besides the sights and events of each day and bonding with his buddies.

But among this huge, often aimless herd, there was a scattering of what must have seemed, at least to the young sailors, odd, even misfit cases: older men with established (or at least advancing) lives, including careers and families, who somehow had wound up in the Navy.

There were, for example, sailors like Hugo Cipriani, a quartermaster petty officer on *Bache*. Cipriani, nearly 32, had enlisted in the Navy in 1942. In the decade before enlisting, Cipriani had bounced around the country in true Depression-era fashion, leaving his Ohio home twice and hitchhiking each time to the promise of California. Cipriani had lived in transient camps, worked as a golf caddy for the likes of Bing Crosby, Bob Hope, and Mickey Rooney—and even wangled his way into a brief enrollment at UCLA.

Another example was torpedoman petty officer Sam Elrod stationed on destroyer *Callaghan* (DD-792). Elrod, also just shy of 32, raised many eyebrows on ship. Back in his town of Hominy, Oklahoma, Sam had been a rural high school teacher and coach. Despite Elrod's petty officer rank (one key to his advancement was his experience coping with boisterous teenagers), it was a little bit like having your teacher leave the front of the classroom and seat himself in the middle of the class.

Elrod was stocky and energetic, with an enthusiastic curiosity about virtually everything around him. To inquisitive shipmates wondering why he was in the Navy at all, Elrod would comment simply that he'd just felt "the urge to be in it." Elrod, a bachelor and the youngest of twelve brothers and sisters, wrote short enthusiastic bursts of (self-censored) letters to his sister Mary Ellen in Oklahoma, with side messages to her husband Tom, his niece Peggy, and nephew Melvin. "Thompsons," began one such letter, speculating on war's end, "have your post-war plans made. If not, here they are, one bunk for an x-sailor, fishing pole, one gun, and ammo. Plenty to eat for thirty days. I guess all the people that were kids when I left are grown up by now. How is fishing Tom? . . . Come out and help us out—just too much to do and, well, it's like driving an 80-penny [nail] with a light bulb."

Usually upbeat, Elrod had nonetheless seen the toll the war was taking and had a cryptic cautionary note for his pubescent niece: "Peggy is almost old enough to get a boyfriend? Tell her to start early. Men will be scarce as dollars after the war."

* * *

From the top down, a tin can's commanding officer (CO) could run and fight his ship as a compact and integrated weapon—something that cruiser and battleship COs (who often had served on destroyers early in their careers) could only wistfully imagine. Meanwhile, from the bottom up, destroyer sailors could both demonstrate and appreciate their individual value to the success and survival of the ship.

There was a well-struck balance—on good ships at least—between commander and commanded (including especially seasoned petty officers such as Elrod, Finn, Bennett, and Mapou and savvy, sometimes miscreant, hands like O'Dette). Ships, even tin cans, were not democracies. Nevertheless, the best and most savvy skippers (and other ship's officers too) learned not just to invoke rank when making the difficult decisions for a warship at sea. These skippers could simultaneously keep a distance and maintain an image of unbending firmness while still conveying a sense of fairness and beneficence toward their crews.

Lots of skippers were not above using their subordinate officers as foils, playing wise, infallible cop against their inflexible, by-the-book cops. In more than one change of command ceremony, for example, a new CO had introduced himself to the crew by saying: "Men, my job is to learn to get along with you," and then, dramatically and ominously eyeing his wardroom officers, continue: "and your job is to learn to get along with me." Destroyer *Lansdale*'s CO had succinctly explained his leadership approach to new XO Robert Morgenthau: "This ship will work if one of us is a son of a bitch. It's not going to be me."

There was no underestimating this dynamic between commanders and commanded. Though many sailors had been motivated to join the wartime Navy by the threat of being drafted into the Army, they were still volunteers. They might be in for "the duration," but usually not for a day more.

By dint of culture, democratic mindset, and naval traditions that were comparatively weak and still emerging, it was fair to say the United States had a Navy quite unlike any other. It was certainly unlike the IJN, which, while trying to outstrip the United States in naval power, blended the rigid command formalities (modeled on the British Royal Navy) with its own national traditions of unflinching control and unquestioning obedience. While U.S. Navy commanders outwardly depended on rigid command structures, the best fully understood that it was a case of leading—and earning the respect of—the willing.

For these reasons—the shared miseries, the cramped quarters, the utter interdependency of being on a small ship in a big ocean and a bigger war—the roughly three hundred officers and crew assigned to good tin cans tended to form unusually strong bonds with their ship and their shipmates. For ships in the Pacific (where equatorial operations were the norm), the bond was sealed, not only by the shared ordeal and tedium of war, but also by "crossing-the-line" hazing ceremonies during which lowly polliwogs (those who had not crossed the equator aboard a ship) were transformed to shellbacks (those who had). If Marines and GIs ashore fought less for a grand cause and more for their buddies, squad, platoon, or company, it was the same with tin can sailors. When it came down to it, most would risk their lives for only three things, in rough order: their shipmates, their skipper, and their ship.

Left Behind

Tin cans were present at Pearl Harbor on 7 December and several, like *Macdonough*, acquitted themselves as well or better than the large ships during the morning's chaos. Indeed, the opening blow was actually struck by a U.S. destroyer. Patrolling the harbor entrance in the hours before the Japanese aircraft arrived, *Ward* (DD-139), an ancient four stacker pulled from mothballs just two months before (and whose skipper, Lieutenant William W. Outerbridge, had taken command just two days before), cornered and sank a small Japanese submarine trying to enter the harbor in the wake of a target-towing vessel. Minutes later, rushing into the harbor to assist *Ward*, *Monaghan* (DD-354), a second and more modern destroyer, struck a glancing blow to a Japanese midget submarine and then promptly dispatched it with depth charges.

Ward's and *Monaghan*'s exploits were the first combat experiences of any sort for both ships' crews, including Richard Farwell, then a green ensign and assistant engineering officer on *Ward*. As it was, Farwell sat out the entire engagement at his GQ station in *Ward*'s No. 2 boiler room. From this hot, airless vantage, Farwell and his black-gang personnel were essentially blind and deaf; *Ward* lacked internal radio communications circuits, depending instead on voice tubes. The only clues they got were the rattling of deck plates and the dropping of small bits of asbestos lagging from the steam lines when *Ward*'s gunners dropped depth charges and fired deck guns. "We all had visions of a torpedo coming through the hull into our compartment," Farwell later recalled. "Still, this was real action."

There was, of course, a lot of action this day—most of it disastrous. This isolated first-day success aside, early battles with superior Japanese ships with better-trained crews, smarter tactics, and more lethal weapons unremittingly proved the U.S. Navy lacked enough good destroyers and battle-tested crews to man them.

This deficiency played out glaringly and tragically at Guadalcanal in the aftermath of the IJN's audacious destruction of four Allied cruisers on the night just after the Marine landings. Three days later, on 10 August 1942, when he decided to send his unprotected supply fleet to the safety of the open sea, Vice Admiral Kelly Turner sent a curt message to the commanding officers of three World War I era destroyers being used as high-speed Marine Raider transports. "I regret I must leave you behind."

One of these three nearly identical ships was *Gregory* (APD-3), a thousand-ton converted destroyer whose already limited weaponry had been reduced further to make room for troop quarters and the four davit-mounted landing craft suspended from her sides. *Gregory*'s newest and youngest ship's officer was Ensign Alvin Gallin, 22, a Brooklyn native and newly minted graduate of the U.S. Naval Academy.

When *Gregory*'s skipper Lieutenant Commander Harry F. Bauer got the order from Turner to stay put while the bulk of the Watchtower fleet left, his disgust, Gallin remembered, was instant and profane. "The son of a bitch doesn't regret this half as much as I do!"

But if Bauer's first reaction was profane, it was also prophetic. At month's end, one of the three fragile APDs, *Colhoun* (APD-2), was sunk with the loss of 51 crewmen during a Japanese low-level bombing attack. Then, on the night of 4 September, after disembarking Marine

Raiders on Savo Island, the two remaining APDs, *Gregory* and *Little* (APD-4), were pounced on by a superior force of three modern Japanese destroyers.

Once again the Japanese ships had crept in close and undetected (neither *Gregory* nor *Little* was equipped with adequate radar and their position was betrayed by overhead flares dropped by friendly aircraft) and aimed their high-power searchlights on the U.S. ships. Gallin was racing to his GQ station in charge of the ship's after 4-inch gun as the Japanese unleashed a torrent of well-aimed gunfire. The topside sailors—including Gallin and his young gun crew—were all caught like deer in headlight beams. Japanese fire concentrated accurately on *Gregory*'s thin-skinned superstructure and bridge. The forward part of the ship was soon consumed by explosions and flame that killed skipper Bauer as well as *Gregory*'s XO and gunnery officer.

With the fight and the ship lost—both *Gregory* and *Little* were sunk that night without inflicting any damage on the Japanese destroyers—Gallin and a handful of sailors abandoned ship in a bullet-riddled landing craft only to have it sink as well. Now, twice shipwrecked, the *Gregory* survivors (two of them brothers) were left dangling in the dark treacherous waters between Tulagi, Savo, and Guadalcanal without enough life jackets to go around. One of the brothers had a badly injured leg, and the other brother refused to leave him when the group considered making a try for shore. And so they all agreed to stick it out while huddling together in the oil-slicked water, taking turns with the life jackets, and clinging to the hope of rescue.

It was perhaps best that they hadn't tried for shore. When morning finally arrived, another of *Gregory*'s boats spotted and retrieved the exhausted band. The men in this boat had tried to reach Lunga Point during the night only to be turned back by gunfire from edgy Marines. As it turned out, the night's bloody, one-sided fiasco cost the lives of eighty-three officers and crewmen, including, in addition to Harry Bauer, *Little*'s skipper Gus Lofberg and Hugh W. Hadley, the commander of a now extinct destroyer division.

Not surprisingly, Gallin carried the ordeal of Iron Bottom Sound with him ever after. The night—and the things he had experienced since—took big helpings of his youth and the self-assurance and sense of invincibility that were youth's birthright. On 1 April 1945, Gallin, now nearing 25, was a full lieutenant, had been decorated with a bronze star, and was a seasoned operations and gunnery officer aboard destroyer *Bryant* (DD-665), a new ship twice the size of *Gregory* with many times its firepower. It was the type of ship, service pedigree, and scope of responsibility that restored self-assurance and, if not invincibility, at least a sense of resiliency. Still, Gallin was mindful of what it felt like in the murderous glare of those Japanese searchlights and in the lonely waters afterward. It made him just a bit fatalistic. If something like that moment—an event over which he had no control—came now, a part of Gallin prayed that it would at least come swiftly and with no pain.

★ Chapter 3 ★

Green Hells

This was a brutish primitive hatred, as characteristic of the horror of war in the Pacific as the palm trees and the islands.

—Eugene Sledge

The Old Breed

A platoon of 6th Division Marines sailed with destroyer *Drexler* when ship and crew left the Solomon Islands en route to the Ryukyus. To every *Drexler* sailor and every Marine passenger, it was obvious this was part of a big push. Why else cram groups of soldiers with all their gear onto ships never intended to carry them?

Space was tight on *Drexler,* so for sleeping quarters the Marines had to make do with cots lined up and lashed down amidships along the railings. The deck force rigged tarps overhead to shelter their guests from the worst of the sun, wind, and rain, but it was a soaked and seasick journey for most of the Marines.

Although they were apt to be wary of interlopers, a handful of *Drexler* sailors did make an effort to befriend their guests over cigarettes and deck-rail chatter. Radar striker Fred Mitchell, not yet 19, struck up a relationship with one Marine who looked to be about his age. The 6th was a newly formed division headed for its first taste of combat. Nevertheless, many individual Marines, Mitchell's new friend included, had seen plenty of action with other units.

The Marine related some of his experiences and asked if Mitchell had ever been in combat. Mitchell hadn't—he was fresh from boot camp and radar training, assigned to a ship that, like the 6th Marine

Division, was heading to its first action. Clearly the saltier of the pair, the Marine offered Mitchell a small bit of combat wisdom he said might come in handy even at sea. "If you sense something coming your way—a shell or a bomb—hit the deck and make yourself as small a target as possible."

The Central Pacific was a war of naval and air power in which the Marines and GIs who made the landings on hostile islands and atolls—eleven assaults in six distinct Central Pacific campaigns—were vastly outnumbered by the shipboard sailors who hosted, delivered, supplied, and shielded them across thousands of ocean miles.

Though statistically outnumbered, it was undeniably the frontline Marines and GIs who suffered most of the casualties—roughly 100,000 killed, wounded, or missing in those hard-fought island battles. The heaviest of those losses spread among just eleven combat divisions: six of them Marine and five of them Army. If not always in terms of total manpower, then certainly in terms of reputation and impact, the war on and beyond the beachheads was identified more with the Marines than it was with the GIs.

The U.S. Marine Corps began its fabled history as the Navy's army—contingents of shipboard troops unleashed for coastal raids and as boarding parties for close-in ship-to-ship combat or for capturing merchant prizes. The biggest modern ships—carriers, battleships, and cruisers—still carried small Marine Detachments.

The Marine Detachment on light cruiser *Nashville* (CL-43) consisted of forty-two Marines, mostly teenagers whose only active service, following boot camp and an orientation course called sea school, was aboard ship. For the most part, these vestigial seagoing Marines performed roles at the highest—and lowest—echelons of shipboard business: serving as orderlies to flag officers and running the ships' brigs. (There were parts of the ship where only senior officers and enlisted Marines could go, and woe betides a sailor sentenced to the brig who had ever publicly badmouthed his jailers.)

It was only during GQ, when no manpower was wasted, that these Marines got any opportunity for combat—as gun crews for ships' AA batteries. Twenty or so men from *Nashville*'s detachment were assigned to 20-mm guns mounted on the port and starboard sides of the boat deck amidships while the rest were mixed in with sailor crews on twin 40-mm mounts. The GQ station for Ben Limbaugh, 20, from Batavia, Illinois, was 20-mm mount No. 13 on the starboard side. Two buddies, Harold Struss and Jim Nelson (the three had gone through boot camp, attended sea school together, and been assigned to *Nashville* at the same time), were stationed on other 20s nearby.

The Marine Detachment's CO was First Lieutenant Tommy Thompson. Thompson, 25, an eight-year Marine veteran, had originally joined the Corps as an enlisted man and received his commission via officer candidate school (OCS) after the war began. Thompson stood 6 feet 2 and comported himself with ramrod bearing and precision. To the younger leathernecks, like Limbaugh, Struss, and Nelson, Thompson seemed a "Marine's Marine"—a term that was part admiring and part disparaging. They speculated that Thompson even slept at attention. They also took secret pleasure in Thompson's actual first name—Rufus.

Virtually all of *Nashville*'s Marines were happy with their assignments. They were not only glad to be part of the Corps, but also glad not to be sharing the travails of their brother Marines in the Fleet Marine Force (FMF) units doing all the fighting on the godforsaken islands they'd only glimpsed through binoculars from *Nashville*'s decks.

When Tommy Thompson graduated from OCS, it seemed that the top performers like him were being selected for sea school and eventual shipboard duty. Seen in that light it was an honor—and part of a tradition that went back to the Corps' earliest days. At the same time, Thompson had no illusions. He knew of the casualty counts being racked up among young Marine officers and was sure his ground combat tour was coming.

These small Marine Detachments aside, the Corps had long since eclipsed its original role to become a multidivision island combat force of nearly half a million men. Unless he was assigned to a ship big enough to have a Marine Detachment (or as in *Drexler*'s case, was temporarily transporting Marines), the average U.S. Navy sailor knew little about the average U.S. Marine—and vice versa. It was as if they were from two different tribes or species. They were shore liberty rivals in ports ringing the Pacific and, by extension, boisterous opponents in boasting and drinking bouts, opposing corners in love triangles, and combatants in the no-holds-barred brawls that shore liberty, boasting, drinking, and wartime romance tended to ignite.

Marines initially scored better in the game of envy: more young men who dreamed of becoming Marines ended up as sailors than the reverse. But with any exposure to combat, the balance of envy soon shifted. Sailors walked on rolling, but sturdy decks, could sleep in actual beds (though in the equatorial Pacific most slept topside whenever possible), and ate full (though monotonous and often unappetizing) meals at regular intervals. The combat Marine shared none of these amenities (at least not for extended periods) while living mostly under open sky or tent canvas and doing his work literally in the Valley of the Shadow of Death.

Indeed, the closer a sailor's work took him to shore, the greater his appreciation of the Marines' mortality—and the more likely he was to catch the scent of his own. Closest of all were sailors on troop transports and on amphibious craft shuttling or escorting Marines, GIs, and their equipment to the beaches.

Some of the larger amphibious ships developed deep allegiances to the Marines they knew. During the September 1944 battle to capture the Southwest Pacific island of Peleliu, the skipper and crew of *LST-661* arranged to deliver a hot meal of pork chops to a company of Marines stationed deep in the island's mangrove swamps. For these Marines who had ridden *LST-661*, this hot meal was virtually the only decent meal they received during their entire time on Peleliu.

The boat crews on the hundreds of tiny amphibious craft that actually delivered soldiers to the beaches on H-hour came closest of all. During beach runs these sailors shared, albeit briefly, the exposure, risks, and mortality of their passengers. Robert "Duke" DeLuca, a signalman on board *Henrico* (APA-45), a troop transport that saw service in both the Atlantic and Pacific, was part of a three-man crew for a landing barge delivering the first wave of troops to Normandy's Omaha Beach. When a German artillery shell blew off the bow of DeLuca's craft, he was wounded on the heel. Their craft demolished, DeLuca and the rest of the boat crew were stranded on the beach for three days before being evacuated; by the time he'd been retrieved and accounted for, DeLuca's parents had received notification he'd been killed in action.

John Brooks, another *Henrico* sailor, had an experience that, while not as close-in, was equally harrowing. Brooks, 21, a motor machinist petty officer, participated in an impromptu pre-landing incursion off the same beach. He was one of ninety sailors embarked predawn on utility boats equipped with racks of 4.5-inch rockets. The sailor volunteers became, in effect, a poor man's version of specially trained and equipped UDT specialists. Brooks' group hardly looked the part: they were hatless and wearing sailor dungarees (shorn of buttons and brass buckles) and shoes without laces. They carried wooden trenching tools and bags of TNT marinated in diesel fuel.

After the utility craft first fired their rocket salvos trying to take out floating mines, the sailors were dispatched in small inflatable canvas boats. They had two objectives: to mark the remaining floating mines with orange flags so that Army Ranger battalions preceding the main landings could avoid them and to explode beach obstacles using their trenching tools and TNT charges.

It turned out to be a chaotic, and quixotic exploit that was all but suicidal. The beach obstacles found by Brooks and the others turned out to be firmly anchored in cement reinforced by I-beams. All they could do was triple the charges on some obstacles, leave others untouched, and then do their best to escape a hail of mortar and small arms fire. Brooks was lucky, emerging from the fray bone soaked, shivering, terrified, but unscarred. More than 70 others were either killed or wounded—all this before a Ranger or GI set foot on Omaha Beach.

By the benchmark of proximity, the average destroyer sailor could understand the average Marine in only an abstract way. Still, if his ship stood close enough to shell the invasion beach and he was stationed topside, a sailor might be able to see the Marines as distant toy soldier-like specks, running, taking cover, or falling in circumstances he could only imagine too well. He might even help some of the wounded being returned on the same landing craft that brought them in. Each destroyer usually had a physician assigned—and these "medical officers" and their pharmacist's mate assistants treated some of the worst and most gruesome casualties.

If a destroyer sailor worked one of his ship's main battery guns, he also understood how his crew's performance might assist, save, or even kill Marines. Harold Scott, the gunnery officer on *Bennion* (DD-662), had barely slept for days before the February 1945 assault on Iwo Jima because he worried over instructions received at a preinvasion briefing. He was told to keep his gunfire one hundred yards ahead of the Marine advance while *Bennion* cruised less than a mile offshore. At such close range and with so little tolerance for error, Scott feared his firing trajectory would be so flat as to risk mowing down the advancing Marines. In the days leading up to the assault, Scott kept his gunner's mates busy experimenting with reduced powder charges to solve the difficult equation of arc and range. Luckily, *Bennion* was detached from the invasion fleet's main body to escort battleship *New York* (BB-34), which was having propeller problems. The slow trip afforded Scott the opportunity to practice at sea using the reduced charges. En route he painstakingly measured and fine-tuned the accuracy of *Bennion*'s 5-inch guns, using both radar and optical spotting. Only just before *Bennion*'s arrival off Iwo Jima was Scott finally satisfied his rounds would not be hitting American boys.

However close or distant, direct or abstract their appreciation of the Marines' dangerous and grimy work, every sailor knew or would soon learn one important thing. And if for no other reason, this one thing made every sailor wish the Marines quick success. It was this: the sooner the Marines bulled their way through Japanese resistance to secure an island objective, the sooner the ships could leave the vicinity of the island, where they were sitting ducks, and return to where they were best able to defend themselves and were hardest to find—maneuvering in the expanses of the Pacific Ocean.

The Marines who fought in the Pacific War's first offensive battles—in "green hells" with already legendary names like Guadalcanal, Cape Gloucester, and Tarawa—were mainly professional soldiers whose service predated the war. Individually they might be young, but as the Corps expanded rapidly with the addition of tens of thousands of new recruits, this core of veterans carried the mantle of the "Old Breed."

Many new Marine recruits—all of them volunteers—joined know-ing little about the Corps and even less about the Old Breed. Eugene Sledge, an Alabaman who dropped out of his freshman year at Marion Military Institute to enlist in the Corps in December 1942 (and pur-posely washed out of Marine officer training early to reach the action sooner), got his first glimpse of the reality of the Corps from the re-cruiting sergeant who signed him up.

Sledge was hardly recruiting poster material. Weighing in at 135 pounds, Sledge (who later would be nicknamed Sledgehammer by his Marine buddies) was slim, quiet, introspective, and mild mannered. The sergeant, contrastingly crisp and professional in blue dress trou-sers, khaki shirt and tie, and white barracks hat, asked Sledge a lot of questions and used the answers to fill out a stack of official-looking forms. But when the sergeant asked about "scars, birthmarks, or other unusual features," the new recruit was curious. Sledge identified an inch-long scar on his right knee, but then asked naively why the Corps needed to know. "So" the sergeant replied, "they can identify you on some Pacific beach after the Japs blast off your dog tags."

During the rigorous months of boot camp and combat training that followed, Sledge would have the opportunity to observe and consider the demeanor of Old Breed Marines. It was not swagger. In-stead, Sledge noticed, each "had an intangible air of subdued, quiet detachment. . . . Sometimes his mind seemed a million miles away, as though lost in some sort of melancholy reveries." Sledge sensed right away that this was a spontaneous look, one that could not be faked or bluffed. He wondered if he would take on that look himself one day. And, if he did, what would be the cost for gaining it?

In February 1944, when Sledge and his buddies completed their stateside training and began their journey to the Pacific, they also got their first exposure to Navy accommodations. Boarding the *President Polk,* a passenger liner converted to Navy use, they were assigned to a belowdecks troop compartment. The compartment was dimly lit, foul smelling and incinerator hot; the Marines' bunks—racks—were stacked seven high with barely two feet of headroom.

Chow was another grim experience: the same hot air, the same sleeping compartment aroma comprised of paint, grease, tobacco, and sweat overlaid by the smells of rancid cooking. "It was enough to turn a civilian's stomach inside out," Sledge recalled, "but we rapidly and necessarily adjusted." Still, if this was what life in the Navy was like, he and his buddies wanted no part of it.

The Marines' only relief from the crowded, malodorous environment belowdecks was to go topside. *President Polk*'s weather decks were jammed as well, but at least there was fresh air. There were also new sensations: the seemingly unbounded ocean, its intriguing sights and smells, and the powerful, throbbing motion of the ship. Exciting at first, these sensations eventually began to subdue the Marines with the realization that *President Polk* was taking them ever farther from home and bringing them ever closer to the unknown.

The novelty of ocean travel and the invigoration of fresh air ultimately failed to offset the boredom of a voyage that dragged on for more than two weeks through an unvarying seascape. Aside from daily muster, the Marines had no place to be or duties to perform. What relief there was took two forms—participating in abandon-ship drills every few days and watching the shipboard gun crews practice their antiaircraft skills against yellow target balloons.

The Marines were not particularly impressed with the Navy guns or their crews. The machine guns—the 20-mm and 40-mm—seemed to do all right, but the barking 5-inch cannons seemed to accomplish little more than hurt the ears. Sledge, who had qualified as a rifle sharpshooter and been trained on mortars, did not think much of their accuracy. "Considering the number of balloons that escaped, we felt the gun crews should have practiced more." But then, he reasoned, maybe the marines "didn't realize what a difficult type of gunnery was involved."

Howlin' Mad

If the Navy's Vice Admiral Richmond Kelly Turner had been a species of sea creature evolving toward an existence on land, it is conceivable he would have emerged from the water transformed into Marine General Holland Smith. More familiarly and justifiably known as "Howlin' Mad," Smith, 62, was, like Sledge, Alabama-born. Unlike Sledge, however, Smith was backwoods reared, boisterous, and volatile. Smith bore an uncanny resemblance (in looks, speech, and mannerisms) to Wallace Beery, a beefy, roughhewn, Depression-era movie character actor—a resemblance he carried from cradle to grave.

Smith developed a special genius for translating Turner's exacting and obsessive ideas about amphibious operations into winning combat tactics ashore. And with experience came another uncanny, more sobering ability. As far as *Time* reporter Robert Sherrod was concerned, Smith "estimated the enemy capabilities better than any other individual I talked to." Smith's casualty forecasts for upcoming assaults were usually accurate—and usually grim. Smith knew the Japanese fought to win and, to overcome them, his Marines needed realistic preparation—training that individual Marines like Sledge learned was "savage, brutal, inhumane, and dirty," but also essential if they were to survive without breaking physically or mentally.

As a teenager Smith had been offered an appointment to Annapolis, but his father, president of the Alabama Railway Commission, refused to let his son attend a Yankee-controlled institution. Instead, the younger Smith pursued law and even set up practice in Mongomery before concluding he hated the profession and needed to escape his father's shadow. In 1905 Smith set out for Washington, DC, hoping to be appointed an Army officer. Finding this path blocked, he settled instead for a Marine Corps commission, even though at the time he had no idea what the Marine Corps was. In the nearly four decades since, Howlin' Mad's estimation of the U.S. Army had plunged about as much as his passion for the U.S. Marines had soared.

In 1939, the then brigadier general Smith had been assigned to oversee the Corps' first foray into amphibious warfare training. Like Turner, once Smith was in, he was all in. Working with Ernest King, at the time a rear admiral commanding the U.S. Atlantic Fleet, Smith basically created an entirely new set of tactics, from instructing Navy gun crews how to fire at shore targets to training Marines how to scramble down rope cargo nets into landing craft.

One huge early problem was the virtual lack of practical landing craft. For a time, Marines were limited to practicing with two ancient and unreliable ship's launches. As training progressed, however, Smith began collaborating with Louisiana boatbuilder Andrew Jackson Higgins. Together they devised and Higgins designed what became the Higgins boat (the navy parlance would be LCVP for Landing Craft Vehicle, Personnel), a stout, plywood, flat-bottom, high-gunwale craft with a retractable rampart bow. The Higgins boat was capable of carrying troops and even light tanks from offshore transports through shallow waters directly onto sandy beaches.

When lowered on the beach, the Higgins boat's full-width bow ramp offered a quick exit route for troops. The innovation made assaults on open beaches possible—Allied Supreme Commander in Europe Dwight D. Eisenhower later extolled Higgins as "the man who won the war for us."*

The Higgins boat was the craft driven by Duke DeLuca and the other APA coxswains to bring the troops ashore at Normandy. Although the Higgins bow ramp was a stroke of genius, its use exacted an enormous cost: disembarking troops became instant targets for shore defenders. The Higgins bow exit quickly became known as the murder hole.

As versatile as the Higgins boat was, it was still a propeller-powered boat needing at least some water under it to maneuver. It turned out nearly all Pacific island objectives were ringed by hard coral reefs. When tides exposed these reefs, unwary boat coxswains sometimes ran aground, leaving boats and troops stranded. If the troops tried to wade ashore, they took particularly heavy casualties. To solve this problem, Smith began experimenting with a vehicle first developed for rescue work in the Florida Everglades. This vehicle evolved into the amphtrac—the Landing Vehicle, Tracked (LVT).

The amphtrac floated on pontoons and rolled on cleated tank treads, enabling the craft not only to propel itself in water but also to climb across exposed reefs and move troop cargoes directly onto the beach and even inland. On the most advanced models, troops used a stern ramp to exit the amphtrac, giving them extra moments before exposure to enemy small arms fire. With all these features, the amphtrac was an ideal amphibious warfare vehicle for the Pacific. Unfortunately, like so many technical advancements introduced early in the war, the

---

*Eisenhower's frames of reference were the gently sloping beaches of coastal Europe rather than the reef-girdled islands of the Central Pacific where LCVPs often could not get past the reefs to reach the beach.

production and availability of amphtracs ended up lagging well behind the desperate need for them.

The war also was well along before Smith actually saw the results of the lessons he'd instilled in thousands of young Marines and GIs. At its outbreak, Smith was a major general and corps commander, but he was still training Marine and Army divisions on Caribbean beaches when Watchtower kicked off.

Transferred to the West Coast in 1942, Smith impatiently marked time in a training role; the closest he got to the action was watching from a circling aircraft as the Army's 7th Division landed on the Aleutian island of Attu. It was only with the opening of the Central Pacific strategy in 1943, when Alexander Vandegrift, the Marines' Guadalcanal leader, left the Pacific to become Marine Corps Commandant, that Smith, still eager and ornery at the age of 60, finally got the combat assignment he always wanted. His first real exposure to the war of beachheads came in the invasions of the Gilbert Islands.

Murder Holes

The Japanese had been taken by surprise at Guadalcanal in what was actually a struggle between two competing invaders. The toll of U.S. dead, wounded, and missing racked up on Guadalcanal gave just a hint of what lay ahead. Casualties of 30 percent were considered a rough benchmark for the most a fighting unit could take and still remain effective. The Guadalcanal casualties, as gruesome as they were, stayed within this benchmark as reinforcements and replacement units cycled in throughout the protracted campaign.

It was not until Turner's first full-fledged Central Pacific operation, the November 1943 landings by 2nd Division Marines on Tarawa in the Gilberts, that Americans learned the real price tag for assaulting heavily defended Japanese bastions. At Tarawa, invading Marines suffered more than 40 percent casualties, including nearly 1,000 dead, all within the space of three murderous days.

In addition to the appalling casualties, Tarawa hit Turner and Smith with a new batch of painful logistic and tactical lessons. The munitions used in preinvasion air strikes and sea bombardment proved too light to root out Japanese troops hunkered down in concrete blockhouses and pillboxes. The Higgins boats could not navigate the offshore reefs, and there were not nearly enough amphtracs to shuttle troops quickly from the reefs to the beaches. A battle projected to last a few hours, instead took three days. In the end Tarawa was conquered only because the Old Breed Marines ashore refused to lose.

Meanwhile, north of Tarawa, the invasion of Makin by GIs from the Army's 27th Division presented problems not nearly as fatal, but in many ways more discouraging and portentous. It turned out there were fewer than 1,000 poorly equipped Japanese defenders on Makin to take on an invasion force of 6,500 GIs. Yet the Makin operation dragged on four days, one day longer than Tarawa.

While Turner was on scene for the gruesome Tarawa assault, Holland Smith observed the simultaneous debacle on Makin. Naval historian Samuel Morison, who witnessed the invasion from offshore, described the assault by the 27th "trigger-happy soldiers" as slow and confused. Their commander, Army General Ralph Smith, had such poor communications with his troops that he rarely knew what happened beyond his command post. The operation's crowning indignity came after the island was finally declared secure, when Holland Smith ventured ashore to visit his Army counterpart. Rifle fire from GI snipers stationed to protect the brass ripped through the canvas of the tent where the two Smiths were meeting. It was just the first episode in a dreadful Marine-Army partnership whose disharmonies and recriminations would escalate to a crisis.

Holland Smith and Kelly Turner would have much preferred to fight the Central Pacific War without the involvement of the U.S. Army, but this just wasn't possible. Even though Corps troop levels at the height of the war swelled to nearly half a million, its manpower was dwarfed by the Army. The Corps simply lacked the manpower—and the armor and artillery—needed to conquer the Central Pacific.

Still, having Marine and Army units co-mingle in a single operation usually proved difficult. Though they both fought for a common flag against common enemies, they were two completely different combat organizations. The Marine Corps was an elite tactical outfit composed of shock troops expertly trained and lightly equipped to hit hard and fast. The Marines were a near perfect, self-contained force for the early Central Pacific offensives—taking small specks of islands, assaulting fierce but lightly armored Japanese garrisons. Sledge and his 1st Marine buddies traveled light, carrying only absolute necessities—much, Sledge imagined, "the way fast-moving Confederate infantry did during the Civil War." Howlin' Mad likely would have agreed with Sledgehammer's observation.

For Pacific Marines like Sledge, there was the conviction—real or imagined—that the Corps did the costly fighting while the clean, crisp, and bountifully equipped "doggies" (GIs) got the easy objectives (Makin instead of Tarawa, for example) and the cushy garrison work. This feeling surfaced during long training hikes on New Caledonia when Sledge's 5th Regiment (part of the 1st Marine Division) would have to make way for Army troop-carrying truck convoys.

As the convoys passed, the Marines barked and yapped, kidding the GIs about being dogfaces. Once a GI hanging out of a truck shouted at Sledge "Hey, soldier, you look tired and hot, soldier. Why don't you make the Army issue you a truck like me?" While Sledge just grinned and yelled "Go to hell," the GI's buddy grabbed him by the shoulder and admonished, "Stop calling that guy soldier. He's a Marine. Can't you see his emblem? He's not in the Army. Don't insult him."

The sense of always having to do more with less was a continuous wellspring for righteous Marine griping, but it was also motivation to adapt and improvise. Once, during the Guadalcanal campaign, Marine commander Vandegrift sent an urgent requisition for a hundred gross of condoms. The requisition raised eyebrows—14,400 condoms for an island still brutally contested where ammunition shortages, not venereal disease, were the primary concern? The condoms, it turned out, did have a prophylactic use—sheathing the barrels of Marine rifles exposed to the Solomons' torrential monsoon rains.

For its success, amply displayed on the other side of the globe on battlegrounds in North Africa, Italy, and eventually Northern Europe, the U.S. Army depended on strategy, room to maneuver, and firepower that overwhelmed. Army leaders had the patience, born of commanding huge troop concentrations and massive logistics, to wait out an enemy. They had the instincts to look for a flanking action and the manpower to envelop or steamroll, much the way the Civil War Union Army had overcome the Confederates.

The Marines instead aimed for quicker victories. The 4th Division was in combat action for only sixty-one days during the war, yet it fought through four complete Pacific island battles. The Marines were inured to taking high casualties—with the conviction that if a campaign dragged on they would ultimately lose even more men. Some might question this conviction. During its combined sixty-one days of combat, the 4th Division Marines suffered nearly 75 percent casualties.

But the Marines had another consideration—their dependence on the availability of U.S. Navy ships, for supply, offshore artillery fire, and carrier-based air cover. As much as the average sailor wanted quick Marine victories, the average Marine desperately needed the Navy to stay in place, supplying him as he hacked his way through Japanese defenses.

Guadalcanal Marines had paid a terrible (and bitterly remembered) price when the transports had pulled out. The Marines and their leaders fully understood that the longer their job took, the more vulnerable their source of supply and support became. This meant the U.S. Marines played war like checkers—fast, blunt, and costly. The U.S. Army meanwhile played it like chess.

The next big Central Pacific targets following Tarawa and Makin—Kwajalein and Eniwetok in the Marshall Islands—had similar topography: small flat parcels of sand-skinned coral floating in crystal-clear lagoons guarded by barrier reefs. The islets dotting these atoll objectives offered neither side much room to stall, hide, or maneuver. Taking the lessons of Tarawa, the Navy stepped up the intensity and explosive heft of their preinvasion poundings and air strikes. Still, once they landed (now mostly via amphtracs), Marines and GIs faced Japanese garrisons ready (after months of preparation digging deep into the coral, setting up interlocking fields of fire, and pinpointing the trajectories of their mortars and light artillery) to contest every square inch of territory.

Even after being driven back from the water's edge, the Japanese would rebound—as they had on Guadalcanal—with night infiltrations and human wave counterattacks. Though the invading America suffered heavily, the costs for the Japanese were always astronomically higher. On Tarawa the unyielding defenders were virtually wiped out. Rarely disposed to take prisoners after witnessing Japanese duplicity and savagery on Guadalcanal, Marines captured only seventeen Japanese out of a garrison of five thousand. This mutual, brutish, and primitive hatred, Eugene Sledge eventually would learn, was as much a part of the landscape of the war in the Pacific "as the palm trees and the islands."

Meanwhile, the uneasy U.S. Marine-U.S. Army combat alliance continued both to grow and sour as the Central Pacific campaign churned northwest. The conquests of Kwajalein (by the 4th Marine Division) and Eniwetok (by the Army's 27th Infantry Division) in the Marshall Islands seemed like almost perfect operations compared to Tarawa and Makin. The number of Japanese killed was just as astounding—3,800 on Kwajalein and 5,000 more on Eniwetok—but the combined Marine and GI death toll numbered under 500. Nevertheless, criticism resurfaced during the assault on Eniwetok and once again it involved the Army's 27th Division, with questions about their training, leadership, and combat spirit. By now Holland Smith was convinced the skills of the 27th's leadership were limited to running "annual balls, banquets, and shipshape summer camps."

Despite these persistent frictions, Kelly Turner and Holland Smith understood there would be an ever greater necessity to put Marine and Army forces ashore together. Succeeding operations were drawing ever closer to Japan and its garrisons on ever bigger islands including, eventually, Japan itself.

★ Chapter 4 ★

Forager, June and July 1944

*Do not stay alive in dishonor. Do not die in such a way as to leave
a bad name behind you!*
— EXCERPT FROM IMPERIAL JAPAN'S *SENJIN KUN* ("ETHICS IN BATTLE")

A Lot of Dead Marines

By the tlme the armada of 506 Navy transport, supply and combat ships
arrived off the Marianas in June 1944, U.S. Central Pacific forces led
by Vice Admiral Kelly Turner and General Holland Smith were experts at pulverizing flat atolls. But now—and pretty much from now
on—they would be up against something different.

The Marianas were not barren coral atolls; instead, though nowhere near the size of New Guinea or the Philippines, these islands
had considerable open space in which the Japanese could maneuver as
well as mountains and caves in which they could dig in for a defense
of attrition. For the Japanese, the stakes were also higher: these islands
were considered true Japanese possessions.

The island chain erupted from the Central Pacific just west of what
postwar hydrographers would call the Marianas Trench—at nearly
seven miles, the deepest reach of all global oceans. The archipelago's
fifteen volcanic islands, the visible residue of the violent sideswiping of
two continent-size tectonic plates, were also the artifacts of centuries-
old upheavals of global discovery, conquest, and colonialism beginning
with the islands' 15th-century discovery by Ferdinand Magellan in service to Spain.

In 1899, during the Spanish-American War, America seized Guam,

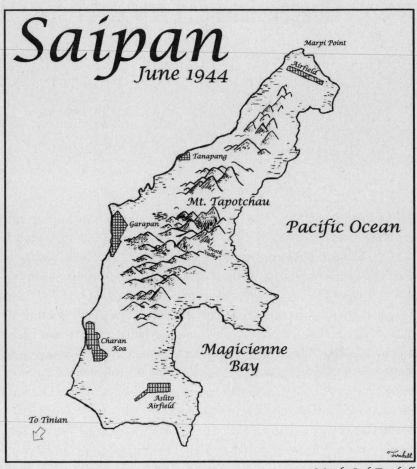

Saipan
June 1944

Marpi Point

Airfield

Tanapang

Mt. Tapotchau

Pacific Ocean

Garapan

Death Valley

Charan Koa

Magicienne Bay

Aslito Airfield

To Tinian

Map by Jack Turnbull

one of the Marianas' principal islands. After the war, defeated and impoverished Spain offered to sell the Americans the rest of its interests in the Marianas, but the McKinley administration balked at the $4 million price tag, and the interests went instead to Germany.

Following World War I's reshuffling of colonial claims, Japan displaced Germany's control over the rest of the Marianas. Under the banner of the South Sea Development Company, Japan began aggressively colonizing and exploiting its "Mandates" Saipan and Tinian—fertile, mountainous islands within sight of each other across a three-mile-wide channel. The ranks of Japanese colonists swelled; within two decades its population of 30,000 included scarcely 4,000 with native Chamorro ancestry.

From its busy perch on Saipan and Tinian, Japan seethed at the nearness of U.S. interests in Guam barely two hundred miles to the south. Within two days of the attack on Pearl Harbor, Japanese troops from Saipan stormed and captured Guam.

The Central Pacific was now one of two distinct and simultaneous Pacific strategic drives*—Kelly Turner and Holland Smith's (overseen by Admiral Chester Nimitz from Pearl Harbor) in the Central Pacific and General Douglas MacArthur's in the Southwest Pacific. It was a measure of the burgeoning power of the United States that it could fight the Japanese simultaneously and effectively in two directions—and have each direction controlled by commanders with sharply divergent approaches to the task. MacArthur disdained Nimitz's island-hopping methods and the casualty levels Marine units sustained. For his part, Nimitz didn't see the point of wasting time and resources in the Southwest Pacific while the Central Pacific promised a quicker, more direct path to Japan.

Still, as both drives gained troops, supplies, shipping, and momentum, they became mutually supportive. Nimitz's Central Pacific thrusts and massive fleet resources drew Japanese sea power, which might have otherwise jumped on MacArthur from the east. Meanwhile, Mac-

---

*At various times there were five areas of American operations in the Pacific War against the Japanese. The other three areas were the South Pacific (now largely left behind); the North Pacific, which, after the Japanese were pushed out of the Aleutians, went dormant; and the China-Burma-India region, used mostly (by Americans) as a strategic air and supply base.

Arthur's Army Air Force resources downed land-based Japanese aircraft that might have devastated Marine beachheads.

Both MacArthur and Nimitz adapted strategies to different landscapes and seascapes. MacArthur's purpose was to move land-based bombers ever forward to secure local air superiority. Nimitz and his admirals meanwhile used carrier air power to shield amphibious landings on key islands that could then be used as stepping-stones—both for subsequent operations and ultimately to put strategic bombers within reach of Japan itself.

Operation Forager, which was to include assaults on Tinian and Guam in addition to Saipan, was designed to secure Central Pacific sea-lanes and capture island bases from which to launch direct attacks on Japan. Saipan came first in the sequence because it had the best airfield in the Marianas and sat one hundred miles closer to Japan than Guam. Saipan could be the takeoff point for nonstop strategic bombing raids using the Army Air Force's immense new chrome-skinned B-29 Superfortresses. It also looked easier to capture.

On 15 June 1944, eight battalions from the 2nd and 4th Marine Divisions—to be reinforced by units from the Army's much maligned 27th Division waiting offshore if needed—landed on a four-mile strip of beach north and south of the small town of Charan Kanoa in southwest Saipan. Seven hundred and nineteen amphtracs packed with troops moved shoreward flanked by gunboats and fronted by a skirmish line of amphibian tanks. The gunboats—Landing Craft, Infantry (LCIs nicknamed "Elsie Items") newly modified and armed with 40- and 20-mm guns and rocket launchers—soon veered from the procession and got into position to fire sheets of 4.5-inch surface-to-surface rockets. The rockets whooshed up, arced, and then plummeted, exploding in the tree lines behind the beaches.

Within a half mile of the shore, the amphtracs fell under intense mortar and artillery fire. Moving at barely five miles per hour, they made easy targets. But most, scuttling like crabs over barely submerged coral, made it across the island's barrier reef, through a shallow lagoon and onto the beaches.

Shielded by tank machine-gun and cannon fire on the ground and by strafing runs from dozens of Navy FM-2 Wildcat fighters launched from escort carriers, more than eight thousand Marines were ashore by midmorning. They fought their way slowly uphill toward the town, a maze of low concrete buildings draped in flowering bougainvillea sitting in the shadow of Saipan's volcanic centerpiece Mount Tapotchau.

The clear but costly success of the first day's landing was contested the next day by a fierce Japanese counterattack from the north. Beaten back, the Japanese left behind 700 killed. But between the landings and the counterattack, the Marines had taken much heavier casualties than expected. The most tragic were wounded soldiers gathered on the beach for evacuation only to be hit again and killed by artillery or mortar fire. On his first day ashore, *Time* reporter Robert Sherrod estimated seeing five dead Marines for every two dead Japanese soldiers. More than 600 U.S. wounded were evacuated from the beach on D-Day alone.

On the 17th the Japanese attacked with tanks, barreling directly down the slopes of Mount Tapotchau's foothills to take a company from the Marine's 6th Regiment (part of the 2nd Marine Division) by surprise. The startled Marines somehow held their composure and their fire, sitting tight as the tanks rolled over their fox holes. Then they jumped up (some soaked in oil from the tanks' leaky engines) to hit the tanks' vulnerable back ends with bazooka fire. It proved to be the end of Japan's armored resistance on Saipan, but just one skirmish in the struggle yet to come. Already the 27th Division had been called in from reserve and plans to invade Guam had been shelved.

By 18 June, 4th Division Marines had slugged their way across Saipan's fertile southern landscape of little farms growing sugarcane, corn, peas, cantaloupes, and potatoes to reach Saipan's eastern coast. From there they were to pivot north for a drive up the island's rugged eastern shore while 2nd Division Marines, positioned on the opposite slope of Tapotchau, moved in parallel up Saipan's western shoreline. In meeting its planned objective, the 4th Division had taken a toll of 2,200 men dead, wounded, or missing.

By now casualty proportions had shifted, but only marginally: Sherrod estimated three dead Japanese soldiers for every two Marines. All the unretrieved corpses he saw were bloated, fly covered, and black. Sherrod could distinguish Marines and Japanese only by differences in their helmets, leggings, and belts.

During lulls in the fighting, the Marines gathered, tagged, and covered their buddies' remains with ponchos. Overworked grave registration details would eventually arrive, document the deaths, and remove the remains for temporary burial.

Meanwhile, the Japanese corpses, after being fieldstripped by souvenir-hunting soldiers (favorite items were gold teeth extracted by Marines using survival knives), were left to the ravages of nature. Before decomposing, these unclaimed bodies looked like pieces of plump, upended statuary struck in grotesque poses. Even as they rotted, some Japanese corpses served as signposts used by patrols to mark (by both sight and smell) otherwise featureless fields or trails. One measure of the duration of the battle for Saipan was that some maggot- and bottle-fly-infested Japanese corpses had decomposed to partially exposed skeletons by the time the island was finally secured.

As usual, few Japanese prisoners were taken. There were, however, civilian internees—a combination of Japanese and Chamorros—to attend to. They were gathered by the hundreds in large makeshift enclosures near the landing beaches. (The numbers were manageable—few of the captors worried about the fate of thousands of other civilians still at large.) Most of the internees, including the Japanese, were frightened, docile, and cooperative. Still, one captured Japanese civilian had reportedly cut the throats of his wife and child and then boasted to his captors, "That is what we will do when you get to the Empire."

Wanting Checkers, Getting Chess

The push north by the two Marine divisions—the 2nd on the west, the 4th on the east—began on 22 June. By then Forager's casualties had climbed to a combined total of 6,000, two thirds of them from the 4th Marine Division.

The two-pronged drive had not lasted long before disconnected Marine lines became overextended. With some reluctance, Holland

Smith ordered the Army's 27th Division, which had stayed behind to mop up Japanese resistance in the south, to fill in the center—its salient feature a long, narrow gulch on the east side of Tapotchau soon to be known as Death Valley.

The GIs under Major General Ralph Smith moved up to take their place in the line. But they moved north cautiously and much too slowly for Holland Smith's sensibilities. Holland Smith still wanted checkers; Ralph Smith was still giving him chess. Incensed, Holland Smith conferred with Vice Admiral Kelly Turner and then both visited their boss Admiral Raymond Spruance aboard his flagship *Indianapolis* (CA-35), seeking permission to relieve Ralph Smith. Spruance gave his approval, Ralph Smith was recalled, and soon the tenuous interservice alliance was spinning out of control.

As the controversy smoldered, stoked stateside by competing elements of the press,* progress through Death Valley remained slow and painful. At stake was gaining the high ground of Mount Tapotchau— and ultimate mastery of Saipan. The 2nd Marine Division delivered one breakthrough on 25 June when its troops fought their way to the west slope heights. Five days later GIs finally broke through the last yards of Death Valley.

Now, the fronts of the Marine 2nd and 4th Divisions and the Army's 27th Division were joined, and the Americans controlled half the island. Saipan's fate was sealed—but not its final costs. After showing anticipated tactics during Forager's opening rounds, Japanese defenders were behaving differently than ever before. In the wake of costly counterattacks on D plus one and D plus two, the defenders had altered tactics to fight a delaying action, largely from the concealment of

---

*The Army's cause was taken up largely by newspapers of the Hearst chain. On 8 July a San Francisco *Examiner* front-page story read, in part: "Allegedly excessive loss of life attributed to Marine Corps' impetuosity of attack has brought a breach between Marine and Army commanders in the Pacific. . . . The controversy hangs upon Marine tactics versus Army tactics, the Marines seeking a swift decision at high cost, while the Army moved more deliberately—at lesser cost." A 17 July editorial in Hearst's *Journal American* made clear Hearst's agenda and his backing of Douglas MacArthur: "The important and significant thing the American people DO know is that equally difficult and hazardous military operations conducted in the Pacific War under the competent command of General Douglas MacArthur have been successfully completed with little loss of life in most cases and with obvious MINIMUM loss of life in all cases."

caves. They were dragging out the inevitable and, in the process, exacting as many American casualties as they could with pinpoint artillery
and mortar fire.

On 1 July—now two long weeks since D-Day—total casualties
had soared to just under 10,000. The four hospital ships assigned to
Forager to evacuate wounded could accommodate only 20 percent of
them. The rest had to settle for bunks on crowded transport ships. As
it was, the boats evacuating the wounded from the beach wandered
from transport to transport, each already overflowing with casualties,
looking for a vessel willing to take the new cases.

To Holland Smith, the escalating casualties pointed to one thing—
the imperative of moving forward. "Our casualties," Smith told Sherrod and other correspondents during a briefing, "are actually lower
when we push forward than when we stand still."

Without Hope or Higher Purpose

Scarcely noticed within the surging population of Marines and GIs
ashore on Saipan was a small unit of two hundred sailors assigned to
Operation Acorn 38. Though they wore the same combat dungarees
as the Marines, Acorn 38's "troops" obviously had none of the leathernecks' discipline, combat instincts, or swagger. One Acorn 38 sailor
was Lorin Nelson, 21, who joined the Navy right after Pearl Harbor
and spent two years aboard destroyer *Dewey* (DD-349) in the thick of
combat at Coral Sea, Midway, and Guadalcanal. In 1943 Nelson was
transferred to *Fanshaw Bay* (CVE-70), one of a new breed of small
aircraft carriers converted from thin-hulled civilian freighters. After
a week's shakedown cruise on *Fanshaw Bay,* Nelson was convinced
his new ship would never stand up in combat. Back in port, Nelson
went AWOL and then compounded his difficulties by running off to
San Diego with a pretty sixteen-year-old girl. When he decided to turn
himself in, Nelson got a short stint in the brig and then got shipped
to Hawaii, assigned to Acorn 38. He'd exchanged the risks of *Fanshaw Bay* for ground combat. After three weeks of infantry training,
Acorn's sailors were put aboard a troop ship to Saipan to land with the

Marines—ready, once a beachhead was secured, to begin building and operating a seaplane base.

On 5 July, with two thirds of the island secured, regiments of the 4th Marine Division were pushing forward between the converging coastlines of Japanese-held northern Saipan. The narrowing frontline prompted Holland Smith to pull the 2nd Marine Division into reserve and hand the island's west side over to the Army's 27th, now under new leadership.

While the Marines sprinted toward Marpi Point, Saipan's northern tip, the GIs held back to clean up pockets of resistance. Smith, ever alert and respectful of his enemy's ferocity, sensed the disorganization and desperation of the cornered Japanese defenders. As the 27th moved in to arrange its defenses, he cautioned them to ready themselves for a last ditch cataclysm of violence. Indeed, each force, in dramatically different ways, was about to witness the final death throes of Japan's futile struggle for Saipan.

Three months after Saipan's fall, during the last days of equally pro-tracted and bitter fighting to conquer Peleliu in the Southwest Pacific, Eugene Sledge would describe, in scribbled notes he concealed between the tissue-thin pages of his pocket-size New Testament, the bizarre be-havior of a beaten enemy. The Japanese could hope neither to drive the Marines off Peleliu nor to expect reinforcements. To Sledge it seemed the Japanese defenders were fighting "solely for the sake of killing, without hope or higher purpose." The Marines were fighting through unimaginable terrain against an unimaginable enemy.

The last Japanese military resistance on Saipan—without hope or higher purpose—was a frantic, pell-mell charge of as many as 3,000 doomed men, which began before dawn on 7 July. The evening be-fore, the defense force's most senior officers—two Army generals and a Navy admiral—ended their lives in a hastily staged ritual suicide. It was now left to a handful of mid-level junior officers to organize and lead the final, desperate thrust.

A small vanguard of perhaps a half-dozen men led the charge when it began at 0430. Flourishing an immense red flag and shouting *"Wah!*

Wah!" they sprinted along the narrow tracks of a sugar cane railroad skirting the beach near the west coast village of Tanapang, about twenty miles south of Marpi Point.

Behind the vanguard followed hundreds of soldiers and sailors, fueled by *sake* and beer, haphazardly grouped and armed with rifles, swords, and bayonet-tipped bamboo sticks. Behind them hobbled hundreds of wounded Japanese, few of them armed, all of them prepared to die.

Collectively, the Japanese in this attack were more a mob or stampeding herd than an organized force, yet they managed to sweep through the front lines of the two battalions of the 105th Infantry Regiment, part of the ill-starred 27th Division. The GIs stood and fought but were soon overwhelmed. In a space of minutes, 650 GIs were killed or wounded. The surviving remnants retreated into the village where they were able to establish a shaky and hard-pressed perimeter close to the beach.

As these infantrymen continued to fall back in vicious house-to-house fighting, a Marine artillery battalion was also being overrun. Before retreating, the Marines lowered the barrels of their 105-mm guns and fired point-blank into the Japanese onslaught.

With the Tanapang perimeter shrinking, some GIs and Marines took to the water. Those who didn't drown were picked up by coastal craft and destroyers such as *Halsey Powell* (DD-686), which also provided close-in support with 5-inch and 40-mm gunfire. Later in the morning, more help finally arrived in the form of a battalion of Army medium tanks. Troop reinforcements followed and, by late afternoon, the Japanese assault was reduced to isolated pockets of survivors.

Sherrod arrived on the scene after the tide of battle had turned to witness Army tanks sweeping the sugarcane fields west of the railroad tracks with machine-gun and 75-mm cannon fire, cutting down Japanese survivors hidden there. Army engineers were also busy rigging charges to blast survivors hiding in culverts and other improvised concealments.

Desperation showed on both sides. As he walked the decimated ground, Sherrod saw pockets of dead U.S. Marines and GIs, most now covered by ponchos. Several surviving U.S. soldiers recounted the pleas of severely wounded buddies to be killed rather than face capture and living defilement by the marauding Japanese. Sherrod also surveyed the carcasses of Japanese dead, noting that many lay in bunches of three to ten and remarking how the Japanese rarely seemed to die alone. He looked for missing hands and blasted heads or chests—telltale signs of suicide death by hand grenade. He saw many, especially among those grouped together.

There were no more desperate charges. Turner declared Saipan secure on 9 July and finalized plans for landings on Guam on 21 July and on nearby Tinian three days following that. On 11 July, mop-up operations by Marines and GIs in the north were still harvesting many dead Japanese soldiers—over 2,000 since the predawn charge at Tanapang. At least one Marine likened the mop-up to a "rabbit-hunt." The Japanese POW count totaled just 86 out of a 30,000-man garrison.

Meanwhile, Marpi Point, Saipan's northern tip, became the crucible of a massive new ritual of death.

Crowds of civilians, it turned out, had fled ahead of the American advance all the way to Marpi Point. Thousands of them—some in groups, others as families, still others as individuals—gathered at the edge of high cliffs overlooking a line of rocks and crashing surf. Soldiers of the 4th Marine Division converged but stood back. They'd come ill-equipped for what were ultimately inner contests between reason (as the Americans knew it) and suicidal passion.

Over public address systems, interpreters and Japanese internees pleaded with the restive crowds: the fighting was done and food, medical care, and shelter awaited them. For many poised above the rocks and boiling sea, however, fear had by now fused inseparably with months of Japanese propaganda and exhortations that the American devils would tear them apart. As Marines ashore and sailors on coastal craft watched (some with indifference but most in helpless awe), thousands of group and individual suicides played out.

While some groups—parents with children, especially—were hesitant as they contemplated suicide, still others staged elaborate ceremonies, some somber, others almost cheerful. One group of nearly one hundred Japanese civilian men and women standing on rocks near the water's edge bowed to Marines watching from the cliffs above. Then,

after removing their clothes, they bathed in the sea. They emerged to
don fresh clothes and stood facing a large Japanese flag spread across
a smooth rock. One man distributed hand grenades. As the grenades'
pins were pulled, the bodies erupted and blood-spattered torsos and
limbs toppled into the sea.

Japanese soldiers were scattered among the civilians; some intent
only on their own suicides, but some still fighting the Americans while
simultaneously expediting the deaths of civilians. As Marines tried to
dislodge one cave-concealed sniper who had killed two Americans and
wounded a third, the sniper redirected his fire to a family—a mother,
father, and four children perched hesitantly at the water's edge. He shot
the father first, then shot the mother, and took aim at the children before a Japanese woman ran over and plucked them to safety. The sniper
then strode defiantly from the cave into a barrage of Marine gunfire.

Other Japanese soldiers made last stands on the island's barrier
reefs several hundred yards offshore. In one case a detachment of Marines was sent out in amphtracs to confront a band of seven soldiers.
As the craft neared the reef, one of the soldiers—most likely an officer—drew his sword as his companions knelt before him on the coral
rocks. The sword-wielding officer then began decapitating the soldiers.
Four heads had already dropped by the time the amphtracs reached
the reef. Sword held high, the officer then charged the Marines who
quickly shot him along with the two remaining soldiers.

Parts of the waters beyond the reef soon became littered with floating corpses, so many that nearby Navy support craft could not entirely
avoid colliding with them. An officer on the minesweeper *Chief* (AM-
315) saw one drowned woman who'd apparently died in labor; the
newborn's emergent head was visible. He also saw a young boy whose
arms were locked around the neck of a Japanese soldier; the dead pair
bobbed in unison amidst the waves and the wakes of nearby ships.

The spectacle of death at Marpi Point turned out to be only the tip
of the holocaust of civilian lives on Saipan. Many civilians were inter-
mingled with the cave and bunker-dwelling Japanese troops and along
with them were extinguished by gunfire, explosives, and flamethrower
bursts. In the end it was hard to say how many lost their lives to tragic
circumstance and how many to conscious self-destruction. But there
did seem to be an urgent compulsion to die. The toll exacted by this

compulsion was steep: 22,000 men, women, and children, more than two thirds of Saipan's civilian population.

The climaxes at Tanapang and Marpi Point forced a question on big-picture strategists such as Nimitz, Spruance, Turner, and Smith—and as well on each Marine and GI who, unlike 15,000 of their comrades, had escaped alive and unwounded and now must prepare for the next beachhead: if this was the unyielding resistance put up by an outpost of the Japanese empire, by a civilian population considered second-class citizens by their home-island countrymen, then what could be expected when those home islands were invaded?

Radio Tokyo, ever boastful while always denying defeat, vowed at every turn that 100,000,000 Japanese stood ready to turn back invaders should they ever reach its shores. Ahead, during the struggle for Peleliu, some Japanese soldiers before being overrun and dying to a man, scribbled a defiant banner reading, "We will build a barrier across the Pacific with our bodies." To Turner and to Smith and to the soldiers, sailors, and airmen whose lives they put in harm's way, these mantras of willing sacrifice seemed far from exaggerated.

★ Chapter 5 ★

The Big Blue Blanket

The American attacks are like waves that beat incessantly on our shores, and I am nothing but a prop in the breakwater that strives to throw them back.

—FLYING OFFICER RYUJI NAGATSUKA

Morning Launch

Task Force 58—four task groups totaling eighteen aircraft carriers, twenty-three battleships and cruisers, and nearly sixty screening destroyers—left Ulithi on 14 March 1945 and steamed north to reach striking distance of airfields on Kyushu, the southernmost of Japan's home islands. The force replenished at sea that same day, continued its advance, and closed to within ninety miles of the southeast coast of Kyushu at dawn on 18 March, ready to launch attacks to support Operation Iceberg.

Task Force 58's principal commander was Vice Admiral Marc Mitscher, who used fleet carrier *Bunker Hill* (CV-17) as his flagship. Mitscher, "Pete" to his Naval Academy classmates and peers, was a diminutive, bone-dry, 57-year-old Midwesterner with the off-kilter face of an aging bantamweight club fighter.

Though it was years of wind exposure and chain-smoking—not boxing—that chiseled Mitscher's pug face, and though the rest of his body was equally pinched and frail, nobody doubted Mitscher's combativeness. He was, in the estimation of his chief of staff Captain Arleigh Burke, wise, simple, direct, and ruthless. Whenever a subordinate task group commander failed to use the forces at his disposal to the best advantage, Burke's job was to fly over to the offender's aircraft carrier, tell the man he was all through, and should take the first available transport back to Pearl Harbor.

Yet as much as Mitscher's parched demeanor matched his tough-minded reputation, he had another, competing reputation: for showing nearly boundless concern for the well-being of his sailors and particularly his airmen.

Mitscher's own career explained this special affection, at least in part. In 1915 he had been among the first U.S. Navy officers to win wings and had flown biplanes from the armored cruiser *North Carolina* (ACR-12) using the first ever ship-mounted catapult rig. In 1919 Mitscher had earned the Navy Cross at the controls of a seaplane in a pioneering transatlantic flight from Newfoundland to the Azores—an exploit that nearly cost him his life.

Mitscher was, in other words, a bona fide naval aviator commanding aviators and fleet carrier operations at a time when many senior naval surface officers without Mitscher's credentials were fighting vainly against the tide of a disruptive new reality: airplanes and pilots, instead of big ships and big guns, were the new keys to gaining and holding supremacy at sea.

His exploits in the Solomons had earned the then commander Arleigh Burke his own Navy Cross, a shared distinction that should have helped Burke pass muster with his new boss. But neither this achievement nor much else about Burke seemed to impress Mitscher—for the simple reason that Burke was a non-aviator. When he'd first been assigned as Mitscher's chief of staff—part of an arrangement that required senior aviation-trained commanders to have chiefs of staff with surface warfare experience—Mitscher virtually ignored him. Later, when Burke finally did gain his boss's grudging respect and confidence, Mitscher would constantly remind him of the priorities within Task Force 58: "Pilots are the weapons of this force."

Mitscher had skippered the *Hornet* (CV-8)* for the audacious Doolittle bombing raid on Tokyo and, several months later, for the Battle of Midway, both prime examples of seagoing airpower's ascendancy—

---

*Hornet (CV-8) was sunk in October 1942 during the Battle of Santa Cruz. The name continued with *Hornet* (CV-12) commissioned in November 1943.

and also electrifying moments of risk taking and decision making. Those moments both came in 1942, with the country just months into the war and its mood, morale, and capabilities for fighting at dismal lows. Now, three years later, prospects had vastly improved.

But changes in war's fortune, no matter how dramatic, didn't diminish the challenge of the next hours. Mitscher, as usual sporting a duck-billed lobsterman's hat to cover a bald head, was in a corner of *Bunker Hill*'s flag bridge ready for the day's work while sitting in a steel armchair facing aft ("Anybody who rides with the wind in his face" he often explained—his own looks notwithstanding—"is a plain damn fool."). He could be found there before each launch, and he stayed there until the last returning aircraft and airman had touched down, stepping away only to munch a midday sandwich in an adjacent sea cabin.

Once again Mitscher was sending aircraft over the heart of Japan, though this time the operation would be more than symbolic. The flying distance would also be much shorter. Instead of sending a small cadre of specially trained volunteers flying a handful of twin-engine medium-range bombers lightened to squeeze out a perilous one-way mission, Mitscher would direct the sorties of hundreds of planes taking off from a dozen carrier decks. Instead of launching and quickly retreating out of range, Mitscher would keep his carriers and escorts in the vicinity, daring the Japanese to strike Task Force 58 while fully expecting that most of his aircraft would hit their targets and return to be refueled, re-armed, and relaunched for day upon day of new strikes. Except for Task Force 58's exposure and for the considerable risks awaiting its pilots at their target destinations, the comings and goings of these aircraft were so regular as to look routine.

The clockwork precision and order of the morning launch seemed to reinforce the image of the routine. As usual, first to leave *Bunker Hill*'s 872-foot-long flight deck would be four F6F Hellcat fighters. Already a Hellcat was positioned on each of its two forward hydraulic catapults (cats), wings unfolded and locked, the pilot beginning to rev the Hellcat's engine, the plane hitched to the catapult's shuttle by a tensioned bridle. Directly behind each of these was another Hellcat, wings also spread full, its pilot waiting his turn on the cat.

Catapulting this handful of Hellcats usually cleared enough space to begin deck run launches. Here, too, the Hellcats had pride of place—full throttle, they could clear the deck after a short 330-foot run. After the Hellcat fighters, the sequence of launch turned to bombers. First the Avenger torpedo bombers followed by dive-bombers—a mix of newer Helldivers (designated SB2C, which many joked stood for "Son-of-a-Bitch Second Class") and older SPD-5 Dauntlesses.

At nine tons fully loaded, the whale-bodied TBF and TBM Avengers* were the largest single-engine airplanes yet flown from a carrier deck. If the Avenger's deficits were its heft and clumsy bulk, the Avenger's air combat virtues—first demonstrated at Midway—were its rugged simplicity, reliability, and versatility as a weapons platform.

The Avenger carried a three-man crew: a pilot, turret gunner, and radioman. The Avenger pilot, an officer, rode in a cockpit situated so high that it was like being on the bridge of a ship. The gunner and radioman, both enlisted petty officers with technical training, boarded the aircraft through a hatch on the starboard side of the fuselage.

One of VT-84's[†] fifteen TBMs was piloted by Ensign Francis Guttenberger, "Guts" to his squadron mate—a nickname imbedded with a hint of mockery. While nobody questioned Guttenberger's fortitude and flying ability, he was short and slight, with a bit of a swagger and a knack for getting into squabbles. There was particularly bad blood between Guttenberger and another VT-84 pilot who stood a full head taller. The two had once come to blows, and the squadron skipper, Lieutenant Commander C. W. Swanson, had called both pilots on the carpet. Now, to keep better track of both, Swanson assigned them to fly as his wingmen—Guttenberger on the port side, his nemesis on the starboard side.

---

*Navy aircraft letter and number designations reflected a combination of aircraft purpose, manufacturer, and model sequence. In the "F6F" aircraft designation, for example, the first F stands for "Fighter"; the 6 stands for the model sequence; and the second F indicates that Grumman Aircraft was the manufacturer. In the "TBM" aircraft designation the TB stands for "Torpedo Bomber"; the M signifies that the aircraft, though designed by Grumman Aviation, was manufactured under subcontract by General Motors. In the SPD-5 designation, the SB stands for "Scout Bomber"; the D indicates Douglas Aviation was the manufacturer; and the 5 for the aircraft model.

†VT-84 is a U.S. Navy aviation squadron designation. The V indicates the use of "heavier-than-air" aircraft, to distinguish it from the U.S. Navy's early and continuing use of "lighter-than-air" flight craft such as balloons and blimps. The T indicates a torpedo bomber squadron. (VF indicates a fighter aircraft squadron, VB a dive-bombing squadron, and VBF, a squadron composed of aircraft responsible both as fighters and as bombers.)

Guttenberger also had a habit of volunteering for special flight assignments, including the potentially hazardous job of towing target sleeves for ships' aerial gunnery. Target towing was putting your life in the hands of young and inexperienced ship gun crews, which was fine if it just involved the pilot. But Guttenberger was also volunteering his two young crewmen—turret gunner Ed Duffy and radioman Tom Kelly. Duffy and Kelly, both New Yorkers (Duffy from the Bronx, Kelly from Queens), both Irish (Kelly had actually been born in Tipperary), and both 19 years old. Duffy and Kelly each liked and respected Guttenberger, but neither was crazy about his volunteer instincts.

Launching each type of carrier aircraft was in effect launching a different type of pilot—with a different psychology and set of skills. During attacks, dive-bombing and torpedo-bombing pilots like Guttenberger (youthful swagger aside) needed nerves of steel and the ability to shut out even life threatening distractions. In a vertical dive or in a wave-skimming torpedo run, Navy "vertical" and "horizontal" bomber pilots were like boxers limited to one punch. While waiting to throw the punch (and never sure it would connect), they couldn't flinch, and couldn't heed the urge to pull up and away to safety.

Navy bomber pilots also carried the extra burden of responsibility for other men—a crew of one or two in addition to the pilot. Shouldering this weight (a heavy one for pilots like Guttenberger and others barely out of their teens and unaccustomed to taking responsibility for anyone beside themselves) was just one of the attractions of becoming a Navy fighter pilot. Another was that in the increasingly remote business of modern war, fighter pilots came as close as was possible to fighting one-to-one, skill-to-skill, with another opponent. Air-to-air combat was a defining concept. It was the opportunity to prove your worth in a struggle that still had some sense of chivalry about it—certainly more chivalry than the impersonal carnage on the ground.

But this opportunity demanded unusual qualities: piercing eyesight, trigger-quick instincts, and total ability to be ever-oriented, ever-anticipating, and ever-reacting. If Navy bomber pilots were stone-nerved, one-punch boxers, then fighter pilots were boxers throwing punches at a kaleidoscope of opponents, most of whom were trying to sneak up from behind, while bobbing and weaving through an infinite arena of sky.

Grummans

Among the aircraft launched from *Bunker Hill* and her sister carriers and winging their way toward Kyushu this day, the F6F Hellcat fighters—what the Japanese simply called Grummans—were the versatile headliners. At a tactical level, the Hellcat rivaled even the B-29 Superfortress as the chief instrument of Japan's destruction from the air.

During the Pacific War's early stages, American navy fighter aircraft had been routinely outmatched by experienced Japanese pilots flying the Mitsubishi A6M Zero—U.S. Navy fliers called them Zekes.* Then in June 1942, an American shore party on a remote Aleutian island recovered a Zeke, belly-up but intact in the muddy muskeg, its pilot's rotting corpse still strapped inside the cockpit. Grumman engineers used this specimen to unlock the secrets of the Zeke's superiority, and the new F6F Hellcat had been expressly designed and built to take it on.

The Navy's early-war mainstay, the F4F Wildcat, could dive faster than the Zeke, a tactic Navy fighter pilots often resorted to in overmatched duels with Zeke pilots. The new Hellcat retained the dive superiority while at the same time being able to outclimb and outmaneuver the Zeke. The Hellcat also protected pilot lives, through the combined use of self-sealing fuel tanks, heavy armor plating (surrounding both the pilot and the engine oil tank), and a bullet-resistant windshield.

The Hellcat could give, avoid, and take punishment in equal measures. Stories of its resiliency became instant legends. Once, during a low-level barge strafing run off the Philippines, a Hellcat flown by Bruce Williams, a *Lexington* (CV-16) VF-19 pilot, was severely damaged. After Williams made an emergency landing on *Lexington*, flight

---

*The code name system for Japanese aircraft used by U.S. forces originated in the Southwest Pacific in 1942 when Army intelligence officer Captain Frank T. McCoy headed a team assigned to identify and classify Japanese aircraft. Captain McCoy, a native of Tennessee, initially assigned down-home names such as Zeke, Rufe, Nate, and Jake to Japanese aircraft. Seventy-five code names were assigned during the first month, and soon these names were in wide use throughout the entire Pacific. In 1944, a joint Army-Navy Air Technical Center in Washington took over responsibility for assigning the names. The code names were then allotted according to the following system: male first names for fighters and reconnaissance seaplanes; female first names for bombers, attack bombers, dive-bombers, reconnaissance aircraft, and flying boats; names beginning with letter *T* for transports; tree names for trainers; and bird names for gliders.

deck crews found his Hellcat's fuselage filled with shards of metal and entire wood planks piercing his wings like arrows.

New to its array of capabilities, the Hellcat could also double as a dive-bomber. This latest use was the brainchild of a second and relatively new Task Group commander, Vice Admiral John Sidney "Jock" McCain.* McCain, a Mississippi native of Scottish descent three years older than Mitscher, was as compulsive a smoker (he rolled his own Bull Durham cigarettes) as Mitscher, and had, if anything, a face more pinched and weatherworn. McCain also indulged a taste for odd headgear; his version was a green fatigue cap accentuated by a black headband and a visor encrusted with gold braid hand sewn by his wife.

As a vice admiral early in the war, McCain (who'd finagled his way into flight school and earned his wings in his fifties) commanded all land-based aircraft during the darkest days of the Battle for Guadalcanal. The self-styled Cactus Air Force, a ragtag assemblage of Marine and Navy pilots (many the orphans of sunken U.S. carriers), flew air cover from Henderson Field, usually outnumbered and too often outmaneuvered by expert Japanese pilots flying superior planes. Once, during a prolonged nighttime air raid on Henderson field, McCain dived for cover into what he thought was a drainage ditch, only to find out it was an active latrine. McCain survived the experience and went on to earn a Distinguished Service Medal and a transfer to Washington to head up the Bureau of Naval Avionics.

Now, returning to the Pacific late in the war, in part to lift some of the command burden from Mitscher's shoulders (and eventually to spell him as principal carrier group commander) and in part to bring a fresh perspective, McCain took command of a carrier task group. McCain's fresh perspective soon brought fresh solutions. One of these was to turn Hellcats into dive-bombers as well as fighters. That way, after dropping its bomb load, the Hellcat dive-bomber reverted immediately to the Hellcat fighter for dueling with Japanese fighters.

While this idea was both fresh and brilliant, it caused a stir in defense factories and carrier ready rooms. The U.S. Navy had invented

---

*McCain's son John S. McCain, Jr., was a submarine commander in the Pacific War and later a four-star admiral. McCain's grandson, John S. McCain III, a former naval pilot and prisoner of war during the Vietnam War, became U.S. Senator representing Arizona and the Republican candidate for the U.S. presidency.

the dive-bomber. Thirty-seven Douglas Dauntlesses flying from *Enterprise* (CV-6) struck fatal blows on IJN carriers *Kaga* and *Akagi* to seal the U.S. victory at Midway. Douglas and Curtiss factories were geared to producing new versions of the Dauntless and its successor, the Helldiver, as the Navy's prime offensive weapons. The switch also meant that thousands of dive-bomber pilots would need to be recycled for training in fighter aircraft. But McCain's own flight operations officer, Commander John S. "Jimmy" Thach, a renowned fighter pilot himself and inventor of the "Thach Weave" fighter maneuver,* was wildly enthusiastic. "This is one of those rare miracles where you get something for nothing," he told *Time* reporter Sherrod. "You drop your bomb; then you've got the world's best fighter."

But there were also two immediate problems: too few Hellcat aircraft to go around and not nearly enough fighter pilots. The solution here lay in solving another problem: the underutilization of a second fighter aircraft in the Navy's arsenal, the fast and powerful gull-winged F4U Corsair.

The design inspiration for the Corsair was the Navy's demand for a carrier aircraft that could match the performance of the best land-based fighter planes (the Hellcat fell short here) yet still be "overbuilt" to withstand the extreme stress of carrier deck landings. In early tests the Corsair became the first U.S. single-engine production aircraft capable of level flight speeds of four hundred miles per hour.

The production Corsair proved to be a controversial aircraft, thought by many to be unsuitable for carrier operations. The Corsair's poor visibility over its long nose (one of the F4U's nicknames was "Hose Nose") made carrier landings tricky, as did the tendency for its port wing to stall before its starboard wing, at slow speeds. And on fast landings, the Corsair's propeller blades came uncomfortably close to scraping the flight deck.

At first, most Corsairs went to land-based Marine Corps squadrons

---

*Thach devised the maneuver as a means to compensate for the greater maneuverability of Japanese fighter aircraft early in the war. It could be executed either by two fighter aircraft side by side or by two pairs of fighters flying together. When an enemy aircraft chose one fighter as his target (the "bait" fighter; his wingman being the "hook"), the two wingmen turned in toward each other. After crossing paths and separating, they would again turn in toward each other, bringing the enemy plane into the hook's sights. A correctly executed Thach Weave left little chance of escape for even the most maneuverable opponent.

who welcomed the aircraft with open arms. Not only could the Corsair, like the Navy's Hellcat, outclimb and outdive the Zeke, it was also faster. Once a Corsair pilot cornered a Japanese aircraft in the killing zone of his plane's six .50-caliber machine guns, the adversary was all but doomed. Like the Hellcat, the Corsair carried 2,300 .50-caliber rounds, enough for a full minute of continuous fire from each gun. Fired in short three-to-six-second bursts, this ammunition capacity made the F4U a devastating weapon against aircraft, ground targets, and even ships.

Late in 1944 new Corsairs, whose bombing and ground support capabilities had long been established, came with modifications that made them more suitable for carrier operations. Among these was the substitution of a four-blade propeller (with shorter individual blades) for the three-blade propeller. And with fewer land operations to support, Marine fighter pilots skilled in flying Corsairs also became available for new assignments.

To meet the sudden new demand for fighter-bombers, Corsairs increasingly found their way back to carrier flight decks, either with Navy squadrons or as part of Marine air contingents. Tricky landings notwithstanding, the Corsair emerged from the shadows as a formidable and versatile carrier-based weapon. By war's end its pilots wracked up an eleven to one kill/loss ratio over Japanese aircraft.

McCain's and Thach's innovations in time extended to better coordination of Task Force 38 air and sea tactics. Screening destroyers equipped with the latest in radar gear were dispatched to stations sixty miles out from the carriers along possible enemy aircraft approach paths.

The job of these "pickets" was to give the carriers early warning of approaching enemy aircraft. Designated destroyers equipped with IFF—identification friend or foe—also had a special "delousing" role, detecting Japanese aircraft trying to sneak through by flying close to the friendlies. Task Force 58's planes returning from air strikes were required to circle these "Tom Cat" destroyers so that CIC teams could use the homing devices to spot the intruders. It then was left to the Combat Air Patrols to confront and splash the intruders.

A final innovation (begun with the December 1944 air raids on Luzon in the Philippines) was the "Big Blue Blanket" (B.B.B for short), a day and night umbrella of fighter planes on station over Japanese air bases to prevent enemy planes from taking off. As B.B.B. fighter shifts relieved each other, flights of bomber aircraft would sweep in to hit any aircraft parked on the ground.

The Hellcat and Corsair combined with revitalized and innovative tactics gave the Americans the advantage over the Japanese in air combat capability and durability—at least on paper. But it was the skill and resourcefulness of U.S. airmen that ultimately made the decisive distance.

U.S. pilots were also simply better trained than their Japanese opponents. Each American who went into action had qualified through two years of intense training and three hundred flying hours. Meanwhile Japan's depleted corps of IJA and IJN aviators had, at best, a year's flight training—eventually chopped to six months and then two, with few actual hours in the air.

Scores of naval aviators such as *Bunker Hill*'s Guttenberger (who along with Duffy and Kelly reached the Pacific in February 1945) were among the newest products of this training. Other relative newcomers included Hellcat pilots, like VF-19's Bruce Williams and VF-17's Willis (Bill) Hardy, and pilot Ted Crosby, flying from *Hornet* (CV-12). Though he was new to operational combat flying, Hardy had been in the Navy for six years, the first four of them as an enlisted aviation machinist mate; he knew his aircraft, its engine, and its capabilities from the ground up.

Combat novices like Guttenberger, Williams, Hardy, and Crosby were also backed by a huge and expanding cadre of veteran pilots with deep combat experience, men like Warren McLellan, 22, a VT-16 TBM pilot, and Art Whiteway, 24, a VF-16 Hellcat pilot, both flying from *Lexington*.

McLellan, a native of Fort Smith, Arkansas, had flown his first combat mission over Tarawa. McLellan's TBM had been hit by ground fire six times, and once, on a glide bombing mission over Palau, he and his two crewmen, radioman Selbie Greenhalgh and gunner John Hutchinson, had been forced to ditch. That had been a scary experience, but luck was with them; within the hour the three airmen were picked up by a float plane from cruiser *Wichita* (CA-45).

New Jersey-born Art Whiteway, who had been flying from *Lexington* since her 1943 commissioning, was a veteran pilot buoyed by his own special sense of luck. During his Pacific deployment, Whiteway's Hellcat always bore the number "13" and the moniker "Lucky Strike." Always, because Whiteway in that time went through four 13s, losing planes to ground fire and carrier deck crash landings. The losses were the occupational hazard of his work, which combined flying C.A.P. and air strikes with air reconnaissance, lone runs to photograph ground targets all across the Central Pacific. Despite these experiences, Whiteway still considered 13 his lucky number. After all, each time he had emerged unscathed even when his airplane had not.

It was one measure of the strength of the U.S. 5th Fleet and its air groups that neither McLellan nor Whiteway was in the Pacific for the March 1945 run up to the invasion of Okinawa. Instead, *Lexington* was in Puget Sound for overhaul; the ship, her crew, her aircraft, and her pilots were not scheduled to return to the Pacific until May.

By contrast, virtually all skilled and experienced Japanese pilots were kept on the front lines without respite until their luck eventually, almost inevitably, ran out. Unlike McLellan and Whiteway, whose "luck" was in large part due to the support ships, aircraft, and personnel sent out to rescue them, downed Japanese pilots were usually doomed Japanese pilots.* As resistant to capture as were Japanese foot soldiers, wounded or distressed Japanese airmen, instead of bailing out or ditching, opted instead for "dare to die" (*kesshi*) tactics: "self-crashing" (*jibaku*) their damaged aircraft into U.S. ships, other aircraft or ground installations.

As the war dragged on, both Japan's army and naval air forces faced gaping deficiencies in equipment, tactics, and, most important, skilled pilots. Cadet Pilot Ryuji Nagatsuka, who completed flight training at an IJA aviation base north of Tokyo in November 1944, was among the last to receive a full year's training.

Nagatsuka began his hands-on training using rudimentary one-man gliders. Launched from hill slopes, the gliders, even if skillfully handled,

---

*Japan, however, did lead the way in stationing its submarines near aerial battles to recover downed airmen.

were able to soar little more than forty feet off the ground. At the end of the "flights," trainees had to haul the gliders back to the summit.

The use of gliders was just one means of conserving precious aviation fuel. From gliders, Nagatsuka then progressed to flying and then to soloing in *Akatonbo* (Dragonflies), slow, fragile biplanes painted a deep yellow with emblematic red circles on the wings and fuselage. On more than one occasion, and for several days at a stretch, even the flying of these craft was postponed for want of aviation fuel.

Japan's air forces were also chronically short of qualified flight instructors. This shortage, coupled with the droughts of aviation fuel, forced innovative but questionable training compromises. Some Japanese aviation cadets, for example, learned tactics primarily by watching filmed simulations. In these crude instructional films, six-foot models of U.S. ships floating in a man-made lake were "attacked" by boom-mounted motion picture cameras at different angles and speeds. It was poor training and no preparation for the meat grinder of real aerial combat.

Lord of Himself

Admiral Raymond A. Spruance, overall 5th Fleet commander, often acted as a counterweight to Mitscher's risk-prone aviator impulses. On more than one occasion, Spruance had cautioned Mitscher not to be tempted by offensive opportunities before him at the expense of shielding beachheads behind him. Spruance's instructions had more the tone of reasoned suggestions than abrupt orders; nevertheless, they had equal impact.

Spruance was, like Mitscher, small and trim—though, unlike Mitscher, Spruance's slender proportions owed to a fitness regimen and abstinence rather than chain-smoking. His sober, studious, and reclusive demeanor extended at least as far back as his midshipman days at Annapolis, where his class book described him as someone who "would never hurt anything or anybody except in the Line of Duty."

Not only was Spruance a nonsmoker, he abhorred tobacco. He forbid smoking in his presence, a policy that required subordinates (including Mitscher) who both worked around Spruance and smoked, to light up furtively and douse quickly according to the rhythm of the admiral's movements, which included marathon deck walks. Spruance was also a teetotaler; perhaps his only indulgent addiction (aside from fitness) was caffeine. His passion for exotic coffees got the perfect outlet as U.S. Navy and Marine operations gobbled up more Pacific island real estate dotted with coffee plantations.

Spruance was thought by many to be the Navy's most intelligent senior officer. Recognized as a cool, composed, and canny strategist—one admirer, Samuel Morison, extolled Spruance as "Lord of himself"—he was also second-guessed for reining in the combative impulses of subordinates like Mitscher. Within the gossipy, war-engorged corps of Navy admirals—those who had "gotten their flags"—where fighting instincts sometimes overruled strategic judgment, glory-deflating caution gained a brand name: "Spruance nuance." Among the elite cadre of "aviation admirals," of course, Spruance had that other shortcoming: he was a surface officer.

As a strategist, Spruance was particularly alert to the elaborate features that gilded Japanese battle plans—intricate schedules and audacious ploys such as those used at the Battles of Midway and Leyte Gulf. Japanese reliance on these sequences and moves often proved foolhardy; still, Spruance learned to factor in these possibilities when deploying his own forces.

Spruance shared proprietorship of the U.S. Navy's massive Central Pacific Fleet: when Spruance and his staff had the helm, it was 5th Fleet; when the less publicity shy, more openly impulsive and aviation-qualified Admiral William Halsey took charge, it became 3rd Fleet. The seed of this seemingly odd arrangement had sprouted in 1942 when Spruance became a last-minute substitute for Halsey—leveled by a severe bout of eczema—in the run up to the Battle of Midway. Halsey had gone to the hospital, while Spruance maneuvered the carriers *Enterprise* and *Hornet* to a sweeping victory.

By mid-1944 the arrangement had evolved to one whereby—at least in the public explanation by Halsey and Spruance's common boss, Admiral Chester Nimitz—the Pacific's fighting ships were kept at sea and the war's momentum was accelerated. "The team remains about the same, but the drivers change." Looked at another way, the switch was a means of keeping two extraordinary but contrasting command talents engaged as well as applying their divergent styles (Halsey's checkers and Spruance's chess) to different Central Pacific operations. The contrasts were dramatic. With Halsey at the helm during Guadalcanal and Leyte Gulf, 3rd Fleet seemed different in more than name from 5th Fleet under Spruance's command at Midway, the Marianas, and, eventually Okinawa. In many ways it was the ultimate irony that Spruance held sway over what were, during June 1944, Navy air's defining and triumphant hours in the Central Pacific: the Marianas Turkey Shoot.

In May 1944, Admiral Soemu Toyoda had inherited command of IJN's Combined Fleet after his more illustrious predecessors, fleet admirals Isoroku Yamamoto and Mineichi Koga, were lost in two separate, disastrous flights. The storied Yamamoto, traveling by bomber to inspect Japanese troops and facilities in the Solomon Islands in April 1943, had been shot down over Bougainville in a daring American aerial ambush. Koga had been lost in March 1944, not even a year later, when a flying boat carrying him west from the Palaus to the Philippines disappeared in a storm.

Koga's presumed death and Toyoda's promotion were kept secret for two months, but once he was finally and openly in command, Toyoda wasted no time responding to the Americans' latest island incursion, the invasion of Saipan. The Marianas were considered home ground—the loss of Saipan, Tinian, and Guam, the major islands of the group, would leave a fatal breach in Japan's beleaguered Central Pacific defensive ring. Toyoda had radioed Vice Admiral Jisaburo Ozawa, Mobile Fleet Commander, to "attack the enemy in the Marianas area and annihilate his fleet."

Ozawa had gained a reputation early in his naval career as an expert in surface torpedo warfare. But Ozawa was also a strategist with a scientific mind and enough of a visionary to have carefully studied carrier tactics and pressed for their use as offensive weapons in the attack on Pearl Harbor. The crown jewels of Ozawa's Mobile Fleet were its six aircraft carriers formed into two carrier groups, one commanded by Ozawa, the other by Rear Admiral Sueo Obayashi. To screen, support, and fuel its carrier divisions' flattops (aircraft carriers), Mobile Fleet also had an entourage of six battleships, thirteen cruisers, thirty destroyers and ten tankers.

Since mid-May, Mobile Fleet ships and aircraft had been gathering and training in the waters surrounding Tawi Tawi, an island near Borneo in the westernmost stretches of the Sulu Sea. The original plan, termed *A-Go* (Operation A), called for Mobile Fleet to lie in wait, baiting the Americans to lunge west and south for an all-or-nothing "decisive battle" close to Japan's interior supply lines. However, as it became clear that the unaccommodating Americans intended instead to invade the Marianas and as American submarine attacks began taking a toll on the ships operating conspicuously near Tawi Tawi, Combined Fleet was forced to its alter strategy.

On 13 June 1944, Ozawa's fleet left Tawi Tawi's anchorages and steamed northeast, bound for the Marianas and a rendezvous with a battleship detachment and support force coming up east of the Philippines. When he received Toyoda's order to execute *A-Go*, Ozawa was one day short of the scheduled rendezvous. The forces converged on the 16th, fueled and organized, and continued east on the 18th.

As the Mobile Fleet drew closer to Saipan and prepared for a decisive battle, Ozawa exuded confidence. Though search planes reported the American task force had twice his number of flattops (the actual number was fifteen), Ozawa reasoned that most of Mobile Fleet's 473 aircraft, built for speed, maneuverability, and maximum fuel capacity, could outdistance America's shorter-range aircraft. He could stay out of striking distance of American aircraft as he attacked.

Ozawa could also use Guam, still in Japanese hands, as a shuttle base for rearming and refueling Mobile Fleet's carrier-based aircraft. Added to that was the support of more than five hundred land-based aircraft on Japanese-held bases throughout the Marianas as well as Japanese island strongholds to the north and south. *A-Go* plans called for these Japanese Base Air Force planes to destroy a third of U.S. carrier forces. In effect, Ozawa believed, Mobile Fleet's combined air combat resources nearly doubled those of the Americans. What Ozawa didn't know was that many of the Japanese land-based aircraft he counted on had already been destroyed by American air raids in the run-up to the Saipan invasion.

Meanwhile, Mitscher's Task Force 58, the origin of those raids, was steaming west of the Marianas, tasked with shielding Operation Forager. But when Ozawa's forces were pinpointed late on 18

June, Mitscher (riding *Lexington*) radioed Spruance (riding nearby on cruiser *Indianapolis*), asking permission to turn, charge, and engage the Japanese. Spruance, fearing an "end around" by other unseen Japanese carrier forces, responded just after midnight with a circumspect but firm demurrer: "Change proposed does not appear advisable . . ." Mitscher was to stay on his tether. Meanwhile, as Task Force 58 edged closer to the Marianas for the night, Mobile Fleet coiled to strike.

★ Chapter 6 ★

Clearing Skies, June 1944

You're the best sight I've seen since I've been living.
—Lt. (jg) Warren McLellan, VT-16*

Dare to Die

The morning of 19 June 1944 broke cloudy and sodden over Mobile Fleet. It was 0730 before Japanese scout planes pinpointed Task Force 58 and already 0830 when two waves of Japanese aircraft—Zekes, bomb-laden Judys, and torpedo-laden Jills, two hundred in all, began winging eastward toward their targets. Two more waves would soon follow.

Meanwhile, Task Force 58 aircraft were busy pouncing on Japanese airfields on Guam. Thirty-three Hellcats were in the midst of dispatching nearly as many Japanese Zekes, when they received the voice signal "Hey Rube!" The use of the old carnival barker's cry—a call and back-handed warning to suckers—had its origins in carrier flight operations back in February 1942, when the first *Lexington*'s fighter aircraft had chased after departing land-based Japanese aerial marauders only to permit a second wave of attackers to slip past them unnoticed. The signal's clear and urgent meaning: "Come back to the ship." It was 1000 and Task Force 58 radar screens were painted full of incoming Japanese aircraft.

---

*Squadron numbers often—but not always—coincided with the carrier numbers to which they were attached—in this case VT-16 was called Torpedo 16; its counterparts were Bombing 16 and Fighting 16. Bomber, fighter and torpedo air squadrons were organized into air groups. VB-16, VF-16 and VT-16 were all part of Air Group 16.

By 1023, with the first wave of Japanese aircraft seventy-two miles distant, briefly slowing, orbiting, and organizing for attack, Task Force 58 turned east into the wind to launch. Mitscher ordered all ships to hold this windward track until further notice. He expected the day to be filled with waves of Japanese aircraft.

Carrier decks were cleared of all bombers to better prepare for what promised to be grueling rounds of launching, recovering, rearming, refueling, and relaunching rotating shifts of fighters. As the Hellcats took off, fighter director communication and control teams, one each to a carrier, vectored and "stacked" the fighter groups to locations and elevations that best positioned them to intercept. The combat C.A.P.s already aloft were now stacked between 17,000 and 23,000 feet as the first Japanese aircraft tried to penetrate. Even as Mitscher issued his commands, fighters from three carriers began tearing into the first wave of Japanese attackers, downing forty-one of them before they reached the line of ships screening the carriers. Just one plane breached this line to score a hit on *South Dakota* (BB-57).

The second, third, and fourth wave of Japanese planes fared even worse. A dozen *Essex* (CV-9) Hellcats made first contact with the second wave and were soon joined by reinforcements to splash almost seventy aircraft. The forty-seven Japanese aircraft of the third wave were directed to the wrong coordinates; a mere twelve were redirected in time to reach the battle area and seven of these were promptly shot down. Misdirection also plagued the eighty-four planes of the fourth wave. After searching for the American fleet without success, most dropped their ordnance in the ocean and flew on to the haven of Orate Field on Guam. During their approach, however, these planes were swarmed by waiting Hellcats. Thirty were shot down and the rest landed so badly damaged that they would never fly again.

The day's air tally—when eventually sorted out and compiled—was unprecedented: 346 Japanese planes downed at the cost of only 15 U.S. Navy aircraft. Several novice fighter pilots had each become "ace in a day" by bagging five or more Japanese aircraft. Alex Vraciu, a VF-16 Hellcat pilot flying from *Lexington* and already the Navy's ranking active fighter ace, added six to his earlier total of twelve.

And the damage inflicted did not end there. Although no American air strikes had been launched against Mobile Fleet, two of its carriers—*Shokaku* and *Taiho*—were sunk, both victims of torpedo hits from stalking American submarines. In one short day, Japan's naval air power, which had once been the triumphant weapon of Pearl Harbor, was irretrievably crippled, and the ranks of even its inexperienced pilots further decimated.

Mobile Fleet Commander Ozawa's flagship *Taiho* received its torpedo hit just as the day's launches began. The damage at first seemed slight, but in the afternoon *Taiho* erupted like a volcano, the victim of the explosive gasoline fumes pumped through its complex of interior ventilation ducts. Ozawa vowed to stay with *Taiho* as the carrier sank, but was persuaded to transfer to a rescue cruiser. The remnants of Mobile Fleet retreated northwest in order to refuel. Despite known losses and many other aircraft unaccounted for, Ozawa, shamed but resolute and still unaware of the scale of the catastrophe, was determined to resume the attack the next morning.

Meanwhile Mitscher, flush with success and backed by Spruance, took three of the four carrier groups southwest in pursuit of Mobile Fleet. Heading in the wrong direction, it was not until mid-afternoon on 20 June that Mitscher's search planes finally located the Japanese at a position reported to be 275 miles west of Task Force 58—just barely within round-trip range of its aircraft.

The afternoon skies were bright and nearly cloudless, but dusk was just a few hours off. Plane launches into an easterly wind would take Task Force 58 even farther from the enemy's position. Aircraft would arrive over the target as darkness fell; returning airmen—all of them exhausted, most trained only for daylight landings and some wounded, flying damaged aircraft or both—would have to grope their way home and somehow land after dark.

Mitscher left his usual perch on the flag bridge of *Lexington* to step into flag plot and confer with Arleigh Burke and the rest of his staff. He pondered his options, but not for long. He made an aviator's decision; he and his airmen would have to take the risk. It would be tight, but they could make it. Mitscher gave the order firmly: "Launch 'em!"

Task Force 58 ships turned once more into the wind, and beginning a little after 1600, Mitscher's carriers launched 216 aircraft—a mix of

Hellcat fighters, Dauntless and Helldiver dive-bombers, and Avenger torpedo bombers. The planes had long since been armed, their engines warmed at intervals, and their fuel tanks constantly topped off.

Shotgun cartridges used to ignite plane engines fired off in skirmish-like volleys as the order came to "Start 'em up." Then, as the engines caught and throttled up, the flight decks were flooded with noise and, as one observer on *Lexington* described it, "halos of pale vapor streaming from the propeller tips."

Once airborne, instead of circling to form up, the aircraft began a running rendezvous to save time and fuel: lead planes turned west immediately after launch and then slowed, allowing others to catch up en route. Avengers and Dauntlesses flew low on the water in three-plane sections shaped like inverted Vs; the faster and longer-range fighters, grouped in four-plane sections, stacked themselves at two thousand to four thousand feet above, weaving to reduce speed and keep station with their flock.

The aircraft were well on their way before pilots learned there'd been a mistake in deciphering the position report first given by the scout aircraft. The one-way radius they had to cover, instead of being 275 miles, was more like 320 miles.

Launches complete, Task Force 58 carriers and escorts immediately turned and sped west against the lowering sun, bent on shortening their pilots' return flight as much as possible. Though many task force destroyers were dangerously low on fuel—a condition both limiting their range and imperiling them if heavy seas were encountered—no time was wasted slowing to refuel.

Mitscher, already beginning to sense the night landing ahead might take a heavier toll on his pilots and aircraft than the attack itself, decided to call off a second strike. He also went on the radio circuits telling all task force ships to be ready to put their searchlights straight up in the air if necessary when the aircraft returned. Five nights before, with Task Force 58 steaming blacked out, Japanese planes had launched four torpedoes toward *Lexington,* two of which had passed within ten yards. Bright lights in a black night and in a sea that might hold aerial or submarine predators would be the risk for those staying behind.

His message went out on intelligence circuits none of the departing air crews could hear. Mitscher knew the pilots had more than enough things to worry about without learning this last contingency.

The Hop Supreme

Torpedo 16's Warren McLellan took off from *Lexington* at 1630, part of Air Group 16's thirty-four plane formation of seven Avengers (this day equipped with bombs instead of torpedoes), sixteen Bombing 16 Dauntlesses, and eleven Fighting 16 Hellcats.

Along the way the group's planes gradually gained elevation, accelerating fuel consumption. Pilots—both eager to strike and anxious about their fuel—flooded the radio circuits with premature target sightings, most of which turned out to be small clouds low on the water. The first real sighting came nearly two hours into the mission—a large oil slick, a bronze-colored trail, that soon led to a formation of Japanese destroyers and tankers.

It was 1835. Already low on fuel, some pilots pleaded to attack the formation, but mission orders were to attack carriers, so the formation, after changing course slightly and using the slick and the tankers as a pointer to the carrier groups that must be ahead, flew on. Ten minutes later, as the planes dipped under the overhang of a huge anvil-topped cumulus cloud, they found what they were looking for.

There were three groups of Japanese ships—more than the scouting reports. One group with three carriers was just ahead, a second carrier group lay to the north, and a third group, uncounted and unidentified, lay even farther to the west. The sky over the carrier group to the north was already crowded with attackers—planes from *Enterprise* and *Hornet*—so the VT-16 Avengers and VB-16 Dauntlesses drew a bead on the ships now just below them.

Descending from eleven thousand feet, VT-16 planes began their approach. McLellan's Avenger was on the port side of his section. Below him, he saw the first blossoming puffs of AA fire. Then, unexpectedly, McLellan felt a jolt from below, and his cockpit began to fill with smoke.

It wasn't AA—he was still too high for that. All McLellan had seen was a spurt of tracers close to his canopy. He pulled his Avenger up sharply to get clear of whatever it was that had hit him, but it was no use. Fire was already flooding the cockpit and he had to get out. As McClellan reached for his microphone to warn his crew to bail out, flames scorched his wrist and the handset fell into the fire. Unable to wait any longer, McLellan bailed out, hoping Greenhalgh and Hutchinson would have the alertness and instincts to follow.

Hurtling in free fall, McClellan grasped his ripcord handle but fought the urge to deploy his parachute. He wanted to get below the AA explosions, and he didn't want to be a slow-moving target for any Japanese fighters in the area. McLellan's plunge carried him below the horizon where it quickly darkened, making it difficult to distinguish sky from sea. Still, McLellan pulled his ripcord in plenty of time. By the time he hit the water, he'd also managed to undo the chest and hip buckles of his chute and pull the lanyard to inflate one side of his Mae West.

McLellan landed in six-foot swells and quickly squirmed free of his parachute harness. He worked simultaneously to unhook the raft pack still attached to the chute harness and the survival pack strapped over his shoulders. It took McLellan precious seconds to free the backpack, and by the time he did, the parachute canopy was filled with water and sinking. McLellan fumbled frantically to release the raft pack but found himself being pulled farther and farther underwater by the sinking canopy. Finally, he let the chute and life raft go. Clutching his survival pack, McLellan now had only his Mae West to give him buoyancy. More than extra buoyancy, he realized he'd lost his best chance for survival—the bright yellow raft would be what search planes would be looking for. Fighting to hold his composure, he pulled the lanyard to inflate the other side of the vest.

Riding atop the wave crests, McLellan finally had a chance to look around. He saw what he took to be the still-floating wreckage of his aircraft. Then he caught sight of what must have brought him down, a Japanese fighter aircraft making strafing runs to finish off its work. McLellan hoped that Greenhalgh and Hutchinson were nowhere near the wreckage.

* * *

Don "Hound Dog" Nelson, a seasoned dive-bombing pilot from *Enterprise*'s Bombing Squadron 10 (VB-10), knew he was taking his SBD-5 Dauntless well beyond its effective radius.

The Dauntless was once thought to be the Navy's hottest aircraft, but its awkward lines and relatively slow speed had since earned it the name "wind indicator." Still, Nelson appreciated his aircraft's ruggedness and dependability as had earlier *Enterprise* Dauntless pilots—the ones who had chalked up two Japanese carriers to seal the victory at Midway two years before.

Those Dauntlesses had been low on fuel when they began their fateful, desperation bombing runs—just as Nelson and his Bombing 10 squadron mates were now. Nelson began the mission knowing it would take him 50 miles outside the Dauntless's usual operating radius of 250 miles. Bombing 10's skipper, Jim Ramage, widened the gap even more by ordering them to bypass their first target sighting, the collection of tankers and screening tankers that Air Group 16 pilots, flying a few minutes behind Bombing 10, would also see first. "We didn't come 300 miles to bomb tankers," Ramage came on the circuit to tell them. They would keep looking for the Charlie Victors, the carriers.

They found what they were looking for twenty miles north—cruisers, destroyers, battleships and—best of all—CVs. Nelson began his dive from thirteen thousand feet and at ten thousand deployed his dive flaps to control speed. His carrier target already looked huge. Nelson saw masses of flashing red dots along each of its sides—the ship's AA guns. Nelson was overjoyed and horrified. It was where he'd dreamed of being, but he wondered if he'd ever get out.

Below him, Nelson's target suddenly shuddered and lost way. There was a large red flash, a bomb hit from another squadron plane on the side well forward. The carrier's mass now stuck right up and down in Nelson's sights. He adjusted his aim to allow for the wind and took the Dauntless still lower to make the target impossible to miss. The carrier was now enveloped in a haze of smoke. Nelson finally yanked the bomb release, felt the bomb fall away, closed his dive flaps, and started his pullout, eyes watering and ears pounding.

Nelson's altimeter bottomed out at 1,500 feet and his speed climbed to 280 knots. Too low and not fast enough, Nelson thought at first, as he dodged his way through what seemed an endless corridor of crossfire. The squadron's prearranged retirement course was supposed to be due east, but for now Nelson took any direction and any altitude that would keep him and his gunner John Mankin aloft and alive. He found himself getting out of firing range from one ship only to drift into the sights of another.

Off one wing Nelson saw a plane burst into flames and slowly float down. Off the other wing, flames enveloped the flight deck of one of the Japanese small carriers. A Japanese cruiser was using its big deck guns to heave shells into the water, probably hoping the attacking aircraft would run into the columns. Sure enough, Nelson saw a Helldiver low on the water lose a wing and crash without a trace of smoke or fire. Nelson briefly drifted into the crossfire of a cruiser and destroyer. Shells burst so close that Nelson could hear the hollow metallic sound of the concussions buffeting his fuselage.

It was dicey for a while, but eventually the gunfire subsided and Nelson managed to join up with another VB-10 bomber. As the sky darkened, the two *Enterprise* Dauntlesses fell in with a formation of *Lexington* bombers. But as Nelson checked his gas, he realized he couldn't—or shouldn't—keep up with this formation. Against the 14 knot headwind, he was running at 2,100 rpm just to hold his place—too much demand on his fuel. Then Nelson spotted another slower formation off to starboard. They turned out to be Bombing 10 planes. Nelson and the other *Enterprise* bomber pilot broke away from the *Lexington* formation to join them.

VF-16 Hellcat pilot Whiteway and his two section mates had lost sight of the VT-16 planes when they'd dipped below the towering cumulus cloud. Assuming their target would be the northern Japanese carrier group, the Hellcat pilots headed that way, only to lose their flock and their own chance at the Japanese. No Japanese plane rose to challenge them, and all they saw below was one flaming carrier and a straggling destroyer. After a half an hour of fruitless searching, the three Hellcats turned for home. As it turned out, the rest of Air Group 16 had a thirty-mile head start on them.

Whiteway was uncertain about his course, so when he spotted a flight of Dauntlesses ahead, his first thought was to follow them. But then he and the other pilots decided to overtake them. The Hellcats' belly tanks gave them more range, and their speed would get them home first so that flight decks could be cleared for the slower stragglers. They climbed to brighter air at seven thousand feet and settled their speed at 170 knots, estimating they'd arrive over Task Force 58 about 2030.

During his first hour in the water, Warren McLellan witnessed quite a show. First, he saw one big carrier that had taken a hit forward of its island structure and a second carrier that was already afire and listing. Then a big ship with the raked stacks of a cruiser swept by McLellan, its bow and starboard side so close he could even discern the color of its sailors' uniforms, all in khaki except one man in white. Next—blessedly farther out—two battleships severed the cruiser's wake.

Finally, in the last of the light, McLellan saw a flight of Zekes circling the burning, listing carrier. Trailing thick, black smoke from its stacks, the carrier continued down wind, leaving the planes without a nest.

It was late—2100—and three of the four tanks on Don Nelson's Dauntless were drained. The last one would be dry soon. Ten minutes before, the pilots received a welcome transmission: "All planes from Commander Task Force 58. Land on any base you see." Still, he—and those others still aloft—would need luck to make it.

Already planes were dropping out—the radio circuits were full of last transmissions. One pilot told his gunner to prepare for a water landing. A Hellcat pilot told his wingman he had been hit in one tank and was going down; the wingman replied he would ditch with him. Nelson watched one group of lights, a whole section of planes, drift lower and lower until the lights extinguished. Bombing 10's formation was hanging in there, but it was ragged. Every few minutes another pilot would come on the circuit, calling a wingman, calling his carrier, announcing he was going in. Each time silence followed.

Art Whiteway was fighting against the effects of vertigo when he and the other two pilots in his section saw lights flashing. They edged south to approach the lights, but the flashes turned out to be lightning. They continued on, seeing nothing through a low blanket of clouds. Now, they too were running low on fuel.

Whiteway was sure they'd passed beyond the task force. They turned northeast, and as they did a star shell flashed nearby. The light blinded Whiteway, and he felt another wave of dizziness overtake him. When he finally recovered and brought the plane under control, he was only two hundred feet above the water, and he'd lost track of his section.

Whiteway's plane was now desperately low on fuel—he thought he might have five more minutes' worth. He began planning to ditch, but as he brought Lucky Strike closer to the water and unbuckled his parachute harness, Whiteway could see, even in the darkness, that the water was rough. Swells were at least ten feet high—not good for landing and not much better for surviving even if he ditched safely. "Good God," he found himself saying aloud, "give me a break."

But rough water or not, Whiteway knew he was running out of options. He lifted the nose of the plane to have one more look around—nothing. He lowered his Hellcat's nose and got ready for the inevitable. His eyes were fully adjusted to the darkness; he at least could tell that the waves had moderated.

Then Whiteway saw a searchlight. It turned out to be a destroyer, but five miles farther on he saw another. As he closed in on this searchlight, Whiteway suddenly saw red truck lights blink below his wing and a carrier's deck pinpoint lights flash on. A Helldiver was already in its landing circle; Whiteway got behind it, followed it around, and after it landed, he got into the groove and landed too. It was 2150. The carrier turned out to be Cabot (CVL-28). There were fifteen gallons in Whiteway's remaining tank—enough, maybe, for one more pass.

Don Nelson's first glimmer of hope came when he picked up Enterprise's homing signal—it meant he had about seventy-five miles to go. Then Nelson saw—or imagined he saw—the arc of a star shell. He thought maybe it was lightning, but then he saw other lights. Definitely star shells. It was 2120. The planes in his formation were still a long way out, but they were approaching the outer screen of the carrier groups. Then, a bit farther on, searchlights: some vertical (markers for the task force spread over several hundred square miles of ocean), others horizontal (pointers to the carriers). Some of the verticals were blunted by low clouds, but the rest stood tall. In the darkness, illuminated until now only by the navigation lights of other distressed planes, the searchlights were exhilaratingly welcoming.

McLellan still had his Very pistol and when things seemed to have settled down, he used it to shoot off a red flare. If Greenhalgh or Hutchinson were in the area they might see it. The descending flare lit up the patch of ocean, a reminder of how alone he was. After two minutes he fired a round from his .38 pistol, and ten seconds later he fired another. McClellan then turned his body slowly in the water—watching and listening, but seeing nothing, hearing nothing.

Even though it wasn't waterproof, his watch ticked on, and as time crept by, McLellan occasionally felt muffled underwater concussions. He reasoned they might be the implosion of watertight compartments in the ships his group had sunk. He tried floating on his back, but the concussions hurt his ears.

Now there was nothing else beyond his thoughts to keep McLellan occupied. He tried to keep his thoughts positive—about things he should do once the sun was up. But then a thought as dark as the night intruded: he had no girlfriend, no wife, no children, and no legacy.

The thought floated with McLellan all that night, sometimes weighing him down in despair, sometimes buoying him with anger and determination. Once he considered putting his pistol to his head and getting it over with. But he shook that off—the Japanese way, maybe, but not his.

Although Don Nelson had reached the Task Force, he quickly realized his troubles weren't over. Around him he saw the lights of arriving aircraft—a traffic jam of red and green and white and yellow. All the remaining aircraft seemed to be converging at once, all starved for gas and desperate to land, somewhere, anywhere, and right now. Though the base circuit had told them to land on any carrier that had a clear deck, Nelson knew all the landing circles would fill quickly, and many pilots would be desperate enough to crowd others aside.

Nelson also saw lights below him, but now they spread more confusion than welcome. Each ship's foremast showed two dim red truck lights—but these might be cruisers or destroyers instead of carriers. Each carrier displayed a distinguishing glow light, but the glow light could only be seen from directly above. The pinpoint lights outlining the flight decks were visible only from close astern.

His fuel gauges showed dry. Nelson knew his best bet was to find a carrier with a clear deck and no other aircraft in its landing circle. Once Nelson lowered his wheels and flaps and took the Dauntless to full power, any remaining fuel would be gone fast. And then unexpectedly he heard what he was praying for all this time: a carrier on the air saying it had both a clear deck and no waiting. The carrier had signaled its position with two blinks of its largest searchlight, and there it was, off to Nelson's left.

Then Nelson got in the groove. Ahead of him he could see the carrier's landing deck lights and the landing signal officer (LSO) astern on the port side, his form defined by the fluorescent light wands used for night landings. But the wands spelled out bad news—wands aloft, crossing and uncrossing. Nelson was being waved off. For an instant he considered landing anyway, but it was too late. He was already passing the LSO. Nelson—fuming—gunned his engine, circled, and began another approach. Another wave-off, this time because a damaged aircraft fouled the deck.

Nelson pulled up his wheels and flaps, climbed a little and throttled back as much as he dared. He was incredibly tired. He doubted that there was enough fuel for another pass—even if he spotted a carrier ready to take him now. Nelson saw lights farther ahead. He kept going, kept gaining on the lights. Sure enough, it was another carrier, a big one.

Nelson went by its port side and looked down. The LSO was giving him a wheels-down land signal. When Nelson circled and got in the groove, he could see the deck was clear. The LSO was signaling high and fast, so he dropped his nose and took off some throttle. When the LSO gave him the cut, Nelson dropped the nose a bit more. The Dauntless wheels touched and bounced, and its arresting hook grabbed a wire. It was a solid, blessed, welcoming yank—almost like a hug.

* * *

When the sun first came up in a mostly clear sky dotted by several small black clouds, Warren McLellan saw an empty ocean—no sign of ships, no sign of aircraft, and no sign of Greenhalgh or Hutchinson. When he'd dozed during the night, seawater had slapped him awake, but it had also flooded his mouth. McLellan's tongue and lips were swollen. He tried taking a sip from his survival canteen, but it only made him vomit. The rising sun at least gave him a direction to head. Saipan, the nearest land, was probably five hundred miles away. Pushed along by a steady trade wind, McLellan kicked off his boots and began swimming.

There was no telling how far his morning swim took him—probably not very far. Maybe he'd covered hundreds of yards or even a mile, but maybe the water's currents had taken that all back and more. Shoeless, his Mae West giving an awkward list to his buoyancy, McLellan stroked the water in a slow paced crawl. He knew it was more an effort of keeping going than realistically getting anywhere. Once, chillingly, his hand slapped the flanks of a large fish.

Then McLellan heard engines. He checked his watch: 0730. The first planes were high-flying Helldivers with Hellcat escorts—no chance he'd be seen. Low-flying Hellcats came next, then came VT-16 Avengers, and with them came a rainfall of life rafts. McLellan finally reached one, inflated it and after several desperate tries, managed to heave himself in. He vomited again—spasms that seemed to turn his stomach inside out—but then he pulled the raft's sail over his head and drifted off to sleep.

Lexington landed twenty-two planes during the night, only ten of them part of Air Group 16. Fourteen planes—including all the returning Hellcats—made it to other carriers. Air Group 16 losses, both to enemy fire and to crashes on the return flight, were 9 out of 34 and 4 out of 64 airmen sent out. Two more men—a *Lexington* flight deck crewman and the gunner from another air group's bomber—were also killed, victims of a flight deck crash during the first landings. "We landed four fighters okay but then it happened," Bob Davis, an electrician's mate manning one of *Lexington*'s hangar deck cranes wrote that night in his diary. "One of our dive-bombers crashed in the middle of the deck, which ruined about seven more planes. Before we could clean the mess up so we could land the rest of the planes, they ran out of gas and about all of them went into the drink."

These losses were a mirror to the losses in the rest of Task Force 58. In the final count (when carriers exchanged information on the planes and crews ending up on their decks and other task force ships reported crewmen pulled from the water), 130 planes had been lost, but all but 38 of the returning flyers—the real weapons of Task Force 58—were saved.

When Air Group 16's intelligence officer debriefed the returning *Lexington* flyers, he asked each to recap his experience. One Avenger pilot seemed to express it best: "Well, I've been jumped worse by Zekes, and there've been missions when I've had to be on the ball more, and I've landed with less gas, but I've never had all that trouble together until now. It was the Hop Supreme."

Warren McLellan, still soaking wet, stood on *Lexington*'s catwalk, being unhitched from a breeches buoy. The ship's loudspeaker was calling him, requesting he go up immediately to the flag bridge. The day was such a blur that McLellan's mind had trouble keeping up with the pace of things. But this was no dream.

His time asleep in the raft—interrupted by bouts of vomiting—finally ended at 1600 to the noise of a flight of Hellcats trailed by four float planes. One float plane settled near McLellan's raft, and its pilot leaned out, grinning. "How about it? Want a lift?"

Though still tongue-tied, McLellan managed to croak, "You're the best sight I've seen since I've been living!"

The float plane flew McLellan to a cruiser. He learned en route that dozens of scout planes were out—sent by Mitscher—and that he'd been spotted close to a huge oil slick. As important, he found out Greenhalgh and Hutchinson had been picked up too.

McLellan was aboard the cruiser briefly—it seemed only long enough to get a pair of dry socks and shoes—before he was strapped into a breeches buoy and swung over to a destroyer. The destroyer, it turned out, had also been sent by Mitscher to fetch him. By the time McLellan was ushered before Mitscher's small, rumpled presence on *Lexington*'s flag bridge, he hardly knew how to begin speaking his thanks through lips and a tongue that were just then beginning to feel like normal.

There was no need. Mitscher quietly shook his hand, welcomed McLellan back, and asked him what he'd seen. McLellan told Mitscher about the two carriers, one with a fiery deck and a fifteen degree list, the cruiser passing close by, the two battleships farther out, and the homeless Japanese aircraft. Mitscher smiled and nodded: "I think we got two carriers last night."

As it turned out, Task Force 58 pilots' bold strike into darkness claimed only one IJN carrier, the *Hiyo;* two others—*Zuikaku* and *Chiyoda*— were hit but only lightly damaged. But this was only one measure of the achievement. Japan's loss of *Hiyo* compounded the loss of *Shokaku* and *Taiho* the day before. A final numbing count would show that Ozawa's Mobile Fleet had lost 92 percent of its carrier aircraft and 72 percent of its float planes. Combined with the loss of fifty Guam-based aircraft, the two-day total climbed near five hundred aircraft—and with them nearly as many skilled flyers.

The two days would soon get an official name—the Battle of the Philippine Sea. Unofficially (and much sooner and more enduringly), they would also be memorialized as the "Great Marianas Turkey Shoot."

But even in this atmosphere of triumph, mixed reviews surfaced. Spruance, in tethering Mitscher and Mitscher's carrier commanders, had both shielded Forager and struck a dramatic blow. Still, as far as the most vocal of the carrier commanders were concerned, Spruance, in not striking earlier and more boldly, had missed "the chance of the century." They were certain it would prolong the war for months.

★ Chapter 7 ★

Returning

A destroyer is all ship. In the beautiful lines of her, in her speed and roughness, in the curious gallantry she is completely a ship, in the old sense.

—John Steinbeck

Fletchers

For what seemed interminable months, the toll taken by Iron Bottom Sound's watery graveyard remained the template for the Navy surface fleet's encounters with the IJN. Despite the signature naval air victories at Midway and the beachhead triumphs of endurance at Guadalcanal and Tarawa, the fact was that U.S. Navy surface ships could at best expect a stalemate when going head-to-head against the ships and aircraft of the IJN.

There was a catalog full of reasons for this overmatch and for too long the thorniest of the shortcomings seemed insurmountable. Imperial Japan's frontline ships were newer, and their skippers and crews were highly (though often blindly) disciplined, better trained, and more proficient, especially when it came to the lightning quick nighttime tactics that gave the IJN a decisive edge in Iron Bottom Sound.

Certain Japanese weaponry was also superior, especially their Type 93 surface-to-surface torpedo—what Americans came to call the Long Lance. The Long Lance's record and reputation bedeviled its adversaries and spurred nightmares among its victims. Packed with more than one thousand pounds of TNT and powered by pure oxygen, the Long Lance produced virtually no wake and no telltale noise as it stalked its prey. It could both outdistance and outrun any torpedo in the U.S. Navy arsenal, reliably hitting targets as far away as eleven miles at speeds approaching 50 knots (and targets twice as far when traveling half the speed). The design secrets of the Long Lance were not fully understood until after the war.

Yet, inevitably, this formidable tide of naval superiority also began to turn, though there was not one innovation, circumstance, or event (such as Midway or Guadalcanal) to conspicuously mark the shift. Instead, it was the accumulation of many factors. Some, like technology and production prowess, were tangible. Other factors, though real enough and vitally important, were hard to pin down: matters of leadership, individual initiative, and teamwork.

First, the United States began to outpace Japan technologically—not so much in pure science as in the genius for delivering an ever-widening and deepening stream of practical and reliable devices to the fleet. Effective (and ever-improving) radar detection was among the first—and most revolutionary—of these technologies.

Radar detection was not new; in fact it had been in use on 7 December 1941. Six truck-sized installations were deployed by the Army in Hawaii, and soldiers at one installation, perched on the northernmost cliffs of Oahu, had spotted, tracked, and reported the incoming Japanese, only to have a drowsy watch officer back at central station unwittingly mistake their sighting for the expected arrival of U.S. bombers.

Early generation ship radars, like those installed on *Colhoun, Gregory,* and *Little* at Guadalcanal were pretty much limited to spotting incoming aircraft, although even aerial targets could be lost when they converged with land masses. Surface targets returned fuzzy images at best, and during the heat of battle, radar was practically useless. There were no radar screens (called repeaters) installed on the ship's bridge; to see an image, the skipper or deck officer had to leave the bridge and go into the darkened radar room.

Radar advances included devising and installing different systems for detecting air and surface contacts and working out system settings for tracking long and short range contacts. A huge advance was the linking of radar tracking—via a then ingenious and revolutionary refrigerator-sized electromechanical computer installed in the internal communications (I.C.) room with the aiming and firing of naval cannons.

On the latest destroyers such as *Drexler,* experienced radio technicians like Pittsburgh native Dudley Gallup, 21, were routinely responsible for servicing exotic technologies that prewar sailors could scarcely have imagined. The newest of these was LORAN, an acronym for "long range navigation" technology, essentially a triangulating system (and the predecessor of today's satellite-driven Global Positioning Systems) of transmitters and antennas used to pinpoint locations for ships at sea. Should a LORAN-equipped ship like *Drexler* be distressed within the bounds of a LORAN grid, its CO could give accurate position reports to units coming to the rescue. LORAN added a thin but important veneer of order to the trackless open Pacific as well as its treacherous coastal waters—large chunks of which remained uncharted.

Another was IFF, a system employing coded radar signals to separate sheep from wolves—incoming friendly aircraft from enemy aircraft. IFF technology was so secret, Gallup recalled, its console's interior wiring was not color coded—a way of protecting IFF's mysteries if equipment fell into enemy hands. To prevent this from happening, *Drexler*'s IFF gear was armed with an internal explosive. It was Gallup's job to trigger this self-destruction mechanism if *Drexler* ever had to be abandoned.

The seemingly unending stream occasionally produced quantum leaps in the technology of age-old weapons. At the end of 1942, following years of research and tinkering with prototypes, antiaircraft projectiles equipped with radio proximity fuses began arriving in the fleet. The fuses used the frequency differences between transmitted and reflected radio waves to trigger explosions. When firing antiaircraft projectiles with these ingenious variable-time (VT) devices built in, the gun crew's aim need only be accurate enough to reach the neighborhood of an oncoming plane. The official terminology for the projectiles was "AA Special," but sailors—many of whom may not have completely grasped VT's principle but fully respected its power—dubbed them "Buck Rogers shells." The first Japanese aircraft victim of the VT fuse fell to AA

Special gunfire from cruiser *Helena* (CL-50) in January 1943. There were many victims of AA Special-type ordnance to follow. By the time of Okinawa, VT-fused projectiles were considered integral parts of a ship's antiaircraft arsenal.

Recalling the early days of the Pacific War and the clear supremacy of IJN's destroyer fleet, Tameichi Hara (then one of IJN's best young destroyer captains and a renowned torpedo warfare tactician) realized Japan's naval leaders "failed to reckon with the miraculous development of electronic weapons by the United States." They also failed to reckon with the torrent of production of which these electronic weapons were just one piece.

Perhaps nowhere was this torrent more evident than in the sheer quantity and steadily increasing quality of new ships hitting the waves. In the case of destroyers, it was the Fletcher Class that set the pace and firmly established destroyers as resilient fleet workhorses capable of going head-to-head with the best of the IJN.

Pringle, Heywood L. Edwards, Bennett, Daly, Cowell, Callaghan, Richard P. Leary, Howorth, and *Bryant* were all Fletcher Class destroyers. So were new incarnations of *Colhoun* (DD-801), *Gregory* (DD-802), and *Little* (DD-803) (their construction and commissioning proved the best sort of revenge for their predecessors' fate). Somewhat like a wartime echo of the dependable, ubiquitous Model T, the Fletcher proved to be the sturdy design for a classic and prolific warship.

The Fletcher was large for a destroyer; at 2,100 tons and 376 feet, a Fletcher weighed more than twice what earlier destroyers weighed and was more than 25 percent longer. Its main deck ran flush all the way fore and aft, increasing the ship's longitudinal strength. The Fletcher's beam was also wider—close to forty feet amidships—which slightly reduced the tendency to roll in rough seas.

Belowdecks, Fletchers' crew spaces were divided in half, separated amidships by propulsion gearing, auxiliary machinery, and four boilers housed in two fire rooms, each supplying a separate, self-contained engine room. The separation of engine and boiler equipment improved the Fletchers' chances to continue fighting even if one of its power plants was knocked out. The plants were powerful and responsive: a combined 60,000 horsepower driving two screws (propellors) delivered flank speed of 36 knots (over 50 miles per hour), and a bit more in a pinch.

Atop the main deck were two flat deckhouses—the biggest extending from just forward of the ship's bridge aft beyond the two raked boiler stacks—containing interior passageways as well as work and storage spaces. Three of the ship's five main battery guns, both its torpedo mounts and many of its smaller antiaircraft guns sat atop these deckhouses.

Below the main deck and forward of the engineering spaces, crammed into three levels, was a honeycomb of watertight compartments for officer and crew berthing, fire control gear, storage, and ammunition. Astern of the engineering spaces were additional belowdeck watertight crew spaces, ammunition storage, and fuel tanks. At the fantail the taper of the Fletcher hull left only enough room for steering gear. In this after-steering compartment, a helmsman could directly carry out emergency steering orders should bridge control signal mechanisms fail. In the event of a power failure, the ship's rudder could still be moved (though slowly and with murderous difficulty) from after steering by hand pumping oil through a transversely mounted hydraulic ram.

The bridge superstructure—the ship's control and communications nerve center—rose three levels above the forward most deckhouse. The second of these three levels contained the bow-facing pilothouse, an enclosed space for navigation and for steering and engine controls capped by an open weather bridge atop which sat the ship's main battery fire control director—informally called the basket. On either side of the pilothouse were exposed bridge wings, convenient places to position lookouts (and, in rough weather, to conveniently vomit downwind).

In the superstructure below the pilothouse were spaces for receiving, coding, and transmitting radio message traffic. Below these, in the deckhouse at the main deck level, was the CIC. CIC, a relatively new configuration pioneered in destroyer *Hutchins* (DD-476), consolidated radar equipment, interior communication, and target-plotting capabilities into a nerve center for coordinating the DDs' battle capabilities—its guns and torpedoes to fight air and surface targets, and explosive depth charges to combat submarines.

Working in a tin can CIC was often exciting, but it could also be a claustrophobic, disorienting experience. The compartment had no portholes to let in external light. It was virtually always a dimmed or darkened space, fleetingly illuminated by the ghostly emanations of the radar repeater screens and the muffled glow of red battle lamps. To stand watch or GQ in CIC, as did Ben Hall, 24, an officer on *Walke* (DD-723), was to be inundated with cryptic information while simultaneously feeling half blind. When under attack by an aircraft, for example, crewmen in CIC would know, often with scary precision, exactly what was about to happen well ahead of anyone else on the ship, yet in their closed-off space they were entirely disconnected from actually seeing it. Hall noticed that this confinement was only made worse because the CIC compartment had just one exit—to port. Before *Walke* reached the war zone, Hall had succeeded in correcting this; shipfitters had installed a second exit on the starboard side.

While CICs on cruisers, battleships, and aircraft carriers were more extensive, better equipped, and a bit less confining, even the tin can CIC was revolutionary. Just as the Fletcher's powerful propulsion plant was a sort of capstone to the capabilities of the industrial age, so CIC consoles, screens, and equipment interfaces were crude harbingers of high technology.

The CIC concept was also a sign that in twentieth-century sea warfare, speed, accuracy, and central coordination of battle information were as important as firepower, propulsion, and seamanship. Coordination from CIC also extended beyond the boundaries of the ship. The demands of joint air and sea operations often required that tin can personnel be able to communicate, coordinate, and occasionally even direct the tactical missions of planes overhead. The tools for doing this—more sophisticated radar, IFF, and the like—were already at hand. What was missing were personnel who were knowledgeable, practiced, and experienced enough to work effectively with pilots and their aircraft, especially when tin cans were on remote picket duty.

Because resources, particularly highly skilled people, were always at a premium, the solution that evolved was the selection and training of specialized fighter director teams, small cadres of officers supported by enlisted technicians who could be dispatched on temporary duty as ship operations and circumstances required. One early volunteer for this duty was a 22-year-old ensign named Franklin Butler. Butler was a native of Providence, Rhode Island, who'd grown up in a multigenerational household so replete with the first name Franklin that early on he answered to Coit, his middle name. Coit Butler had left Bowdoin College to enter naval flight training but then volunteered to switch to fighter director training when the opportunity came up. The idea of controlling high-speed fighter aircraft to intercept and shoot down enemy bogeys was exciting. It also helped that the three-month training program would be held at a Navy-commandeered luxury resort on Georgia's Saint Simon Island.

The first Fletchers were launched and reached the fleet late in 1942. A few, including *Fletcher* (DD-445) itself*—the lead and namesake of the class—even saw action at Guadalcanal. During 1943, Fletcher construction accelerated: more than 50 were launched and average construction time fell below six months. By war's end 175 Fletchers were delivered to the Navy—the most ever for any one major warship class.

During this massive production cycle, there were occasional missteps. There had been, for example, an abortive effort to equip a handful of Fletchers *(Pringle* was one) with catapult-mounted scout aircraft after the fashion of battleships and cruisers. The alterations included removing a torpedo mount and strengthening the keel. But in early tests, recovering a launched aircraft onto a small, narrow-beamed ship in any kind of rolling sea proved to tricky and hazardous, so the idea was abandoned.

But missteps such as this were also offset by lessons learned and new modifications. Among the most vital modifications was the addition of all sorts of mid- and short-range AA guns installed on resurrected battleships like *West Virginia*. By the time of L-Day, new and

Fletcher and the destroyer class were named for Admiral Frank Friday Fletcher, a late-nineteenth and early-twentieth-century admiral who'd been commander in chief of the Atlantic Fleet just before America's entry into World War I. Frank Friday Fletcher was the uncle of Vice Admiral Frank Jack Fletcher, who commanded the carrier task force supporting the invasion of Guadalcanal. It was Frank Jack Fletcher who had limited carrier-based air cover for Guadalcanal, much to Kelly Turner's distress.

overhauled Fletchers, in addition to their five dual-purpose 5-inch-38 cannons, bristled with medium- and short-range antiaircraft weapons: ten 40-mm guns* and seven 20-mm machine guns. On several Fletcher destroyers, the removal of a torpedo mount made way for the installation of more AA guns, one more sign that the ships' real predators were aircraft, not other ships.

The Fletchers were such consummate ships that the succeeding destroyer class—the *Allen D. Sumner*—changed little in design. The Sumners were one hundred tons heavier and were equipped with two rudders to complement the two propellers, a feature that made the Sumners—like *Drexler*—a shade more maneuverable. The *Sumners* also increased main battery firepower by adding one gun; the five single gun mounts were replaced by three twin gun mounts.

These newest additions to the destroyer line in fact represented an excess of riches. With the war in Europe nearing its end (and high-seas combat operations in the Atlantic and Mediterranean significantly curtailed), many existing ships, including some DDs, were rerouted to the Pacific—an opportunity for a "double dose" of war.

As a result, some of the latest ships ended up being reconfigured before they saw any action. Ships such as *Harry F. Bauer* (DD-738/DM-26) (named for Al Gallin's skipper on *Gregory*), *Shea* (DD-750/DM-30), *J. William Ditter* (DD-751/DM-31), and *Lindsey,* launched as *Sumner* Class DDs, were refitted as high-speed minelayers.

A few of these newly launched ships (essentially destroyers rigged for special duty) benefited from the availability of veteran officers and crews. *Harry F. Bauer*'s XO, for example, was Robert Morgenthau, whose destroyer *Lansdale* had been shot out from under him by a German aerial torpedo during an April 1944 convoy run in the Mediterranean Sea. Following survivor's leave, Morgenthau was ordered to Maine where *Bauer* was under construction. On his way he stopped at the Naval Gunnery Factory where many of *Lansdale*'s surviving crew (47 were lost to the sinking) were assigned. Morgenthau managed to

---

*The 40-mm guns, designed by Bofors, an arms manufacturer once owned by Alfred Nobel and based in neutral Sweden, were licensed for use by both Allied and Axis powers during the war. The Fletchers' ten 40-mm Bofors guns were installed in five open twin mounts—two mounts forward, two amidships, and one aft.

handpick forty men for duty on *Bauer*—including four of the black commissary men who had performed so well as gunners on *Lansdale*.

Despite examples like *Bauer*, Okinawa was war's introduction for these ships and the bulk of their crewmen. *Hugh W. Hadley* (DD-774), a destroyer named to honor Al Gallin's destroyer division commander, had been launched in July 1944, commissioned in late November, and finished shakedown just days before her departure from San Diego on 21 February 1945.

For more than a few among the ranks of *Hadley*'s officers and crew, finally heading for the Pacific, it was a little bit like getting in under the wire. The war of beachheads would end soon, and they would get a triumphant taste of it before it did.

So the departure had the mingled aura of a bittersweet celebration. As *Hadley* passed Point Loma, Bill King, one of the ship's young assistant engineering officers streamed a huge handmade kite high above the stern. The sailors stationed on the fantail for sea and anchor detail thought him odd for doing that, but his young children, Billy and Susan, watching from shore with their mother, knew exactly where their father was.

Little Beavers

Changes in some naval tactics, like advances in shipboard technology, came in a steady, cumulative stream. Some innovations took seemingly mundane (though surprisingly profound) forms. Still others arrived almost surreptitiously—the products of persistent and near subversive efforts of a new generation of leaders to upend the formality and temerity leading up to Pearl Harbor and Iron Bottom Sound.

Underway replenishment ("unrep"), undoubtedly the least glamorous (yet most profound and enduring) of these tactics, while having little to do with immediate success in battle, had ultimately all to do with winning the war.

Simple in concept, unrep was the capability to transfer fuel, food, ammunition, supplies, mail, and people between supply and combat ships running side by side at sea without the need to enter a sheltered harbor, slow down much, or long interrupt ongoing operations. Mind boggling in detail, the process was an intricate choreography of communication, logistics, manpower, navigation, and seamanship.

And it was a proprietary U.S. invention: experimented with as early as 1900, perfected in the 1930s, and kept so secret (its mysteries were protected nearly as vigilantly as radar, as VT fuses, or as any other technology, including the atom bomb) that the United States was pretty much the exclusive practitioner of unrep through and beyond the war. Unrep vastly extended the range and striking capability of U.S. naval task forces such as the fast carrier groups in the East China Sea. Skippers on ships with depleted stores of fuel, water, and food, knew they could usually reach one of these fast-moving depots with time to spare.

Sometimes, however, unrep's availability and flexibility created its own problems. Like (prewar) highway motorists running near empty but with lots of ground to cover, task unit, group, and force commanders such as Admiral Halsey were tempted to push the operations envelope. When they did, tankers and customers might end up battling high winds and heavy seas to refuel.

Even under the best conditions unrep was a challenge to ship handling. To accomplish underway refueling, for example, ships steamed side by side barely yards apart (often with a ship keeping station on either side of the oiler), connected by an intricate umbilical of hoses and lines while force-feeding gallons of volatile liquids.

The challenge was especially great on the bridge. Whoever "had the conn" during refueling needed nerves of steel and skills that blended endurance, finesse, and exactitude. It was not often the sort of responsibility comfortably delegated by a ship's skipper, but it was on *Mississinewa* (AO-59), *Miss*, a newly commissioned auxiliary oiler, which had reached the Pacific in July 1944. *Miss*'s skipper Philip Beck, a hard-drinking prewar merchant captain, preferred prowling the well decks during refueling, so he divided ship-handling chores between *Miss*'s executive officer and Charley Scott, a reserve Lt (jg). Brooklyn-born Scott, just shy of 24, had excelled at navigation in his 90-day wonder studies at Notre Dame. Scott also had prior experience on a convoy oiler in the Atlantic, but being trusted to conn *Miss* was, he recalled years later, "one of the most important things I ever did."

Exacting skills were not confined to the oiler's wheelhouse. Keeping *Miss*'s refueling hoses and lines out of the water was left to the hand-eye coordination of sailors like Herb Daitch. Daitch—"D" to his shipmates—was a string bean 19-year-old from Queens, New York, who operated *Miss*'s No. 2 cargo winch during refueling operations. Daitch's skills were such that occasional adolescent lapses (he once fell asleep in some cargo netting and was believed missing over the side) got him little more than a verbal slap on the wrist.

It was no stretch to say that ship damage control—a second, equally mundane but equally vital war tactic—was made possible only because America's full wartime mobilization gave it unique access to the know-how of a wide cross section of professional specialists. Stung by the vast—and sometimes avoidable—destruction wreaked by fires and explosions on the ships at Pearl Harbor and Iron Bottom Sound and spurred by the advocacy of two reserve naval officers who, in civilian lives, were deputy chiefs in the New York and Boston fire departments, the U.S. Navy, beginning in 1942, set up a string of shipboard damage-control schools.

Using ship mock-ups for hands-on practice and a curriculum aimed at getting "the fear of fire out of the sailor," the schools trained damage control parties from every new ship under construction. The former New York and Boston firefighters also introduced pieces of civilian fire-fighting technology to the Navy. Most important was the fog nozzle, which atomized water to a fine spray and doused a blaze much more quickly and efficiently than a solid stream of water. But there were others as well: light, gas engine-powered water pumps called "handy billies"; standardized hoses and couplings, foamite fire suppression systems, portable breathing devices, and oxyacetylene steel-cutting equipment.

In all, the training and equipment introduced a revolutionary notion to propeller-powered sea warfare—that the ability to survive after sustaining battle damage was just as important as the ability to inflict battle damage. In these terms, when damage struck, the fight, instead of ending, had just begun. As much as they pushed this idea, the evangelizers of this tactical doctrine still had little idea just how vital this damage control doctrine would prove to be.

* * *

A third, more directly battle conscious tactical innovation was also, in its way, unique to the U.S. Navy and especially to the hard-charging independence and aggressiveness of its younger commanding officers. Commander Arleigh Burke (the same Navy officer who would eventually be assigned as Vice Admiral Marc Mitscher's chief of staff) was the exemplar of an emerging generation of seagoing leaders built on the ballsy, hard-driving foundation of William Halsey.

Burke had begun the war sitting behind a Washington desk, but by January 1943 he'd connived his way to the South Pacific. Put in charge of a destroyer squadron (DesRon) in the thick of the Solomons' morass, Burke gained an enduring moniker—"31-Knot Burke"—for the way he constantly pushed his destroyer skippers to pursue and engage Japanese targets at boiler- and engine-busting speeds.

Burke pressed for operating doctrine making it possible for on-the-scene squadron commanders (like him) to initiate offensive action without waiting for permission from far-removed authority. In one four-month period during the Solomons Campaign, Burke's Squadron 23 "Little Beavers"* destroyed one Japanese cruiser, nine destroyers, one submarine, and thirty aircraft.

The inspiration for the squadron name Little Beavers was a logo painted on one of destroyer *Claxton*'s (DD-571) torpedo mounts. The logo depicted the Native American character in the then popular *Red Ryder* comic strip. The original *Claxton* version displayed an amply endowed Little Beaver warrior wearing little more than a G-string and aiming his arrow point blank at the upturned posterior of a character named "Tojo." (The destroyer squadron logo was cleaned up somewhat by giving Little Beaver more clothing, reducing his undercarriage, and removing Tojo altogether.)

Also indicative of the DesRon 23 mystique was a classic—and near disastrous—episode involving destroyer *Spence* (DD-512). After sustaining battle damage and a crippling sideswipe with squadron mate *Thatcher* (DD-514) during the Battle of Empress Augusta Bay, *Spence* was blacked out and limping from the scene when she came under 5-inch gunfire from the direction of her own picket lines. *Spence*'s skipper

---

*Destroyer Squadron 23 consisted of destroyers *Aulick* (DD-569), *Charles Ausburne* (DD-570), *Claxton* (DD-571), *Converse* (DD-509), *Dyson* (DD-572), *Foote* (DD-511), *Spence* (DD-512), and *Thatcher* (DD-514).

was quick to the Talk Between Ships (TBS) circuit, shouting excitedly: "We've just had a bad close miss! I hope you're not shooting at us!"

In fact, it was Burke shooting. Faced with a radar screen full of conflicting target blips, Burke had decided to "throw a shoe," a crude means of sorting out enemies and friendlies. "Are you hit?" Burke asked anxiously. "Negative," *Spence*'s shaken CO replied, "but they're not all here yet!"

"Sorry," was Burke's classic rejoinder, "but you'll have to excuse the next four salvos. They're already on the way."

Burke, most of the skippers, and many of the crewmen who formed the core of the original Little Beavers had since moved on. (When promoted to be Mitscher's chief of staff, Burke's first reaction was that "somebody is trying to railroad me out of these lovely destroyers."). Still they'd left behind a legacy that added swagger to every tin can and every tin can sailor. And many of the DesRon 23 ships who'd shared in these exploits—*Claxton, Foote* (DD-511), and *Thatcher*—were on hand at Okinawa.

Let 'Em Walk

In October 1944, all these factors and forces—the cumulative weight of technology, production, process, and tactics in the hands of a new generation of naval commanders leading crews of citizen sailors—converged off the Philippines in the Battle of Leyte Gulf.

For General Douglas MacArthur, retaking the Philippine Islands from the Japanese was the crowning strategic and symbolic objective of his long campaign slog through the Southwest Pacific. Beginning with an invasion foothold on Leyte (code name Operation King II), an island in the central Philippines fronted on the east by the deepwater Leyte Gulf, MacArthur's 6th Army and 7th Fleet (bolstered by the surface and aerial forces borrowed from Halsey's 3rd Fleet) were to move on and around the most strategic pieces of real estate in the sprawling archipelago, culminating in the eventual capture of Luzon, the Philippines' northernmost, largest and most populous island, and its capital Manila.

It was an idea MacArthur had effectively sold to President Roosevelt. His plan required that Admiral King and Nimitz drop the idea of invading Formosa and simultaneously share Halsey's 3rd Fleet air and ship resources with 7th Fleet commander Admiral Thomas Kinkaid.

MacArthur's campaign of reconquest would stretch for months. (It continued still on the eve of Operation Iceberg, and the persistent demands on Nimitz's resources created friction.) But its all-important first step came on 20 October 1944 with the landing of troops on six beach sectors north and south of the Leyte coastal town of Tacloban.

For the most part, the initial landings went easily. GIs took some mortar fire on the northern beaches and troops in the south had to break through tough resistance centered on 1000-foot-high Catmon Hill. But across the whole, rapidly expanding front, there was little indication the Japanese intended to hold this particular ground.

Early that afternoon, MacArthur made his signature return to the Philippines. Embarked on a barge from his flagship *Nashville,* MacArthur expected to tie up at a pier and step ashore "immaculate and dry." But most piers had been damaged or destroyed during the bombardment and assault, and, being told of MacArthur's arrival, a no-nonsense Navy officer serving as beachmaster simply growled, "Let 'em walk!"

When the barge ultimately broached short of the northern landing beaches, MacArthur ordered the ramp lowered, and he and his retinue were forced to splash ashore in knee-deep water. Watching through binoculars from *Nashville*'s flag bridge was Ben Limbaugh, part of the ship's Marine Detachment. Each day a Marine was assigned to be MacArthur's orderly. Yesterday it had been Limbaugh's turn; today it was Jim Nelson, and Limbaugh could see his buddy slogging stride for wet stride beside MacArthur. Limbaugh figured the general must be pissed. Indeed, the indignities of squishing shoes and spoiled creases in his khaki pants competed with MacArthur's composure and instinct for historical stagecraft; the look on his face hovered between determination and annoyance at the upstart beachmaster.

After walking inland to inspect the terrain and the results of the preinvasion bombardment, MacArthur paused on the beach, delivered a rallying speech into a waiting cluster of microphones, and then returned to *Nashville.* Though MacArthur's inspiring performance was one for the ages, it masked the bloody slogging going on in the jungles ahead of him. It also gave no hint of a real danger soon to glide into the waters at his back.

★ Chapter 8 ★

Narrow Straits, October 1944

The straight dope is that they're whipped. But good.

—ORVILL RAINES

Body Crashing

Within minutes of the United States' first forays into Leyte Gulf, news of the impending invasion was on its way to Japanese Combined Fleet headquarters where Admiral Soemu Toyoda, Combined Fleet commander in chief, triggered the *Sho Go* or "Victory Operation" plan. *Sho Go* had several contingent versions, each a response to a different possible invasion target. The plan for the Philippines was *Sho 1*.

Japanese Vice Admiral Takeo Kurita's First Striking Force, the biggest piece in the *Sho 1* plan, was to enter Leyte Gulf at dawn on 25 October to attack American amphibious and supply shipping. Kurita decided to split his forces, taking the bigger portion—twenty-nine battleships, cruisers and destroyers—through San Bernardino Strait, the narrow water passage separating Luzon and Samar, to strike at Leyte Gulf from the north. Meanwhile, Second Striking Force, a smaller group of two battleships, a cruiser, and four destroyers under Vice Admiral Teiji Nishimura, would swing up from the south via the Sulu and Mindanao Seas and sweep into Leyte Gulf through Surigao Strait.

Far north of the Philippines, Vice Admiral Jisaburo Ozawa commanding the tattered remnants of Japan's Mobile Striking Force— six carriers with only a handful of aircraft, three cruisers, and eight destroyers—was tasked with luring America's potent carrier fleet (Halsey's Task Force 38) with its air groups away from Leyte. If the

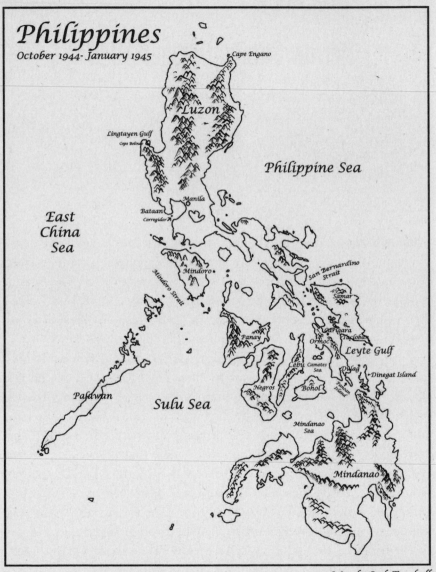

Philippines

October 1944- January 1945

Cape Engano

Luzon

Lingtayen Gulf

Cape Bolinao

Philippine Sea

East
China
Sea

Manila

Bataan

Corregidor

Mindoro

Mindoro Strait

San Bernardino
Strait

Samar

Carigara
Ormoc
Tacloban

Leyte Gulf

Panay

Cebu
Camotes
Sea

Dulag

Dinegat Island

Palawan

Negros

Bohol

Panaon
Island

Sulu Sea

Mindanao
Sea

Mindanao

Map by Jack Turnbull

deception worked, First Striking Force's battleships, cruisers, and destroyers, joining as pincers (and augmented in the south by a small Second Striking Force under Vice Admiral Kiyohide Shima), would find a clear path into Leyte Gulf and chew up MacArthur's vulnerable invasion fleet.

Sho 1 (alternatively termed *A-Go*) was an elegant, elaborate, almost reverential plan. But like many Japanese war plans, its success depended on meeting tight schedules across many days, vast distances, and unforeseeable circumstances.

Sho 1 also had elements of the sacrificial and delusional. Mobile Striking Force, for example, was a carrier force in name only; painfully aware of his force's lack of aircraft and the pilots to fly them, Ozawa fully expected his ploy, even if successful, would end in utter ruin for his ships, his men, and himself.

Meanwhile, *Sho 1* planners deceived themselves into believing effective air cover for First and Second Striking Force ships would somehow come from land-based Japanese squadrons in the Philippines. But when the new First Fleet air commander Vice Admiral Takijiro Onishi arrived in the Philippines to organize air cover, he found fewer than one hundred operational aircraft to work with. It convinced him that a new and radical tactic would have to be tried if Japanese air power was to have any impact on the momentous struggle ahead.

Onishi, a short, stocky, and dyspeptic 53-year-old with coarse features and the coarse reputation and manners to go with them, had helped build the Japanese naval aviation powerhouse, only to watch its systematic decay and destruction. In the process he had seen entrance requirements lowered and curricula slashed for both navy and army aviation training programs. Given the reality of intense and bitter interservice rivalries, Onishi knew he could expect little help from IJA's air force. He also knew that even if he had more navy planes and pilots, they simply could not win with conventional tactics against America's superior planes and expert pilots.

Onishi was a staunch devotee of the samurai way and fighting Japanese spirit—*yamato damashi*. He was also an early proponent of using special attack (*tokkō* was the Japanese abbreviation) operations infused with body-crashing spirit—*taiatari seishin*. Onishi's advocacy eventually bore fruit. Even before the loss of the Marianas and his fall from grace, Prime Minister Hideki Tojo of Japan had sanctioned preliminary studies of the concepts. Facing dire circumstances, Imperial Japanese Headquarters now cleared the way for any tactical expedient necessary to make *Sho 1* succeed.

Assembling squadron leaders at Mabalacat Naval Air Station northwest of Manila on Luzon, Onishi first conveyed the need to counter American carrier-based air power as Japanese ships converged on Leyte Gulf. Then he delivered a stunning assessment. The only feasible way to accomplish this, he believed, was to employ body-crashing tactics: organizing the handful of Philippine-based aircraft into suicide squadrons, each plane carrying a 250-kg bomb and each targeting an American aircraft carrier.

Onishi then opened the floor for discussion, most likely knowing that there would be little dissent even to this most unprecedented idea. Onishi was a flag officer, and traditions of loyalty, deference, and respect (the very foundations of Japanese society) were only heightened in military settings, even when the stakes were raised to certain death.

The idea flowed through an audience of pilot officers who, willingly or unwillingly, had inherited the samurai mantle.* Many had lost both comrades and honor in humiliating battles with American aircraft, especially during the Battle of the Philippine Sea. Even the best of them flew inferior aircraft using inferior fuel—low-octane aviation gasoline "spiked" with turpentine and alcohol. Here was the opportunity to erase shame; it was the sacrifice of one pilot and one aircraft for the destruction of a warship with a crew of three thousand and fifty or more aircraft. Although the mood among Onishi's audience probably ranged from rabid enthusiasm to stoic resignation to pure dread, those who finally spoke asked only to be allowed to organize the force themselves.

Finally, *Sho 1* required the cooperation of an enemy with impulsive leadership and overextended resources. Here, in at least one aspect, Japanese planning was on the mark. Combing the waters to the north

*During Japan's 19th Meiji Restoration a fractured feudal system run by warlord masters and their samurai was unified under one emperor (Meiji) and one constitution. The leveling of Japan's elaborate caste system, instead of discarding the tenets of *bushido*—the way of the warrior—had infused them in the military officer corps. Since most of these officers were drawn from the ranks of the middle and lower classes, *bushido* had, in a sense, been democratized.

of the Philippines, Halsey's scout planes finally spotted Ozawa's decoy force: flooding the airwaves with radio traffic and maneuvering conspicuously in a desperate effort to be spotted. Almost immediately, Halsey took the bait and, charging north with his fast carriers and their screens, left an unguarded San Bernardino Strait in his wake. Before Halsey departed, though, Task Force 38 air groups had already pummeled a good portion of First Striking Force, both weakening Kurita and Nishimura's split forces and unraveling their delicate timing.

Surigao

If Halsey's departure left San Bernardino Strait vulnerable, there was no such vulnerability at the northern exit from Surigao Strait into Leyte Gulf. Aboard the U.S. ships anchored off the invasion beaches in San Pedro Bay or patrolling Leyte Gulf, 7th Fleet commanders still nursed collective, painful memories of the 1942 disaster at Savo Island. Scout planes tracked every move of Nishimura's seven ships as they advanced between the islands of Negros, Cebu, and Bohol on the west and Mindanao on the east. Preparations were guided by a singular obsession: to avoid repeating Savo Island. The U.S. forces got into position to deal uncompromising destruction to the approaching Japanese.

The primary agent of destruction was to be a battle line of six 7th Fleet battleships parading back and forth across the northern entrance to Surigao Strait. Of the six—*West Virginia, Tennessee, California* (BB-44), *Maryland, Mississippi* (BB-41), and *Pennsylvania* (BB-38)—only *Mississippi* had not been a Pearl Harbor victim three years before. In all, the battleships mounted sixty-four main battery guns with either 16- or 14-inch muzzles.

Fronting the main battle line were split lines of cruisers, eight in all, each armed with either 6- or 8-inch main battery guns. Absent from these lines was MacArthur's flagship *Nashville,* pulled away despite his protests and tucked behind a protective screen of tin cans and patrol craft in San Pedro Bay.

Battleships and cruisers were lined up to confront the incoming Japanese on the perpendicular. The textbook tactic, called "crossing the T" put the American ships in position to bear all their guns on the Japanese while in turn masking—blocking—the aim of nearly all the Japanese main batteries. Crossing the T was the ultimate checkmate move in naval surface warfare. Forty years before, during the Battle of the Straits of Tsushima, the IJN used the tactic to ambush and systematically decimate a Russian fleet during the Russo Japanese War. Tsushima marked the emergence of Japan on the world stage and began the IJN's ascendancy as a global naval force. Now, the tables were set—and about to be turned.

But not before two vanguard units took brief, nuisance shots at Nishimura's ships. The first, a flotilla of thirty-nine motor torpedo boats (PTs)—split into thirteen sections of three boats each—was positioned in the approaches to Surigao Strait. The small, fast, mahogany-hulled PTs were to act as harassing skirmishers, radioing Japanese positions before attacking independently—and most expected futilely—with torpedoes.

More—but not necessarily much more—was expected from Nishimura's next hurdle: 22 DDs from three destroyer squadrons being sent south in three closely timed thrusts to stab at the Japanese flanks. Instead of gunfire, the tin cans would use speed, hoped for stealth and surprise, and their still-suspect, seldom-used torpedoes.

Advancing in short single columns along the strait's eastern and western shores and into its center, the tins cans would pivot to unmask and fire torpedoes, and then flee toward the lines of friendly cruisers and battleships. If their entry, torpedo launches, and flight were timed correctly, the tin cans would pass safely away from or under the arc of the big ships' outbound salvos.

Not all the tin cans making that nighttime charge into Surigao Strait were later present for L-Day at Okinawa. But many were, including *Bache, Bennion, Daly, Heywood L. Edwards, Leutze, Newcomb,* and *Richard P. Leary.*

The fast but fragile PTs accomplished the chief part of their job: sending ahead position and speed reports on the Japanese to the big ships upstream. Their torpedo runs were indeed futile—thirty fish fired with no strikes. But the costs, though painful, were modest—three men killed, 20 wounded, one PT run aground.

By the time Nishimura's seven ships had shrugged off the PTs and come within range of the first wave of destroyers, though, stealth and surprise were largely gone. Japanese illumination flares popped and hovered in the sky, and searchlight beams danced across Surigao Strait in an effort to pick up the attackers. Guns silenced going in so that muzzle flashes would not betray them before they had a chance to fire torpedoes, the tin cans—a column of two on the west side of Surigao Strait, a column of three on the east—plowed on. If stealth and surprise were gone, they still had speed: with the Japanese formation heading north at 25 knots the southbound columns of tin cans accelerating to roughly 30 knots, the two forces were converging at a land speed exceeding sixty miles per hour.

At the mouth of the Strait, some of the parading battleships and cruisers had firing solutions on their targets even before the first two waves of destroyers finished their runs. The Japanese ships began showing as blips on *West Virginia*'s surface search (SG) radar at twenty-five miles distance. Soon, main battery plot reported that Spot 2, *West Virginia*'s aft fire control radar, had picked up the targets. As the minutes ticked on, Spot 2 never relinquished its aiming lock.

The battleship and cruiser lines held their fire but could do so only so long. The accuracy of their long-range cannons required distance, and the armor piercing (AP) projectiles in the gunhouse breeches required arc and elevation to be most effective. In a way, it would have been difficult to prevent them from firing—there were eager hands at the ships' firing keys.

For individual sailors on the tin cans racing into and out of the dark waters of the strait, the perils of that night (the Japanese, of course, but also the gunfire of their own ships and the chance of being hit by another tin can's fish) were heightened or dampened by two circumstances: whether you had something to do and whether you were able to see what was going on.

On *Daly*, one of six tin cans hugging the west side of Surigao Strait for the second wave of torpedo runs, Jim Kelly, a 21-year-old coxswain stationed in the ship's aftermost 5-inch gun, watched from an open hatch in the gunhouse. Even with *Daly*'s guns silent for the run toward the target, Kelly at least had a good vantage. He saw Japanese illumination flares; to his relief they were falling short, exposing the Japanese ships more than the line of destroyers. Kelly had great faith in *Daly's* skipper R. G. Visser, mainly because he always told it to them straight. Hours before, Visser had assembled the crew on the fantail to describe to them precisely what they'd be doing.

After launching torpedoes, *Bache,* the lead tin can steaming ahead of *Daly,* opened fire with 5-inch batteries. *Daly* and then *Hutchins* followed the same sequence. This abruptly ended sightseeing or anxious waiting for the tin cans' 5-inch gun crews.

Each gun was enclosed in a steel gunhouse giving more shelter from wind and water than incoming fire. In tropical waters, with nighttime temperatures hovering in the eighties, these steel enclosures—and all the compartments below them—were oven hot.

Ammunition (separate steel projectiles and brass-encased propellant charges) was passed by hand from the ships' fore and aft ammunition magazines to "ready ammunition" handling rooms just below the gunhouses. Kit Hall, a New Hampshire-born deck seaman on *Bache* was assigned to the No. 2 mount handling room. He and several other men who'd been crouching nervously in its hot, buttoned-up, and sightless confines began loading the carousel of projectile and powder hoists lifting ammunition to the gunhouse.

Eight-man crews did the work in the gunhouse—a grunting, profanity-laced corps de ballet of gun captains, pointers, trainers, sight setters, fuse setters, loaders, hot shell men, and ammunition handlers. On *Daly* No. 3 gun, 19-year-old Charlie Dunn's job was to drop the gun's breach block after each round was fired to expel a hot shell casing. An experienced gun crew like Dunn's could fire twelve to fifteen rounds per minute. On this night the guns were being fired in automatic, so his crew's job was to stay on their feet as *Daly* lurched and to keep filling the loading tray.

As the first two waves of DDs finished firing their torpedoes and bent into their escapes, the ships' skippers and crews had no idea if they'd succeeded—or would survive to find out. Annoyed that he hadn't gotten a report about his own ship's torpedoes, Barry K. Atkins, the skipper on *Melvin* (DD-680)—a tin can in the first wave—finally asked his

CIC "When the hell do our torpedoes arrive?" Two more minutes he was told.

Rather than retreating in column (doing this would provide a big combined target, a juicy "knuckle" for the Japanese guns to aim at), the ships fled independently. The tin cans belched obscuring smoke, zigzagged, and chased splashes as they went—heading directly for the closest splash of a Japanese incoming shell with the expectation the next one would land elsewhere.

Atkins had been straddled by Japanese gunfire before when he'd commanded a PT squadron off New Guinea. He wasn't bothered by the probing searchlights—he knew they weren't very effective at more than five thousand yards distance. Atkins tried to calm the edgy men in *Melvin*'s pilothouse by assuring them the Japanese shells would never hit them, though in his own mind, he realized they just might.

Suddenly, over Atkins shoulder, the strait was bathed in a light so fierce it seemed like instant dawn. And then—after an instant strangely and completely bereft of sound—a cataclysmic chain of explosions. A ship—and its ammunition magazines—erupting.

West across Surigao Strait from *Melvin*, soaked in seawater and watching from the gunhouse hatch of No. 5 gun on destroyer *Monssen* (DD-798), gunner's mate Virgil Melvin witnessed the same explosion. He could see plainly it was a Japanese ship. Its forward mount, he recalled, "popped straight up in the air like a big hand had picked it up and thrown it away." The eruption turned out to be *Fuso*, the next-to-last ship in the Japanese column.

Fuso was struck amidships by one torpedo. Exploding underwater, virtually all the force of the torpedo warhead's eight hundred pounds of TNT transferred to *Fuso*'s armor. The force breached *Fuso*'s hull and ruptured fuel tanks, igniting fires that spread to an ammunition magazine. The magazine explosion—the final cataclysm—split *Fuso* in two. *Fuso*'s severed torso and trunk drifted on the surface, disgorging dead, wounded, and dazed Japanese sailors, most destined for the bottom of Surigao Strait.

Meanwhile, Bob Durand, a quartermaster at the wheel in *Richard P. Leary*'s pilothouse, was both seeing enough and doing enough to contain his fear—at least for the moment. *Leary* was in a three-ship column led by *Newcomb* and trailed by *Albert W. Grant* (DD-649); two other three-ship columns—one to the east and the other to the west, all part of Destroyer Squadron 56—flanked *Leary*'s column. For these tin cans just beginning their run into the area vacated minutes before by *Melvin* and the other ships in the first wave, any faint hope of surprise was long gone. Even before launching torpedoes, the last ships were being straddled by Japanese gunfire. To Durand, his hands tight and trembling on the wheel, the stakes of the night condensed into keeping *Leary*'s prow aligned with the wake of *Newcomb*, just ahead.

The lines of battleships and cruisers were on an eastbound leg when they received permission to open fire. The battleship skippers fired first, expecting their projectiles to arrive after the tin cans were clear of the killing ground. The Japanese were then thirteen miles away from the U.S. battle line, their hulls not yet up on the horizon. Topside on the battleships, the eruptions of noise, smoke, and flaming gas from the immense muzzles of each multi-gun mount was volcanic. But inside the thickly armored gunhouses (spaces that more resembled factories than artillery emplacements) the noise was muffled: a *whoosh*—an immense whisper—followed by the lunging hydraulic recoil of tree trunk-sized barrels and breeches. On their climb up and their plunge down, the guns' big projectiles rumbled with a distinctive freight train clatter. Near the top of their trajectories—some directly over the tin can cavalry—the projectiles glowed like constellations of red-hot coals.

When the Japanese closed to nine thousand yards, an orgy of cruiser gunfire joined in. In a space of eighteen minutes, cruiser cannons unleashed more than four thousand 6- and 8-inch rounds. The pace of gunfire became practically unstoppable.

The first and second waves—eleven of the twenty tin cans involved—launched nearly eighty torpedoes. The third wave would add another twenty-eight, but Surigao Strait was already wildly crisscrossed with the wakes of torpedoes and ships—the hunters and the hunted. Muzzle flashes and deep concussions from the guns of both sides filled the predawn sky.

* * *

The window of escape was closing fast on tin cans of the third wave. Last into Surigao Strait, they'd each dodged a gauntlet of gunfire to come closest of all to Nishimura's advancing line. Now, they stood to pay for their persistence. Standing at his GQ station high on *Leutze*'s after stack, gunner's mate John Perkins, 21, had seen shell splashes as tall and ordered as a line of telephone poles on either side of the ship. It amazed him none were hitting. Now, on the way out, it only seemed worse, as if everyone had chosen *Leutze* as a target.

Confusion spread like a fever across communications circuits. Targets once so unmistakable were now scattered like peas in a dozen different shell games. On the bridges and in the CICs of the battleships and cruisers, the taste for blood swelled with the confusion. It seemed to say: blow everything out of the water and sort out the details later.

Sensing the splashes getting close, Ray Hoffman, 19, a fire controlman perched in *Newcomb*'s main battery director got on the circuit to ask his buddy in plot to find out what was going on. "Hoffer" his buddy replied, "CIC thinks it's our own cruisers firing on us!" Jesus, Hoffman thought to himself, can't we just tell them to stop?

The fever finally broke over *Grant*, the trailing tin can in the last wave. *Grant* went dead in the water after being hit nearly twenty times; it quickly became clear most were 6- and 8-inch rounds from U.S. cruisers.

When *Newcomb*'s skipper got word that *Grant*'s doctor was dead, he ordered *Newcomb*'s whaleboat lowered and its own doctor sent to help. Bob Reid, a boatswain's mate who'd been with *Newcomb* since construction, was assigned to operate the boat; as *Newcomb* circled to approach *Grant*, Reid and the doctor set out across the quarter mile still separating the two ships. Now, with word of the damage to *Grant* spreading, the battleship and cruiser guns fell silent. The breezes coursing through Surigao Strait carried smoke and the smell of cordite.

It was beginning to get light as *Newcomb*'s whaleboat approached *Grant*. Once Reid and the doctor were aboard, they went their separate ways, the doctor to treat the most seriously wounded being brought to the crew's mess and Reid to wander on deck, helping as best he could.

Reid carried a kit of medical supplies and knew a little first aid— enough to apply sulfa powder, inject Syrettes of morphine, and start plasma IVs. Still, he was unable to help—or cope—with much of what he saw. Those wounded but able to function were already busy assisting with damage control. The rest were grievously mauled, either just about to die or certainly eventually to die. Most were so full of holes, it was nearly impossible to find a place to inject morphine or start an IV.

Damage to the ship seemed as grievous as the damage to its sailors. An explosion had torn apart *Grant*'s No. 5 gun and the crew's berthing compartment below. A gash at the waterline flooded *Grant*'s forward engine compartment, storerooms, and other berthing spaces. A hit to a forward 40-mm gun ignited nearby ammunition and set raging fires. Part of *Grant*'s superstructure was flattened and its radar stanchions toppled. An explosion amidships had killed its doctor, and along with him, five radiomen and nearly all of a repair party. Reid saw *Grant*'s skipper T. A. Nisewaner, stalking disconsolately through the ruins, raging and swearing to kill the cruiser men responsible.

At sunrise three PT boats skimmed the Mindanao Sea heading back to Tacloban. At one point they were shot at by a Japanese cruiser. "It was wounded," one of the sailors recalled. "Its topside was a real mess." The PTs ducked behind a cluster of small islands to get out of the way. When the PTs resumed their journey, their crewmen spotted objects floating in the water. At first they thought they were coconuts, but finally saw they were the heads of Japanese sailors.

As one boat passed close to a few stragglers separated from the main group, a Texas-born sailor drawled to his buddy nearby: "I bet there's an admiral in there somewhere that's been busted to a seaman deuce by now."

History seldom gives instant conclusions. When observers reach them, the results are apt to be exaggerated, misleading, or conflicting. Even as events are being sorted out—especially among victors—many owners step in to claim disproportionate shares. This was certainly true of the 25 October 1944 action in Surigao Strait. It would take two postwar years of interviews; the scanning of deck logs, position maps, and other data; and analysis and argument to sort out who could reasonably claim credit for what.

Still, no one—Japanese or American—could dispute the visible results: Battleship *Fuso* and destroyer *Yamagumo* ("Mountain Clouds") were sunk, soon followed by Nishimura's flagship *Yamishiro* and destroyer *Michishio* ("Tide Running Full"). Destroyer *Asagumo* ("Morning Clouds"), shorn of its bow, was in retreat with the badly damaged cruiser *Mogami* and destroyer *Shigure* ("The Frequent Rains of Fall and Winter")—the only Japanese ship to emerge virtually unscathed.

Meanwhile Shima's following force—three cruisers and four destroyers—arrived just as First Striking Force's wounded survivors fled. Though Shima's ships managed to avoid most of the wrath of the 7th Fleet, they quickly claimed a full share of ignominy. Shima's ships only offensive contribution was the firing of eight torpedoes at small islands mistaken for enemy surface targets; and *Nachi*, one of his cruisers, managed to collide with slow-moving *Mogami*. At the end of a ragged morning chase into the Mindanao Sea, a small unit of U.S. destroyers and cruisers eventually caught and dispatched bowless *Asagumo* with gunfire. Naval aircraft soon tacked *Mogami* to the morning's toll. This left destroyer *Shigure* as the only survivor of Nishimura's sacrificial thrust into Surigao Strait.

On a morning so replete with victory, it was natural to bathe in self-congratulation. The cruiser and battleship sailors could reasonably boast of their guns' supremacy, even though most Navy leaders understood it was a valedictory performance. The destroyer skippers and their crews could equally well claim the battle was over even before the cruiser and battle lines fired the first round: tin can torpedo salvos, despite many more misses than hits (and many of those hits on ships not actually aimed at), had sunk, slowed, or crippled five of Nishimura's seven ships.

But in the case of the Battle of Leyte Gulf (a battle still raging even as the guns in Surigao Strait fell silent), which eventually came to encompass four days of engagements across thousands of square miles of oceans, the real meaning was deeper than the vindictive satisfaction of battleship, cruiser, and destroyer men. Leyte Gulf would prove an inflection point, a juncture in history signaling the irretrievable collapse of one naval power and the indisputable ascendancy of another. As Japan's naval air threat had disintegrated during the Great Marianas

Turkey Shoot, so had Japan's surface navy threat essentially vanished during Leyte Gulf. Facing the unacceptable prospect of unconditional surrender, her political and military leaders had only desperation in reserve.

In a 30 October letter to Ray Ellen, *Howorth*'s Orvill Raines wrote: "Well, the big fight for the Navy is practically over with out here. In spite of Jap claims, their fleet is on the run and like a dog with a can to its tail: Every jump they take, the American Navy is banging away at them. The straight dope is that they're whipped. But good."

★ **Part Two** ★

THE *KAMIKAZE* BOYS

★ Chapter 9 ★

Becoming Young Gods, October 1944

Having stepped up to the task, you have all become young gods with no earthly desires.

—Vice Admiral Takijiro Onishi

Off Samar

It was midmorning when Tom Van Brunt nursed his Avenger back to *St. Lo* (CVE-63)'s formation. He was relieved to see other planes circling and lining up to land. Since 0645, when Van Brunt and a handful of other pilots from Task Unit 77.4.3—Taffy 3—first spotted the parade of Japanese warships stampeding south under cloud-pocked skies off Samar Island on 25 October 1944, Taffy 3's formation of six escort carriers and six tin cans had been fleeing a superior force and unable to recover aircraft.

It was clear from that first sighting that Taffy 3's ships could neither outgun nor outrun this adversary—what turned out to be the northern pincer of Admiral Takeo Kurita's First Striking Force. Although days of U.S. air and submarine strikes had whittled down Kurita's armada from twenty-nine combatants to twenty-two, First Striking Force remained potent. Collectively, the 18-inch guns of super battleship *Yamato,* the 14-inch guns of three older battleships, and the 5-inch guns of eight cruisers easily outmatched in range and punch the 5-inch guns on any Taffy 3 ship. And all of First Striking Force's ships, not least its ten screening destroyers, could easily overtake Taffy 3, whose effective speed was constrained by the lumbering escort aircraft carriers (CVEs).

Despite the odds, Taffy 3 commander Rear Admiral Clifton Sprague somehow fashioned order and fighting purpose out of surprise and imminent disarray. First, Sprague transmitted a plain language plea for help to two other task units—Taffy 1 and Taffy 2—positioned just over the southern horizon. Next, he turned his formation into the east wind long enough to launch aircraft. Only then did Sprague point his escort carriers southeast, away from the advancing Japanese, but also away from First Striking Force's primary objective—the invasion fleet in Leyte Gulf. Meanwhile, the skippers of Taffy 3's DDs and DEs doubled back to shield the carriers—surrounding them in smoke, then charging the Japanese like terriers at ankles to shoot torpedo spreads and 5-inch salvos.

Kurita, for his part, while he had come for a fight, had expected it to be with the Leyte invasion force. The carrier convinced him he must have stumbled on one of Mitscher's fast carrier groups. He hoped that it was isolated; if so, this was a golden opportunity not to be passed up, no matter what the original objective.

Though already in the midst of realigning his formation to guard against enemy aircraft, Kurita could still have reeled the ships into battle line and used First Striking Force's superior fire power to pick apart the American formation systematically. Instead, he signaled General Attack, an order unleashing his captains and leaving them to their instincts to pick both targets and tactics. The ships charged on, and Kurita's opportunity to obliterate both Taffy 3 and the transports in Leyte Gulf began to slip away.

Despite these missteps, Kurita still seemed to have the upper hand in surprise, maneuvering, and firepower. Each of his ships added a distinctly colored dye to its projectiles as a means to track gunfire accuracy; a rainbow of splashes was already advancing up the wakes of the retreating Americans. Yet, as the morning lengthened and First Striking Force failed to outflank, envelop, and demolish Taffy 3, it became increasingly possible the Americans might make good their escape—though at a price. The aggressive, sacrificial tactics of the DDs and DEs bought time for the fleeing CVEs and dealt outsized damage to several Japanese cruisers and destroyers. Eventually though, Japanese firepower claimed three tin cans—*Hoel* (DD-533), *Johnston*

(DD-557), and *Samuel B. Roberts* (DE-413)—and escort carrier *Gambier Bay* (CVE-73).

In the end, though, it was probably Sprague's decision to delay retreat long enough to launch aircraft that made the crucial day-saving difference for the Americans. Taffy 3's squadrons of Wildcats and Avengers though launched hurriedly—many without full loads of fuel or ammunition—began making nonstop runs at the Japanese ships.

Rather than climbing high and circling to build formations, Taffy 3's plane crews picked up teams at low altitude and roared north in makeshift echelons. Ed Huxtable, CO of *Gambier Bay*'s VC-10,* led a pickup team of Avengers and Wildcats from several carriers. Huxtable steered his formation just above the base of the cloud deck and then pointed them directly in.

Burt Bassett, an Avenger pilot and VC-10's executive officer, flew on Huxtable's wing. When Huxtable gave the signal, Bassett peeled off and made his run, only to have his tail section shot up. He dropped his bomb by instinct and then wrestled with his controls just to keep his plane aloft.

Meanwhile, Huxtable radioed: "Fighters in to strafe." Hearing this, VC-10 Wildcat pilot Joe McGraw, a Syracuse native barely three years out of high school, peeled away from his escort position on the port side of Huxtable's formation. In front and below him McGraw saw a cruiser and what looked like two battleships. McGraw pushed over to strafe the cruiser's bridge, jinking up, down, and sideways as he went by to avoid the disorganized flak. He next approached the bigger of the battleships—probably *Yamato*—to make a strafing run on its bridge.

Gene Seitz, 24, another VC-10 pilot, teamed with a Wildcat pilot from *Kalinin Bay* (CVE-68), also swooped in on a battleship. He aimed for the bridge and flew through a lot of AA. After pulling out and seeing the AA fire was still chasing him, Seitz couldn't help but yell indignantly: "Don't shoot me, Goddamn it, I've already made my pass!"

Instead of hitting these bigger ships, *Gambier Bay* Wildcat pilot

---

*The C stood for Composite—VC-10 and other CVE squadrons consisted of both fighter aircraft (usually Wildcats) and torpedo bombers (Avengers).

Dick Roby, another 24-year-old, joined with three other Wildcat pilots to work over two Japanese destroyers. Coming in above a thin cloud layer, Roby made a sixty degree dive—almost vertical—and pulled out at three hundred feet. Every round in his wing guns was armor piercing, and he aimed amidships, trying to get boilers and engine equipment. "You could see the hits and the damage and it turned them around."

Even after expending bombs, torpedoes, and machine-gun ammunition, Taffy pilots continued to attack, either flying wing for other pilots with ordnance or diving to draw fire and disrupt maneuvering. Only when low on fuel did the pilots break off and look for a place to land. Many, including *Gambier Bay*'s Bassett, Seitz, and Roby, were diverted to Tacloban, site of a dirt landing strip newly wrested from Japanese control and barely operational. Many of these—including Bassett and Roby—either crashed on landing or experienced mechanical problems or got their plane wheels so hopelessly mired in the Tacloban mud, they were unable to get back in the fight.

During the first chaotic minutes of the running battle, Van Brunt dropped a depth charge (his only ordnance for what began as a predawn antisubmarine patrol) along the flanks of a Japanese cruiser. He then flew south, where he was able to land on *Marcus Island* (CVE-77), a Taffy 2 carrier. The Avenger refueled, rearmed, and teamed with four other aircraft, Van Brunt, his rear gunner Jack South, and radioman Lester Frederickson launched into a slicing crosswind that nearly took the plane down. "We're leaving a wake!" Frederickson shouted from his perch in the plane's belly, as Van Brunt fought with the controls and finally got them airborne.

During their second strikes, McGraw, Seitz, and Van Brunt returned to a vastly different battle. The sky was filled with reinforcements—a handful of refueled and rearmed Taffy 3 aircraft like theirs, but also fresh Wildcats and Avengers from Taffy 1 and Taffy 2. And below, inexplicably yet undeniably, the Japanese formation—still scattered, many without escorts and some trailing oil slicks—had turned and begun heading north.

Van Brunt picked out the biggest target he could find among the stragglers—he assumed it to be a battleship. As Van Brunt maneuvered the Avenger, he got an impromptu fight talk from gunner Jack South.

"Sir, here comes the best goddamn torpedo plane in the United States Navy! Let's make it count!"

Van Brunt dropped his torpedo square in the ship's path. There was an explosion as he pulled up—his wingman later confirmed a direct hit—but then the Avenger's left rudder promptly went limp. Van Brunt tested the controls; he could climb and turn with his right rudder but knew his next challenge would be to land safely—and soon.

When he reached *St. Lo*'s landing circle, Van Brunt radioed the Landing Signal Officer. Van Brunt's gentle pine-woods drawl, an artifact of his prewar life as a schoolteacher in southern Georgia, belied both his fatigue and his anxiety about getting down safely: "Gabby, can you bring me in on a right-hand turn? I've got no left rudder." Gabby radioed he could as long as Van Brunt had good control, but he'd have to wait until everybody else got aboard.

Both Van Brunt and the LSO understood the risks. The Avenger was by far the Navy's heaviest carrier-based plane and *St. Lo* was an escort carrier. Its six-hundred-foot flight deck sat atop a flimsy prefabricated hull. Like nearly all the Taffy CVEs, *St. Lo* had been built in Kaiser Industries' assembly line West Coast shipyards. Equipped with virtually no protective armor, the ships were sardonically called Kaiser Coffins.

The CVEs were short and boxy; their truncated flight decks, perched like tabletops on bathtubs, were interrupted forward by a small, open-island superstructure—something like the flight tower at a small dirt airstrip. Escort carriers were originally conceived for two specific wartime roles: in the Atlantic to provide mobile airborne antisubmarine defense for supply convoys (an idea concocted by President Franklin Roosevelt); in the Pacific to shuttle replacement aircraft to the fleet carriers (the brainchild of Admiral Chester Nimitz). By the end of 1943, the war of beachheads fashioned a new use: full-time, end-to-end air support for Pacific island invasions. With the CVEs constantly on hand—each carrying about thirty fighter and torpedo bomber aircraft—the bigger but scarcer attack carriers could be used for wide-ranging strikes closer to Japan.

Van Brunt circled *St. Lo* as the other squadron planes got into the groove. He kept the Avenger at a normal 1,500 feet altitude but, flying against the grain, stayed well outside the counterclockwise landing circle. The circuit chatter indicated there were incoming bogeys, so Van Brunt also kept a weather eye to stay clear of friendly Triple A, including *St. Lo*'s single 5-inch.

Dare to Die . . . Sure to Die

When news of Taffy 3's plight reached Taffy 1, its commander Rear Admiral Thomas L. Sprague (NO relation to Clifton Sprague, Taffy 3's commander) began to organize assistance. Taffy 1, operating 130 miles south of Taffy 3, had already launched a deck load of planes to join the chase for Japanese stragglers of the night action in Surigao Strait. Once recovered, these planes would rearm and fly north to help Taffy 3. In the meantime, Taffy 1 CVEs became bases for Taffy 3 refugees. It was about 0730 when the Taffy 1 planes began returning. But nearly coincident with the friendlies, the first body crashers arrived.

These first planes, which had taken off an hour earlier from Mindanao, lunged for escort carriers *Santee* (CVE-29), *Petrof Bay* (CVE-80), and *Suwannee* (CVE-27). *Santee* took the first suicide hit to the forward port side of its flight deck. The plane penetrated to the hangar deck where its flaming wreckage ignited fires that threatened a stack of bombs.

As *Santee* damage control parties fought to control the fires, gun crews on *Sangamon* (CVE-26), *Suwannee*, and *Petrof Bay* combined to shoot two more would-be crashers. *Suwanee*'s guns then took on a third, but this plane, though hit and trailing smoke, rolled on its back and plunged into *Suwanee*'s flight deck just forward of the after elevator. This plane's bomb exploded, causing scores of casualties to flight deck and hangar personnel and disabling the elevator.

Suwanee's damage control parties quickly doused these fires. *Santee*'s crew managed to contain their ship's damage as well, only to be rocked by the explosion of a torpedo fired by an undetected submarine. *Suwannee* (along with *Santee*, part of a class of sturdier escort carriers converted from fuel tankers) absorbed the hit, sustaining some damage and a slight list from flooding, but sailed on at near flank speed.

It was nearing 0800. The skies over Taffy 1 were again clear, and her crews, after treating casualties, turned to the business of recovering aircraft and sending them off to help Taffy 3. Though the phenomenon of desperate pilots (more often Japanese, but occasionally American) crashing ships was hardly new to the Pacific War, the next hours and days would prove that a new inexplicable and terrifying twist had taken the stage. "Dare to die" had become "sure to die."

Poster Boy

At about the time these first body crashers struck, a formation of nine more took off from Mabalacat. Leading the group was Lieutenant Yukio Seki, one of twenty-four volunteers who stepped forward—every Mabalacat aviator, to a man—after Vice Admiral Takijiro Onishi's 19 October meeting.

Seki, 23, was at once an odd and natural choice to command the mission. An Imperial Japanese Naval Academy graduate fresh out of advanced flight school, Seki was a skilled pilot with some carrier-based combat experience. Seki had more in common with the Taffy 3 pilots than the Japanese flight novices whose deficiencies in age, skill, and experience would make them prime "body crashing" fodder in the months ahead. At the same time, though, Seki was a poster boy for the best in Japan's latest generation of military manhood. He was wolfishly handsome, trim, and ramrod straight. As the son of a widowed mother, Seki's pedigree was unpretentious and unassailable. He was the personification of the new samurai, a role model and sacrificial example for others—many others it turned out—to emulate and follow.

The group's official name became the *Shinpu* (a compound noun, written using the Chinese characters for "god" and "wind").* Special Attack Unit with Seki as commander. Composed of all the pilots and remaining aircraft of what had formerly been the navy's 201st Air Group, *Shinpu* Special Attack Unit was organized into four flight sections, each section's name chosen to symbolize an essential virtue of

---

*According to some sources, U.S. translators initiated the use of *kamikaze* to describe Japanese suicide attacks in general. According to these sources, *kamikaze* was seldom used by the Japanese during World War II as a reference to organized military suicide attacks. (*Kamikaze* was used in other contexts though: for example as the name of an early 20th century class of Japanese destroyers.) After World War II, however, *kamikaze* increasingly crept into Japanese usage, probably influenced by the U.S. occupation and the exposure to American media.

Japanese manhood. The aircraft resources—twenty-six Zekes—were further divided: half would be used for body crashing, half for escorts and witnesses.

Ready to go and perhaps as motivated as they might ever be, Seki and the other original volunteers nevertheless had to linger several days before realizing their fate. During that time, there were a number of missions, but each was either aborted or produced dismal results—mistaken target coordinates, mechanical failures, planes lost in bad weather, or jumped by American C.A.P.s. As new aircraft filtered into the Philippines during these frustrating days, they became part of *Shinpu* Special Attack Unit. Organized into new flights with their own glorious names, the planes were ferried south to airstrips on Cebu Island and then onto Mindanao to be closer to the developing action.

Meanwhile, while every Mabalacat mission got its ceremonial send-off, the fanfare for each became increasingly self-conscious and subdued. Whether mission takeoffs sparked pride, resignation, or dread, "failed" returns implicitly carried the stain of shame. When grounded, the original volunteers sat idle, free to relax (if they possibly could) and to contemplate their destiny. Though squadron mates offered encouragement and consolation, an ominous question loomed: Just how many times could a person set off prepared to die and return alive?

As it was, for all the glory that had been initially showered on this first contingent of body crashers, they might end up as no spearhead at all. Though officially unsanctioned, there'd already been earlier body crashing episodes—some perhaps as early as mid-1944. Now these new units—not to mention ones being formed by the IJA—might grab the first glory, dulling the first volunteers' legacy while eventually leaving them just as dead.

Then, at 1020 on 25 October, Seki's formation of Zekes broke through and made contact with Taffy 3.

Now Things Will Start Rolling

One Zeke dived at *Kitkun Bay* (CVE-71). Ron Vaughn, an 18-year-old Texan positioned as a lookout on *Kitkun Bay*'s after port catwalk, watched as the plane climbed, rolled, and plunged straight down toward the flight deck. *Kitkun Bay*'s 40-mm gunfire battered the plane. Vaughn saw a portion of the plane's tail section crumple, causing it to veer drunkenly from its trajectory. One of the attacker's wings managed just a glancing blow to the ship's port-side catwalk—but its bomb exploded in the water just off the bow, with blast and shrapnel claiming a score of casualties.

Moments later, *Kalinin Bay* took a deeper mauling from a plane that succeeded in crashing its deck. Two other Zekes were shot down and two more driven off by gunfire from *Fanshaw Bay* and *White Plains* (CVE-66). But then the remaining three planes drew a bead on *St. Lo.*

The wing of one Japanese plane, shot down by *St. Lo,* fluttered right in front of Tom Van Brunt, barely missing his Avenger. Then he saw another plane career toward *St. Lo* and watched as it too was shot out of the air. What Van Brunt didn't see—and what *St. Lo* gunners missed as well—was a third Japanese plane approaching astern. Van Brunt recalled later: "He came right up the wake, pulled up, nosed over, and then crashed into the flight deck."

Aboard *St. Lo,* crewmen were caught in the abrupt squeeze of contradictory events. First, they'd exhaled and stood down after spending the early morning square in the crosshairs of a Japanese fleet. Then they—and particularly the flight deck crews—were working furiously to recover aircraft. And now back to GQ as bogeys snooped in.

Few eyewitnesses agreed completely about what happened next. Many were convinced the entire Japanese aircraft sliced through *St. Lo*'s flight deck, igniting fuel and ordnance in the hangar area below. Brock Short, 19, a signalman positioned on the island just aft of *St. Lo*'s conning bridge, instead was sure he saw a bomb drop from the plane's wing just before the plane itself disintegrated atop the deck. It was this bomb, Short was convinced, which "doomed our ship."

This much was certain. In the next twenty-seven minutes, as explosions rocked and fractured *St. Lo,* all its crewmen abruptly turned their attentions to the singular, urgent business of survival.

Larry Collins, 29, one of *St. Lo*'s communications officers, was in the wardroom when GQ sounded. He jumped up and sprinted toward his GQ station on the fantail. His accustomed route was through the hangar deck, "but the Lord steered me another way." Collins went up the usual ladder, but instead of getting off at the hangar deck, he kept climbing to the gallery level. The plane hit while he was still climbing. Collins turned and ran forward. Explosions seemed to chase him. They came one after another—maybe a half dozen—and with each explosion the ship shuddered.

Hearing blasts, Radar Technician Evan H. "Holly" Crawforth ran from the mess deck to a forward ladder also leading to the hangar deck. Someone cautioned him: "Don't go up." He started to turn back, "but I just had to see." Crawforth glimpsed smoke and fire sweeping across the deck and a huge hole in the flight deck just behind the elevator. He ducked back below and took a roundabout series of passageways back to his duty station in Radio 2.

Radio 2 was dark but filled with sailors. "I told them to get the hell out. We went over to radar, which had a door opening onto the catwalk." The door was jammed but they quickly unhinged it, tumbled out, and ran forward along the starboard catwalk, away from the smoke and fire. Crawforth inhaled the acrid scent of exploded ordnance. After emerging unscratched from the morning's ordeal, it was hard to believe they'd finally been hit.

Joe Lehans, 27, *St. Lo*'s radar officer, was in that same gallery level radar compartment when he felt the first jolt of the crash. Dust puffed from the air ducts and settled across the room. Then there were explosions—and it was clear the ship was listing. The radar equipment and everything associated with it were classified Top Secret. Lehans knew what he had to do. First, he grabbed an armload of messages and instruction manuals and stuffed them into a weighted canvas bag. Next, he loaded and cocked his .45-caliber pistol. With the weighted sack in one hand, Lehans backed out of the compartment like a bank robber with his gun blazing, shooting up screens and consoles. When he got outside to the catwalk, he heaved the weighted bag overboard.

Briefly, inexplicably, Lehans then started toward his stateroom intent on retrieving his Remington electric shaver. Very quickly he let that idea go. Lehans did, however, dip back into the darkened radar room to retrieve a canvas bag stuffed with his own assortment of survival gear—gloves, an extra life belt, several .45 ammunition clips, and pieces of chocolate in watertight containers.

On *St. Lo*'s bridge Seaman Bill Pumphrey was getting final instructions from the ship's skipper Captain Francis McKenna. Pumphrey, a 20-year-old from the West Texas plains town of Paint Rock, was the Captain's Bridge Talker, a position of both privilege and isolation. Several minutes before, McKenna had calmly given the order to abandon ship and would by tradition be the last man to leave. Now McKenna was releasing Pumphrey so he could go over the side. He thrust a sheaf of papers into the young sailor's hands, ordering Pumphrey to take care of the papers, but by no means to be killed or captured while they were in his possession. Pumphrey gulped audibly, rolled the papers into a tube, thrust them under his shirt and belt, removed his talker's headphones, saluted McKenna, and started for the ladder leading to *St. Lo*'s flight deck.

Meanwhile, Larry Collins joined lots of others jammed onto *St. Lo*'s forecastle. He'd been there less than five minutes when another ship's officer called down from the flight deck. "Captain says abandon ship." Some men headed for knotted escape ropes being rigged over the side. Some jumped. One man near Larry hopped immediately to the rail, perched there for a moment, then leaped. Windmilling his arms and legs, the sailor gleefully shouted "30 days leave!" all the way into the water.

When Holly Crawforth got forward, sailors were evacuating the wounded—putting life jackets on them, looping lines around their torsos, and lowering them painstakingly to the water. The process, Crawforth remembered, "was just too slow. Finally, all we could do was put jackets on them and drop them over the side."

Crawforth got to a knotted line hanging from one of the forward gun tubs. He didn't get very far on the line—maybe ten feet. "The man above me lost his grip and peeled the rest of us off as he fell." Crawforth hit the water hard and plunged deep. When he finally surfaced, Crawforth tried to use his life belt but it was torn: the last of the CO_2 used to inflate it just bubbled out. He ditched the belt and began swimming.

Larry Collins jumped from the rail still wearing his helmet, and when he hit the water the chin strap wrenched his jaw and his teeth dug deep into his tongue. Collins' mouth filled with blood as he swam away to windward. Finally, he turned on his back and inflated his life belt. Survivors gathered together and waited. *St. Lo* was drifting downwind and still exploding. "Her whole port side flew up in the air, and pretty soon she was gone."

It had taken the wounded *St. Lo* barely thirty minutes to sink. She carried with her to the bottom of the Philippine Sea the extinguished lives of 140 sailors and airmen. There were more muffled explosions once she'd submerged and then, all at once, silence. The Divine Wind had claimed *St. Lo* as its first kill.

There was little for Tom Van Brunt and his shaken crew to do now. A landing refuge had been pulled out from under him and, along with it, who knew how many good friends and squadron mates. Using right rudder, Van Brunt nosed the Avenger west toward Leyte and Tacloban where, with more than a little luck, he, Frederickson, and South were able to land in one piece. Burt Bassett, Van Brunt's University of Florida fraternity brother was standing near the runway as Van Brunt's shrapnel-ridden Avenger touched down and taxied to a stop. He was surprised to see Van Brunt emerging from the cockpit—they'd not seen or heard from each other since before the war. They had some catching up to do. The day was over for both, they'd each lost a ship, but they'd each come through it without a scratch.

Back in his headquarters in Manila, Onishi received reports from the surviving observer pilots from the morning missions out of Mindanao and Mabalacat. The first strike reported hits on at least two carriers, with each set ablaze. The results of the second strike—Onishi knew it had been led by Seki—were even better: four American carriers hit, with at least two severely damaged. Sensitive to the imperative of supplying inspiring results to his emperor and his countrymen, Onishi fairly leaped to the conclusion that his body crashers' morning work had sunk six aircraft carriers. "Okay," he muttered, leaning back in his chair. "Now things will start rolling."

Beyond Recognition and Hope

It turned out the day's ordeal was not quite over for Taffy 3. Within moments of *St. Lo*'s sinking, both *White Plains* and *Kitkun Bay* weathered close brushes from two more body crashers, while a third crashed directly on *Kalinin Bay*'s flight deck. While each attack caused some damage—and bad damage to *Kalinin Bay*—luck held for these CVEs. They escaped afloat and with relatively few casualties. When things started rolling again on the 26th, however, it was Taffy 1's turn to grapple with catastrophe.

During that next afternoon, a flight of twelve Japanese planes approached Taffy 1's formation. Taffy 1's C.A.P. accounted for nearly all of them, but one penetrated to target *Suwannee* as aircraft were being recovered.

Paul "Cactus" Walters, an aircraft machinist mate and Hellcat plane captain, was one of the flight deck crewmen standing forward on the flight deck when this lone bogey arrived. Walters, though not quite 21, was among *Suwanee*'s most seasoned flight deck crewmen. He had even been part of the ground crew for the renowned "Cactus Air Force."

Walters' Hellcat had landed, been spotted near the bow, and its pilot had gone below decks for debriefing. Walters was helping spot other aircraft when he first glimpsed the intruder. The Japanese plane was coming in on the heels of an Avenger just then taxiing toward the forward flight deck elevator. The Avenger's after gunner had seen it too; his guns were just then tracking the plane and sending up a stream of .50-caliber fire that continued until the very instant it hit.

The day before, Walters had been below decks and on his way topside when *Suwannee* received its first hit. He'd seen only sparks and flashes as shrapnel—a cinder-hot piece of which hit his arm—pierced through the deck. This afternoon, though, Walters got the full show.

The incoming plane careened into the Avenger, igniting an explosion that demolished both aircraft, the flight deck elevator, and the port side catapult shack. Men, some of them aflame, were blown or jumped over the side. To escape the first flash of flames and explosions, Walters sprinted forward and leaped down to the slice of the ship's forecastle extending beyond the flight deck. He and others, many severely burned or wounded, many dead or about to die, were trapped on this cul-de-sac by explosions and a flaring wall of flame held back only by the ship's forward motion.

Charlie Casello, 23, a "yellow shirt" aviation boatswain mate petty officer from Lexington, Massachusetts, was standing near *Suwannee*'s bridge when the explosion and flames erupted. Casello, whose usual spot was also forward of the flight deck, knew that most of his yellow shirts were right in the middle of it. He sprinted forward, first to help remove the wounded and eventually to work the fire hoses. Casello found George Dobson, another yellow shirt and Casello's good liberty buddy, sprawled on the deck aft of the flames. Dobson was badly wounded, with most of one shoulder all but torn away. Casello dragged Dobson to the shelter of the port catwalk but was pretty sure Dobson was a goner.

Lieutenant Walter B. Burwell, *Suwannee*'s medical officer, was treating other wounded on the flight deck when he learned about the sailors trapped on the forecastle. Accompanied by a corpsman and carrying first aid bags filled with morphine Syrettes, tourniquets, sulfa, Vaseline, and bandages, Burwell commandeered a fire extinguisher and used it to suppress flames as he and the corpsman worked their way forward from below decks. He reached the forecastle to find that the stranded sailors had been showered with flaming aviation gasoline from the flight deck. Some had leaped aflame into the sea, while others were incinerated before they could leap. These men, he reported later, were "burned beyond recognition and hope."

Although the flow of gasoline had by then mostly consumed itself, the decks and bulkheads remained blistering hot and ammunition clips in the small arms locker on the deck below popped like strings of firecrackers. Men poised on the rail and still ready to jump had to be restrained during the hours it took finally to quash the fires. When Walters, exhausted, trembling, and feeling much older than his twenty years, at last made his way back to the hangar deck, he left behind him a scene of carnage and devastation unlike any imagined by him.

Though a picture of the scale and import of these first attacks was still being shaped, it was abundantly clear that aircraft carriers were the targets of choice. Their decks and more precisely the aircraft elevators built into those decks were the bull's-eyes. And each successful attack embodied three synergistic weapons—the plane, of course, but also the bomb (or bombs) usually attached, and, finally, the reserves of aviation gasoline in the plane's tanks.

Both the escorts and the attack carriers were alike in having wooden decks. Early on, naval planners had quashed the idea of installing armored steel flight decks on carriers as adding too much weight and sacrificing too much speed and maneuverability. Crashing planes penetrated easily; the layer of timber barely slowed the impact and made the torching of aircraft, fuel, and ordinance staged below practically inevitable. Cavernous carrier hangar decks couldn't be buttoned up like other compartments. The first detonations could—as had happened on *St. Lo*—quickly unleash a chain of fires and explosions to race through the ship, claiming a grim toll of damage and casualties. Even though *Suwannee*—likely owing to its sturdier construction—had escaped sinking, its casualties from the series of attacks were both grievous (just short of *St. Lo's*) and portentous. Eighty-five men were killed, 58 were missing and 101 were wounded; within days most of the missing and many of the wounded—nearly all of them burn victims—would cross the ledger to join the dead. These were casualty numbers Marine and Army commanders of the war of the beachheads had grown accustomed to. But they were new, sobering, and unprecedented to the Navy.

★ Chapter 10 ★

To Get In and Get Aboard, November 1944

It is very discouraging to . . . have a very fine ship with some 345 officers and men on it defeated by one lousy Japanese.
—COMMANDER ARTHUR PURDY, USS *ABNER READ* (DD-526)

Bull's Run

Feeding on the smallest morsel of success, body crashing ballooned to a strategy that coupled with sending massive troop reinforcements through Ormoc and Carigara, two ports on the western side of Leyte, might yet evict the Americans from the Philippines. Japanese general Sosaku Suzuki, charged with defending Leyte, was supremely confident of retaking Tacloban within days and afterward demanding not only the surrender of MacArthur's Philippine forces but the return of New Guinea as well. With this as backdrop, the crosshairs of *tokkō* shifted to the American invasion and supply fleet in Leyte Gulf.

Adding to the resources of Vice Admiral Takijiro Onishi's *Shinpu* Special Attack Unit was an influx of *tokkō* raiders joining Lieutenant General Kyoji Tominaga's Fourth Air Army. Although apparently never collaborating with Onishi on planning, resources, or tactics, Tominaga had nonetheless been busily assembling army pilots and aircraft at forward bases even before the American landing. Tominaga's fighter planes were sent to Negros Island, west of Leyte, and his combined resources probably exceeded the IJN's. The newly assigned army pilots—many unknowingly ticketed for *tokkō* missions—were hastily deployed and, up to the point of their departure for the Philippines, were told only that they were part of a "special assignment" involving the Leyte campaign. As far as most were concerned, the Pacific War with the Americans was a navy predicament—one that the navy had gotten itself into and from which it would have to extricate itself.

Meanwhile, Onishi's exaggerated claims of success spurred the flow of fresh reinforcements to his *Shinpu* Special Attack Unit. Although IJN's Philippine aircraft arsenal had dipped to fewer than two hundred planes just before the invasion, the numbers now swelled as planes flew in from Japan and Formosa. Though there was no consistent tally of departures and arrivals, about two hundred reinforcements made it to Philippine bases before the end of October; another six hundred would arrive in November; and a final one hundred in the first days of January. There would be, at least in the decisive weeks to come, enough fuel for the fires ignited by Onishi and now stoked by Tominaga.

These influxes of Japanese pilots and planes, coupled with the temporary erosion of U.S. capabilities, began to tip the balance of local air superiority in Japan's favor. Compounding the outright loss of two Taffy CVEs—*Gambier Bay* and *St. Lo*—were the losses of several other escort carriers whose flight decks were out of commission for days and possibly weeks. The worst of these—*Suwannee*—was bound for three months of stateside dry dock repair. And things weren't much better for Halsey's Task Force 38—suffering both from blows to its ships and, in some ways, an even bigger blow to its reputation.

Halsey and Mitscher's part in the overall Battle of Leyte Gulf had been to pounce on Vice Admiral Jisaburo Ozawa's northern decoy force with three carrier task groups, racking up a thorough, but ultimately hollow victory. Ozawa's forces boasted only 166 aircraft to contest the Americans (who would end up flying over five hundred sorties against the Japanese), and he anticipated complete annihilation. Task Force 38 air strikes claimed five Japanese ships, four of them carriers (including *Zuikaku,* the last surviving carrier of the six that staged the attack on Pearl Harbor), and task force surface units sunk three more. But eight Japanese ships, including a light cruiser carrying Ozawa, made good their escape.

Halsey's biggest casualty, in what became known for the record as the Battle for Cape Engaño, turned out to be his reputation. As air strikes were just barely getting underway on the morning of the 25th,

Halsey received a plain-language cry for help from 7th Fleet's Thomas Kinkaid who was appalled to learn Halsey had gone north.

For his part, Halsey fumed and briefly stalled, but eventually detached a surface group that sped south but arrived too late to help. Halsey was stung by criticism, some of it from his boss Admiral Chester Nimitz (it reduced Halsey to tears) and much of it unspoken. Halsey, however, did get support from one important corner. When Douglas MacArthur overheard some of his own staff officers badmouthing Halsey, he jumped quickly to his defense. "That's enough!" he shouted. "Leave the Bull alone! He's still a fighting admiral in my book."

Still, after this sullied victory and its harvest of second-guessing (to some 7th Fleet sailors, Cape Engaño would forever be known as the "Battle of Bull's Run"), Halsey likely itched to get back on the offensive in the South China Sea. It was not to be.

On 28 and 29 October, two of Halsey's carrier groups clobbered Luzon, trying to wipe out Japanese aircraft already operating from its airfields and to staunch the flow of new planes coming in. The fighter and bomber sweeps had some success, knocking down about seventy Japanese planes and demolishing another dozen on the ground.

Then, like a boxer taking punishment so he can land his own blows, the Japanese launched body-crashing missions toward the carriers just offshore. The first counterpunch landed on 29 October—a flaming suicide plane demolished a port side gun tub on *Intrepid* (CV-11) extinguishing the lives of ten sailors and wounding six more.

The next day, five planes, part of a larger horde of *kamikazes,* managed to sidestep C.A.P. and reach a second carrier group. The five were picked up by radar and three of them were splashed as they descended, but one suicide pilot crashed *Franklin* (CV-13) and a second crashed *Belleau Wood* (CVL-24). The blows punctured the flight decks, destroyed nearly fifty planes and killed more than 150 sailors. Expert and heroic damage control saved the day for all three ships, and none was ever in danger of sinking. But it was clear that just one crash to a carrier could trigger a conflagration capable of exacting a huge toll.

These suicide blows could not have come at a worse time for Halsey. After weeks of virtually nonstop operations, Task Force 38 desperately required a breather to rest, replenish, and rearm. Exhaustion showed in big matters and small. One task group had been at sea sixty-four consecutive days spelled only by replenishment stops at advance bases. *Franklin,* now grieving over so many lives, was also worn down by pileups of lesser casualties. At one time or another, half of *Franklin*'s crew had gone on the binnacle list with heat rash.

On 28 October John McCain's carrier task group departed for Ulithi. On 30 October two more groups (one of them the group to which *Franklin* and *Belleau Wood* belonged) followed, leaving remaining units shackled indefinitely to the undiminished needs of the Leyte invasion. Departing with them was Mitscher, relieved as planned by McCain. Mitscher was clearly spent and in need of a breather, a human barometer of the Task Force 38's overall condition.

Respecting if not yet fully comprehending the scale of this new suicide air threat, Task Force 38's new boss McCain strengthened C.A.P. and moved his remaining carriers farther out to sea. While this meant better protection for Task Force 38, it also limited the availability of strike aircraft and the time they could spend over targets.

This sudden airpower imbalance might still have been avoided by the deployment of AAF fighter planes to newly captured Leyte bases. But these planes were slow to arrive and, thanks to Tacloban airstrip's unyielding monsoon mud, even slower to become operational. The Japanese, though struggling to marshal enough aircraft and pilots, had two things in their favor. They had firmer runways to fly from and, when attacking U.S. ships, could use the islands' terrain to avoid radar detection.

I Can Finish Leyte in Two Weeks, but I Won't

Interservice rivalries flared during the first weeks of the Leyte campaign. As the invasion fleet lay exposed off Leyte, on land the army once again seemed to be playing chess instead of checkers. MacArthur had a lot of ground to conquer and terrible conditions (thirty-four inches of rain fell during King II's first forty days) to slow his progress. Still, MacArthur seemed to be just inching along. Sixth Army, led by Walter Krueger, a stolid, unimaginative German-born general, always paused at Japanese strong points to wait for artillery to flatten enemy defenses.* When questioned about this by a usually supportive press corps, MacArthur, chin forward, was ready with his choicest rhetoric: "If I like I can finish Leyte in two weeks, but I won't!" he disclaimed (speaking, as he often did, both to his listener and to history). "I have too great a responsibility to the mothers and wives in America to do that to their men. I will not take by sacrifice what I can achieve by strategy."

For his part, MacArthur was enraged by Nimitz's caution in the face of the new aerial suicide threat. Never one to short sell his capabilities, MacArthur had long chafed at not being named Supreme Commander—the "Pacific Ike." It galled him to have to bargain over the use of ships and aircraft resources "on loan" from 3rd Fleet. MacArthur's vocal support of Halsey as a "fighting admiral" may simply have been a bow to the loyalty and respect Halsey had shown him. But it may also have been meant as a backhanded slap at Halsey's more circumspect boss—and MacArthur's Pacific rival—who now seemed to be upsetting MacArthur's timetable.

Reporters at MacArthur's headquarters on Leyte one day overheard the general reading the riot act to 7th Fleet's Thomas Kinkaid. Nimitz looked to be stalling on plans for MacArthur's early December thrust to Mindoro, an island close to Luzon on the west side of the archipelago. MacArthur needed Mindoro as a staging point for the climactic assault on Luzon, but Nimitz didn't want to risk Central Pacific ships without reliable land-based air cover. MacArthur railed against what he saw as the U.S. Navy's motheaten tradition of heaping disgrace on captains who lost their ships. "What do they have ships for?" he demanded of Kinkaid. "What do the American people expect you to do with all that hardware if not throw it at the enemy?"

There was some truth in MacArthur's complaint. Whenever a ship was lost, Naval regulations required a court of inquiry to establish responsibility and fix any blame. The prospect of facing a court of inquiry— "captain breakers"—tempered the willingness to take risks of ship captains and fleet commanders alike.

But these investigations were serious business not just because of

*MacArthur called Krueger one of his "Three Ks." The other two were 7th Fleet admiral Thomas Kinkaid and George C. Kenney, commander of Allied air forces in the Southwest Pacific.

"hardware" loss. One bad decision at sea—in peace or in war—could also cost the lives of hundreds, even thousands of men. MacArthur undoubtedly understood this. But, at least during this unguarded moment, MacArthur evidenced little responsibility to the mothers and wives of the sailors aboard ships he wanted thrown against the enemy.

Defeated by One Lousy Japanese

The holes in the flimsy shield surrounding the Leyte beachheads showed from the very first day of November. That morning, beginning about 0930, a menagerie of Japanese aircraft—single engine and multiengine, both army and navy, some suicide, some not—eluded radar and C.A.P., to descend on a group of 7th Fleet battleships, cruisers, and tin cans guarding Leyte Gulf.

A flight of Val dive-bombers arrived first—and apparently included the first *kamikaze* to take aim at a tin can. The menacing profile of the Val, an IJN two-seater with fixed landing struts dangling like the forelegs of a wasp, was familiar to most Pacific sailors and airmen. Once the staple of Japanese carrier air strikes, the Val was now a slow, outmoded relic whose chief virtues were its reliability and—in the months ahead—its expendability.

Buffeted by stiff antiaircraft fire, one Val pilot aborted his dive on Australian cruiser *Shropshire* and dipped briefly into a low-hanging cloud, apparently to regroup and go again. Instead, the Val pilot abruptly heaved his plane at destroyer *Claxton* (DD-571).

Condition "one easy" was set for *Claxton*'s crew, meaning most men were at their battle stations but had some freedom to move around. Bob Proudfoot, one of *Claxton*'s fire controlmen basking in the morning sun atop the ship's main battery director, heard the plane before he saw it wing over and drop like a stone. In that instant Proudfoot felt a sensation shared by thousands of sailors in the days, weeks, and months ahead: the plane and its pilot were aiming at him.

While the attack seemed to happen in slow motion, it took just seconds. Before Proudfoot and the rest of the crew could leap into the basket, the Val had splashed astern just off *Claxton*'s starboard side.

The plane hadn't missed the ship entirely. Bill Monfort, *Claxton*'s chief radioman, standing just aft of the radio shack, saw one of its wings plow into a 40-mm gun and its crew before hurtling into the water. The impact of the crash tossed a huge wave across *Claxton*'s fantail. Then the plane and its bombs exploded, rocking the stern, severing steering control, and swamping starboard compartments. With ship's engines still churning but unable to maneuver and the hull settling to starboard, *Claxton*'s skipper M. H. Hubbard slowed his ship in an effort to stem flooding.

Working topside, *Claxton*'s damage control personnel improvised a giant carpet of mattresses anchored by bunk frames to drape as a patch over the starboard side. Belowdecks, others groped underwater to secure the patch by tying lines to compartment stanchions in the flooded spaces. Meanwhile, ship engineers offset the list by pumping liquid ballast—fuel and water—from starboard to port tanks or over the side. *Abner Read* (DD-526) also dropped from formation to stand by.

Destroyer *Killen* (DD-593), was the next besieged, shooting down four planes, but taking a bomb hit from a fifth angling across its bow. During the worst of it, *Killen*'s skipper H. G. Corey—nicknamed "Glory Corey" by some crewmen—had galloped between bridge wings, at each crossing wresting the wheel from the helmsman's hands and giving it a roulette spin to either port or starboard.

Pharmacist mate Ray Cloud, watching from the fantail near *Killen*'s after battle dressing station, saw the plane—a sleek twin-engine Frances fighter-bomber—swoop in low across the port side. As its pilot released his bomb, Cloud said to himself "he dropped it too soon," and then watched transfixed as the plane roared by—pursued and chewed up by fire from *Killen*'s 40- and 20-mm guns.

Cloud guessed wrong. The bomb hit the water, skipped once, and then pierced *Killen*'s port side hull forward, exploding between No. 2 and No. 3 magazines. The blast tore a gaping hole in *Killen*'s port side and water poured in. By the time Donice Copeland, 18, one of *Killen*'s radar petty officers, emerged on deck from the radar shack, the bow was all but submerged and the ship nearly dead in the water.

George Muse, *Killen*'s executive officer, who'd bounded from the radar shack seconds after the explosion, was already over the side and underwater inspecting the damage. When Muse surfaced, Harold Johnson, another radarman, helped haul him back on deck. "The damage is pretty bad" Muse called up to Corey, who was leaning down anxiously from the bridge wing, "but she'll float."

Ray Cloud, meanwhile, dashed up the ship's starboard to find A. A. Thurlo, *Killen*'s medical officer, whose battle station was in the wardroom. The two men ended standing ready but helpless at the fringe of the carnage. All but a few casualties were trapped below decks. Even two unwounded sailors, stuck in the ship's emergency generator room and able to communicate by sound-powered phone, soon drowned. The final tally of dead eventually climbed to 15.

Killen's tormentor was not quite done. Now trailing smoke, the pilot aimed his Frances toward *Ammen* (DD-527). Bill Hart, gun captain on *Ammen*'s forward most 5-inch gun was certain the Frances would strike the bridge. So was Hubert Hunzeker, *Ammen*'s torpedo officer who was standing on the port bridge wing, directly in the plane's path. Hunzeker instinctively ducked, covered his head with his arms, and braced for a life-ending explosion.

There was no explosion—at least none Hunzeker heard. Instead, there was an enormous clatter and a huge, prolonged hissing of steam. The Frances, it turned out, hit by *Ammen*'s 40-mm gunfire, had veered aft to strike broadside between *Ammen*'s twin smoke stacks.

Each of the plane's wings had crumpled the top of a stack, scattering debris, some to the decks and some overboard. Most of the wreckage went overboard, but one wing and engine lodged in the starboard railing. Superheated gases hissing from the misshapen stacks briefly ignited a backwash of gasoline that spread across the deckhouse.

Ammen's Supply Officer John Moynahan, in charge of a cluster of 20-mm mounts, was crouching on the main deck aft of No. 2 stack when the plane hit. Like Hunzeker, Moynahan was surprised how little noise there'd been. Seeing the tops of both stacks gone, Moynahan realized with a start that Charles Helmer, one of his supply clerks stationed as a talker on a platform atop No. 2 stack had undoubtedly been killed. Likeable, fast, efficient Helmer—was gone.

Ammen's damage control parties smothered the fires, dislodged the plane's wing, and heaved it over the side. Flames gave way to thick, stinging clouds of steam. The wounded and burned (Bill Hart saw one man with his arms locked straight out, dripping sheets of flesh) walked or were carried off for treatment.

Despite the damage, *Ammen* continued to maneuver at flank speed, but now her power plant was close to shutting down. Each stack did double duty—an inner cylinder belched exhaust smoke while an outer sleeve gulped fresh air. Now, with both stacks smashed, boiler exhaust mingling with smoke, flame, and steam from the wreckage displaced fresh air to feed—and choke—*Ammen*'s furnaces. To prevent this, Leon Carver, one of *Ammen*'s engineering officers, helped devise a sort of emergency tracheotomy: rigging canvas sheets to close off the amputated stacks' intake ducts while opening fire room hatches to create temporary fresh air intakes.

As *Claxton*, *Abner Read*, *Killen*, and *Ammen* fought their morning duels with predators in Leyte Gulf, ten miles south a second group of Japanese planes swept in from the west. Eluding radar detection by hugging the contours of Panoan Island, they skimmed Surigao Strait's mirror-calm waters to set upon *Anderson* (DD-411) and *Bush* (DD-529).

It was now about 0920 and *Anderson* was anchored offshore after escorting landing craft into Cabalian Bay. *Bush* lookouts spotted one of two Bettys—navy twin-engine bombers—launching a torpedo toward *Anderson*. *Anderson* guns soon opened fire.

Bush went to GQ, turned west toward the action and accelerated to 15 knots and then 25 knots. *Bush* was soon attacked by a different Betty approaching to starboard. Fortunately for *Bush* and its crew, the tin can's 35-year-old skipper Rollin (Westy) Westholm was a skilled and confidant ship handler—a burly former torpedo boat squadron commander in the Solomons and off New Guinea.* Ordering full rudder turns, Westholm repeatedly swung the ship, both to keep her guns pointed toward attackers and to dodge strafing fire, bombs, and possible torpedoes.

So close to land, the Japanese planes maneuvered like bushwhack-

---

*Westholm's Patrol Squadron 2 included *PT-109*, skippered by Jack Kennedy, a young naval reserve officer from Boston and son of the U.S. Ambassador to England. Westholm taught Kennedy to play acey deucy, a fast-paced navy variant of backgammon, and Kennedy returned the favor by teaching Westholm the finer points of backgammon itself.

ers, flying behind the crest of a ridgeline overlooking the Surigao Strait before dashing across the water. Since radar was no help with these planes, more sets of sharp eyes were needed in a hurry. Lieutenant Tony Lilly, who joined *Bush* during construction as gunnery officer and had since become Executive Officer, was already on the bridge. Lilly's GQ assignment was in CIC, but he'd come topside after realizing *Bush* was too "landlocked" for him to be of much use there. Westholm and Lilly choreographed their moves—Lilly positioning himself on the bridge wing opposite the one where Westholm stood. Robert Aguilar, a storekeeper petty officer who'd grown up as a keen-eyed hunter in Arizona, was one of several sailors called to the bridge on the double, handed a pair of binoculars, and told to keep his eyes peeled on the ridgeline.

At 0942 *Bush* crewmen felt the muffled thump of an underwater explosion and then readied for the approach of a second Betty, this one to port. The strengths of the twin-engine Betty, like so many other IJN-designed planes, were its lightness, speed, and long range. But its compromises—insufficient armor and vulnerable fuel tanks—earned it the nickname "flying lighter."

Now limbered up, *Bush* main battery gunners were ready for this target. Jim Collinson, a 28-year-old Rhode Islander and mount captain on No.1 gun (named "Helen" in tribute to his wife), was perhaps *Bush*'s most seasoned gunner's mate. His experience with the 5-inch-38 extended to service on cruiser *San Juan* (CL-54) in Iron Bottom Sound. To the newest sailors on Collinson's gun crew this might be a frightening, adrenaline-filled moment. To Collinson it seemed almost like a day at the office.

Pivoting Helen in local control, Collinson locked the gun on the Betty and squeezed off a steady stream of shots on what to him was the best kind of target—one closing dead on, getting bigger, and scarcely maneuvering. With *Bush*'s other guns locked on and firing as well, it was impossible to tell which mount's projectile finally connected with the Betty, igniting the flying lighter and sending its fireball into the water one hundred yards away.

The crash earned the *Bush* gunners a brief chorus of appreciative shouts, but they had less success with the next two attackers, a third Betty coming from astern to drop a poorly aimed bomb and, ten minutes later, a fourth Betty angling in on the bow. While topside gunners exhaled and readied for new attacks, ship technicians battled the equipment gremlins. A radar system, sonar gear, several radio circuits, and power to two of *Bush*'s 40-mm mounts went on the blink; whether the result of the mystery explosion or simply the nonstop hammering of ship's guns, the gremlins had to be chased down.

By now *Anderson* had pulled anchor and was under way, maneuvering in the V-shaped contours of Cabalian Bay and gaining speed. As *Bush* gun crews took on the covey of Bettys, *Anderson* gun crews were firing at two new beasts: the first a low-flying twin-engine Lily bomber, the second a diving Oscar single-engine, single-seat fighter—both aging IJA transplants from the China front. After making their brief runs, the Lily and Oscar both retreated west to the cover of land, soon to be replaced by a Betty coming from the north and low on *Anderson*'s starboard bow. This intruder flew to within one thousand yards before launching a torpedo. *Anderson*'s skipper rang up flank speed and ordered a turn hard to starboard. The torpedo's wake cleared close astern.

It was now 1012. While *Anderson*'s guns cooled, *Bush*'s banged away intermittently for an hour more, first at two Bettys attacking to port with torpedoes and strafing and then at a Zeke diving out of the clouds.

Standing exposed on the port bridge wing, Tony Lilly caught a piece of machine-gun shrapnel from one of the Bettys. It was another of those slow-motion moments: the Betty so close as it dropped its torpedo and passed the bow that Lilly swore he saw the pilot's face, and then the punch to his shoulder. The wound momentarily staggered and nauseated Lilly, but he kept to his feet and stayed on the bridge. Meanwhile, the pilot of the valedictory Zeke dropped a bomb, strafed *Bush*'s decks, and tried, perhaps, a suicide crash before disintegrating into the water off *Bush*'s starboard quarter.

The skies over both *Bush* and *Anderson* then went quiet, though hardly empty. Planes were still visible, buzzing faintly, annoyingly like mosquitoes out of reach. *Bush*'s radar screens remained flecked with unidentified bogeys even farther out. *Anderson* had fired about four hundred rounds of 5-inch 20- and 40-mm ammunition at its two predators. *Bush* gunners meanwhile had expended much more—close to

four thousand rounds in all. In *Bush*'s No. 4 mount, the firing pace
was so hectic that when the hot shell chute jammed, no time could be
spared to clear it. The gunhouse filled with acrid, choking smoke, and
it wasn't until the fracas ended that Ed Bennett, the mount's hot shell-
man, finally had time to clear the chute of brass casings.

Things also seemed to have quieted to the north, though damage control parties on *Claxton*, *Killen*, and *Ammen* still had their hands full.
From a distance, *Ammen*, with its stacks cocked and compressed like
hobo top hats, may have looked the sorriest victim, but it was actually in the best shape and would continue to operate for several more
weeks before being pulled for repair. *Killen*, stable but still bow down,
was inching its way to the sheltered notch of San Pedro Bay.

Out in Leyte Gulf, *Abner Read* still hovered near *Claxton*'s port
side, both ships plodding along at about 5 knots. Though the morning crisis seemed to have passed, it continued to be a nervous time.
With Tacloban itself cleaning up after Japanese air attacks, requests
for army air cover came up empty. Shortly after 1300, *Abner Read*'s
skipper Arthur Purdy, hoping to speed things up, dispatched a boat to
Claxton, sending with it his medical officer, a pharmacist's mate, and a
team of repair personnel.

Some sailors on *Abner Read* already had a taste of the sort of disaster *Claxton*'s crew was now contending with. In the dead of night little
more than a year before, while *Abner Read* was patrolling off Kiska
in the Aleutian Islands, the ship struck a floating mine. The explosion
punched a huge hole in *Abner Read*'s stern. Men sleeping in the after
berthing compartment awoke only to be overcome by smoke and then,
when the stern snapped off, were abruptly dropped into the frigid water. Lee Chase, a ship's mess cook, was one of a group of men lucky
enough to be thrown clear when the momentum of the still-spinning
propellers upended the detached stern. Chase struggled underwater
for what seemed an eternity before surfacing and finding his way to a
floater net. Hauled into another ship's lifeboat, Chase was brought on
board that ship (he never learned its name) and deposited in front of
a blower, buck naked (the way he'd left *Abner Read*) shaking, puking
fuel oil, and gasping for air.

Abner Read's losses were heavy that night—70 men dead or missing in the frigid water and another 50 injured—and she was eventually towed to Puget Sound for months of shipyard repair. (Most of the fantail survivors, including Lee Chase, ended up in hospitals, never to see the ship again.) At Puget Sound a new fantail had literally been bolted onto *Abner Read,* leaving a huge athwart-ships welding scar as a visible reminder to both veterans and replacements—and, it turned out, as a portent.

Abner Read's boat was still on its way over to *Claxton* when two undetected Vals dropped through low-cloud cover and lunged for both ships. The first Val briefly strafed *Claxton* and then pulled away. Purdy (who'd taken command after the Aleutians) rang up more speed to get *Abner Read* clear of the second, but this Val had already nosed into a steep dive. As the plane closed with *Abner Read,* its pilot released a bomb which, according to witnesses, dropped through No. 2 stack like a pocketed pool shot and exploded in the after boiler room. In the process, the Val lost a wing to *Abner Read*'s triple-A fire and cartwheeled to a collision with the ship's starboard side.

The Val's wreckage slammed into a 40-mm gun and then scraped diagonally across the deckhouse before tumbling to a stop on the main deck below. Fires from spilled aviation gasoline and from the after boiler room's explosion began cooking off *Abner Read*'s topside ready ammunition supplies. Heat also triggered the five torpedoes in the forward mount, sending each of them into the water on a blind trajectory. For a few frantic minutes, skippers on nearby battleships and cruisers ignored the air threat and maneuvered wildly to avoid the errant fish—and each other.

Suddenly *Abner Read,* which had stood by all morning to shield *Claxton,* became the ship in desperate need of help. *Claxton* tried briefly to approach *Abner Read* to fight fires, but exploding ammunition made it too risky. On *Abner Read,* amidships fires blocked escape routes to bow and stern and, with water pressure gone, it was impossible to flood belowdecks magazines. Another huge internal explosion sealed *Abner Read*'s fate. When Purdy ordered abandon ship at 1405, most crewmen who survived the amidships inferno were packed like cattle on either the forecastle or fantail.

Even before the order came, Sam McQueen, a gunner's mate on one of the main deck 20-mms had decided his only way out was over the side. As McQueen reached the railing, he bumped his left arm and noticed it had no feeling—he'd caught a big piece of shrapnel. McQueen managed to leap into the water, but he was a poor swimmer under the best of circumstances. With his left arm useless, he was sure he was going down.

Bob Brewer, a buddy in the water near McQueen offered to help, but McQueen urged Brewer to stay back—he'd just drag Brewer down with him. Brewer ignored McQueen's warning, grabbed him by his left arm and pulled him to a floating ammunition canister. McQueen was able to swing his good arm around the canister and stay afloat.

Less than ten minutes after Purdy's abandon ship order, *Abner Read* rolled to starboard and sank stern first. McQueen and Brewer were among the first survivors rescued—scooped up by *Abner Read*'s whaleboat and deposited on *Claxton*'s deck. *Claxton* gradually edged closer and so did destroyer *Richard P. Leary*, newly dispatched to the scene. Efforts to haul in some survivors raised horrible shrieks as rescuers' hands ripped swaths of burned skin from roasted limbs.

Frank Gauthier, a sailor assisting the rescue on *Leary*'s main deck, watched helplessly as one survivor tried to climb up a cargo net only to have the skin, flesh, sinew, and muscle of one arm rip away up to his elbow as the dying man tried to grasp the netting. Someone on *Claxton* finally thought to use the bed frames still strewn on the deck. With lines attached, the frames were lowered and suspended underwater. Survivors able to move were coaxed to paddle over the submerged frames and then were hoisted aboard like fish caught in a seine.

Recovery efforts paused for a final intruder; this time it was a Val in a shallow dive obscured by the veil of smoke from *Abner Read*'s fires and explosions. Finally, locking on the plane, gun crews from both ships threw up fire that ripped the Val to pieces and sent it into the sea.

Between them, *Claxton* and *Leary* eventually rescued all but 22 of *Abner Read*'s more than 300 crewmen. Despite all the terrible burn injuries, this was good fortune—a fraction of the lives lost a year before in the Aleutians. For the survivors aboard *Claxton*, another piece of good fortune was plucked from an otherwise awful day. *Abner Read*'s own doctor and pharmacist mates were now aboard *Claxton* and ready to give aid.

* * *

Dusk finally tossed the last kindling on the fires of a long day. Shortly after 1800, *Anderson* lookouts spotted three Oscars, the closest approaching bow-on just five thousand yards from the ship's starboard side. When an *Anderson* 5-inch round set the Val aflame, its pilot reacted by reversing direction, streaming up close along *Anderson*'s port side and ending his life in a side swipe crash. Most of the Val ended up in the water, but there was a brief loss of bridge steering control and gasoline-fed flames claimed five lives, including *Anderson*'s medical officer. By nightfall *Anderson,* its steering control restored, had joined up with *Bush* for mutual protection. *Bush* had survived the day without being hit and with only two casualties. As *Anderson* orbited *Bush*, *Bush*'s medical officer and two pharmacist's mates were sent over by boat to help.

What had happened in Leyte Gulf harked back to the Navy's worst days at Guadalcanal. While the attacks seemed amateurish, impromptu, and uncoordinated, they'd also been crudely effective. Within a few hours, using just a handful of aircraft, the Japanese had sunk one warship and badly damaged four others. Added to *Killen*'s 15 dead and *Abner Read*'s 22 were 4 from *Claxton* and 5 from *Ammen*. Only *Bush* had come through almost unscathed.

The attacks also added a new wrinkle. Beholding a buffet spread of three battleships and four cruisers, the predators had instead seemed to go for side dishes. While it was impossible to get inside the dead pilots' minds, it seemed, at least to *Abner Read*'s skipper, that each bomber was "very much on his own, and it was up to him to pick his target and make his attack."

In the case of *Claxton*, it was as if the Val pilot, determined to exchange his life for a ship but unable to reach *Shropshire,* had instead set upon *Claxton* as a more vulnerable target. Hubbard, *Claxton*'s skipper, admitted his surprise at being singled out. "It was expected the plane would re-attack that cruiser," he wrote in his action report, "and the lookouts were concentrating in that area."

Still, whatever the choice and whatever the motivation behind it, many of the tin can skippers and crews were certain of the Japanese pilots' intent. Barely a week since the first *kamikaze* success, the tactic's reality had now seeped into U.S. thinking and vocabulary. In his action report, Hubbard, for example, was sure the dive on *Claxton* was "of the suicidal type." And in *Bush*'s deck log, the final maneuver of the last Zeke to attack that morning was tallied as "an attempted suicide crash dive."*

The men also had a sense of the ironies and implications of the day's battles. "It is very discouraging," lamented *Abner Read*'s skipper Purdy (now ticketed for a court of inquiry) in his action report, "to . . . have a very fine ship with some 345 officers and men on it defeated by one lousy Japanese."

---

*Reflecting years later on the morning's events, Tony Lilly, *Bush*'s executive officer, was not so certain. The Japanese pilots, Lilly concluded, were more likely just inexperienced and inept rather than driven by suicidal fervor.

★ Chapter 11 ★

HI-RI-HO-KEN-TEN, November 1944

The Japs have got the kamikaze boys, and nobody else is going to get that, because nobody else is built that way.

—COMMANDER JOHN S. THACH

Elephants Fly

For the Japanese, *Sho-Go*'s dismal results were now at least partly offset by the promising new arc of *tokkō*. Body crashing might never win the war, but it could very possibly hold the Americans at bay and surely instill in them a dreadful sense of the cost of encroaching any farther on the Empire. Exaggerated reports of *tokkō* success could also bolster the morale of a home population starved for inspiration and begin paving the way for sacrifices that might be required of them later.

The news may even have raised hopes for a home front sideshow taking shape in the fall of 1944. Operation Flying Elephant, as it was called, involved launching thousands of large hydrogen-fueled balloons laden with explosives high into the Pacific jet stream. Its origins were long-shelved prewar experiments by the Japanese Military Scientific Laboratory, an outfit that also experimented with remote-controlled tanks and lethal high-voltage stun guns.

Carried east at 120 miles an hour in high-altitude "rivers of fast moving air," Flying Elephant's incendiary balloons would, it was estimated, reach the skies over America's Pacific Northwest in about sixty hours, there to descend, crash, and trigger their payloads, it was hoped, to ignite firestorms in Washington, Oregon, and Montana.

Considered a means for Japanese civilians to exact revenge after the humiliation of the 1942 Doolittle raid, Flying Elephant was also a way for them to participate in the spirit of *tokkō*—a way short of sacrificial death, at least for now. The balloon spheres (painstakingly assembled in theaters and stadiums by a workforce of paperhangers, schoolgirls, and sex industry workers), were fashioned by pasting overlapping strips of rice paper—600 strips to a sphere. To prevent damage to the balloons, workers were required to pare their nails and remove any sharp objects such as bobby pins. Suffering the effects of draconian wartime food rationing, younger assemblers were often scolded for eating the balloon paste.

Flying Elephant's "attacks on North America" kicked off with a flourish on 1 November, and in the next six months some 9,300 balloons were released from launch points all along Japan's eastern shores. Though it was ultimately too quixotic an effort to pose a meaningful challenge to American might, Flying Elephant's incendiary intentions foreshadowed a much more systematic and lethal campaign soon to rain down on Japan's own cities. Meanwhile, the desperate ardor that symbolized Flying Elephant churned away to produce more Special Attack pilots and devise even more radical Special Attack weapons.

Gods Graduate

In October 1944, while IJA pilot Ryuji Nagatsuka was stationed at a base north of Tokyo and still in fighter pilot training, another aspiring IJA flyer named Toshio Yoshitake was about to complete training as a reconnaissance-assault pilot. Yoshitake, 22, a graduate of Japan's elite Imperial Military Academy (IMA) was, in many ways, the mirror image of Yukio Seki, then about to become the icon of *Shinpu* Special Attack Unit in the Philippines. Like Seki, Yoshitake was the product of a prestigious military academy, and his family origins, while more traditional and upwardly mobile than Seki's, were also relatively modest.

In October, as Seki readied for the mission that would end his life, Yoshitake fine-tuned the skills so essential for flying on the China front: strafing, skip bombing, controlling artillery barrages, and directing the movements of ground troops. He was a promising pilot, especially in navigation and instrument flying. But even as Yoshitake and his buddies prepared for combat over China, the needs of the Pacific War prevailed. When they graduated, the eager novice pilots were told that instead of being posted to China, they would instead be dispatched to the Philippines to repel the American invasion. At a briefing in early November came even more startling news: they were to fly Special Attack missions.

With little time to adjust to a fate they'd not so much chosen as acquiesced to, Yoshitake and eleven other pilots took possession of brand new Mitsubishi *Ki-51* Type 99 assault aircraft. The *Ki-51* (American code name Sonia), a dive-bomber considered too slow and fragile for the rigors of the Pacific War, had proven its mettle as a ground attack plane in the China-Burma-India theater, largely because of its ability to operate from rough or muddy airfields. The planes assigned to them were specially modified to carry 500-kg bombs for suicide attacks. The pilots were given orders to ferry the *Ki-51*s via *Kyushu* and Formosa to an airfield near Manila on Luzon.

Oceans Shake, Dragons Crawl

October 1944 also marked the graduation of four hundred students from the Naval Torpedo School at Kawatana, near Sasebo. Following the departure ceremony (and another ceremony to greet the next class of four hundred), veteran destroyer captain Tameichi Hara, who'd been the school's commander since May, began his own farewell. Come December, Hara would take command of light cruiser *Yahagi*; he was as thrilled about going back to sea as he was relieved to be leaving Oppama's frustrations and disappointments behind. Japan's clumsy efforts to design conventional torpedo boats had produced terrible results, and Hara's students, though smart, eager, and dedicated, were mostly mismatched washouts from preliminary flight training.

During his time at the school, Hara watched from the sidelines as Japan's naval fortunes plummeted. In July he was ordered to shift the focus of his curriculum almost exclusively to tactics for fighting along Japan's coasts. It left Hara enraged at the ineptness of the IJN's top leaders, especially Takeo Kurita and Jisaburo Ozawa, and the rage only deepened with the disastrous October news filtering in from the Philippines.

But now that he was leaving—and taking a post where he could better control his own fate—Hara was upbeat as he welcomed Captain Toshio Miyazaki, the new senior instructor and an old friend. Miyazaki arrived by special train, bringing with him a top secret cargo he was anxious to show to Hara. The cargo, which had arrived stored in a separate car under armed guard, was transferred discretely to an abandoned torpedo firing range for Hara's inspection.

What Miyazaki unveiled for his friend were three small boats and a dozen sets of lightweight diving gear. The boats looked to Hara like ordinary motorboats, each built from plywood and powered by an automobile engine. "This craft is a surface *kamikaze*," Miyazaki announced to Hara in a stage whisper. Hara was appalled.

The boats, it turned out, had warhead bows that were to be packed with explosives. The diving gear would be used by frogmen carrying compact explosive charges to attach to the rudders and propellers of enemy ships. The boats with the warhead bows were given the name *Shinyo*, meaning "Ocean Shakers"; the frogmen would be *Fukuryu*, "Crawling Dragons."

Miyazaki explained to Hara that the much-touted use of *tokkō* volunteers in the Philippines had cemented decisions to use the concept on all fronts. The Torpedo School's four-hundred-man incoming class would be given the choice of conventional torpedo boat training or training in these new "sure to die" weapons.

Hearing all this, Hara felt sorry for his old friend and more relieved than ever he was leaving. The equipment looked flimsy, and the new students would be ill prepared to learn to operate it. Hara stayed at the school only long enough to help with the volunteer process. Once he got the results (two hundred chose conventional training, 150 opted to become Ocean Shakers, and the rest to become Crawling Dragons), Hara departed as quickly as he could, vowing never to look back.

Earth Turns Toward Heaven

One early November morning, personnel at Otsushima, a submarine base on a barren island near the southern tip of Honshu, mustered for a special ceremony. Officers, sailors and trainees lined up at attention under a cold, cloudy sky on either side of a long walkway sloping from the headquarters building of Special Base Unit One down to the docks. Three IJN submarines—*I-36, I-37,* and *I-47*—were lined up, their crews turned out and standing at attention along the subs' rails. Mounted atop the deck of each sub, forward of the conning tower, were four objects which, considering their size, shape, construction, and deep black hue, might have been each big sub's set of quadruplets.

On cue, a coterie of twelve men, each wearing a sleek new, one-piece uniform topped by a gleaming white ceremonial headband (called a *hachimaki),* emerged from the headquarters building. They strode briskly through the cordon of cheers, under the fluttering banners and past the toots and thumps of a small brass band. Leading the twelve was Sub-Lieutenant Sekio Nishina.

A year before, then Ensign Nishina and another IJN junior officer, Lieutenant Hiroshi Kuroki, had sown the seeds of this day's send-off. Both were stationed at Otsushima and consumed with devising ways to make better use of the IJN's best, but woefully underused, weapon— the Type 93 torpedo, what Americans called the Long Lance. In losing at Midway and being chased from the Solomons, the IJN had found ever fewer opportunities to use the Type 93 against American Navy ships.

The solution Kuroki and Nishina struck upon was both elegant and audacious: increase the Type 93's explosive payload, expand its hull to accommodate a human pilot, and configure it to be launched underwater from the deck of a fleet submarine. The two young officers then weathered months of bureaucratic intransigence to successfully champion a weapon whose final form was remarkably similar to their initial vision.

The first *kaiten* (roughly translated as "turn toward Heaven") was in fact a Type 93 torpedo split and widened to make room for its pilot, additional fuel and oxygen tanks, and an explosive payload triple the size of a conventional Type 93 warhead. Throughout the development process, *kaiten* planners and designers had gone through the motions of including ways for *kaiten* pilots to flee the craft just before striking a target. Indeed, an escape hatch was built into the bottom of the craft. Still, nearly all its trainees considered the *kaiten* to be a subsurface *Tokkotai* weapon—a "sure to die" coffin.

Just two months before, *kaiten* prototype testing had cost Hiroshi Kuroki's life. Trapped underwater for hours in a *kaiten,* Kuroki had dutifully made observations and taken notes up to the moment of his asphyxiation. This day, as Nishina made his way to the waiting sub-marines, he carried a ceremonial box containing Kuroki's ashes. When the twelve men (each, including Nishina, now a fully trained *kaiten* pilot) reached the docks, there was a hushed pause as the pilots bowed before a Shinto shrine. Then, in groups of four, the *kaiten* pilots went aboard the subs to which they'd been assigned.

Each climbed atop one of the *kaitens* and, brandishing ceremonial swords they'd received as gifts, waived triumphantly to the cheering well-wishers. Crewmen soon cast off lines, and the subs got under-way for a top secret destination and one-way missions for the twelve *kaitens.*

And Cherry Blossoms Fall

While the three *kaiten*-laden submarines neared targets known only to their captains, back in Japan small cadres of IJN student pilots were being introduced to yet another top secret new "super weapon." Be-fore getting a first peek at the mystery weapon, potential volunteers at Konoike Naval Air Base east of Tokyo (its gate sign read "Navy Thunder God Corps"), were given one last chance to opt out with the reminder: no one using the weapon could expect to come back alive.

Already, first sons, only children, and children of single parents had been winnowed from the pool of possible volunteers. The vol-unteer process itself had been timed to occur simultaneously on the same August 1944 day all across the ever shrinking but still immense,

Japanese empire. The call for volunteers went out to all the instructors and pilots of IJN single-engine aircraft—fighter planes, reconnaissance planes, carrier-based attack planes, and dive-bombers.

At that time, the pilots—a mix of both officers and enlisted petty officers—were given limited but explicit information: Japan was losing the war and would be unable to carry on without taking extreme measures. One of those extreme measures was a "very special instrument of certain death" developed by the Imperial Navy. "If you hit even the largest enemy aircraft carrier with this new weapon," they were told, "it will sink for sure!" Then the other shoe dropped before them: "The weapon has been designed as a one-way trip. There is no way the pilot can return alive."

Virtually all who received the call ended up volunteering—some with rabid enthusiasm, most with quiet acquiescence or fatalism. Each air corps had been required to categorize its volunteers as to mood: Very Eager, Eager, Earnest (reserved for those who submitted their acceptance in blood), and Compliant; and as to ability: Excellent, Good, or Fair.

Now, weeks later, at this threshold moment, with one last chance to back out, the pressure was sometimes enough to jolt a few into withdrawing. For those few who withdrew, it was both a step back toward life and social exile. They were unceremoniously removed from the room, never to see the weapon or to be seen again by those who stayed.

What was at last unveiled for the remaining volunteers was at once breathtaking and unremarkable. If the *kaiten* resembled a torpedo with a miniature conning tower, this top secret device resembled a torpedo with a cockpit.

The craft was about six meters long with stubby, mid-fuselage wings, and twin tail rudders made of fabric-covered plywood. The fuselage was metal alloy and a cluster of three rocket nozzles protruded from its tail. The craft's undercarriage consisted of a simple wooden skid. After being trained in the use of this slight, sleek craft, the volunteers were told proudly, they would ride them into battle as Divine Thunder pilots.

* * *

The long title for the superweapon was the Project *Maru Dai* special attack craft. *Maru* meant "circle" and *Dai* (which can be read "O") was a way of incorporating the name of the project's remarkable inventor: Special Service Sub-Lieutenant Shoichi Ota.

Young, broad-shouldered, and fully-bearded Ota, a character who would increasingly be shrouded in mystery, seemed to arrive out of nowhere at the doorstep of Japan's Naval Aeronautical Research Laboratory (NARL), part of the sprawling Yokosuka Naval Base. Ota was trained as a navigator, not a pilot, but he arrived with an idea—captured in a crude brush drawing—for a "glide bomber" with rocket engine boosters to be carried to the target vicinity by a twin-engine Mitsubishi G4M medium bomber (American code name Betty). Its "guidance system" would be a suicide pilot (he immediately volunteered himself) requiring only minimal flight training.

Ota's emergence would forever be suspect. The senior Japanese militarists advocating *Tokkotai* tactics often asserted they were being pressured from below by restive young frontline officers (like Nishina, Kuroki, and now Ota). Still, it seemed odd that Ota was somehow able to shepherd his crude idea through Japan's technical, manufacturing, and military labyrinths, and some wondered whether Ota was merely the face of a scheme hatched high up.

Whatever its true origins, Ota's man-guided glide bomber idea neatly capitalized on two converging circumstances—the desperate war conditions and Japan's increased commitment to developing rocket-based weapons using technology supplied by Axis partner Germany.

Maru Dai also smashed a convention. Everyone assumed airborne *Tokkotai* would be regular aircraft adapted for suicide use. Ota supplied a radical new concept (what today might be called a paradigm shift)—a craft built expressly for aerial suicide. The notion at first startled and dismayed the NARL designers. To this point they had designed traditional weapons; though adaptable for suicide use, suicide was not their origin. With *Maru Dai,* NARL designers' complicity would be complete: They would create weapons in which other men would invariably be consigned to die. "Before this war is over," muttered one researcher to another at the conclusion of Ota's astonishing concept presentation, "we, too, will have to take a dive on that plane."

* * *

Shoichi Ota's radical idea got the fast track. Ota made his pitch to the NARL staff in July 1944—within weeks of the fall of the Marianas. On 5 August, his concept was presented to the Naval General Staff, then at work on Operation *Sho-Go.* By mid-August, NARL received orders to begin trial production. In the meantime, the net was cast wide for volunteers to fly—and die—in *Maru Dai.*

Maru Dai specifications were explicit. Its fail-safe, armor-piercing warhead (weighing 2,600 pounds and triggered by six redundant fuses) would account for fully 80 percent of its loaded weight. Its speed would exceed that of any enemy aircraft encountered. At the same time, *Maru Dai* operational capabilities would be bare bones: precise enough to detach it from a transport bomber, stable and maneuverable enough to glide to the target. Most of the craft would be built from wood and other materials that were easy to obtain, assemble, and transport. *Maru Dai*'s range would be short and unquestionably one way.

Maru Dai's design and testing inevitably required compromises. Some trade-offs were routine: the craft's stubby wings needed to supply lift, but not so much that it would collide with its mother ship after release. Others were unfortunate but unavoidable: while most components could be wood and fabric, the fuselage required use of costly metal alloys.

Cruising range proved to be the biggest problem. As designed, the craft could not fly more than ten times the altitude from which it was dropped. Since the Betty's maximum altitude ceiling was 20,000 feet, *Maru Dai*'s maximum range would be forty miles. This, however, assumed ideal conditions. A more realistic cruising range was five rather than ten times drop altitude. This meant twenty miles, which meant the transporting Betty could have to get dangerously close to the target—within range of U.S. fighter screens and maybe even ships' guns. To increase the chance of success, *Maru Dai* missions would require fighter escorts—perhaps as many as four for each Betty transport.

The final design (along with this crucial caveat) was submitted to Navy General Staff. No one seemed to blanch; indeed a prompt go ahead was given to produce one hundred operational planes by the end of November. The first two planes emerged from manufacturing in early September and full production began immediately.

By then *Maru Dai* received a shorter and more inspirational name: Ōka, meaning "Exploding Cherry Blossom." Five symbolic pink cherry blossom petals were painted on the side of each craft's warhead nose.

In Revenge for 100 Million People

On 1 October 1944, the Navy Divine Thunder Unit was officially organized. Designated the 721st Naval Flying Corps, the unit included, in addition to its Special Attack component, Betty transport and fighter escort squadrons (though as yet no fighter planes). Ota was among the first personnel assigned to the 721st. Because he was not a pilot, Ota could not, strictly speaking, be an Ōka volunteer; instead, he would ride a Betty transport and be tasked with reporting mission results.

Before actually riding the Ōka, Divine Thunder student pilots were first trained on *tokkō* tactics using banged-up old Zekes. Only just before final graduation were students scheduled to get a single Ōka practice drop in a version of the craft stripped of booster rockets, ballasted with sand instead of explosives, and rigged with the wood landing skid.

Each pilot's "drop" was quite literally a "do or die" test of proficiency. Even without the boosters, the students got a wild two-minute ride followed, hopefully, by a high-speed "one-point" landing on a grass-covered field. About 10 percent of the practice drops resulted in crippling injury or death.

The successful graduates of this training made an odd lot. They included a sprinkling of young Naval Academy graduates (these "little gods" had important symbolic value), as well as older, rough-hewn, and boisterous petty officer fighter pilots. Even then, a few were hard to pigeonhole.

One of the enlisted pilots was Higher Flight Petty Officer Keisuke Yamamura. Because of his fighter combat experience, Yamamura supposedly had a dual role—both as a potential Ōka pilot and as a fighter escort pilot (if and when the promised escort planes arrived). For his part though, Yamamura wanted nothing more of traditional fighter operations. He was fully committed to flying the Ōka and branded those who expressed second thoughts as cowards. To dramatize his intent, Yamamura fashioned for himself an elaborate *hachimaki* that tailed to his waist. On it he inscribed his death statement: "Turning myself into a fireball, I shall now take revenge for 100 million people!" Though he may not have arrived that way, Yamamura fell squarely in the Earnest category.

In contrast to Yamamura, Reserve Sub-Lieutenant Saburo Dohi was not so easily tagged. Before volunteering for the IJN, Dohi had been training to be an elementary school teacher. He was shy and soft-spoken, but he could also be a profound thinker and a lively conversationalist about topics for which he had passion (like literature and philosophy) and with people he had gotten to know. Dohi was usually calm and composed during training—sometimes to the point of seeming to nod off. But he was also well versed on the Ōka and willing to share his insights with pilots new to the 721st Naval Flying Corps. On the scale of commitment, it was all but certain Dohi had not been rated Earnest or Very Eager, probably not even Eager. Compliant was probably the term that best suited him.

With manufacturing and pilot training both in full swing, Navy General Staff began deciding where and how to stage the weapons in suitable forward area air bases. These decisions came in November with America's invasion of Leyte well under way and the first Saipan-based American B-29 bombers making reconnaissance forays over Tokyo.

Ōka production targets leaped from 100 to 150. While Navy General Staff could not be entirely sure of the direction of America's next strategic jump, they decided to send 30 of the first 100 planes to the Philippines and the balance to Formosa.

On 8 November, the 721st made a move from its temporary location to Konoike Naval Air Base. Along with them went a promise from higher up to meet all their equipment needs, including twenty training Ōkas, thirty Bettys converted to transports, twenty Zeros, and an adequate cadre of support personnel—beetles.

At Konoike, in addition to its official Navy Thunder God Corps sign, hung a banner installed by the 721st's voluble mission commander Lieutenant Commander Goro Nonaka. It read: HI-RI-HO-KEN-TEN. ("Irrationality can never match reason; Reason can never match law; Law can never match power; Power can never match heaven.")

★ Chapter 12 ★

Target Paradise, November 1944

*For us, the American fighters were like dangerous microbes: we
had to exterminate them one by one and wipe out their breeding
ground, the aircraft carriers.*

—RYUJI NAGATSUKA

Everyone Needs Halsey

The Japanese had tossed two wrenches into MacArthur's Philippine
campaign. One had been experienced before, but the other, if not entirely new, at least had new implications. The Japanese troop reinforcements pouring through Leyte's back doors at Ormoc and nearby
Carigara were simply the latest rendition of the Tokyo Express. The
offensive-minded and (apparently) orchestrated airborne suicide hits
aimed at ships, however, were cause for alarm and caution.

They were already having a psychological impact. In little more
than a week, scuttlebutt about the phenomenon spread like a contagion through 7th Fleet ships. Sailors gloried in the strengths and capabilities of their ships but also knew their Achilles' heels. In that sense,
the contagion had already struck the psyches of carrier and tin can
sailors.

Few "Kaiser Coffin" sailors doubted their ships could be taken out
with one punch. Fleet carriers sailors could be proud of their ships'
resiliency, but also unnerved by the heavy casualties from secondary
explosions and fires. Tin cans had fought well on 1 November, but destroyers operating alone or on the point made tempting bait.

And what about the cruisers and battleships—they'd so far escaped, but how long could that hold? They would have to find out soon. Although 7th Fleet's biggest ships hadn't ventured beyond Leyte Gulf and Surigao Strait, they'd need to—and in force—in order to shut Leyte's back doors, capture Mindoro, and prepare to invade Luzon.

Maligned though he was, everyone now clamored for Admiral William Halsey's help. Halsey, who'd longed to have Task Force 38 planes beat the B-29s to the skies over Tokyo, saw that prospect fading. Instead, he'd have to cover MacArthur—but for how long and with what? The unavoidable answer was to bring back task groups from Ulithi ahead of schedule. Halsey's first move was to split off a ten-ship surface task group and send it racing westward to bulk up the forces in Leyte Gulf. The second was to recall two carrier task groups and position them east of Leyte. And the third was to advise Admiral Chester Nimitz that if Task Force 38 was to be used, as many carrier groups as possible should be mobilized. He would have to be allowed to do a thorough job while still protecting Task Force 38 from the new suicide menace. Nimitz gave Halsey the green light to begin air strikes on 5 November.

The air strikes across Luzon—two days of dawn fighter sweeps followed by rotating deck loads of fighter-escorted bombers—began as scheduled thanks to a break in the weather. *Lexington* fighter pilot Bruce Williams led a Hellcat section in a raid on airfields south of Manila. It was a tough mission against heavy flack and several squadron planes were lost, including one flown by VF-19's well-regarded XO Smiley Bowles. Pilots on other strikes got better results though: fewer casualties, lighter resistance, and good hunting, both against aircraft and shipping. Nearly 60 airborne kills were claimed on the first day, and combined aircraft destruction tallies (aloft and on the ground) exceeded 400. Bomber and torpedo crews also had a field day over Philippine bays and harbors. The biggest antishipping catch was IJN *Nachi*, Vice Admiral Kiyohide Shima's flagship during the Battle of Surigao Strait.

The Blue Ghost's Fourth Life

But the Japanese also snuck in a counterpunch early in the afternoon that same day. Despite heavy defense precautions, a raid of Zekes pounced on McCain's flagship *Lexington*. During more than a year of Pacific fighting, *Lexington* had been sunk three times according to Japanese propaganda bulletins earning the sobriquet "Blue Ghost". The closest call had been a December 1943 torpedo that temporarily crippled her steering gear. *Lex* CO E. W. Litch, met this latest menace—four incoming bogeys—with a hard turn to starboard to unmask *Lex*'s air defense guns.

As the 5-inch, 40- and 20-mm barrages began, Dick Fullam, a *Lex* catapult officer, was standing in the port catwalk. He saw two of the Zekes, one trailing the other and both flying at about two thousand feet, cross *Lexington*'s bow from port to starboard. For a moment, *Lexington*'s forward main batteries had the only decent shot, but then the Zekes' flight path unmasked starboard 40s and 20s as well. Quad 3—a 40-mm mount forward of the island above the main batteries—opened up. Quad 3 was a new station, but not a new job for first loader Ray Dora. Just five days before he'd been moved forward from Quad 11, an identical gun tub behind and below him on the starboard side of the island. Same job, different place—Dora knew his buddies on Quad 11 were about to join the shooting party.

Well beyond the bow, Zeke 1 and then Zeke 2 swung right to parallel *Lexington*'s starboard side and became ducks in a shooting gallery. Every starboard gun of every caliber had a clear shot. But as the Zekes reached the beam, both again turned right, now low on the water, and powered straight toward *Lexington*'s island. For the guns on and near the island, the Zekes presented smaller profiles on growing targets. From his oblique view on Quad 3, Dora could see the Zekes taking hits, but still coming in.

On the port catwalk, Fullam saw the Zekes' wing guns wink and instinctively ducked. When he popped up, Zeke 1 was gone, but Zeke 2 was still inbound. Fullam ducked again.

Quad 3's crew kept firing as Zeke 2 grew bigger in their sights. Dora heard a riot of sound around him—it was like being in an echo chamber—but he kept dropping clips into the loading hopper. The crew was still working fast, desperation overtaking precision.

Meanwhile, in the buttoned-up spaces of the island, Charlie Ryberg, a radioman in Radio 1, and Ralph Truax, a signalman in After Control, followed the action in much the way *Lexington*'s belowdecks sailors did—by the acceleration of the ship, the heavy turn to starboard, and the sequence of the guns: first 5-inch, then hammering 40s, and last, the fast percussion of the 20s. Eager to see what was happening, Truax stepped to a catwalk outside After Con. Expecting a wash of light, a cool wind, and a bird's eye view, Truax instead got a backside whoosh of searing heat.

In Radio 1, Charlie Ryberg heard a muffled crash followed by a big, shuddering bang. The power was still on and equipment functioning, but smoke poured from compartment air vents. Andy DeWald, the Radio 1 lead, reported casualties above. With DeWald's okay, Ryberg grabbed a first aid kit and went to help.

Zeke 2 had struck the island's third level, and its bomb blast opened a seam in After Con. Fire fueled by aviation gasoline pushed through the seam, incinerating most of the men inside. On After Con's port catwalk, Truax stood just at the disaster's fringe: still alive and in one piece, but with flash burns on his head, neck, arms, and hands.

Collision and blasts rained fire and shrapnel down on gun crews in the 40- and 20-mm tubs as well as the starboard catwalk beneath. At Quad 3, Ray Dora was tossed to the deck. Quad 11, Dora's old station, had been wiped out.

Dick Fullam heard neither crash nor explosion from the port catwalk, but he did hear his talker shouting, "We've been hit!" Jumping to the flight deck and sprinting aft, Fullam soon saw *Lexington*'s XO Thomas Ahroon standing outside After Con's inboard hatch. Ahroon's face was beet red from flash burns, but he was already shouting for hoses to be brought over.

For the moment, Ralph Truax had no idea what had happened and no inkling he'd been burned. He tried to get back to After Con, but he saw that was impossible. Instead he stumbled forward toward the signal bridge looking for his buddies there.

Charlie Ryberg carried the first aid kit up a level to the starboard side of flag plot. The hatch was blown open, and Ryberg saw four or five wounded men inside, including Lieutenant Barney Carmen, a Signal Division officer. Carmen was sprawled face down, the back of his shirt awash in blood. Ryberg knelt down next to him, but Carmen, groaning, told Ryberg to check the others. (Carmen's back, Ryberg would later learn, had been pierced by the trigger mechanism of one of the crashed Zeke's machine guns.) Ryberg injected Carmen with a morphine Syrette and moved to help the others.

Up on the signal bridge, conditions were just as bad. The signal room hatch was blown, and through it Ryberg saw Truax. Moffet, a signalman, lay dead, his head severed, near Truax's feet. From this perch, Ryberg and Truax could see the destruction in the 40- and 20-mm gun tubs below. Ryberg stood unbelieving as others—*Lex*'s dentist, its Catholic chaplain Father Cope, and several pharmacist's mates—arrived and spread out to assist. Somebody took Truax below to sick bay. Ryberg returned to Radio 1.

Fullam, after manning a fire hose near After Con, worked his way up through the island to rescue wounded. He helped one burn victim clad only in shorts and another with a nearly severed leg; as with Charlie Ryberg, the most anguishing sights were the gun tubs. Fullam particularly remembered one dead sailor whose knees were hooked on the rim of the tub sponson, the remainder of his body positioned as though he were attempting a headstand. "Boy what a mess there was up there," the ship's electrician Bob Davis would write in his diary entry for the day. "Legs and arms, head and all parts of bodies all over the place."

Despite the mayhem, the *Lexington* was able to resume air operations. When VF-19's Bruce Williams returned from a sweep, he could see the damage as he made his approach. When he touched down, Williams noticed at once the awful smell of burnt metal and steel and the sight of the carnage around *Lex*'s island. Someone pointed out the remains of the Japanese pilot, still dangling from the island amid a tangle of metal and wire. The pilot's body would not be cut down until the next day.

Late that afternoon, when Bud King, 19, one of Fullam's catapult crew, headed across the deck on his way to the crew mess hall, he was waylaid by a pharmacist's mate rounding up volunteers for a work detail. The day's fatalities (the final tally would be nearly 50 dead with another 130 wounded) needed to be carried to the after elevator for the trip to the hangar deck and preparation for burial at sea. King was normally no volunteer, but as tired and hungry as he was, he knew it wasn't a request he could shrug off. The detail worked until nightfall, and after the job was done, it seemed days before King could sleep or eat.

After this first intense round of air strikes, Nimitz's naval representative, meeting in Tacloban with MacArthur and his staff, lobbied MacArthur to release Task Force 38 for three to four weeks of East China Sea operations. Nimitz's—and Halsey's—case seemed to be bolstered by Task Force 38's interception of a troop and supply convoy as it off-loaded a mile off Ormoc. Air strikes on 11 November sank virtually the entire convoy. The transports, it turned out later, carried about 10,000 troops and only a handful escaped.

It was a near replica of the blow that turned the tide at Guadalcanal, but MacArthur remained adamant. He expected the Japanese to keep trying to reinforce and defend Leyte to the bitter end. And now, after a brief fair-weather interlude, monsoon weather was back, further delaying the construction of Army air bases on Leyte. MacArthur wanted no chance of a stalemate.

Nimitz broke the news to a disappointed but subdued Halsey on the 13th. Air strikes concentrated next on Philippine area shipping. Lulls caused by foul weather or refueling were used, ironically, to allow the Japanese to "restock" the Islands' bays and harbors with fresh target opportunities.* It was the first formal unveiling of McCain's Big Blue Blanket concept.

On into November, Task Force 38 began taking a predictable, time clock approach to its work. As sure of their might as they were of their crews' fatigue, it was almost as if Halsey and his planners had lost

---

*One carrier group was also diverted to strike Yap, a bypassed Japanese-held island east of the Philippines and southwest of Ulithi. Air strikes there produced disappointing results, and blame fell on the faulty performance of a new secret weapon, an incendiary chemical jelly called napalm. The task group admiral complained that if napalm couldn't be rejiggered to ignite more reliably, his planes might as well be armed with empty beer bottles.

focus and urgency. The Big Blue Blanket smothered Luzon every six or seven days, usually originating from the same spot in the Philippine Sea and following the same launch routine.

Because of scheduled refit rotations, Task Force 38 was now usually down to two carrier groups on station with a third group en route to Ulithi and a fourth returning. Task Force 38 faced a constant resource dilemma: how to balance punishing air strikes with keeping a leak-proof C.A.P. umbrella overhead.

For their part, the Japanese were getting wise to the pace and place of U.S. Navy operations. Snoopers tracked the comings and goings of task group ships from Ulithi—a target paradise if they could slip by its defenses. They rightly sensed opportunities against an enemy basking in the glow of spectacular victories and unchallenged domination. The Japanese also saw chances to test the prowess of their evolving Special Attack arsenal.

Cauldron of Sleep

Ulithi, seen through the periscope of Japanese submarine *I-47* on the morning of 19 November, was indeed a target paradise. The *I-47* hovered just below the surface near islands on the west side of the atoll. Lieutenant Commander Zenji Orita, *I-47*'s skipper, sighted three cruisers and, beyond to the southwest, the outsized profiles of battleships and aircraft carriers. Other ships were moored at the center of the harbor, and distant wisps of stack smoke confirmed the presence of still more.

There was no need to doubt the accuracy of aerial reconnaissance reports relayed to the *kaiten* mother submarines. Ulithi lagoon was crammed: four fleet aircraft carriers, three battleships, and numerous cruisers, destroyers, transports, oilers, and other auxiliary vessels—perhaps two hundred ships in all.

Beginning with Sekio Nishina, *I-47*'s CO Orita gave each of the *kaiten* pilots a chance to look through the scope. Nishina stared for two long minutes before abruptly relinquishing the scope to the next man. Later that day he wrote in his diary of the "golden opportunity to use *kaiten*."

* * *

Two days before, Toshio Yoshitake and eleven of his *tokkō* squadron mates had reached Pollack Airfield on Luzon. The trip from Japan, expected to take two days, had stretched to more than a week because of mechanical problems.

Following a day of rest, the pilots set off on the 19th to pay a courtesy visit to Fourth Air Army headquarters in Manila. They rode on the back of a flatbed truck, and as the truck neared Manila, they heard distant explosions and saw huge plumes of black smoke. Smoke rose above what they assumed was Clark Airfield, a short distance from Pollack.

One of the ships Orita, Nishina, and the three other *kaiten* pilots may have seen through *I-47*'s periscope on the morning of the 19th was auxiliary oiler *Mississinewa (Miss)*, part of Service Squadron (ServRon) 10. After completing an early underway replenishment (unrep) in the Philippine Sea, *Miss* had returned to Ulithi on 15 November. The crew spent all the next day filling *Miss*'s tanks to near capacity: 404,000 gallons of aviation gas, 9,000 barrels of diesel oil, and 90,000 barrels of fuel oil. *Miss* then moved to anchorage in berth No. 131 near sister oilers *Lackawanna* (AO-40) and *Cache* (AO-67).

For *Miss*'s three-hundred-man crew the days were mostly filled with routine drudgery and overwhelming heat. At night, though, there might be a break (at least for those not on watch)—a chance to watch a movie under Ulithi's open, secure skies. The movie for the night of 19 November was *Black Parachute*, a spy thriller about secret agents battling Nazis.

After the movie, some sailors headed belowdecks to bunks in the sauna-like berthing compartments. Others, like Winston Whitten, 22, chose to spend the night topside. Whitten, a tool and dye maker before the war and now a 1st Class motor machinist's mate, had taken in the screening of *Black Parachute* before standing midwatch in *Miss*'s engine room. Relieved from watch at 0400, Whitten and a buddy, instead of bunking below, strapped hammocks to stanchions on *Miss*'s after cargo deck. They joined dozens of other *Miss* crewmen already asleep here and on the forward cargo deck. It was cooler—at least compared to the engineering spaces and berthing compartments. Through breaks in the ever-threatening monsoon clouds, they also got a tropical sky full of stars.

Earlier that same evening, over a farewell dinner, the *kaiten* pilots toasted their mission with fine sake in ceremonial lacquer bowls, a gift reported to be from the Emperor himself. After dinner the four men purified themselves with spring water and all, except Sekio Nishina, shaved and trimmed their hair. They then retired to their bunks and their thoughts.

At 0300, Nishina and another of the *kaiten* pilots crawled through watertight access tunnels connecting *I-47*'s interior with the bottom hatches of their *kaitens*. These hatch exits—ostensibly installed as escape routes for the *kaiten* pilots—now doubled as entrances. Unfortunately, it had only been possible to equip each mother submarine with two of these conduits. Accordingly, just after midnight, *I-47* had surfaced briefly to permit the two other *kaiten* pilots to enter their craft to await the launch. Then *I-47* submerged for its final approach into Ulithi.

The launches began at 0415. Nishina's craft was released first; the others followed at five-minute intervals. All four *kaitens* were underway by 0430, each tracking independently to a specific target area within the lagoon, each scheduled to strike at 0500.

The *kaiten* pilots could adjust their crafts' depth, attack course, and speed by manipulating controls for diving planes, a rudder and a valve mechanism that helped steady the craft by letting in seawater as fuel was consumed. The ideal speed was 20 to 30 knots, the ideal depth was fifteen feet—a piloting challenge under the best of conditions and a consummate feat for men about to die. For all intents and purposes, each traveled blind. Instructed not to rise to periscope depth until just before impact, the pilots depended on initial target bearing and range, adjusting en route to the readings of their gyro-compasses and stop-watches.

By 0545 the day had already begun for many of the crewmen on ships moored at Ulithi. The sky was filling with light and predawn C.A.P.; the calm harbor waters below were scribbled by the wakes of whaleboats, harbor shuttles, and patrol craft. Aboard *Miss*, Fernando (Cookie)

Cuevas, 33, had been awake since well before reveille. Cookie Cuevas and two other cooks were busy in *Miss*'s crew galley, located in the deckhouse aft, readying breakfast.

Herb Daitch, the ship's No. 2 winch operator was also awake and sitting on the edge of his bunk when, at 0547, *Miss*'s aviation forward gas storage tanks exploded. The blast concussion tossed Daitch and other sailors in the compartment to the deck like bowling pins. Cookie Cuevas was checking a galley oven when he was knocked down too. Cuevas didn't know what it was, but it felt big and bad. He grabbed a life jacket and headed to the crew quarters one deck below.

Sleep turned to a cauldron—a waking, living, and dying nightmare—for men who'd been sleeping on *Miss*'s forward cargo deck. Most were set on fire, 15 were killed instantly. On the after cargo deck, sailors like Whitten, who'd suffered no worse than a hard fall from his hammock, raced forward on the starboard side only to be chased back by the intense heat.

In officer's country above decks on the port side, the blast woke Charley Scott with a start. He instinctively jumped from his upper bunk only to land on the shoulders of his roommate Jim Lewis. Once they'd untangled themselves, Scott and Lewis looked through their porthole, but couldn't see what happened. Both men jumped into trousers and shoes, and ran out to investigate. Though he had seen nothing yet, Scott was all but certain *Miss* was doomed.

On his way from the galley, Cookie Cuevas woke sailors in the berthing compartments. When he reached the stern, the ship's midsection was rocked by another explosion. The noise of this explosion rose above the screams of injured men. Then came the panic-mad whoops and bells of calls to battle stations from ships all across the lagoon.

Already, a flaming oil skim was hugging *Miss*'s hull forward, flowing aft like a turgid river. While there were some patches of black slick near the stern and more forming, there were also huge swaths of translucent lagoon water—a sight once so ordinary now turned vital for those trying to escape. Some sailors jumping into the water picked their spots carefully, while others dove blindly. Winston Whitten, one of the first over the port side, was scooped up by *Miss*'s own whaleboat, which soon headed for oiler *Lackawanna,* loaded to the gunwales with survivors.

For a few minutes Charley Scott thought he was trapped on *Miss*'s superstructure, but he managed to find a ladder leading down to the main deck. He also jumped off the port side, well clear of the oil, and swam a strong stroke to get as far away as possible. A whaleboat from *Cache* stopped and offered to pick him up, but Scott declined, motioning the coxswain to keep heading toward *Miss*.

Herb Daitch was purposely not wearing a life jacket as he readied himself to jump—and he urged others around him to take theirs off too. Daitch knew if he ended up surrounded by oil, he'd have to get underwater fast. Cookie Cuevas, meanwhile, faced a momentary dilemma. Frank Lutz, *Miss*'s Chief Commissary Steward, standing calmly on the fantail kept telling Cuevas: "You've got plenty of time." Lutz was Cuevas's boss, and he didn't want to seem disrespectful, but finally he couldn't wait any longer. "I'm gone!" Cuevas yelled back to Lutz as he dropped over the side.

At 0830, *Miss* rolled and sank into the sandy bottom of Ulithi's spotless lagoon. Many of her 63 fatalities went with her, entombed in a hulk that continued to leak oil for decades. Others, including Frank Lutz, failed to make it out of the water alive. Survivors Daitch and Whitten ended the morning on *Lackawanna* and Cookie Cuevas on *Enoree* (AO-69). Charley Scott finally made it to *Cache*, which also sheltered Jim Lewis and *Miss* CO Philip Beck. Scott doubled as *Miss*'s communications officer, so he spent the rest of the day on *Cache*'s bridge, communicating by TBS with other ships to track down the locations of survivors.

Lexington was then at Ulithi undergoing round-the-clock repair. Blue Ghost diarist Bob Davis sensed the pace of repair would soon send them back at sea. Meanwhile, in the way of sailors who learned to compartmentalize war's tragedies, Davis had only a brief entry about the "two-man subs" across the lagoon. "Luckily we spotted them before they did too much damage. They did blow up one of our tankers, tho."

False Starts, Great Triumph

Later that same day, when Yoshitake and his squadron mates returned from Manila, they found Pollack Airfield a shambles. The explosions and smoke they'd seen the day before were from an American air strike that left all twelve of their planes either completely demolished or badly shot up. Under most circumstances the pilots would have simply waited at Pollack for new aircraft to arrive. Instead, crews bustled to salvage what they could and, within two days, were able to piece together four flyable *Ki*-51s.

As soon as these planes were ready, four pilots—one of them Toshio Yoshitake—were ordered to fly them south to Negros. Within moments of takeoff, however, the weather turned so foul that all four made emergency landings at another airfield near Manila. Once more, fate intervened. Both Yoshitake and his plane were grounded—Yoshitake with a dose of bone-rattling dengue fever, his makeshift *Ki*-51 with elusive engine problems.

On the night of 24 November, American B-29s began saturation bombing of Tokyo, raids that shocked and devastated all of Japan. Because the raids threatened to disrupt *Ōka* production, a move was under way to move the *Ōkas* to Kure, a port city at the southern end of Kyushu. From there, they would be deployed to Formosa and the Philippines. *Ōka* manufacturers were then working nonstop to complete the first one hundred aircraft. It was not until late in the evening of 27 November that these were packed and sent off to be loaded aboard the huge new supercarrier *Shinano*.

Shinano itself was fresh from final construction at Yokosuka Naval Shipyard. Originally envisioned as a super battleship on the order of *Yamato* and *Musashi*, *Shinano* had begun a mid-construction conversion following Midway. *Shinano* emerged in November 1944 as the largest aircraft carrier ever in terms of both tonnage and length. To protect the ship while it was being fitted out and made ready for deployment, it was decided to move it to the Inland Sea. En route the *Shinano* would off-load the *Ōkas* at Kure.

* * *

After the Ulithi attack, submarine *I-47* had stayed at periscope depth as long as its skipper Zenji Orita dared. Finally, however, he had no choice but to crash dive and escape attacks by American destroyers. Before leaving the area, *I-47* recorded a handful of explosions in the harbor, including two large ones around 0600.

Ten days later, *I-47* and sister submarine *I-36* reached the Japanese naval base at Kure.* *I-36* arrived with three living but shame-faced and disconsolate *kaiten* pilots; their *kaitens* had jammed in the racks during repeated launch attempts and were still strapped to the sub's deck. Two days later a large conference was convened to evaluate mission reports by the two submarine skippers.

For his part, *I-47*'s skipper Zenji Orita did not think the mission had gone that well; he hoped to convince planners to focus on using *kaitens* in enemy shipping routes instead of protected anchorages. Senior participants, however, were all too eager to extrapolate from scraps of evidence—Orita had witnessed two columns of fire while *I-36*'s skipper detected two explosions.

Japan needed heroes and sacrificial readiness now as much as it needed results. Ignoring the possibility that the fires and explosions may have risen from one target, the meeting participants enthusiastically endorsed hopes for the *kaiten* and simultaneously honored the memories of the dead patriots. Nishina, the summary concluded, had sunk an aircraft carrier; each of the other four *kaiten* pilots had sunk a battleship.

---

*Submarine *I-37*, its *kaiten* still attached, was sunk during a coordinated attack by destroyer escorts *Conklin* (DE-439) and *McCoy Reynolds* (DE-440) near the entrance to Kossol Passage in the Palau Island group.

Chapter 13

Suicide at Its Best, November–December 1944

Only the present exists for a pilot. Farewell, past!

—RYUJI NAGATSUKA

Phantoms of the *Intrepid*

Task Force 38's high-risk juggling of strike missions and C.A.P. faltered midday on 25 November as its two carrier groups were simultaneously readying a strike—the third of the day—and recovering planes. Within a half hour, *Hancock* (CV-19), *Essex* (CV-9), and *Cabot* each took painful but glancing suicide-style hits. Meanwhile, *Intrepid* reeled from two staggering blows just minutes apart.

The first plane came in high and took out a 20-mm gun crew on its way into *Intrepid*'s flight deck. The plane might have sliced cleanly through to the hangar deck had its bomb not exploded at the gallery level, blasting upward into a ragged dome of splintered timbers and downward into a spray of hot shrapnel, which quickly touched off fires and threatened ready stores of aviation gas and ordnance.

The second punch—less than five minutes later—was more shallow, a *kamikaze* swooping in low from astern to a skidding crash that flung debris and shrapnel from the impact point well aft all the way to the bow. Sal Maschio, a portside 20-mm gunner, leaned down to inspect what to him resembled a gasoline rag. Another gunner saw it, realized it was part of the pilot's scalp, and tossed it over the side.

The plane's bomb, which pierced the flight deck near the crash point, exploded at the hangar level, sending a new round of secondary blasts rippling through the ship. In flag plot, three levels above the flight deck, task group commander Vice Admiral Gerald F. (Bogey) Bogan, fidgeted a few minutes before finally removing the admiral's stars from his shirt collar. Instructing his senior officers to do the same, Bogan headed down to the flight deck, his staff in tow. Jake Fegely, 19, the flag plot radar operator, left his set and fell in line behind the brass. Fegely spent the next hours manning a fire hose.

Ed Coyne, an aviation machinist's mate stationed forward on *Intrepid*'s flight deck, was a safe distance from the fires, but two of Coyne's best buddies, weren't. Right after the first crash, Raymond Rucinski, who was part of the same fueling team as Coyne, was released to go below and help out. Coyne realized Rucinski had likely reached the hangar deck before the second crash. And Coyne was certain his other buddy, Sern (Shorty) Nelson, had been down there all along. Both, it turned out, were among the many *Intrepid* sailors killed that afternoon.

Coyne, Nelson, and Rucinski had all been assigned to the same hangar-level berthing compartment. Although only a bulkhead separated it from the burned-out hangar, the compartment itself had been spared. Coyne and other sailors who tried to bunk there that night were spooked by what some swore was the sound of funeral music coming from *Intrepid*'s electric organ.

The organ (a donation from a stateside church) sat atop a bulkhead-mounted pedestal on the far side of the hangar, intact but inoperable. Still, the specter of a phantom organist seemed of a piece with the day. Coyne knew it was just the wind or a trick of jittery imaginations performing to susceptible ears. Still, he found it impossible that night and in the days ahead to nudge the ghosts of Nelson and Rucinski from his dreams.

Valedictions

The next afternoon, *Intrepid*'s crew buried its dead. It was a remarkably calm day in the Philippine Sea, and *Intrepid* seemed to move through it at funereal pace. Ranks of dungaree-clad sailors were assembled three and four deep in an open hangar bay aft of the port side deck elevator. Debris had been cleared to make room, but a malodorous pall of smoke and burned flesh remained. Flanked by *Intrepid*'s two chaplains, its CO and XO, a Marine color guard, and the ship's band, the dead lay in ordered rows, each corpse encased in a canvas shroud weighted with a shell canister.

Two sailors stood at attention by each of the shrouded bodies. These escorts, pooled from various ship's divisions, were responsible for lifting and moving the bodies forward as the service progressed and, finally, with dropping them into the sea. Don Lorimer, a 20-year-old seaman who had joined *Intrepid* in December 1943 (enough time to have attended other of these ceremonies and memorized the Navy Hymn's first verse), was a gunnery division delegate. The day before, Lorimer was stationed aft in one of the port side 40-mm gun sponsons. Both planes hit forward of where he had stood, and servicing the gun had kept him from seeing the chaos they caused. Lorimer suspected his crew had fired at one or both of the bogeys, but there was no way to be sure they'd done anything or could've done any better.

The corpse assigned to Lorimer was among the last to go over. He and his partner had to lift the body several times, and each time shuffle it one row closer to the side. As they did, Lorimer wondered about the dead sailor he was carrying to his grave. He had recognized only one name from the casualty list, a sailor he'd met once when both pulled mess cook duty. Lorimer also realized the shroud might contain just a mismatched collection of body parts from several dead crewmen. Whoever it was made for a heavy load and probably would sink even without the shell casing. By the time the two sailors reached the deck combing, lifted the body, and released it over the side, Lorimer was completely exhausted.

Within days of the funeral aboard *Intrepid* (and ceremonies like it on *Cabot* and *Essex*), Admiral William Halsey got his respite from the Philippine operations. While its individual task groups had been spelled intermittently to refit and replenish, Task Force 58 had been operating in the crucibles of the South China and Philippine Seas for eighty-four straight days; five fast carriers (*Intrepid* and *Cabot* now joined *Lexington, Belleau Wood,* and *Franklin* on the list) needed major repairs. Instead of "further casual strikes," Halsey pointedly argued in his departing summary report, "only strikes in great force for valuable stakes or at vital times would justify exposure of the fast carriers to suicidal attacks."

Halsey firmly believed this "great force, valuable stakes, vital times" measuring stick no longer held for Leyte. Time and space were running out for Japanese defenders there. All through November, U.S. 6th Army troops pressed a slow two-pronged advance across Leyte's coastal roads, mountains, and jungles. The Japanese countered with more infusions of troops and a stubborn resistance that took advantage of formidable terrain and interior lines.

Both sides were fighting the weather as much as each other. To advance, Americans literally had to bring their own roads; Army engineers hauled loads of gravel to cover swamped-out stretches of Highway 2, the conduit for the push from the north and east. Infantrymen on each front were plagued with "immersion foot," a polite name for the ravaging condition GIs in Europe called trench foot.

After first closing Leyte's back door at the Carigara on 4 November (less by assault than by the Japanese abandoning it), GIs converged on Ormoc. GIs got stalled but finally bulled through fierce resistance at Breakneck Ridge, the northern anchor of Japan's defense line on Leyte. Breakneck was a gateway to a ravine GIs later called "Death Valley" after they found immense piles of bloated Japanese corpses—reinforcements mowed down by American artillery.

Meanwhile, an amphibious landing on Leyte's southeast coast speeded progress for units pushing overland from the first beachheads near Tacloban. By 1 December, 6th Army pincers joined to give MacArthur control of all of Leyte except its westernmost peninsula and a Japanese defensive perimeter around Ormoc. Twenty-four thousand Japanese troops had died in the process, and the remaining 35,000 were hemmed in with their backs to the sea.

As Japan played for time in the Philippines, the *Ōka* project took what looked to be a prudent, almost precautionary step toward deploying the craft to Formosa and the Philippines. After a consignment of one hundred *Ōkas* was loaded and stowed on board, aircraft carrier *Shinano* and three escorting destroyers left for Kure, there to off-load the *Ōkas* and a cadre of support technicians.

It was a short trip—several hundred miles hugging close to Japan's southeast coast. But almost from the start, the convoy was shadowed by *Archer-Fish* (SS-311), a U.S. submarine standing offshore to rescue downed crews during the first B-29 raids on Tokyo. *Archer-Fish* stalked the convoy for two days as it zigzagged toward Kure. Finally, on 29 November, *Archer-Fish* struck. Four torpedoes hit *Shinano* squarely and eight hours later she went down, taking most of her crew and passengers and all of her top secret cargo.

The loss of *Shinano* and of the consignment of *Ōkas* initially seemed a crippling blow. A veil of secrecy fell: survivors who knew about *Shinano*'s secret cargo were quarantined to contain word of the loss. At the same time, with the war telescoping in on Japan, the loss of a supercarrier was not the devastating blow it might once have been.

As for the *Ōka*, the small wood-and-aluminum-constructed craft were cheap and easy to assemble. Indeed, production churned along. On 1 December 88 *Ōkas* were shipped overland to Kure. From there thirty were to be sent to Clark Airfield in the Philippines and the balance to Formosa. Another fifty craft were ordered to partly offset the loss of the first one hundred.

Meanwhile at sunset on the day of the *Shinano* disaster, "traditional" suicide aircraft took their parting November swipes at a Leyte Gulf task group now scaled back to just twenty-five ships—nine of them battleships and cruisers. With no beachheads to pound, the big ships— in concert with sixteen destroyers—were being used primarily to shield inbound and outbound re-supply convoys.

Two days before, while heavies and tin cans refueled from a tanker in Leyte Gulf (using a merry-go-round formation, two ships fueled while the rest circled), thirty Japanese torpedo planes and dive-bombers dropped through a screen of low clouds to attack. Answering to a raucous chorus of GQ alarms, fueling stopped, ships dispersed, and steel curtains of antiaircraft fire went up.

James Fahey, a sailor manning a 40-mm gun aboard *Montpelier* (CL-57) (then just returning to the Southwest Pacific after a stateside overhaul), confided to his diary that the melee was the crew's first ever exposure to aerial suicide. "Before the attack," Fahey wrote in his entry for the day, "We did not know they were suicide planes, with no intention of returning to their base." Fahey saw one attacker crash cruiser *St. Louis* (CL-49) and another hit battleship *Colorado* (BB-45) before *Montpelier*'s got its turn. "We knocked our share of planes down, but we also got hit by three suicide planes. . . . Lucky for us they dropped their bombs before they crashed into us."

The ships were not completely without air cover. A few Army Air Force P-38s (twin-engine, single-seat fighter-bombers with their unmistakable twin tail booms) skirted the raid's fringes but seemed wary about getting involved. "When we opened up on the Jap planes," Fahey noticed, "they got out of range of our exploding shells. They must have had a ringside seat of the show." Meanwhile, the sky above the ships seemed to fill up like a junkyard with planes, bullets, bombs, and debris, most of which would have to fall. Sure enough, Fahey later wrote, "It looked like it was raining plane parts."

This midday Monday ambush was then followed by Wednesday's attacks—two *kamikaze* raids piercing a sunset which seemed, at least to historian Samuel Morison's eyes, "a theatrical setting for a suicide attack." GQ—to Fahey's ears "an awful loud frightening sound" with "trouble written all over it"—actually first rang at 1630 on *Montpelier*.

A preliminary probing thrust—only a few planes bombing and strafing but "a tussle while it lasted,"—was followed minutes later by the real thing. Fahey saw one plane miss with a bomb run on cruiser *Portland* (CA-33) and then run across the formation, miraculously escaping shell blasts and gaining altitude before finally banking in a power dive toward battleship *Maryland* (BB-46).

"This was suicide at its best," Fahey wrote later with an almost admiring detachment. "He came down so fast that if he dropped a bomb, he would have beaten it to the ship." The *kamikaze* ended up striking between *Maryland*'s forward main batteries, a collision, explosion chain, and sky-lighting bonfire that took 31 sailors' lives and burned or wounded 30 more. Like the blows to the fleet carriers, *Maryland*'s casualties and damage were one more testimony to the steep price one suicide aircraft impacting one blue water heavy could exact.

* * *

The big ships now had their baptism. Yet, even as *Maryland*'s pharmacist's mates and yeomen tallied the casualties, a separate six-plane *kamikaze* contingent was circling new prey: two picket destroyers, *Saufley* (DD-465) and *Aulick* (DD-569), patrolling the eastern entrance to Leyte Gulf.

Saufley, one of the early Fletchers, first saw action in the Solomons, had survived a lot of combat since, and was fresh from a West Coast overhaul like cruiser *Montpelier*. *Aulick*, another veteran Fletcher, owned a tough-luck past: in 1943 the ship had run hard up on a reef at flank speed. The damage had cost *Aulick*'s skipper his command and the ship and its crew the good part of a year sitting in repair.

There was no second-guessing these pilots' intentions. Each aimed for a ship's bridge and each had a separate lesson to teach. The first: it was no sure thing for one moving plane to hit one moving ship. The second: when *kamikaze* pilots acted in concert, this tactic was more apt to succeed. And when it did succeed, the results were devastating.

Jim Coulling, a *Saufley* officer, saw his ship's attacker diving from the port quarter heading straight for the bridge. *Saufley* CO Dale Cochran (Coulling wrote years later), "did it by the book. He backed full astern causing the *kamikaze* to overshoot." Missing the bridge, the *kamikaze* clipped a wing on *Saufley*'s No. 2 mount before slicing into the water off the starboard bow. Its explosion dented the bow and deluged *Saufley*'s decks with saltwater and fuel. But there were no fires and only one casualty (though a fatality): a panicked sailor who apparently jumped ship and was lost to darkness and an unforgiving channel current.

Aulick meanwhile battled two planes, the first coming up its stern and hitting a radar antenna before crashing into the water fifteen yards off the port bow. *Aulick*, whose skipper had backed to avoid this attack (and largely succeeded), now pulled ahead full to engage the second plane. This pilot, like his predecessor, was trying to gain a path up the stern, using the twilight sky and backdrop of Dinegat Island at Leyte Gulf's southern entrance as camouflage. *Aulick*'s skipper continued banking the ship to starboard to keep guns unmasked, but the plane gradually gained its angle, first on *Aulick*'s port quarter and then her stern.

Aulick backed again, but the second pilot had likely learned a lesson: come in low so as not to overshoot. The plane was on fire when its left wingtip struck the starboard bridge wing. From there it was simple, brutal mechanics and pyrotechnics: its fuselage swung inboard and down to the forecastle deck; its bomb exploded close to the No. 2 gun; and blast and fire touched off a secondary explosion of handling room gunpowder. It was this second explosion—and its blowback to superstructure (including the wardroom aid station) and bridge—that did the most damage and claimed the most lives. One third of *Aulick*'s crew would be killed or wounded.

That night *Aulick* took shelter in San Pedro Bay and moored alongside an LST (Landing Ship, Tank). Her 60-plus wounded were gathered in the crew's after berthing space, and with *Aulick*'s own doctor counted among them, medical officers and pharmacist's mates from two other ships came aboard to help. Meanwhile, the 31 dead, nearly all from the No. 2 mount, its handling room, the bridge, and flying bridge, were collected on the fantail and covered with canvas while arrangements were made for burial ashore.

The descriptions of injuries to the dead (as later recorded in *Aulick*'s official deck log) read like a litany of clinical insults, each capped with a death stamp: "Fracture, compound, right ant. skull (dead); . . . wounds, multiple, extreme (dead); . . . burns, multiple, third degree, 100% body (dead); . . . wounds, punctured back and chest (dead) . . ."

By the next day, when the bodies were finally taken ashore, the canvas shrouded remains had already begun stewing in the equatorial heat. To Brian Masterson, a radioman from Long Island, New York, who was pitching in on temporary repairs, the stench of burnt flesh mingled with the metallic smell of welding was overpowering. For the rest of his life, the odor would invariably return, as strong as ever, whenever he saw, heard, or smelled any type of construction work.

Season of Peace

December 1944—the Season of Peace in another year of war. Thanksgiving Day had already passed with little or no celebration on most front line ships, though skippers usually promised rain checks for a quieter time. Cruiser *Montpelier* delayed its Thanksgiving until 4 December, when it was well away from the Philippines at anchorage off Palau. "It was worth waiting for," James Fahey recorded in his diary. "We really had quite a feed." For destroyer *Spence* (DD-512), then operating with 3rd Fleet, 23 November was a doubly blessed day. "Today is Thanksgiving you know," Torpedoman Roy Merritt wrote his sister Florie in South Carolina. "We had roast turkey and just lots of good things. I also got lots of mail today, got your letter and about 15 others." In wartime's skewed calendar, a holiday was any day when mail arrived, especially in the form of passionate letters—sugar reports—from wives and sweethearts.

MacArthur (who celebrated Thanksgiving ashore with news that Congress had elevated him to five-star rank) had big ambitions for December. If he had stuck to his timetable, the Season of Peace (such as it was) in the Philippines Campaign would have been broken on 5 December with the invasion of Mindoro—and broken again with the invasion of Luzon ten days later. Meeting with MacArthur at month's end, however, his "Three Ks" urged caution. Mindoro lay a good 250 miles northwest of Leyte, deep in Japanese territory. With Task Force 38 battered and exhausted and George Kenney's AAF still bedeviled by delays in readying air strips and bringing in aircraft, there was no way of promising enough air cover.

Although he once contemplated sending troop and supply transports to Mindoro without air cover if need be, MacArthur relented. He postponed Mindoro until 15 December and Luzon until the second week of the New Year. With this timetable decided, Halsey got the nod to stand-down. Task Force 38 would get an extended breather at Ulithi, return with air strikes on Luzon from 14 to 16 December, and launch more strikes 19 to 21 December, after a pause for refueling at sea.

Postponement of Mindoro, however, did not mean a hiatus for either 7th Fleet or 6th Army. The opportunity would be put toward an amphibious assault near the Japanese bastion at Ormoc—the closing of the final back door to Leyte. The date chosen was 7 December, the third anniversary of Pearl Harbor.

* * *

The date set for Ormoc thus also marked the beginning, for Americans at least, of the fourth year of war. Three full years seem an eternity in young lifetimes and, for this particular eternity, many servicemen had all but suspended the portions of their lives not related to the war. The very youngest, the teenagers, could afford to—that is, assuming they survived. For those who couldn't or wouldn't wait, however, life events went on even in the shadows of separation and possible death—betrothals, marriages, and especially the arrival of children.

The events were shuffled to fit the uncertainty of war and the obdurate certainty of military schedules. For Pacific war sailors and carrier-based airmen, any semblance of life was usually crammed into the cycle of stateside overhaul of their ships. During these two-to-three month periods, ships' crews (in two shifts—port and starboard) spread out to visit hometowns, families, and lovers across the country.

For some ships, the 1944 holidays arrived early. When Destroyer *Hull* (DD-350) returned to the Pacific following an August through October stateside overhaul, it was collectively boasted that fully 13 *Hull* sailors had left pregnant wives behind. Sonarman Patrick Douhan was among the expectant fathers; to augment his $75 monthly paycheck in anticipation of this event, Douhan signed up to be *Hull*'s part-time mail clerk.

Not surprisingly, the seeds of these visits home had a way of reaching harvest while the father was literally half a world away. Tom Clyce, destroyer *Claxton*'s chief radio technician, for example, learned (by letter from his wife Mabel nearly a month after the fact) of the birth of his son Tom Jr. while *Claxton* was still covering operations in the Philippines.

In still other cases, life events became package deals. After a propulsion plant breakdown in April 1944, destroyer *Bush,* much to the crew's delight, headed stateside for repairs. *Bush* arrived at Mare Island near San Francisco in early May, and most veterans on the roster were given alternating sixteen-day leaves. Boatswain's Mate Wesely Northey began his leave on 21 May and made it home to Wisconsin to wed Mary Ann Federman in the first week of June. Northey's son Dennis was born on 25 February 1945.

Even for crewmen without family-planning agendas, stateside overhauls afforded a cherished opportunity—however brief—to connect with loved ones they'd not seen in years. The family of 28-year-old *Hull* Electrician's Mate Robert (Scotty) Wilson—his sister Bess Strannigan and her three children, his brother Jackie, Jackie's wife Bea, and their two sons—drove all the way south from the small coal mining camp town of Winton, Wyoming, to Gardiner, New Mexico, to visit him while he was home on leave. The three adults and five children piled into one automobile, the Strannigans' Plymouth, for the ride. To prepare for the trip (a nearly two-thousand-mile journey for a three-day visit), the family had pooled gas coupons and taken newer tires from Jackie's car to put on the Plymouth. Work demands kept Scotty's brother-in-law Andy, a mine foreman in Winton, from making the trip. But some miners had chipped in with gasoline coupons to make the drive possible.

Wilson lived in Gardiner with his young wife Ruby, a nurse at Gardiner Hospital. Wilson's older brother Jim was also there on leave from the Army and service in the Aleutians. Then eight-year-old Liz Strannigan remembered Scotty (she called him Uncle Rob), as blond, blue-eyed, and outgoing, though a bit of a tease to her and her 19-year-old sister Margaret. Once, Liz had confided to her mother that she'd pulled the whiskers of the Strannigans' cat Wilkie. She was astonished when Uncle Rob knowingly told her, "Wilkie tells me you've been pulling his whiskers." The Wilsons were not Catholics, but Scotty Wilson made a point of wanting a cross to carry with him, so Liz' sister bought one when the family reached Gardiner and gave it to Scotty as a going-away present.

Sailors on *Hull, Claxton,* and *Bush* were luckier than sailors on a few ships who lost out on a chance for a stateside overhaul. In mid-1944, for example, when destroyer *Reid* (DD-369) pulled into Pearl Harbor, her crew fully expected they were onward bound for a West Coast overhaul. *Reid,* a Pearl Harbor attack survivor, had served virtually nonstop in the Solomons and New Guinea since 1942. Anticipating *Reid*'s imminent refurbishing, her skipper Samuel McCornock readily agreed to allow the transfer of crucial shipboard systems and equipment to other ships staying in the war zone. Division and squadron commanders were livid when they learned of McCornock's unauthorized generosity. As punishment, arrangements were made to conduct

Reid's overhaul in Pearl Harbor rather than sending her—and her crew—stateside.

There were scant holiday thoughts among the embattled Japanese servicemen in the Philippines or elsewhere in Japan's shrinking empire. New Year's, perhaps Japan's most important holiday, was just weeks ahead. There was bitter irony in the New Year's tradition of holding *bonenkai* ("year forgetting") parties to leave the old year's worries and troubles behind. If there was ever a year to forget it was 1944.

In December Ryuji Nagatsuka was assigned to an army air base on the southwestern tip of Honshu. Backed by mountains to the east, the base bore the brunt of icy winds sweeping off the Sea of Japan. As part of their continuing training as fighter pilots, Nagatsuka and twenty-six others were attached to a squadron responsible for defending Kyushu against raids of American B-29 bombers flying from bases in China and now from the Marianas.

The pilots flew Mitsubishi *Ki*-30 Type 97 light bombers (American code name Ann), which, though sturdy and maneuverable, were outclassed by American aircraft. *Ki*-27s, for example, had been scrambled to chase Jimmy Doolittle's escaping B-25s, but had not been able to overtake them.

But Nagatsuka also rode as an observer in the backseat of a more advanced fighter aircraft—a twin-engine Kawasaki *Ki-45 Toryu* (American code name Nick)—scrambled to confront a formation of B-29s. The huge silver bombers—to Nagatsuka they resembled "flying castles"—were now equipped with automated gun turrets. At maximum speed the B-29s could outrun their smaller, lighter attackers.

Powered by four engines and equipped with self-sealing fuel tanks, the flying castles were virtually indestructible, but there had been one landmark success. During an August 1944 B-29 raid, one IJA pilot had downed two flying castles—one by direct ramming, the second as a result of the explosion to the first.

The Japanese pilots' best hope was to catch a B-29 unaware, approaching from below and firing at the cockpit in hopes of killing the plane's pilot and co-pilot. Nagatsuka's pilot tried this tactic on two B-29s, but ran out of ammunition without stopping either of them. It was a sobering experience for Nagatsuka. In a few days' time, it would be his turn to try. Reflecting on his experience, Nagatsuka would write in his dairy: "It is a pilot's duty to do the impossible."

The first days of December found Toshio Yoshitake still on Luzon and still aching and unsteady from his bout of dengue fever. After repeated unsuccessful tinkering, mechanics—the pilots called them beetles—at last decided to change the engine on Yoshitake's plane. Finally, on 4 December, Yoshitake flew on to Negros, buoyed with the prospect of joining his comrades.

Once again, Yoshitake's trip was rough. The clouds and rain forced him to an emergency landing on a muddy airstrip far from where his squadron mates were billeted. Still, Yoshitake had succeeded in reaching Negros, and he was reunited with his squadron that same night.

Early next morning he awoke groggily to the news that an American resupply convoy had been spotted on its way to Ormoc and a *tokkō* mission would take off within the hour. It looked like the moment had arrived. As the other pilots dashed to the flight line, Yoshitake stayed back to get news on the condition of his own plane.

Once again dismal news. His plane's new engine had absorbed a soaking that again put it out of action. All Yoshitake could do was stand at the edge of the runway and cheer on his comrades as they flew off to their destiny.

As the 7 December date for the Ormoc landing approached, (CNO) King and Central Pacific Forces Chief Chester Nimitz had reason to be concerned that the terms of the Philippines Campaign—supporting the stately MacArthur as his Army slogged through the conquest of continent-size pieces of real estate—meant protracted exposure for their ships and sailors.

The Bull's Run episode had shown what could happen when an impetuous task force commander such as Halsey was shoehorned into a defensive roll. And now, tethered within the gulfs, bays, and bottleneck passages of the biggest of the Philippines' more than seven thousand islands, Navy ships were facing the aerial suiciders without adequate air cover of their own. Though the conquest of Leyte was nearing completion (but at a pace set solely by MacArthur), other more distant and more vital pieces of Philippine real estate were still ahead. It must have occurred to them that the next weeks might bring escalating encounters with Japan's inscrutable suicide machine: Ormoc and Mindoro might each be worse than an already bad Leyte Gulf; and Lingayen might be worst of all.

Chapter 14

The Far Side of Leyte, December 1944

*What do the American people expect you to do with all that hard-
ware if not throw it at the enemy?*

—General Douglas MacArthur

Tune-Ups

It had an almost perverse symmetry. As pressure increased on Ormoc,
7th Fleet ships operated ever closer to enemy-held airfields, allowing
the Japanese to shorten their range, increase their ability to spot targets,
and improve their aim. Simultaneously, planning and logistics needs
for Mindoro and Lingayen pulled more U.S. ship resources off-line.
Convoys and task groups for ongoing Leyte operations such as Ormoc had to make do with smaller, slower, more vulnerable supply craft
screened by fewer and smaller combatants—usually older destroyers.
With Halsey's carrier groups on hiatus, they also had to make do with
the shortcomings of Army air cover. As a result, increased opportunities to mount suicide attacks coincided with a more exposed and less
potent set of targets.

The Ormoc tune-ups—raids to clear Japanese shipping from the
Camotes Sea approaches and a mission to resupply 6th Army troops
already ashore and advancing toward Ormoc along Leyte's western
shore—indeed proved costly.

The first and worst casualty was *Cooper*, one of three destroyers
staging a moonlit 2 December raid on Ormoc's doorstep. *Cooper* was

split in half by a Long Lance torpedo and sank in a matter of seconds, her disjointed hull twisting and rolling to starboard so quickly that several of her 5-inch guns still fired as she went down.

Many *Cooper* sailors belowdecks were trapped; most who survived were stationed topside. One of these lucky ones was 19-year-old signalman Tom Hogan perched high up on the flying bridge. By the time Hogan went over the side, he was literally able to step into the water.

Another was Harvey Huff, 23, a seaman with a wife, one child, and another on the way back in Indiana. Huff, a loader on a port-side 40-mm, was holding an ammunition clip when the torpedo exploded. Certain that *Cooper* was going down fast, Huff dropped the clip and slid down a hot shell chute into the water.

Jim Villiers, the Brooklyn-born torpedoman who once went AWOL to avoid being transferred off *Cooper*, emerged as perhaps the luckiest. Just days before, Villier's GQ station had been switched from the forward to the after torpedo mount. The forward mount was demolished by the blast; Villiers meanwhile was thrown clear and overboard. He surfaced just in time to see *Cooper*'s stern point up and sink.

When the explosion occurred, Marvin Davis, handling room captain for No. 1 gun, scrambled up through the handling room emergency hatch and into the gun turret. By then, *Cooper*'s bow was already pointing up steeply, and Davis, along with several others, simply fell through the gunhouse's open rear hatch, over the rail, and into the water. Davis saw *Cooper*'s stern sink as did Villiers, but he also saw the bow submerge, leaving a huge trail of bubbles. With a handful of other survivors, some badly wounded, Davis clung to the edge of one of the ship's floater nets. Two hours after the sinking, a Japanese submarine glided by on the surface, perhaps fifty yards away. Minutes later, two large Japanese landing craft also passed close by. Apparently none of the craft spotted the men.

Debris from Ormoc's shell-riddled docks and warehouses littered the water. Jim Villiers and three other survivors managed to snag a floating timber big enough for all four to cling to. When it grew light, the sailors heard strange voices and soon spotted two clusters of Japanese sailors—themselves clinging to logs—on either side of them not twenty yards away. The groups passed warily and mostly in silence, though one Japanese sailor made a gesture that, at the time, sent shivers through Villiers—a hand swiping across his throat.* Rescued by seaplanes† that same afternoon, Villiers, Hogan, Huff, Davis, and other survivors were returned to Leyte Gulf where they learned 191 sailors—over half the crew—were lost.

The next dustups began late morning on 5 December as a Leyte-bound supply convoy (eleven landing craft screened by four prewar tin cans) filed through Surigao Strait and into the homestretch. Eight Japanese planes—among them quite possibly the Sonias flown by suicide pilots from Toshio Yoshitake's squadron—caught them in ambush. Two planes crashed into the cluster of slow and defenseless landing craft, sinking one and crippling a second, while a third plane's port wing scraped destroyer *Drayton* (DD-366)'s bow, in the process killing six sailors and wounding twelve more.

The day closed with a sundown strike by two Vals on destroyer *Mugford* (DD-389) as she escorted the damaged convoy ships into San Pedro Bay. Jim Cofer, a 24-year-old firecontrolman (and, before the war, a Chattanooga Golden Gloves champ) tracked one Val through the main battery director's rangefinder as its pilot bungled a bombing run on *Mugford*. One bomb dropped prematurely and harmlessly into the water while a second still dangled, apparently stuck to the Val's wing rack. George Garmon, a gunner on *Mugford*'s only 40-mm, saw the plane head toward land and soon heard an explosion from that direction—most likely the bomb had shaken loose.

Moments later the Val was back, this time low on the water and aiming for *Mugford*'s port side. As *Mugford*'s guns fired, the approaching Val ballooned in Cofer's rangefinder optics. It became a blur before crashing at *Mugford*'s waterline—taking out No. 2 engine room and killing eight sailors. Though *Mugford* reached San Pedro Bay under her own power, she was out of the war.

For the veteran sailors on *Drayton*, *Mugford* and other prewar

---

*Villiers would later conclude that the throat slashing gesture by the Japanese sailor was actually meant as a warning to men he assumed were Japanese: shipwrecked IJN sailors who drifted ashore risked summary execution by Philippine natives.

†Clarence Brinker, another survivor, recalled the seaplane that rescued him being so packed with *Cooper* sailors that the plane's pilots taxied several miles before managing to get it aloft.

tin cans, the Ormoc shuttles stirred bad memories of the Solomons. The Philippines seemed to combine the "Slot's" most unnerving aspects—little room to maneuver, spotty air cover, nonstop at GQ—with the Pacific War's newest terror—the suicide aircraft. With the Ormoc landings less than two days off and Mindoro just a week beyond that, veterans and raw recruits alike needed little convincing that the far side of Leyte was a world brimming with hurt.

Full Day, Empty Magazines

Most were thus relieved—but wary—at how uneventfully the Ormoc landings actually went. Though shadowed by Japanese reconnaissance aircraft, a preinvasion sweep by four veteran Fletchers scared up no opposition. The intercoastal invasion fleet—twelve destroyers screening a handful of troop transports and dozens of smaller amphibious craft, minesweepers, and support craft—arrived off the invasion beaches largely without incident. Aboard *Howorth*, yeoman Orvill Raines took in the beauties and perils of the trip to Ormoc and later described his feelings to Ray Ellen. "Darling, the 'West Side' is beautiful. We weave through the numerous small islands, continually changing course. Always uncertain what lies beyond the next point . . . It reminds me of when I used to play 'rubber-guns.' . . . We'd hide from each other and then sneak around trying to find ourselves, always expecting a quick slap and sting in the face or back."

The landings began early on a warm 7 December morning—five waves of beach-bound landing craft preceded by a twenty-five-minute overture of gunfire and rockets. GIs encountered little resistance ashore—the landings had actually fooled the Japanese who concentrated instead on the diversionary probes by GIs farther south. A Japanese supply convoy was detected approaching from the west, and land-based Marine fighter planes scrambled to cut it off. Everything, in short, was going according to plan and better than expected until radar on destroyer *Lamson* (DD-367) spotted incoming bogeys.

The melee that followed, one pitting U.S. Navy ships and Army C.A.P.s against Japanese aircraft in what historian Morison ranked as among the "most devastating air assaults of 1944," began at 0948 and raged unbroken into the night.

Picket ships *Ward* (APD-16) and *Mahan* (DD-364) took the morning's first blows. *Ward*, the unlikely hero of the war's first hours when her crew sunk a Japanese midget submarine at Pearl Harbor, had since been converted to an attack transport and served in a string of invasions from Tulagi through to New Guinea and now the Philippines. Richard Farwell, *Ward*'s assistant engineering officer in December 1941, was now a full lieutenant and *Ward*'s CO. When he saw the first formation of attackers—nine twin-engine Frances fighter-bombers approaching from the north—Farwell rang up *Ward*'s speed and began circling to evade. At first these planes swept right, bound for *Mahan*.

Farwell's lookouts soon spotted a second group, six planes flying in from the west, with Army P-38s close behind. By now, though, several Japanese planes from the first formation had turned their attention to *Ward*. Farwell stopped the ship's circling. instead ordered a quick series of hard rudder turns, hoping to make the fish-tailing *Ward* a less predictable target.

Farwell also held fire. *Ward*'s heaviest weapons were antiquated 3-inch single-purpose guns supplemented by 20-mms; realizing his armament was short on punch and range, Farwell may have hoped the intruders wouldn't single out *Ward*. Farwell finally released his guns when all three winged over into steep dives straight toward *Ward*. It was too late. Two planes were hit and deflected by *Ward* salvos—one crashed well astern, the other near the bow—but the third Frances, sneaking in on the port side before guns could bear, crashed just above the waterline abaft the bridge.

Ward was then heeling so far to starboard that the collision nearly toppled her. There was a large explosion; survivors later told Farwell the force of the blast propelled one of the plane's engines all the way through the ship's midsection. *Ward* slowed and lost power. Farwell ordered cease fire and turned his crew's efforts to fighting fires.

Meanwhile *Mahan*'s sailors were enduring a comparable ordeal: crippling crashes by three planes in a matter of minutes; the most calamitous a direct hit to the superstructure near the No. 2 gun. *Mahan*'s CO at first tried to race for the cover of other screening ships, but speed only fanned flames. *Mahan* slowed, but by then fires blocked access to flooding controls. With flames at the bulkheads of the ship's forward magazine, *Mahan*'s skipper ordered abandon ship.

A lot of green recruits had come aboard *Mahan* during her recent West Coast overhaul. One of them was 19-year-old George Pendergast, part of *Mahan*'s engineering black gang. When he reached the main deck from No. 1 fireroom, Pendergast was decked out in garb that made him resemble a young Casey Jones, complete with red bandana neck scarf and starched engineer's cap.

Pendergast saw the heaviest damage was to the ship's superstructure—most of it was sheered off. Topside was an "orderly mess" with belowdeck sailors like him trying to figure out what was happening, others already jumping ship, and *Mahan*'s harried torpedomen trying to jettison *Mahan*'s torpedoes without hitting other ships. Pendergast left *Mahan* by the fantail and was later picked up by *Walke;* he reached her main deck only after a tough climb up a balky Jacob's ladder, but was rewarded by a swig of medicinal whisky doled out by a *Walke* pharmacist's mate.

Even as *Mahan*'s sailors fought to save their ship, Farwell concluded he had little choice but to give up on *Ward*. Topside ready ammunition supplies were already cooking off and, like *Mahan*'s CO, Farwell feared his ship's main magazines might soon erupt. "We had no power," he recalled. "We were dead in the water, and the sky was still full of *kamikazes.*" Farwell ordered his crew over the side.

Ward had casualties—some with severe burns—but no fatalities. With ship's power gone, two of *Ward*'s four Higgins boats couldn't be lowered. However, the remaining two LCVPs were already in the water fighting fires. Crews in these boats gave up that effort and instead began hauling in survivors. Two other ships—destroyer *O'Brien* (DD-725) and transport *Crosby* (APD-17) also stood by. Destroyers *Walke* and *Lamson* were by then picking up *Mahan* survivors. Many would be saved, but the three *kamikazes* had claimed ten sailors' lives and wounded scores of others.

Both *Ward* and *Mahan* remained afloat, almost inconveniently so, with more attacks threatened and little real prospect of taking either in tow for the long fight back to Leyte Gulf. Sinking them was the best option. Torpedoes and gunfire from *Walke* delivered *Mahan*'s coup de grace. *O'Brien* meanwhile became *Ward*'s executioner. For *O'Brien*'s skipper it was a task laden with irony—and doubtless with regret. Precisely three years before then Lieutenant, now Commander William Outerbridge, had skippered *Ward* to her singular moment of glory.

It was already nearing 1100, but the day's *kamikaze* marathon was just beginning. The convoy and its screen (absent the damaged stragglers and two landing craft stuck on the beach) formed and turned southwest, bound for Leyte Gulf, a swarm of Zekes in hot pursuit.

In quick succession several ships sidestepped or deflected the aim of crashing suiciders. One target was fast transport *Liddle* (APD-60), a converted destroyer escort named for a pharmacist's mate killed on Guadalcanal. Gun crews on *Liddle* and *Cofer* (APD-62) combined to shoot down one attacker, but minutes later another suicider approaching bow-on smashed and exploded directly into *Liddle*'s flying bridge. The strike demolished the ship's pilothouse, CIC, and radio room, taking the lives of 38 men (including *Liddle*'s skipper) and seriously wounding a score of others.

"Wounded treated throughout the day and night," wrote bespectacled *Liddle* pharmacist's mate Harold Deal in his journal for the day. *Liddle*'s doctor Jerome Greenbaum was killed, leaving the 25-year-old Deal (a pharmacist in New Berlin, New York, before the war), and *Liddle*'s other pharmacist's mate Milfred Poll to tend the wounded until more medical help arrived from *Cofer* and destroyer *Hughes* (DD-410). Deal closed his journal entry by describing the fatalities' final predicament. "What few dead it was possible to move were taken to the Mess Hall. Many of the dead were caught in the wreckage, and it was impossible to extricate them."

Afternoon found the Ormoc Attack Group passing the coastal town of Baybay on its way clear of the Camotes Sea. Fighter-director ship *Lamson* by now had twelve C.A.P. P-38s at her disposal. After vectoring several toward a snooping Japanese reconnaissance plane, *Lamson* herself was attacked, first by the snooper and then by a *kamikaze* skimming in low and undetected from the cover of land.

Flying thirty feet off the deck, this second plane closed *Lamson* quickly. It nearly passed clear amidships, but its wing clipped the after stack, and the impact spun the fuselage hard into the deckhouse aft of the bridge. Its propeller blades chewed through layers of steel like a buzz saw before finally locking in a bulkhead. Gasoline-fed flames spread forward to the No. 1 gun. Heat chased some survivors to the forecastle, others all the way aft. A rescue tug traveling with the convoy approached *Lamson*, at first to battle fires but then to take on survivors when abandon ship was called.

Darkness finally pulled down the curtain on the worst of the day's attacks, but the next morning the battle resumed, continued even as the firepower of four more ships joined the convoy, and concluded only as its scattered elements finally cleared Leyte's southern cape.

Remarkably, one of these elements included *Lamson*. Some thought was given to sinking *Lamson* in the manner of *Ward* and *Mahan*, but losing yet another ship may have been too much for the convoy commander. Eventually the rescue tug took *Lamson* in tow with *Flusser* as escort. The trip was tough for *Flusser*'s gunners, who had to fend off a host of predators. In the process, they emptied the ship's magazines, and escort responsibility fell to destroyer *Reid*, the ship whose crew had earlier lost out on an opportunity for a stateside overhaul. *Flusser* was the only ship to return without a bullet, but others probably came close. During the running battle back to San Pedro Bay, group ships combined to shoot more than eighteen thousand antiaircraft rounds.

Mindoro's Allure

Postponing the Mindoro operation until 15 December seemed to do little to diminish its perils. Still, Mindoro's strategic allure was strong. At their closest, Mindoro and Luzon were separated by Verde Island Passage, just seven miles wide. Mindoro's northern tip also lay just ninety miles south of Manila, the nerve center of Japanese resistance. Mindoro was mostly wild and mountainous, but its southeastern coast boasted the requisite features of a logistics base so essential for invading Luzon: a sheltered bay, good landing beaches, four abandoned airstrips with stretches of suitable space to build more.

Through all his conquests in the Southwest Pacific, Douglas MacArthur prided himself in never permitting his reach to exceed his air cover, but he had already done so on Leyte. The sobering prospect for Mindoro was that his 6th Division GIs and 7th Fleet ships and sailors would be operating deep within the Sibuyan Sea closely surrounded by Japanese-held islands and airbases. Until Mindoro could be captured and its runways reactivated, the closest U.S. airbase (Dulag) would be a full 260 miles distant.

As the kickoff for Mindoro neared, the going was never more treacherous for units involved in the capture of Ormoc. Desperate Japanese defenders were trapped (the town itself would fall on 10 December), but the GIs' logistic needs were ravenous and couldn't be met using Leyte's narrow, mud-clogged mountain and coastal roads alone. Accordingly, two supply echelons—one on 9 December, a second two days later—were assembled to run the gauntlet.

The first convoy made its roundtrip without a scratch, perhaps because the Japanese opted instead to take a crack at shipping in Leyte Gulf on 10 December. The primary victims that day were a liberty ship, a landing craft, and a PT boat—all sunk—and *Hughes,* suicide-crashed amidships by a Betty bomber.

Hughes survived the attack but with a huge crater in her main deck, crippled propulsion gear below, and the loss of nearly 30 dead and wounded, most from her engineering spaces. Gordon Sayner, 20, the loader on one of *Hughes'* 20-mm guns, remembered a picture-perfect day inexplicably interrupted by heavy rain drops advancing across a mirrored sea. The splashes turned out to be bombs dropping, several close enough to disable *Hughes'* propulsion plant and make her a sitting duck. When the Betty crashed aft of the ship's single stack, flames whisked along the topside decks like a speeding tide, lapping at sailors' feet and ankles before receding just as quickly.

Hughes flashed a Mayday alarm, and soon a flight of P-38s dispersed circling Japanese planes. Oliver Jones, a 19-year-old deck seaman who'd left No. 2 handling room to help with the casualties, was tasked with distributing tiny bottles of medicinal whiskey to wounded awaiting transfer to a nearby destroyer.

The picture-perfect day became an inky, rain-soaked night throughout which many hands stayed at GQ stations. The next morning,

Gordon Sayner woke from a fitful sleep at the base of his gun to find *Hughes* being towed by destroyer *Laffey* (DD-724) through waters suddenly crowded with ships, including carriers and cruisers. Later that day, *Hughes* sailors not standing watch were assembled amidships by the ship's XO, who asked for volunteers to go below. Sayner, who stood a rail-thin six feet three, was one of many volunteers organized in ten-minute shifts, who snaked their bodies through the asbestos dust, fumes, twisted piping, and crushed machinery of the forward engine and after fireroom, searching for *Hughes'* missing and dead.*

The ships Sayner had seen materialize in Leyte Gulf were elements of the Visayan Attack Force—the Mindoro invasion fleet. The Force's three component groups—the Mindoro Attack Group, the Close Covering Group, and the Torpedo Group—made for an unusual collection of the very big and the very small, nearly 160 ships in all. At the small end were over one hundred PTs, landing craft, and small minesweeps screened by a score of destroyers. The groups' heavyweights were four cruisers, including flagship *Nashville.*

There was even more heft in a separate Heavy Covering and Carrier Group assembled to support the invasion from open waters of the Sulu Sea. In addition to six escort carriers and eighteen tin can screens, the group boasted battleships *West Virginia, Colorado* (BB-45), and *New Mexico* (BB-40) plus cruisers *Denver, Columbia,* and *Montpelier.* The Heavy Covering and Carrier Group was one response to the continuing air-cover debacle. The other, of course, would be the return of Halsey's fast carrier groups to operations in the Philippine Sea, set for 14 December.

Terrible Second

Dispirited at being left behind for his squadron's 5 December *tokkō* mission, Yoshitake's mood only worsened, first because of lingering repair problems and then, with those resolved, a stretch of bad weather. At last, doubly good news: a break in the weather and an American

---

*Sixty years later Sayner would be diagnosed with asbestosis.

convoy heading for Ormoc Bay. Yoshitake and three other pilots were set for a mission flying out the next morning, 12 December.

After all the waiting and inaction—through illness, mechanical problems, and weather delays—Yoshitake felt relieved by the prospect. Death would be a welcome release, especially if he could take with him hundreds of the enemies who had humiliated his country. He feared only failure, of somehow letting down his comrades or being forced to return to base for some stupid, shameful reason.

The gathering of the Visayan Attack Force may have bolstered the morale among the sailors in Leyte Gulf. But until this armada actually left for Mindoro, the Ormoc supply forces would remain the point of the spear (or, perhaps more aptly, the canary in the cage) for 7th Fleet operations in the Philippines. A stark reminder of this was not long in coming: the ease and tranquility of the first resupply echelon gave way on 11 December to the ordeal and carnage of the "Terrible Second."

The bare-bones convoy (thirteen landing craft with six destroyer screens) departed Leyte anticipating trouble; after the loss of *Cooper, Ward,* and *Mahan,* most ships left classified documents and crew pay-roll records behind. As backup, at least on convoy flagship *Caldwell* (DD-605), key personnel received mimeographed lists with the names, ranks, rates, and file service numbers for all shipboard personnel. They would come in handy.

Trouble began mid-afternoon on the outbound leg when the convoy was spotted by a snooper aircraft. By 1700, a formation of nine Nakajima B6N *Tenzan* (Heavenly Mountain) torpedo bombers was overhead. The large IJN three-seat single-engine plane (code name Jill) was originally conceived as the staple torpedo-bombing weapon for new generations of Japanese aircraft carriers. Its outsized rudder had even been angled forward to give it clearance on carrier elevators. Now, however, with Japan's carrier fleet all but eliminated, the Jill had been relegated to a land-based role.

The Jills at first came in with torpedoes and bombs. Gunners on *Caldwell*—helped by Marine Corsairs flying C.A.P.—fought off several and splashed one. Bombs from others dropped near but clear of convoy small craft.

Meanwhile, four Jills concentrated on destroyer *Reid,* lead ship on the convoy's inboard side. Pestered or wounded by C.A.P. and convoy AA, some Japanese pilots switched to suicide dives. *Reid*'s gunfire hit the lead Jill, but the plane crashed *Reid*'s main deck amidships. The Jill's wing splintered *Reid*'s starboard whaleboat before its fuselage crashed at the waterline. A second plane hit *Reid*'s No. 3 gun, igniting explosions of aviation and ready ammunition on the stern. The ship rolled to starboard, hung there momentarily and then sank stern first—all in a couple minutes' time.

For crewmen like 19-year-olds Jesse Pickeral and Len Olsen, both at forward gun mounts, there was no time to grab nearby life jackets. *Reid* went down in waters thousands of feet deep; as she dropped, muffled subsurface explosions—the eruption of her boilers—roiled the surface. Convoy ships managed to rescue 166 *Reid* crewmen.

About forty new recruits had joined *Reid* at the conclusion of her midsummer Pearl Harbor overhaul. Replacement pool assignments were often drawn alphabetically—in *Reid*'s case the new sailors' names almost all began with the letter O. Len Olsen (a survivor, as was Jesse Pickeral) was one. The 103-man fatality list read like a dictionary page with the names of others.

Night brought some respite to the Terrible Second; still, the dark sky blossomed with flares, occasional strafing passes, and (as one ship's action report put it) nonstop aerial "heckling" until the convoy finally arrived off Ormoc's beaches at 2300.

As off-loading progressed, destroyer *Caldwell*'s surface radar detected a Japanese supply convoy apparently trying to reinforce and supply its own forces. *Caldwell*'s radar-controlled gunfire chased it. When off-loading finished at 0400, the U.S. convoy re-reformed and set off under rain-pocked skies for its return trip through the gauntlet. Plane sightings continued during the predawn, but at 0700 the welcome umbrella of Marine air cover arrived.

★ Chapter 15 ★

The Shadow of Lingayen, December 1944

Before the innovation of suicide attacks by the enemy, destruction of 80 or 90 percent of his attackers was considered an eminent success. Now 100 percent destruction of the attackers is necessary to preserve the safety of the task force.

—Vice Admiral John Sidney McCain

Ice Candies

Toshio Yoshitake and three other pilots were dozing in the operations shack at Bacolad airfield when the order to attack came at 0700. Morning on Negros Island had begun under a light drizzle, but soon there was light in the Eastern sky and the prospect the sun might burn away the low clouds.

Yoshitake bounded enthusiastically for his plane, but when he climbed into the cockpit and started his engine, black smoke belched from the exhaust. Trouble again, he realized, but he also knew it was now or never. Despite the smoke and low engine rpm, Yoshitake was determined to give it a go. He taxied his balky aircraft onto Bacolad's muddy runway, waited his turn, and began his takeoff run.

The plane bumped and wheezed along the runway until Yoshitake finally managed to take off. He struggled to maneuver the *Ki-51* clear of the tree line at the runway's end. One landing strut clipped a palm frond with a loud *thwack,* but Yoshitake was aloft at last. As the formation headed east, his plane continued to trail smoke. Yoshitake tried to keep up, but the other three aircraft gradually pulled away.

* * *

At 0800, with the Ormoc convoy still southbound through the Camotes Sea, Japanese aircraft—estimates were as high as twenty-five planes—suddenly bore in from the direction of Cebu. Crews on screening ships and Marine pilots flying C.A.P. aircraft prepared to take them on.

Luck at first held for the screening ships in the morning melee. Destroyer *Conyngham* (DD-371) nimbly dodged a suicide dive, and bomb runs on *Smith* (DD-378), *Edwards* (DD-619), and *Coghlan* (DD-606) also failed. But then devastation hit *Caldwell,* first in the form of a low-flying Zeke streaming down her port side through a curtain of 20- and 40-mm fire. The plane crossed just astern in a steep bank to starboard, rolled on its back, and nose-dived into *Caldwell.* One Zeke wing clipped the ship's bridge, the other the starboard main deck near the bow. Its fuselage plowed into the superstructure just below the bridge. This impact, and the gasoline fires that followed, killed everyone inside the ship's main radio compartment.

Once they'd crossed Cebu and reached the Camotes Sea, the three other aircraft in Toshio Yoshitake's flight were little more than distant specks. Yoshitake was straining his eyes to keep them in sight when new specs began to join them in the sky. He realized these must be puffs of antiaircraft fire. If so, the American convoy was ahead, and he could just keep flying toward the puffs. Then, all at once, a deep blue shape crowded his vision—a U.S. Grumman.

For a moment the American pilot, whose big red face and torso seemed to crowd the Grumman's cockpit, flew wingtip to wingtip with Yoshitake, apparently sizing him up. Then the plane pulled up and zoomed away, leaving Yoshitake to swivel his head, trying frantically to locate his adversary. Soon, a fluorescent stream of tracer rounds—what the Japanese pilots called ice candies—straddled his canopy.

With barely a thought, Yoshitake pulled his plane's drop tank lever releasing the undercarriage bomb. It was his only choice if he hoped to evade the Grumman, but it also meant shedding his primary weapon. Instinctively (despite his sacred intentions) he had chosen, at least for the moment, the elusive possibility of life over the certainty of death.

Yoshitake dropped altitude. He was now over water, but in the distance he could also see a small tree-lined island. Yoshitake steered his *Ki-51*—now much more maneuverable minus the weight of the bomb—in its direction. As he approached, the water below changed color from translucent blue to sand yellow. He spotted a clearing on the island and the flat outline of an airstrip runway.

In losing altitude, the *Ki-51* lost speed, but if the American wanted to take careful aim, the Grumman would have to decelerate as well. And if it did, Yoshitake's *Ki-51* might just have the advantage with its low-level, low-speed maneuverability. Yoshitake might also reach the island, land safely, and, yes, live another day.

Yoshitake jinked his aircraft close to the wave tops, his mind racing with options for evasion and escape, when suddenly his cockpit collapsed in an implosion of shattered glass, debris, dust, and smoke spiced with the aroma of aviation fuel. As instantly as it began, the fracas shifted to silence, except for the rush of wind. The tormented *Ki-51* engine had died.

The plane crash on *Caldwell* triggered at least one explosion when the Zeke's undercarriage bomb flew forward, richocheted off *Caldwell's* No. 2 gun, and detonated close to No. 1 gun. Meanwhile, bombs from another aircraft were seen straddling *Caldwell,* and one may have reached the ammunition handling room just below No. 2 gun. The room contained an assortment of projectiles, some with proximity fuses, others packed with WP—flakes of incendiary white phosphorous for shore bombardment use. Several proximity warheads exploded, raking the forecastle and bridge with shrapnel. The WP warheads leached fumes and intense heat.

The effects of the blasts carried all the way to the flying bridge where Vaughn Adjemian, 22, *Caldwell's* assistant gunnery officer, was knocked off his feet and briefly into unconsciousness. When he came to and collected his wits, Adjemian worked his way down to the bridge where he found *Caldwell's* skipper George Wendelburg. Wendelburg was still in command, but seriously wounded and clearly in pain—a piece of shrapnel had entered the palm of one hand and propelled its way well up into his forearm.

Explosions and fires chased many crewmen aft, including most of the forward damage control party. This left Mel Cratsley, *Caldwell's* damage control officer, and Wesley Wadsworth, its Chief Electrician's Mate, as the only two fighting fires and helping survivors. Cratsley was a mechanical engineering graduate of Carnegie Tech where, at six feet four, he was a star basketball player. Wadsworth, a 28-year-old Iowan, had joined the Navy in 1937. Both were trained in damage control and in handling WP. Now they teamed up to suppress fires, steer wounded toward battle dressing stations, isolate damaged electrical circuitry, and jettison some two dozen projectiles still loose in the wreckage.*

Caldwell's fatality count quickly spiraled to 25, including virtually all its radio personnel and many from the forward gun crews. Forty more, including Wendelburg and Adjemian, were wounded. Nine men missing in action were all but certain to be dead.

After this attack, the Terrible Second's ships and crews returned to Leyte without further incident. En route, *Caldwell*'s fatalities, laid out on mattress frames sheathed with zippered, heavy-canvas covers, were buried at sea. Wesley Wadsworth was assigned to head the detail.

When Toshio Yoshitake regained his senses, he was hanging upside down, suspended by his harness, in the wreckage of his *Ki-51*. Though disoriented and badly banged up, Yoshitake was still alive. His rescuers—IJN personnel on Mactan Island, just off Cebu's eastern shore—were at first horror-struck by Yoshitake's appearance. A big piece of his scalp had been peeled like a carpet from his skull, but it turned out he was in no danger of dying. After having his wounds treated on Mactan, Yoshitake was transported back to Pollack Field on Luzon, there to await another opportunity for a *tokkō* mission.

Brassville

As ships of the Terrible Second cleared Leyte's southwest coast, their crews cast eyes on what turned out to be the advance elements of the

---

*Wesley Wadsworth, a vigorous 91, disputes several key aspects of the *Caldwell* after action report from which this account is drawn. Wadsworth, for example, recalls that the plane crashing *Caldwell* with such devastation approached directly from astern, rather than coming from the bow and reversing direction. He also argues that *Caldwell* was neither straddled nor struck by bombs from other Japanese aircraft. Instead, he believes, an 8-inch artillery projectile, jury-rigged as a bomb and fixed to the undercarriage of the suicide aircraft, detached to penetrate the forward handling room bulkhead. In the handling room, the exploding Japanese shell detonated the *Caldwell*'s own artillery rounds—especially those with proximity fuses—to cause most of the post-crash casualties and damage.

Mindoro invasion fleet—though advance might have been the wrong word. It was Slow Tow Convoy, a motley assortment of six Army and Navy tugs, an Army aviation gasoline tanker, and two Navy landing craft screened by five tin cans. Slow Tow had left San Pedro Bay at 0600, just hours before the Terrible Second was attacked. Now the two echelons—one inbound and limping, the other outbound but somewhat disorganized and barely making headway—crossed paths near Panaon Island. As they passed, Terrible Second sailors may well have mistaken the Slow Tow vessels for another Ormoc resupply group. If so, they likely eyed them with a mix of relief and pity. Meanwhile, Slow Tow crews, sensing what might lie ahead for them, looked on with more than a touch of unease.

Though Slow Tow was the first Mindoro unit to embark, it would be last to arrive. The muscle and meat of the invasion fleet—the transports and screens of the Mindoro Attack Group, the cruisers and destroyers of Close Covering Group—overtook Slow Tow early on 13 December—at last a true point on an impressive spear.

For air cover, the two faster groups had overlapping C.A.P. umbrellas drawn from escort carriers (then just entering the Sulu Sea to the west) and Leyte-based Marine Corsair squadrons. Slow Tow reached the pass point unmolested and was well down on the southern horizon by mid-afternoon when the Attack and Covering Groups took a sudden pounding.

Nashville, flagship for the Mindoro Attack Group, had been MacArthur's home during King II's opening days. His eagerness to see firsthand the 25 October gun duel in Surigao Strait had prompted Navy brass to discretely shield *Nashville* behind a bodyguard of tin cans in San Pedro Bay—well out of harm's way.

For this operation, *Nashville* embarked 50-year-old Rear Admiral Arthur D. Struble, who six months before had been chief of staff for Navy forces during Overlord, the invasion of Western Europe. Hosting a flag was both privilege and hardship. For junior officers and sailors it meant stricter dress and grooming requirements, more crowded berthing and mess spaces, and (perhaps worst of all) more senior officers to salute.

Nashville bulged with brass and VIPs. Besides Struble there was

Brigadier General William C. Dunckel, overall commander for more than twenty-five thousand Army invasion personnel. Accommodating both an admiral and a general, *Nashville* (*Brassville* to some sailors) also carried staff captains and colonels, not to mention a pool of civilian reporters.

On this day the VIPs offered no dispensation to *Nashville*. The 9,500-ton cruiser, her nine hundred sailors and especially her forty-two-man Marine detachment, were about to step directly in harm's way.

It was a serene afternoon, sunny overall, though spotted with cumulus clouds riding overhead like the ships of a celestial Great White Fleet. *Nashville* held the terrestrial formation's post position as Struble's Attack Force cleared the southwest tip of Negros and turned northwest into the Sulu Sea. IFF detected a bogey in the vicinity, but all that Tommy Thompson, CO of the ship's Marine detachment, could see at first were two low-flying Marine Corsairs about to cross directly over *Nashville*'s stern.

Thompson was responsible for AA Control Aft: a cluster of twin 40- and 20-mm batteries on the boat deck amidships and astern. The bulk of Thompson's enlisted Marines were mixed in with crews on 40- and 20-mm gun mounts amidships—split between Thompson and AA Control Forward. Thompson's junior officer (JO), Second Lieutenant Paul Pedersen, was stationed forward while Detachment First Sergeant Alton Chambers had charge of several fantail guns.

Too late, lookouts spotted the source of the IFF alert—a lone Japanese Val with a bomb strapped to each wing. The plane had been masked from radar by approaching over land and had cast doubt on IFF reports by tailing the Marine Corsairs.

The Japanese plane at first seemed to be making for a ship astern of *Nashville* when suddenly it banked to port and aimed instead for the cruiser. As this maneuver unfolded, Ben Limbaugh, one of Thompson's Marines, was sitting on the port side of the boat deck. A buzzer sounded and Limbaugh jumped up to dash to his station—No. 13, 20-mm across the boat deck on the starboard side.

The Val's pilot was still completing the sharp, sweeping turn, his starboard wing angled to the water, as the plane neared *Nashville*'s port side and got into the sights of its guns. Thompson got word to release his guns, but the Val was on top of them so fast only a few guns could squeeze off rounds. The Val seemed pointed directly for *Nashville*'s bridge when its inboard wing instead snagged a 40-mm gun barrel amidships just forward of Thompson's station. The impact spun the Val—a complete suicide package of pilot, plane, fuel, and bombs—into a port-side 5-inch mount aft of Admiral Struble's flag cabin.

Aviation fuel gushed from the Val's shorn wings, and both its bombs exploded, mowing down boat deck sailors and Marines with shrapnel. The collision sparked the fuel and for a few moments flames towered above *Nashville*'s stacks. Ready stocks of ammunition cooked off and detonated, pulsing streaks of tracer rounds across the decks. Bodies and bloody body parts flew through the air. Some men were blown into the water while others vaulted over the side to escape.

Damage control parties contained the fires within twenty minutes, and *Nashville* stayed in formation with its other gun batteries ready for new targets. There was heavy damage, though, including the destruction of *Nashville*'s flag bridge, CIC, and communications office. Boat deck gun crews, meanwhile, took the very worst of it. As sailors fought fires and pulled dead and wounded clear, Tommy Thompson was relieved at his station and went to check on his Marines.

Ben Limbaugh never reached gun No. 13. Instead, he came to lying amid the ruins of the boat deck, surrounded by canisters of 20-mm ammunition, with what felt like a bell clanging inside his skull. His green Marine dungarees were torn and his hands and arms were hurting and bleeding. Limbaugh raised himself to his feet. His head continued ringing so much it was hard to make out what two other Marines were shouting as they stumbled toward him out of the smoke enveloping the deck.

As his senses returned, Limbaugh could see and smell (but not yet hear)—not so much *what* had happened, but rather the *result* of a sudden, cataclysmic, but still unfathomable, event. A torpedo? A bomb? A stroke from God? Marines were everywhere, but they were mostly dead Marines or pieces of dead Marines. For a while it seemed only the three of them survived, but as forms stirred around them, each hoped there might at least be a few others.

These stirrings finally pushed the three men to action. They moved about, checking on bodies. Where they saw movement or detected breathing, they lifted or dragged the man aft. When there seemed to be no more living, they returned for the dead, tears streaming down their faces. Soon, competing sensations—joy at being alive, guilt at not dying with the others—began washing over them.

Medical personnel were treating casualties both in the *Nashville*'s wardroom and in the enlisted mess. They tended a wounded population that eventually reached 190, including General Dunckel. A Navy captain and two senior Army colonels were among an eventual total of 133 dead, some already being laid out aft in *Nashville*'s aviation hangar.

The awful news for Tommy Thompson was that his Marine Detachment, save for its leaders Chambers, Pedersen, himself, and a few others—had been wiped out. Nearly half Thompson's Marines—those assigned to boat deck guns—had been killed outright. All the rest (save Limbaugh and his two buddies, who were ambulatory) were seriously wounded.

Each loss was personal and wrenching to Thompson, none more devastating than the wounded boy the ship's medical officer brought Thompson to see. The doctor was encouraged. The Marine would likely lose his arm but would just as likely survive. Apparently overhearing this prognosis, the Marine seemed to lose his spirit right before Thompson's eyes. The young Marine died soon after.

Destroyer *Stanly* (DD-478), the ship assigned to help in just these circumstances, pulled alongside to fight fires while other ships retrieved dozens of *Nashville* survivors from the water. Once damage was assessed, *Nashville* turned and headed back to Leyte Gulf (and eventually stateside repair) with *Stanly* as escort. Meanwhile, Struble, the wounded Dunckel, their staffs, and four reporters were transferred to destroyer *Dashiell* (DD-659), which unexpectedly found itself hosting a dozen VIPs.

Frightening, to Put It Mildly

In the Sulu Sea—and about an hour after the attack on *Nashville*—sailors of the Heavy Covering and Carrier Group were busy with incoming bogeys. There were seven *kamikazes* and three fighter escorts to begin with, but C.A.P. waylaid and splashed all but three, and two more fell to ship AA on the rim of the group's formation. When the last plane exited the gauntlet, its pilot climbed, banked into a dive, and aimed for destroyer *Haraden* (DD-585), then speeding to an air defense station.

Haraden gun crews barely opened fire on the diving aircraft before it careened into the ship's starboard side, its inboard wing slicing across the starboard bridge wing and its engine and fuselage uprooting the forward stack. The momentum of impact catapulted both plane and stack wreckage over *Haraden*'s port side while the explosion of the plane's bomb cratered *Haraden*'s forward fire room.

To Thomas Inman, a machinist mate petty officer in charge of the forward engine room just aft of the fire room, the collision was a loud *boom* followed by a cloud of fiber and dust from the room's forest of steam piping. Steam pressure plummeted, leaving Inman no choice but to ring up stop and secure the throttle. When engine room lights dimmed and the steam generator began vibrating wildly, he secured the entire engine room and took his gang topside.

When he reached the starboard-side boat deck, Inman saw destruction everywhere: the forward stack gone; the main mast bent; a piece of the bridge sliced away; bright scraps of signal flags strewn across the deck; bulging deckhouse bulwarks; torpedo warheads riddled with shrapnel and leaking molten TNT; a whaleboat splintered, afire and hanging from one davit.

Inman crossed the deck, stepping carefully to avoid tripping over bodies. On the port side he spotted the canister-shaped turret housing that sat atop No. 2 torpedo mount (what torpedomen called the "dog house") lying on its side, the head of Chief Torpedoman William Sproule crushed beneath its rim.

Haraden lost power to its remaining boiler and engine room, leaving the ship momentarily dead in the water, without water pressure or communications, its guns only able to fire in manual control. Damage control personnel converged on the scene and split into teams. While power and water main pressure were out, men used gasoline-powered portable pumps to battle fires. Others, including Carl Spiron, 19, an electrician's mate in the after damage control party, began retrieving dead and wounded.

The day before, Spiron had been reassigned from the amidships repair party. The men in this party were among those bearing the brunt of the crash and explosion. One wounded sailor Spiron ended up helping was the very man with whom he'd just switched assignments.

The casualties—they would total 14 dead and another 24 wounded—were brought forward by stretcher to a triage area set up in a passageway near the ward room. *Haraden*'s medical officer (this time, at least, no medical personnel were wounded or killed) sorted through a collection of casualties mirroring the plane's trail of destruction. Fatalities, in addition to the ship's chief torpedo man, included a water tender, a signalman, a quartermaster, another torpedoman, and a fire controlman. The wounded men who stood a chance of surviving were carried inside; others were removed to a stretch of main deck nearly awash in blood.

Destroyer *Twiggs* (DD-591) was along *Haraden*'s port side within minutes of the crash, using her own fire main pressure and hoses to help contain fires. As with destroyers *Stanly* and *Dashiell* closing with cruiser *Nashville* to render aid, *Twiggs'* time alongside *Haraden* was a chance for her sailors to get a firsthand look at the destruction caused by one plane and its suicide pilot. *Twiggs* and *Haraden* were both Fletcher-class destroyers, so it was a little bit like coming upon an identical twin after a horrible accident—like seeing your own self in ruins and wondering just how that happened and how it might feel. To Robert Melville, 19, a quartermaster on *Twiggs'* bridge, "It was frightening, to put it mildly", to see *Haraden*'s bridge (Melville's own station on *Twiggs*), in such bad shape.

Unrolling the Big Blue Blanket

The elements of a major Japanese aerial strike on the Mindoro convoys—186 planes launched from fields scattered across Leyte, Luzon, Negros, and Panay—were readied for 14 December. Japanese planning was well coordinated but based on a faulty assumption: that American ships were bound for Negros or Panay instead of Mindoro. Japanese aircraft—including almost fifty *kamimazes*—launched that morning and vectored to the west coast of Negros never found their intended prey. What they found instead—what found them—were Task Force 38 fighter aircraft just returned from Ulithi. Eager Hellcat pilots splashed nearly two thirds of the errant attackers and the rest fled to shelter on smaller island airstrips.

The 14th coincidently signaled the start of McCain's Big Blue Blanket concept. B.B.B.'s new offensive tactics—engaging Japanese planes in the air while simultaneously covering airfields to destroy others who dared take off or land—were enhanced by new sea and air defensive tactics. These included the use of picket destroyers equipped with the latest in radar and IFF, plus the deployment of Jack Patrols—fighter aircraft stationed at the four corners of each task group to intercept low-flying intruders.

By evidently consolidating its aerial commands and dispersing its aircraft, Japan had, in Admiral William Halsey's begrudging estimation, "at last evolved a sound defensive plan against carrier attacks." He countered with his own moves. Task Force 38's four task groups were reduced to three, each with more carriers and a more substantial screen. Each carrier air group also got more fighter-bomber aircraft and fewer dive-bombers and torpedo planes.

McCain's B.B.B. held sway for three days. Task Force 38 fighter-bombers (joined by Marine Corsairs and CVE aircraft in the Sulu Sea) eventually claimed sixty air combat kills and more than 200 planes destroyed on the ground.

Meanwhile, the Mindoro Attack and Close Covering Groups transited the Sulu Sea undetected and arrived off Mindoro. At 0530 on 15 December, destroyers *Fletcher*, *LaVallette* (DD-448), *O'Bannon* (DD-450), and *Hopewell* (DD-681) deployed to begin firing at Mindoro's southern beaches. At 0700, thirty minutes before H-Hour, lookouts saw crowds of sightseeing Filipinos thronging the landing beaches. Bombardment was delayed while warning shots were fired to disperse the crowds.

These would-be greeters proved to be the only immediate obstruction to the landings. General Dunckel, who years before had toured Mindoro in a Model-T Ford, transferred from *Dashiell* to a PT boat for the ride to shore. The day's objective—the large town of San Jose—was in American hands by noon.

At the beachhead and offshore, however, the day was having its costs. A horde of *kamikazes* with escorts—nearly forty aircraft in all—evaded the Big Blue Blanket, some heading for the CVEs of Heavy Covering and Carrier Group, others for LSTs still off-loading troops, equipment, and supplies.

C.A.P. and AA splashed eight *kamikazes* over Heavy Covering and Carrier Group. Two ships—destroyer *Ralph Talbot* (DD-390) and CVE *Marcus Island*—each bagged one, although for both ships the margin of escape was narrow. In *Marcus Island*'s case, the suicide plane crash was just twenty feet off the starboard bow. As it roared by, the plane's wing clipped a lookout platform, severing the head of the sailor standing there.

On destroyer *Howorth*, the margin was close as well in a brush with two suicide planes. "Honey," *Howorth* yeoman Orvill Raines wrote days later to his wife, "they turned right at us and to every man on the ship it looked like they were coming at them personally. The feeling of chance and uncertainty was almost unbearable. Right in their faces the boys kept firing. They were hitting them all over. I can't imagine what held them together."

Howorth fishtailed to escape one plane but a second plane soon followed, chopping away *Howorth*'s mainmast radar antenna before bouncing off the forecastle and into the sea. "I never saw such fear on anyone's face," Raines wrote. "They stood almost frozen . . . scared out of their wits. I easily understood it because the three seconds between the time they shouted 'duck' and when he actually hit, I have never felt so far from you Darling and yet so close."

Though none of the crew had been injured, plane wreckage was strewn across *Howorth*'s decks, including, according to Raines' letter, "a piece of the Jap's cheekbone picked up by the medical officer."

The Mindoro landing craft had come up on ideal beaches—wide, gently sloping, with firm sand underfoot. For once, GIs walked ashore with dry shoes. Trucks and tanks raced inland unimpeded by mud. For men who'd endured two months of Leyte's muck and mire, it was a blessing to be free of the typhoon belt and astride dry land.

Ideal conditions expedited off-loading, but they also served the needs of Japanese planes. Army C.A.P. alerted ships to a covey of Japanese aircraft flying up from the south. C.A.P. pilots trimmed the raid from twenty planes to ten, but these ten swooped low across the shoal waters between the landing beaches and invasion fleet's main body to target two slow-moving LSTs—*738* and *472*.

Gunfire from the LSTs and destroyer *Moale* (DD-693) claimed four planes, but two were able to crash. One plane hit *738* near the waterline, exploding its stores of ammunition and aviation fuel; the other rammed *472*'s main deck forward of the superstructure, its bomb penetrating to explode on the tank deck below. *Moale* came alongside *738* to fight fires only to be caught by an explosion that holed her bow and wounded 10 sailors. *O'Brien* and *Hopewell* tried to assist *472*, but were turned back—thereby escaping a second explosion.

There were only a handful of casualties, but both LSTs burned like beacons until sunk by destroyer gunfire later in the afternoon. By nightfall, invasion transports and landing craft were clear of Mindoro's beaches, formed into a convoy with *Dashiell* (still a temporary flagship) and eight other destroyers as screen, and were on their way back to Leyte.

There would be no bogeys to torment the return journey of the Mindoro Attack Group—but no protective air cover either. The weather—so fine and clear at Mindoro—turned grim over Leyte, spreading its own blanket of wind and rain to ground Japanese and American aircraft alike.

Meanwhile, in the eastern half of the Philippine Sea, Task Force 38's carriers, battleships, cruisers, and destroyers suspended battle operations on 16 December and converged for refueling set to begin early on 17 December. Many Task Force 38 ships rode high—low on fuel but also "de-ballasted" in anticipation of soon topping off. They were scheduled to rendezvous with a replenishment group out of Ulithi: ten oilers, five CVEs (with replacement aircraft for Task Force 38's carriers) plus an entourage of tin cans and fleet tugs. The rendezvous point would take them outside the reach of any Luzon-based Japanese aircraft. It would, however, plant both groups in the path of a stealthy and particularly savage typhoon.

★ Chapter 16 ★

Uncompensated Losses, December 1944

For some reason that goes deep into the soul of a sailor, he mourns over shipmates lost through the dangers of the sea even more than for those killed by the violence of the enemy.

—SAMUEL ELIOT MORISON

Divine Wind

Typhon, a hundred-headed mythological monster, so frightened the Greek gods (not least Zeus) that they ran in terror on first seeing him. In one Chinese dialect the word *tai-fung* translates to "Formosa Wind." For Japan, whether called *shinpu* or *kamikaze*, the "god wind" or "divine wind" phenomenon achieves the sacred: tradition holds that fierce typhoons were responsible for destroying Mongol invasion fleets poised to overrun feudal Japan.

The Western Pacific typhoon season runs from April through December; during these months as many as two dozen mature typhoons either threaten or assault the Philippines, Japan, and China directly. The storms are the survivors of a season's stockpile of embryonic tropical depressions that meander westward, gathering moisture and energy from warm equatorial seas and spin from the earth's rotation. When tropical depressions reach critical typhoon mass, the center of the spin—a vortex called the eye—becomes a netherworld of mountainous ocean swells and plunging barometric pressure rimmed by palisades of torrential downpours and high winds.

* * *

During World War II, typhoon early warning systems were crude at best—much less advanced, for example, than systems for spotting, identifying, tracking, and firing at enemy targets. Organized storm-warning methods were all but undone by wartime secrecies, fast-changing battle operations, and foul-ups in communications and ship handling, both small and colossal. The most reliable "systems" turned out to be simple, age-old nostrums rooted in practical seamanship and common sense.

In the midst of a typhoon, modern communications might also supersede good judgment. In making decisions for his ship and crew, a nineteenth-century sailing captain had to rely on his knowledge, wits, and conscience. With advances in long-range communications, however, a twentieth-century warship captain also often had to answer to the judgments of experts and superiors far from the scene.

In such circumstances, it was almost worse if the radio or telegraph circuits went silent. Storm or no storm, the warship captain had his orders. What did the silence mean? Was he to keep going at all cost? Should he wait for further instructions or take action now? Such dilemmas were defining tests of leadership and self-confidence, especially for young captains on small ships in a big war on an even bigger sea.

Small Ships, Big War . . .

Destroyers *Hull* and *Monaghan,* both Pacific War veterans, were escorts for the Ulithi refueling group. *Hull*'s experience included Guadalcanal as well as wide-ranging operations throughout the Northern and Central Pacific. During the attack on Pearl Harbor, *Monaghan* had been the second tin can (after *Ward*) to draw blood. In the three years since, the ship and her crew had earned twelve battle stars in emblematic sea-air battles such as Coral Sea and Midway.

Hull had just returned in August from a West Coast overhaul during which the now aging tin can (she'd been launched in 1935) was updated with the latest in armament (especially 20- and 40-mm guns), radar, and communications equipment. The modernization enhanced *Hull*'s serviceability and fighting power, but also compromised seaworthiness.

As a result of the overhaul, *Hull*'s 1,395-ton launch weight ballooned beyond 2,000 tons, with most of the added weight installed at the main deck level and in the superstructure. *Hull*'s (and *Monaghan*'s) original design included two outsized smoke stacks—taller than those on the Fletchers and absent any streamlining "rake." The stacks acted almost like fully rigged sails; now they combined with the top heaviness to make ships such as *Hull* and *Monaghan* less trim and stable in any kind of sea.

Hull, to say the least, had become a ship-handling challenge for even an experienced skipper and crew; yet she returned to the war with many untested recruits as well as a new young CO, Lieutenant Commander James Alexander Marks. Though he was a Naval Academy graduate (class of '38) with nearly three years' actuals on destroyers in the Atlantic, Marks was still learning the ropes in his first full-fledged combat command.

Described by another young destroyer skipper as "very serious and very regulation," Marks was no favorite of the crew's veterans. He suffered by comparison with *Hull*'s previous skipper who had forged strong wartime bonds with his chiefs, petty officers, and sailors. Soon soured by Marks' "by-the-book" demeanor, the crew also considered his ship handling suspect—another sharp contrast with his predecessor. A running joke among crewmen was that with Marks at the conn, no dock was safe. The ship's chiefs soon settled on their own sardonic nickname for the skipper: lengthening his first initials "J. A." into "Jackass." About twenty other sailors were even believed to have voted with their feet—going AWOL while the ship was still in overhaul and turning themselves in only when *Hull* was well on the way to the Pacific.

Monaghan also had a new skipper, Lieutenant Commander Bruce Garrett, a Naval Academy classmate of Marks and also in his first combat command. *Monaghan*'s crew had no opinion—pro or con—about Garrett. Garrett had assumed command barely twenty-four hours before the fueling group left Ulithi. There simply hadn't been time to get to know him—or he them.

Replenishment operations on 17 December were perilous from the start. Fueling went slowly; towlines snapped; hoses frequently parted, spilling oil across already treacherous decks; and collisions almost occurred more than a few times. Still, Admiral William Halsey was reluctant to belay fueling. He knew his destroyers' bunkers were low, with many tanks even drained of seawater ballast in readiness to take on fuel. Moreover, Halsey had promised General Douglas MacArthur that Task Force 38 would be ready to resume air strikes on 19 December. Still nursing a bruised ego from the Bull's Run fiasco of late October, Halsey was loath to renege on his commitment.

Eventually, though, just after midday, Halsey concluded fueling efforts were only inviting disaster and ordered them stopped. Several ships especially low on oil, among them destroyer *Spence* (DD-512), were ordered to stay with the oilers and look for an opportunity to fill up. The rest were sent to a new rendezvous point to the northwest, with fueling to resume at first light on the 18th.

Soon, however, with combatants and replenishment ships alike still floundering in mountainous seas against gale-force winds, there were new doubts about conditions they'd find at the new location. Halsey's staff aerologist was increasingly convinced the beast (naming typhoons was not yet a tradition) was also tracking northwest. Toward nightfall, accordingly, Halsey set yet another rendezvous point—this one southwest of the initial site and far south of the second.

Ships steaming northwest turned more to the southwest. Under the prevailing conditions, even slight course changes were risky. Poor timing or finesse risked broaching and becoming "locked in irons"— caught athwartships in a deep trough between wave crests. Once the new courses were set, however, some skippers noted moderating seas and rising barometers. For a few hours, in what amounted to a high-stakes game of blind man's bluff (in which the pursued couldn't spot the pursuer), the westbound ships managed to outpace the storm's speed by several knots. It gave the illusion the worst might be over.

Patrick Douhan, a *Hull* sonarman (and one of the ship's thirteen "expectant fathers") never dared leave the bridge during the night of the 17th. Conditions were so bad that *Hull* rolled as far as seventy degrees on either side of her keel. At the limits of each roll, green water poured over the exposed bridge wing.

Douhan's watch station was in the combination sonar and radar compartment behind the bridge. Both systems were brand new but completely inoperable following hours of wind, salt spray, and pounding sea. Douhan knew even if they were functioning, neither sonar nor radar would be of much use under current conditions. But this didn't seem to keep CO Marks from hounding the radar techs to get the systems up and running. It was clear to Douhan that the techs were only risking their own lives in a hopeless effort. Equipment and fixtures were breaking loose as the techs tried to work—and either actually crashing to the deck or literally flying across the compartment.

Hull's worst vulnerabilities—its age and smaller size, its top-heaviness, and its hardheaded skipper—did not include low fuel. Overall fuel reserves were about 70 percent. Conditions for *Hull*'s sister ship *Monaghan* were even better: her bunkers were more than three quarters full. The fuel situation, though, was much worse for destroyer *Spence*.

Spence, a Task Force 38 tin can, was a newer, heavier, and sturdier Fletcher Class ship. A few of her veterans, including Albert Rosley, 20, a torpedo petty officer from western Maryland, were charter members of Arleigh Burke's DesRon 23 Little Beavers. Most, though, were not. Like *Hull, Spence* was just back from a West Coast overhaul with both a new skipper and many teenage recruits. The new CO, Lieutenant Commander James Andrea, was a Naval Academy man in the class just ahead of *Hull*'s Marks, but the two new skippers seemed worlds apart—at least in the estimations of their respective crews. Unlike Marks, Andrea had gotten off on the right foot with his crew (including veterans such as Rosley), largely by making frequent rounds of his ship, stopping for coffee and conversation whenever he came across one of the impromptu enlisted "coffee messes" that flourish on virtually any Navy ship.

While *Spence* was more seaworthy than either *Monaghan* or *Hull,* her fuel reserves were dangerously low at ten to 15 percent—barely enough to steam another twenty-four hours in placid seas.

By the afternoon of the 17th, when *Spence* was detached from Task Force 38 to remain with the oiler group, side-by-side "parallel" refueling was already out of the question. The ships resorted instead to stern-to-bow methods. At first the oilers trailed inflated canvas balls attached to ropes; the idea was for destroyer deck crews to grapple the balls, tie off the lines, and use them to transport fuel hoses. The problem was that *Spence*'s sailors couldn't spot the balls in the turbulent seas—much less snare them and haul them aboard. Oiler crews also tried to pass lines by attaching them to floating empty forty-two-gallon drums and even a jury-rigged surfboard, all to no avail.

Before midnight on the 17th, when it was evident that none of his ships could reach the third rendezvous in time, Halsey once again set new coordinates—these to the northwest and, it turned out, even more squarely into the storm's path. During the next hours, wind and sea only intensified. At 0500 on the 18th, the latest rendezvous was scratched, and all ships were ordered to make best speed south.

All these changes in rendezvous coordinates, courses, and speeds had scattered Halsey's flock across roughly 2,500 square miles of ocean. Some ships found themselves in better conditions and some in much worse. Carrier *Hancock* (CV-19) reported only scattered showers while, for carrier *Wasp* (CV-18), midmorning seas ranged from "very high" to "mountainous." At one point *Wasp* passed so close to the storm's eye that it painted distinctly on the ship's SG—surface search—radar; an image taken of the screen was probably the first ever photograph of a typhoon's cyclonic core.

Hancock and *Wasp* withstood the seas well, as did the other big carriers, the battleships, and most cruisers. On the light carriers, however, it was a much different story. Despite doubled tie-downs and flattened tires, hangar deck aircraft rolled, banged, and occasionally caught fire. Eighteen aircraft on *Monterrey* (CVL-26) were destroyed. For carrier *Cowpens* (CVL-25)—nicknamed "The Mighty Moo"—the toll was seven aircraft, as it was for *San Jacinto* (CVL-30).

The damage to the carriers was bad but containable. The ships that fared worse were the smaller, narrow beam vessels—especially the DDs.* Among these, the ones who fared worst of all were those riding high like *Spence* or those whose captains stubbornly tried to fight the storm as they might fight the Japanese—by charging ahead, at all costs.

---

*The even smaller DEs seemed to ride the storm better, in part because their topside profiles presented less "sail area" to typhoon winds.

Lieutenant Commander J. H. Wesson, the skipper of destroyer *Hickox* (DD-673) had it about right. "You cannot fight a typhoon," Wesson reported to higher-ups before buttoning up and heaving to—and thereby saving his ship. Wesson's pragmatism may have been aided by luck or by God. By midmorning on the 18th, however, neither good fortune nor divine pity would intervene to save destroyers *Hull*, *Spence*, and *Monaghan*.

. . . Bigger Sea

Patrick Douhan had stood by helplessly on *Hull*'s bridge for eighteen straight hours. Though conditions had only deteriorated, Douhan decided to head aft to his sack in the after berthing compartment and to try to get some sleep. At last sensing his chance (and in his haste leaving his life jacket), Douhan made a dash for it. He somehow reached the after deckhouse, got down to his berthing space, and crawled exhausted into his bunk, only to have a huge roll toss him hard to the deck. Bruised, frustrated, and scared, Douhan climbed back up to the after deckhouse, where about twenty other terrified sailors huddled.

By now *Hull* was locked in irons, wallowing helplessly in a deep trough. To make things worse, the deck house starboard hatch had blown off, exposing the sailors inside to cascades of seawater each time *Hull* leaned to starboard. The winds on the port beam seemed to be howling more loudly than ever. It was approaching 1100 and Douhan was certain *Hull* was on her last legs.

After failed refueling attempts on the 17th, *Spence*'s tanks were below 10 percent by dawn on the 18th. Skipper Andrea, despite earlier advice from old hands, was only now ordering seawater ballasting of his tanks. It was too late and ballasting efforts had to be abandoned. Meanwhile, saltwater was getting into topside ventilators. Water reached a compartment containing the ship's master circuit board and began shorting out panels and circuits. Soon power was all but gone throughout the ship and the rudder was locked hard to starboard. Water was a foot deep in most compartments, and damage control parties were struggling to shore up failing bulkheads. The after deckhouse collapsed totally, and a gaping hole ripped open on the fantail as depth charge racks were torn loose and carried away. *Spence* took more rolls, each time recovering, but only partially. A final roll to port pushed *Spence* onto her beam ends. *Spence* hung there, her entire starboard side from keel to mast top exposed, awaiting the verdicts of sea and sky.

Had the sea paused in its verdict, more of *Spence*'s sailors might have escaped. As it was, the sea's decision was swift, uncompromising. *Spence* continued to roll until the bottom of her capsized hull bulged like a huge grave marker atop the water. Many men were trapped inside.

North of where *Spence* capsized, destroyers *Hull* and *Monaghan* were losing their struggles as well. When *Hull* made her fatal roll to starboard, pure panic erupted among the sailors in the after deckhouse. With the starboard hatch blown off, there was nothing to hold back the incoming sea. The port hatch was dogged down, and men dangled from its latches to stay above the rising water, in effect blocking the one path to escape. Patrick Douhan managed to grab the hatch's handle, braced a foot against an overhead vent (essentially a bulkhead fixture now), and pushed up with all his might. But it was no use—the hatch was held down by too much human weight.

Douhan knew there was nothing else to do if any of them were to get out. He used his free foot to kick at the hands clutching the latches. This cleared several latches and other hands fell away as men sensed the opportunity. Finally, the hatch swung wide and most of the men got through. Douhan found himself prostrate and without a life jacket on the outer bulkhead of the deckhouse, with *Hull* already awash and settling beneath him.

Monaghan was most likely the last of the three tin cans to succumb. Despite his inexperience and the loss of power, CO Garrett and his crew had somehow managed to keep *Monaghan* from broaching by running before the wind. At about 1100, in hopes of leveling *Monaghan*'s stern, Garrett ordered ballasting of *Monaghan*'s after tanks. As on *Spence*, the futile effort came too late. Overheads in the engine and fire rooms were now literally being peeled back from structural bulkheads. By 1130 the last of *Monaghan*'s generators gave out and the ship spaces went completely dark. One crewman counted seven giant rolls before *Monaghan* broached and was carried high up the slope of a swell. Near the top, *Monaghan* slipped and skidded back like an edgeless ski athwart a steep cliff. Finally, in the trough, an avalanche of water buried *Monaghan* and her crew.

Fighting On

Crammed with other torpedo gang sailors into a shack atop the forward deckhouse, *Spence*'s last capsizing roll took Albert Rosley by surprise. The roll may have buckled the shack or forced its door and simply shaken its occupants loose. At any rate, Rosley found himself without a life jacket in an upside-down, underwater world, pinned against the flash shield of a 20-mm gun. After squirming free and getting reoriented, Rosley stroked resolutely to reach the surface.

To his great relief, Patrick Douhan found a stray life jacket. As he finished putting it on, a rush of water swept him forward, depositing him amidships near a 40-mm gun bay. As Douhan grabbed a railing, he saw another sailor who was pinned under a big life raft still lashed to *Hull*'s forward deckhouse. Douhan knew him—a Pearl Harbor veteran always ready with a raised fist and a cry of "Fight on!" It was the man's response to all of life's trials, petty or monumental. His fist was raised now, Douhan could see, though there looked to be little chance he would get free.

Just then Douhan lost his grip and was swept clear of the wreckage. He found himself in open water in the middle of a cluster of sailors, all grabbing at two more big life rafts cut loose from the ship. The rafts seemed to be strung together: as wave crests passed, men and rafts were all tossed into the air. Douhan got a handhold on one raft, only to watch it smash the other with such force that it crushed the heads of several men caught between like popcorn kernels. Douhan recoiled, let go, and was almost instantly swept away.

For the first time since he'd been pulled from the ship, Douhan got a full sense of how small he was compared to the waves. It was like being at the bottom of an endless stampede of formless giants. And the sky was no better. It was raining so hard that Douhan had to shield his face from what felt like a shower of needles. Then he was suddenly being pulled down, so fast and so deep his ears seemed about to pop. Douhan was all but certain he was being sucked into the propellers of another ship.

A cluster of *Spence* survivors found themselves surrounded by pieces of floating debris and several rafts and floater nets. Because *Spence* had been so low on fuel, there was not much of an oil slick, although more than enough to coat the men with a patina of black, stinking goo. Albert Rosley popped to the surface near one of the floater nets. Rosley was a good swimmer, but he was also without a life jacket, so it was a relief to grab something that promised buoyancy. Rosley saw other men gathered around the floater net, perhaps as many as twenty to twenty-five. That was a relief as well—not to be alone.

Another man on this floater net was Al Krauchunus, *Spence*'s supply officer. Just before the sinking, Krauchunus had been lying down in the wardroom, trying to sleep when *Spence*'s chief engineer ran in and warned him the ship was taking water down its stacks. At first he was too exhausted to heed the warning, but when Krauchunus finally got up and reached the door, he was slammed by a torrent of water that nearly sucked him back into the wardroom. Krauchunus used all his strength to cling to a bulkhead railing, his body flapping "like a flag in a gale."

Finally, when the ship lurched back and the flood receded, Krauchunus filled his lungs and scrambled through an access hatch to the main deck. The next thing Krauchunus knew, he was floating just a few feet from *Spence*'s inverted hull, trying to breathe while simultaneously vomiting fuel oil and seawater. Krauchunus was also without a life jacket, but several floated within reach; he grabbed one and tied it around his legs.

For the moment, bobbing on the lee side of *Spence*'s upturned hull, he was protected from the worst of the waves and wind. But Krauchunus knew he had to get away or risk being pulled down. He waited for his retching to subside, gulped some air, and pushed off from the hull into the sea. Somehow, Krauchunus found his way to the floater net.

In calmer seas, the net—an expansive fishnet-like rectangle buoyed by cork floats—would have ridden flat. But each big wave rolled it up like a carpet, throwing some men free while entangling others. After each wave, the survivors struggled to untangle the mess. Occasionally a new survivor would appear, but time and the sapping of individuals' strength and resolve constantly whittled away at the number of survivors.

By midafternoon the winds and seas at last began to moderate. Before sunset, some ships were able to report brightening skies, and near nightfall, wind speeds were down to 60 knots. At 1848, Halsey ordered all Task Force 38 ships to post additional lookouts to spot missing sailors washed overboard.

It was after midnight when Halsey first learned any ship had been lost—a signal relayed from destroyer escort *Tabberer* (DE 418) that her crew had rescued survivors from *Hull*. Shaken, Halsey quickly ordered an all-out search, one that would take three days and the full-time efforts of seven ships.

It was the end of Halsey's plan to resume strikes against Luzon on 19 December. Most ships were grappling with storm damage or low on fuel or both. Fueling operations resumed on 19 December, but as ships readied to launch strikes on 21 December, the storm remnants settled over Northern Luzon. Flight operations were all but impossible, so Task Force 38 continued on to Ulithi for rest, repairs, and Halsey's appearance before a court of inquiry.

Wind from Below

The Mindoro landings stunned Japanese planners who realized Mindoro's capture threatened supply routes to Luzon and hopes to finally halt the American advance toward Japan. The *Ōkas* would be important weapons in this struggle, but only if their deployment could be accelerated.

By mid-December, a shipment of thirty *Ōkas* reached Kure and another fifty-eight reached Sasebo on Kyushu's western coast. Now the rush was on to move the craft by sea to the Philippines. Aircraft carriers *Unryu* and *Ryuho* were assigned the mission and their departures— *Unryu* from Kure, *Ryuho* from Sasebo—were moved up to 17 December.

Simultaneously, deployment also accelerated for the Thunder Gods Corps. Planes and pilots from a Betty-equipped squadron were assigned to the Corps, as were pilots and planes from a Zero squadron. In total, fifty-four Bettys and sixty Zeros were to be rushed to the Philippines.

Most, but not all, the Ōka pilots were also being sent to the Philippines with a small contingent to remain in Konoike and train new volunteers. This decision set off strong emotional ripples among the more fanatic Ōka pilots like Keisuke Yamamura. Yamamura and the other early volunteers had been promised the lead in suicide attacks and, accordingly, a unique place in the hearts of the Japanese people. Now, however, such attacks were already occurring in the Philippines using conventional aircraft and pilots with no special training. The cachet of the Thunder Gods was beginning to wear thin, costing the men honor and stature.

As these frustrations boiled, operational planning suffered another huge setback. On 19 December, not quite halfway to Luzon, carrier *Unryu* met the same fate as *Shinano,* this time by torpedoes from *Redfish* (SS-395). *Unryu*'s loss gave Japan's fleet headquarters second thoughts about sending any of the Thunder Gods to the Philippines. *Ryuho* was rerouted to Formosa and her 58 Ōkas were off-loaded there. Japan had lost two aircraft carriers and 138 Ōkas without the Thunder Gods program striking its first blow. Except for the Ōkas already in Formosa, no more craft were to be deployed long distances by sea. The operational range of the Ōkas would be bounded by the range of the mother planes flying from mainland bases.

Dreams of Rescue

When Patrick Douhan popped back to the surface, he realized waves, not ship's propellers, were pulling him down. It happened time and time again: as surely as Douhan was pulled under, he would bob up again. Though he never lost his fright, Douhan quickly learned not to fight the inevitable. In doing so, he managed to conserve his strength. Douhan also somehow managed to focus on the positive—that he would get out of this alive and return to his wife and new baby.

* * *

By early afternoon on the 18th, the worst of the typhoon was over for *Spence* survivors on the floater net. The men established what order they could, spacing themselves around the net so as not to unbalance it. They also counted heads, learning their number was down to twelve. Besides Krauchunus, there was one other ship's officer, and there were ten sailors, among them Albert Rosley. They were elated when they snared a canvas bag containing an inflatable 20-man raft. After inflating the raft, four men, including Krauchunus, climbed on. He quickly sensed the raft's stability couldn't be trusted in such heavy seas and returned to the net. The three others, though, decided to take their chances with the bucking raft. It carried them away and they were never seen again.

The afternoon lengthened into a tranquil evening and a cold night. The morning of the 19th brought placid seas, but also a sun burning high, hot, and long. The men had some water rations—a swallow every three hours from a keg attached to the net—but little else besides knives and a small hatchet. The hatchet was used to crack open a drifting canister of what turned out to be vegetable shortening, which the men used to smear their exposed heads, shoulders, arms, and feet. A few even tried eating it. Some wondered whether the shortening would repel—or attract—sharks.

By daybreak on the 20th, the group was down to six—Krauchunus, Rosley, and four others. There were several plane sightings, but none very close. All were by now beginning to hallucinate. When the profile of an escort carrier hove into sight, the men screamed themselves into delirious exhaustion, but with no apparent success. Rosley was convinced the carrier was a huge automobile speeding down a glistening highway.

It seemed hours before the waves eased and Pat Douhan set his mind to other worries—first and foremost the possibility of sharks. During the first night, when Douhan felt something bump the back of his neck, he was so keyed up he froze in panic. The bump turned out to be a large wooden sweeper's broom stenciled with the letters "USS HULL." For a moment, Douhan felt like he'd found a lost friend. He also found

The Alligator: Vice Admiral Richmond Kelly Turner on board USS *Rocky Mount* (AGC-3) off Saipan, 17 June 1944. NAVAL HISTORICAL CENTER PHOTOGRAPH

The Bull: Admiral William F. Halsey, Commander, Third Fleet *(right)* conferring with Vice Admiral John Sidney (Jock) McCain, Commander, Task Force 38 *(left)*. NAVAL HISTORICAL CENTER PHOTOGRAPH

Admiral Ernest J. King, Commander in Chief, U.S. Fleet *(center)* with Admiral Chester W. Nimitz, Commander in Chief, Pacific Fleet and Pacific Ocean Areas *(left)*, and Admiral Raymond A. Spruance, Commander, Fifth Fleet *(right)*, July 1944. NAVAL HISTORICAL CENTER PHOTOGRAPH

Vice Admiral Marc A. Mitscher Commander, Task Force 58 *(right)*, confers with his chief of staff, Commodore Arleigh A. Burke *(left)*, on board TF58's flagship, USS *Bunker Hill* (CV-17), during operations off Japan in February 1945. NAVAL HISTORICAL CENTER PHOTOGRAPH

Vice Admiral Thomas C. Kinkaid *(left)* with General Douglas MacArthur *(center)* on the flag bridge of USS *Phoenix* (CL-46). NAVAL HISTORICAL CENTER PHOTOGRAPH

Admiral Raymond A. Spruance, Commander, Fifth Fleet *(left)*, and Lieutenant General Holland M. Smith, USMC, Commander, Fifth Amphibious Corps on Saipan, 10 July 1944. NAVAL HISTORICAL CENTER PHOTOGRAPH

USS *Quincy* (CA-39) illuminated by
Japanese searchlights during the Battle of
Savo Island, off Guadalcanal, 9 August
1942. *Quincy* was sunk in this action.
NAVAL HISTORICAL CENTER PHOTOGRAPH

U.S. Marines rest in the field on
Guadalcanal, 1942. NAVAL
HISTORICAL CENTER PHOTOGRAPH

Executive officer Robert M. Morgenthau
(later District Attorney of New York
County) at the July 1944 commissioning
of USS *Harry F. Bauer*, named in honor of
the commanding officer of the USS *Gregory*
(APD-3), who was killed at Guadalcanal.
NAVAL HISTORICAL CENTER PHOTOGRAPH

Battle of the Philippine Sea, June 1944.
Pilots in a ready room on board USS
Monterey (CVL-26), after landing at
night following strikes on the Japanese
fleet, 20 June 1944. U.S. NAVY
PHOTOGRAPH

USS *Belleau Wood* (CVL-24) burning after being hit by a suicide aircraft, 30 October 1944. USS *Franklin* (CV-13), also hit during this attack, is afire in the distance. NAVAL HISTORICAL CENTER PHOTOGRAPH

Japanese suicide plane disintegrates in flames after hitting USS *Intrepid* (CV-11) during operations off the Philippines, 25 November 1944. NAVAL HISTORICAL CEN-TER PHOTOGRAPH

Burial at sea for crewmen of USS *Intrepid* (CV-11) killed during aerial suicide attack, 25 November 1944. U.S. NAVY PHOTOGRAPH

Crewmen cleaning up the port side gun battery of USS *Nashville* (CL-43) after the ship was hit in that area by a *kamikaze*, 13 December 1944, while en route to the Mindoro invasion. NAVAL HISTORICAL CENTER PHOTOGRAPH

USS *Langley* (CVL-27) rolling sharply as she rides out the "Great Typhoon" of 18 December 1944. NAVAL HISTORICAL CENTER PHOTOGRAPH

USS *Pennsylvania* (BB-38) and battleship of Colorado class, followed by three cruisers, move in line into Lingayen Gulf preceding the landings on Luzon. NAVAL HISTORICAL CENTER PHOTOGRAPH

Marines of the 28th Regiment, Fifth Marine Division, hoist the U.S. flag on a piece of pipe, at about 1020 hours on 23 February 1945, after capturing the summit of Iwo Jima's Mount Suribachi. This was some seventeen minutes before the famous flag raising immortalized by Associated Press photographer Joe Rosenthal. NAVAL HISTORICAL CENTER PHOTOGRAPH

USS *Franklin* (CV-13) afire and listing after being hit by a Japanese air attack while operating off the coast of Japan, 19 March 1945. NAVAL HISTORICAL CENTER PHOTOGRAPH

Damage to USS *Lindsey* (DM-32) after being struck by suicide planes off Okinawa, 12 April 1945. NAVAL HISTORICAL CENTER PHOTOGRAPH

USS *Intrepid* (CV-11) afire, after she was hit by a *kamikaze* aircraft off Okinawa 16 April 1945. A Fletcher class destroyer steams by in the foreground. NAVAL HISTORICAL CENTER PHOTOGRAPH

U.S. Navy F6F Hellcat from VF-16 being launched from USS *Lexington* (CV-16). NAVAL HISTORICAL CENTER PHOTOGRAPH

U.S. Navy TBM-1C "Avenger" of Torpedo Squadron 51 takes off from USS *San Jacinto* (CVL-30). NAVAL HISTORICAL CENTER PHOTOGRAPH

Carrier-based F4U Corsair (wings folded) being armed with rockets. U.S. NAVY PHOTOGRAPH

Japanese Mitsubishi *Zero-Sen* "Zeke" fighter bomber on Philippine airfield, equipped with a bomb and preparing to take off on a suicide mission during the Leyte operation. NAVAL HISTORICAL CENTER PHOTOGRAPH

Japanese Aichi "Val" dive bombers take off on a suicide mission from an airfield near Manila in the Philippines. NAVAL HISTORICAL CENTER PHOTOGRAPH

Mitsubishi "Betty" medium bomber with *Ōka* special attack craft mounted underneath fuselage. NAVAL HISTORICAL CENTER PHOTOGRAPH

Damage to USS *Hazelwood* (DD-531) from aerial suicide attack, 29 April 1945. U.S. NAVY PHOTOGRAPH

USS *Aaron Ward* (DM-34) in the Kerama Retto anchorage after being hit by several Japanese suicide planes off Okinawa, 3 May 1945. NAVAL HISTORICAL CENTER HOTOGRAPH

Flight deck scene on USS *Bunker Hill* (CV-17) following *kamikaze* hit, 11 May 1945. NAVAL HISTORICAL CENTER PHOTOGRAPH

Casualties from USS *Evans* (DD-552) are brought aboard USS *PCER-855* from USS *Ringness* (APD-100) after *Evans* was damaged by *kamikaze* attacks while on radar picket duty off Okinawa, 11 May 1945. NAVAL HISTORICAL CENTER PHOTOGRAPH

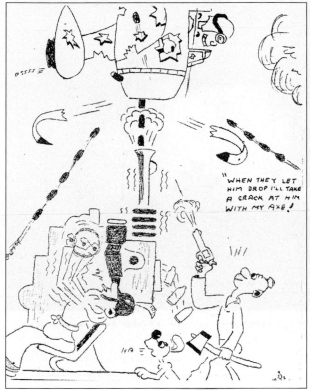

"Keep shooting until his prop brushes your whiskers. In the last thousand yards he still has a lot of smart flying to do to hit you." (Illustration and excerpt from "Calling All Destroyers," a training pamphlet prepared by crew of USS *Wadsworth* [DD-516] and later widely distributed.) U.S. NAVY DOCUMENT

"Now hear this. One Val headin' for our fantail. Sweepers standby to starch 'ur brooms!" (The "pooch" shown in these illustrations is "Willie," the *Wadsworth* mascot.) U.S. NAVY DOCUMENT

USS *New Mexico* (BB-40) hit by suicide aircraft at dusk, 12 May 1945, while off Okinawa. NAVAL HISTORICAL CENTER PHOTOGRAPH

A marine of the first Marine Division draws a bead on a Japanese sniper during fighting to take Wana Ridge near the town of Shuri in May 1945. NAVAL HISTORICAL CENTER PHOTOGRAPH

USS *William D. Porter* (DD-579) sinking after a near miss by a suicide aircraft off Okinawa, 10 June 1945. Two LCS(L) amphibious craft are alongside, taking her crew off. NAVAL HISTORICAL CENTER PHOTOGRAPH

USS *New Mexico* (BB-40) anchored in Tokyo Bay, late August 1945. Mount Fuji is in the background. *New Mexico* was hit twice by *kamikaze* aircraft, resulting in a combined casualty of more than 80 men killed and more than 200 men wounded. NAVAL HISTORICAL CENTER PHOTOGRAPH

Mel Cratsley *(left)*,
USS *Caldwell* (DD-605).

Patrick H. Douhan,
USS *Hull* (DD-350). PHOTOGRAPH
COURTESY PATRICK H. DOUHAN

Left: Lawrence C. Finn,
USS *Bennett* (DD-473).

Right: Nick J. Korompilas,
USS *Mannert L. Abele* (DD-733). PHOTOGRAPH COURTESY
NICK J. KOROMPILAS

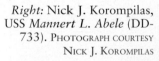

Left: Malcolm Fortson, Jr.,
USS *Leutze* (DD-481).

Right: Paul (P. D.) LaRochelle,
USS *Lindsey* (DD-771/DM-32)

Richard M. McCool,
LCS(L)-122.

Donald A. Lorimer, USS *Intrepid* (CV-11).

Left: Warren E. McLellan,
USS *Lexington* (CV-16),
VT-16. PHOTOGRAPH COURTESY
WARREN E. McLELLAN

Right: Joseph A. Lehans,
USS *St. Lo* (CVE-63)
PHOTOGRAPH COURTESY
DARA LEHANS

Left: Fred W. Mitchell,
USS *Drexler* (DD-741).
PHOTOGRAPH COURTESY
FRED W. MITCHELL

Right: Aristides S.
Phoutrides, USS *Laffey* (DD-
724). PHOTOGRAPH COURTESY
ARISTIDES S. PHOUTRIDES

Rufus B. Thompson, Jr.,
USS *Nashville* (CL-43).
PHOTOGRAPH COURTESY
RUFUS B. THOMPSON, JR.

Harold M. Scott, Jr.,
USS *Bennion* (DD-662). PHOTOGRAPH
COURTESY HAROLD M. SCOTT, JR.

Left: Charles D. Towers,
LCS(L)-118.
PHOTOGRAPH COURTESY
CHARLES D. TOWERS

Right: Al Turnbull
(center), USS *Bunker Hill*
(CV-17), VT-84.
U.S. NAVY PHOTOGRAPH
COURTESY AL TURNBULL

Left: Arthur P. Whiteway,
USS *Lexington* (CV-16),
VF-16. PHOTOGRAPH
COURTESY ARTHUR P.
WHITEWAY

Right: Paul K. (Cactus)
Walters, USS *Suwannee*
(CVE-27). PHOTOGRAPH
COURTESY PAUL K. (CACTUS)
WALTERS

he could rest his arms and hands on the broom and restore some feeling to his fingers.

Once, Douhan spotted a searchlight beam. It quickly raised hope but just as quickly disappeared. Hours later, though, Douhan spotted a second light, this one much dimmer. He shouted and this time got a reply. It turned out to be a raft filled with fifteen other *Hull* survivors. He was glad to see them, but there was no water or food on the raft. Men were packed tightly inside, standing in torso-deep water, supported only by the raft's "floor"—a loose latticework of slats.

Just after midnight, first one man and then several more spotted a shape on the horizon. Hopes of being near an island were dashed by the prospect it was Japanese held. Some even smelled the characteristic sweet, pungent odor of Japanese cooking; despite their hunger, it made them tense and nauseated. Then another undeniable scent—diesel oil: it must be a Japanese submarine surfacing to recharge its batteries. The raft went silent and stayed that way even after the apparition disappeared.

By the morning of 20 December, as small, widely dispersed clusters of survivors began the ordeal's third day, dozens of more fortunate men—most from destroyer *Hull* including her CO James Marks—were rescued and aboard destroyer escorts *Tabberer* and *Swearer* (DE-186) and destroyer *Knapp* (DD-653).

DE *Tabberer*'s sailors were the biggest heroes in the first hours after the sinkings. Still battling the storm (during which she lost her main mast and most radio communications) and using searchlights whose beams barely topped the wave crests, her crew spotted and picked up ten *Hull* survivors before midnight on the 18th. Each rescue came at great risk: *Tabberer*'s CO Lieutenant Commander Henry Lee Page steered fifty yards upwind of his target, stopped *Tabberer* and let the wind and waves carry her to the "floater." More than one survivor washed up on *Tabberer*'s deck like a large fish.

Riding gentler waters next day, *Tabberer* pulled in twenty-eight more *Hull* sailors. This catch earned Page and his exultant crew the right to continue the hunt through 20 December. It was about then that the first *Spence* survivors turned up. *Tabberer* rescued several before sunup, and at 1030, *Swearer* found the floater net holding Krauchu-nus, Rosley, and four other sailors.

Douhan had seen *Tabberer*'s searchlight on the night of the 18th. Between the time of the *Hull*'s sinking and rescue by destroyer *Brown* (DD-546) midmorning on 21 December, survivors in the life raft had drifted nearly seventy miles. The raft, it turned out, did offer some protection against sharks, Douhan's worst fear. On the morning after the sinking, dorsal fins began to circle. The sharks—some men guessed they were twelve to fourteen feet long—made exploratory passes during that first day, but took no bites.

The sharks' restraint was rewarded by the 20th, as men succumbed to exposure, dehydration, kidney failure (from gulping seawater), and desperation. After a prayer and the redistribution of their garments, corpses were cast loose to the sea and the waiting sharks. There was even some live meat. One man left the raft bound, he believed, for a ship's galley stocked with sandwiches and 7 Up. When another man tried to retrieve him, a shark bite gouged his upper arm while other sharks converged on the delirious swimmer.

By the 21st, none of the remaining dozen men were fully coherent. Douhan's optimism had all but vanished after nearly seventy-two hours. If a raft mate took a sip of salt water, it was barely noticed and rarely protested. Lost in personal delirium, the men rarely interacted; when they did, it was with a glare or a curse. Few took note the sharks were circling ever closer.

Rescue seemed out of the question, so when rescue finally arrived in the shape of destroyer *Brown*, it had a dream-like quality. The fury of the sharks robbed of a feast; gunfire from *Brown* sharpshooters to kill the sharks; the arms lifting them onto a cargo net and helping them aboard; other arms that all but carried them belowdecks to bunks; even the sips of water and mugs of steaming pea soup—all became aspects of each man's hallucinations. Douhan, for example, was convinced he was aboard a Russian submarine and didn't understand how the men helping him could possibly be speaking English.

Also lost to these men was the rescue's sad postscript. Twenty minutes after pulling in the *Hull* survivors, *Brown* found a raft carrying six delirious men off destroyer *Monaghan*. The six were *Monaghan*'s first, last, and only survivors.

Admiral Breaker

By Christmas Eve, destroyer *Brown* had reached Ulithi and transferred the *Hull* and *Monaghan* survivors. When Pat Douhan was carried aboard Hospital Ship *Solace* (AH-5), the path his stretcher took was flanked by a chorus of nurses singing Christmas carols. Douhan, like most, was already springing back. He'd regained his senses and a few of the fifty pounds he'd lost. His legs, though, were covered with painful saltwater abscesses, eventually requiring surgery.

Tabberer was the first rescue ship to reach Ulithi, and her "catch" of *Hull* and *Spence* survivors was already aboard *Solace*. It was time for a series of joyous and impromptu reunions, though the mood soured when the latest influx of survivors became the last. Only then did each man begin his personal tally of lost shipmates and buddies.

The final combined losses would be staggering. In addition to the sinking of three warships and serious damage to scores of others, there was the human toll: nearly 800 officers and sailors drowned, including all but 24 of *Spence*'s crew and all but 6 of *Monaghan*'s. In Admiral Chester A. Nimitz's judgment (in a January 1945 letter that remained classified for ten years), it was the Navy's greatest loss "without compensatory return" since the 1942 Battle of Savo Island.

For several days, beginning 26 December, a court of inquiry chaired by three admirals convened at Ulithi in the wardroom of destroyer repair ship *Cascade* (AD-16). More than fifty witnesses were called to testify.* Lieutenant Commander James Marks, the lone surviving captain among the three lost destroyers, became the inquiry's sole "defendant." Mark's face was still covered with saltwater sores, and his eyes were still swollen nearly shut when he took the stand. His defense of his own actions was that *Hull* had not been released from station until

---

*Albert Rosley sat in on part of the inquiry, but did not testify. Patrick Douhan did not attend the inquiry.

early morning on 18 December. Though losing all in efforts to stay in formation, he was simply following orders. When asked, by court custom, whether he had accusations against any of his crew, Marks said he did not. When the court addressed the same question in turn to each *Hull* witness, their answers were the same.

The court's most prominent witness, of course, was Admiral William Halsey. He appeared on the first day and, as anticipated, his testimony was staunch and unbowed. Solid evidence of an actual typhoon had not been confirmed until early morning on the 18th. By then, in his words, "the horse was out of the stable." His commitment to resuming air strikes on Luzon, he conceded, "was uppermost in our heads right up to the last minute."

On 3 January, the court of inquiry returned a two-hundred-page, single-spaced report replete with 157 "Findings, Opinions, and Recommendations." The report attributed losses of *Hull* and *Monaghan* to their inexperienced captains, older designs, and top-heavy retrofits. *Spence*'s skipper James Andrea was also faulted posthumously for his failure to ballast his ship's stern tanks and for not removing topside weight.

While there were other admonishments—to Task Force 38's aerologist for relying too much on remote weather reports rather than the situation at hand and to task force commander McCain for briefly turning his carrier task groups squarely into the typhoon's track— overall responsibility fell to Halsey. Yet, in judging the actions of a still-popular fleet commander, the court's words were measured, if not equivocal. The report's carefully parsed bottom line was that Halsey's "mistakes, errors, and faults" were ones "of judgment under stress of war operations" rather than "offenses."

The court's findings, opinions, and recommendations, of course were just that. Actions, if any, were up to Pacific Fleet's Chester Nimitz, whose terse 22 January memorandum approving the court's proceedings and findings, stepped back even more from judgment's brink. No further proceedings were ordered for *Hull*'s Marks. As to Halsey, his mistakes and errors (the term "faults" was stricken), in addition to being mitigated by the "stress of military operations," also stemmed "from a commendable desire to meet military requirements." Nimitz's actions may have been intended to mollify Halsey—already stung by the words in his commander's frank, though classified, letter. Halsey's fighting qualities, after all, were essential for the hard road still ahead.

None of this, of course, brought comfort to those closest to the men lost at sea. All the while as the court of inquiry took testimony, it issued its report, and the surviving principals awaited its conclusions, word of the 800 deaths was making its way toward families and communities. At first the word was tentative. On 13 January 1945, for example, Mr. and Mrs. William Harvey Merritt in Easley, South Carolina, learned via telegram that their son Roy Merritt, a *Spence* torpedoman, "is missing while in the service of his country X As you undoubtedly know the ship to which he was attached was lost in a recent typhoon in the Pacific area X." Only on 9 February did the contents of a second telegram—"Careful review of all facts available relating to the disappearance of your son . . . leads to the conclusion that there is no hope for his survival"—confirm the worst.

If these telegrams were clipped and stark, the condolence letters that followed were less so. Al Krauchunus, signing himself as "Senior Survivor," wrote a letter to the parents of *Spence* sailor Robert Louis Strand that perhaps was as hard for Krauchunus to write (custom versions were likely sent to hundreds of next of kin) as it was for Strand's loved ones to read. "At the time of capsizing, Robert was not able to get off the ship and into the water. He was not seen by any of the survivors at any time after the ship rolled over."

The most resonant letters of all came from surviving shipmate buddies. When *Hull* survivor Kent J. May wrote Robert Wilson's wife Ruby in New Mexico, he told her that "Bob and I were very close friends. We had lots of good times together. I thought an awful lot of him." Wilson and May had both escaped *Hull* and reached a raft. Wilson seemed all right recalled May, "But very soon a large wave hit us and I didn't get back to the raft at all and doubt if he did either." And if May's opening words about his friendship with Wilson rang with warm truth, his later words likely rang with quiet finality: "I can't offer you any hope for his life. To the best of my knowledge and belief he is deceased."

All these communications joined sadness with perplexity. Many back home were prepared for violent wartime death, but not from a storm. (Liz Strannigan, Wilson's nine-year-old niece had no idea what a typhoon was.) Though the men were as surely dead as if they had been shot, bombed, or torpedoed by the Japanese, there would be few awards for heroism or sacrifice—not even Purple Hearts.

In normal times, the loss of 800 men and three warships in a single catastrophe, man-made or natural, would grab headlines and collective emotions—a small but important consolation for those enduring individual grief. But January 1945 was no normal time. News about thousands of losses in Europe's Battle of the Bulge crowded papers and signaled that victory in Europe—and probably the overall war—was nowhere at hand.

Meanwhile, in the Pacific, the climactic battle for the Philippines—the invasion of Luzon—was under way. The battle ashore seemed to be going well, although it would drag on to claim huge casualties among combatants and civilians alike. But the struggle's first violence struck earlier, during the very first days of January, when the skies above Lingayen Gulf seemed to become the very dome of Hell.

★ **Part Three** ★

THE CRUELEST MONTHS

★ Chapter 17 ★

Corpses That Challenge the Clouds, January 1945

In serving the sky, be a corpse that challenges the clouds.
—JAPANESE "SONG OF THE WARRIOR"

Under Way for Some More Fighting

In the first days of the invasion of Luzon, an American Army sergeant interrogated a captured Japanese sailor—a rare opportunity. Speaking through an interpreter, the sergeant asked the prisoner if he thought Japan could hope to win the war. Japan would certainly win, the prisoner responded—and for one indisputable reason: "Japan is one mind." The prisoner's actual words—*yamato damashi*—were new to the sergeant, so he asked the interpreter for more of its meaning. There was no equivalent English word or phrase according to the interpreter. "Fighting spirit" perhaps came closest, but *yamato damashi* actually meant much more. "If you think of a willpower that no force on earth, short of killing its possessor, could discourage, and add to that the stubborn, cold belief of a bigot, you might get a little closer to its meaning."

Troops for the invasion of Luzon—GIs from five separate 6th Army divisions—were assembled from over a dozen South and Southwest Pacific bases, all but one captured from the Japanese. Each base was a reminder in concrete and Marsden matting of how fully the tide of Japan's East Asian Empire had ebbed, while Japan's powerful, well-equipped, well-trained, well-housed, and well-fed enemies moved ever closer to its shores.

GIs from the 37th and 40th Divisions boarded transports at Bougainville (once a dreaded Japanese strongpoint in the Solomons) and embarked 15 December as Task Force 79 (the Lingayen Attack Force), sailing first across the Solomon Sea for a landing rehearsal along New Guinea's southeast coast and then north to Manus in the Admiralties, their final staging point for the Philippines. Lacking deepwater harbors, the transports and LSTs for Task Force 78 (the San Fabian Attack Force) spent the same period laboriously shuttling two Army divisions' worth of men and equipment from beaches farther up the New Guinea coast.

The Luzon Attack Force (designated Task Force 77), meanwhile, finished assembling in Leyte Gulf just as the New Year turned. Its fleet of 164 ships included firepower from six battleships, six cruisers, and nineteen tin cans, plus aircraft from a dozen escort carriers. On 3 January, its lead elements sailed through Surigao Strait and into the Mindanao Sea.

Counting the Task Force 78 and 79 elements simultaneously converging on the Philippines from Manus and New Guinea, General Douglas MacArthur, now riding *Boise* (CL-47) after the disabling of *Nashville,* commanded an invasion force of 280,000 GIs, sailors, and airmen. *Howorth* yeoman Orvill Raines summed it up in a 2 January letter to his wife: "Underway for some more fighting."

MacArthur's Luzon adversary, Lieutenant General Tomoyuki Yamashita, commanded what seemed, at least in numbers, a formidable defense: upward of 270,000 ground personnel. Yamashita, 59, known as the "Tiger of Malaya" for his ruthless conquest of the Malaysian Peninsula at war's outset, had spent much of the war in disfavor. Sidelined to duty in Manchuria, Yamashita was recalled only when Japan's hold on the Philippines was finally imperiled. Yamashita took command in Manila just days before the American invasion of the Philippines and had been fighting a delaying action ever since.

Yamashita was confident, even boastful, in public. He was bluntly dismissive about the fall of Leyte and Mindoro: "The loss of one or two islands does not matter." Yet inwardly, Yamashita despaired, knowing his supply and logistics channels were all but choked off. Following high command orders, he had reluctantly dispatched tens of thousands of reinforcements to certain death in Sosaku Suzuki's futile defense of Leyte. The best Yamashita could do in defending Luzon was to buy time while the home islands prepared for a final stand.

Though he didn't know the timing of the inevitable American invasion of Luzon, Yamashita was sure of its entry point. It would come at Lingayen Gulf, over the same ground used by Japan's own forces in the 1942 conquest of the Philippines—and for the same reason. The broad, flat central Luzon plain—the doorway to Manila and an ideal maneuvering ground for tanks and ground troops—was accessible only from Lingayen. Girding for his best strategic option, a lingering battle of attrition, Yamashita decided to evacuate Manila and shift nearly all his forces, including those entrenched at the Lingayen beachheads, to positions in remote mountain jungles east of the capital.

Meanwhile, at Clark Field outside Manila, evacuation to Formosa was being arranged for Shigeru Fukudome, Takijiro Onishi, and other Naval Air leaders. Ground personnel were being organized into brigades destined ultimately for ground fighting.

Though the end was near for Japanese airpower in the Philippines, there were still hundreds of planes earmarked for aerial suicide parked in concealed revetments and pilots standing by to battle the invasion once it began. The only thing lacking was realistic hope that these planes and pilots could defeat the Americans using conventional strafing, bombing, and torpedo tactics. *Taiatari seishin*—the substitution of guts for skill—was the only alternative.

After December's operations at Ormoc and then Mindoro, the waters beyond Surigao Strait had become almost casually familiar—though U.S. skippers and crews knew they traveled within easy range of Japanese airfields and close to shores that masked bogeys from radar detection. Already, on the first day out, a suicide Val had crashed an oiler while another *kamikaze* was shot down close astern of escort carrier *Makin Island* (CVE-93). The two episodes demonstrated just how perilous the Mindanao and Sulu Seas remained.

After steering southwest past Bohol and Cebu, Luzon Attack Force rounded the southern tip of Negros, repositioned its flocks of amphibious and support craft into two large groups shielded by CVE C.A.P.s, and pointed northwest, with the western shores of Negros and then

Panay to starboard. Late in the afternoon of 4 January, as lead elements approached Mindoro Strait, a low-flying Betty plowed into the flight deck of carrier *Ommaney Bay* (CVE-79).

There'd been virtually no warning before this near perfect hit. None of *Ommaney Bay*'s guns got off a shot. Clifford Grant, 24, a loader in the 40-mm gun tub on the forecastle, realized something had happened only after the Betty had already crashed *Ommaney Bay*'s island and flight deck. One of the plane's two bombs exploded in the hangar deck, the other in the forward engine room. *Ommaney Bay*'s fierce fires were soon capped by billowing oily black smoke.

The first blasts seemed to mark *Ommaney Bay* as a goner. Within minutes, the most seriously wounded sailors were being strapped into stretchers and, with kapok life jackets affixed, lowered over the side. Grant, a veteran who'd been on *Helena* during Pearl Harbor and later survived the cruiser's sinking in the Solomons, tried to calm sailors who were scared they might be trapped. With no hope of containing the conflagration, sailors used finally fire hoses as descent lines to the water.

As *Ommaney Bay* lost headway, several tin cans raced in to pick up floating survivors and even send over salvage parties. Then, flames reaching torpedo warheads stored on the hangar deck triggered explosions that sealed the ship's fate. After a half hour in the water, Grant was picked up by a whaleboat from destroyer *Burns* (DD-588). Grant reached *Burns*'s deck in time to see a spread of torpedoes fired into *Ommaney Bay*, sending her to the bottom.

Ommaney Bay's casualty count was steep—93 killed or missing and 65 wounded—and included repair parties from other ships. For *Eichenberger* (DE-202), the afternoon's effort was a devil's bargain: her whaleboat rescued three *Ommaney Bay* sailors, but three of her own were killed aboard *Ommaney Bay*.

Next day, the Luzon Attack Force was in the South China Sea abreast of Luzon. After the loss of *Ommaney Bay*, men who'd not been nervous before now had every reason to be. The ships were their closest to Manila's airfields, and C.A.P. had already intercepted and thinned out morning and midday raids of about fifteen bogeys each.

As expected, the day's heaviest raid—twenty bogeys—approached at dusk. There followed a quick string of suicide crashes and bomb hits to cruiser *Louisville* (CA-28), two Australian cruisers, and two tin can screens. The biggest victim, carrier *Manila Bay* (CVE-61), absorbed a suicide flight deck crash by a bomb-laden Zeke and barely dodged a second. Unlike *Ommaney Bay*'s, though, *Manila Bay*'s fires were quickly contained.

As darkness fell on 5 January, with ships due to reach Cape Bolinao, the portal to Lingayen Gulf, before sunrise, Task Force 77's Vice Admiral Jesse Oldendorf (the architect of late October's victory in Surigao Strait) had reason to be both satisfied and apprehensive. He had led his fleet on its farthest advance yet into Japanese waters on the west side of the Philippines. The passage had cost him one ship, varying degrees of damage to ten others, and just over 400 battle casualties.

However, 6 January's agenda—invasion preliminaries for 9 January's S-Day*—would place attack group ships within even easier reach of Japan's Philippine-based airpower.

Unmatohed by Any Other

For the U.S. ships at Lingayen, 6 January was to be a day unmatched by any other since the *kamikaze*'s debut. It began with Task Force 77 separating into groups—the CVEs to open sea northwest of Lingayen, fire support ships to bombardment stations off either shore at the entrance to Lingayen Gulf, and a quartet of destroyers to shield minesweepers from coastal batteries. C.A.P. intercepted a morning raid of ten bogeys, shooting down five and chasing the rest, but even more were overhead before noon. A near miss dive by one *kamikaze* on destroyer *Richard P. Leary* kicked off a relentless hour of direct hits to *New Mexico,* destroyer minesweeper *Long* (DD-209/DMS-12), two destroyers, and a transport.

New Mexico's big guns were firing at targets along the eastern shore of Lingayen when a Japanese plane already in flames crashed her port

---

*Ever since June 1944 when D-Day—the 6 June schedule for the invasion of Northern Europe—had overshadowed and been confused with the 15 June D-Day for the invasion of Saipan, U.S. Pacific War planners had been careful to designate invasion dates with letters other than "D."

bridge wing. Casualties were heavy—30 dead, 87 more wounded—and included the ship's CO, a senior British liaison officer and Robert Sherrod's *Time* colleague William Chickering.

Fifteen minutes later, a Zeke crashed *Long*'s port side, igniting huge fires that prompted a rush to abandon ship. Sister ship *Hovey* (DD-208/DMS-11) sped to the scene to scoop up survivors: just one fatality, but dozens with severe burns.

Meanwhile, gunners on destroyer *Walke* (one of the minesweeper screens) battled four attackers. They shot down two, but the wing of a third—a Zeke armed with a bomb—sliced into the bridge. Bill Rugh, 19, a port side 20-mm gunner stationed just below the bridge, ducked an instant before the plane's wing hit. When Rugh got to his feet, his shirt and dungarees were burning, but he quickly put out the fire, sprinted to the railing, and leaped feet first to the main deck. Fleeing barely a stride behind Rugh was Pete Ryan, the gun's loader. Ryan had been soaked in gasoline and burned like a torch until Rugh and several other sailors were able to tackle him and smother the flames.

The Zeke's bomb had broken loose on impact but failed to explode; instead it zipped clear through CIC, passing just inches from the head of Ben Hall, *Walke*'s sonar officer. Splashes of gasoline followed in its path. Hall, though shaken, was untouched by either gasoline or flame, but a sailor standing across from him was instantly wrapped in flame—burning, Hall later recalled, "like a corncob."

Though now out of commission, the CIC space itself was still intact, while the officers' wardroom—the forward battle dressing station during GQ—was in ruins. With no other place to take the wounded, they were carried into CIC.

Among the worst of the casualties was *Walke*'s new skipper Commander George Davis, who'd taken command less than two weeks before. Hall liked Davis and thought him by far the best of the three skippers he'd worked under. Davis, clad now only in shoes, a watch band, and dog tags, was horribly burned. He was in desperate need of plasma, but it was hard to find a spot to attach an IV. *Walke*'s doctor finally discovered a patch of unburned skin near Davis's groin. Davis got his plasma but died within hours.

Like Davis, Rugh, and Ryan, most of *Walke*'s casualties (47 in all with 13 dead, including George Davis and, several days later, Pete Ryan) were burn victims. All three had literally been set ablaze, while others, often just as badly injured, were instead scalded by superheated steam. When Ben Hall tried to grasp the hand of one of these victims, a damage control officer, a sheath of elbow-length skin slipped off like a glove.

On 6 January the chaotic noon hour gave way to a somewhat less hectic though no less unnerving afternoon. There were two mid-afternoon *kamikaze* hits: first to cruiser *Columbia* (CL-56) and then to destroyer *O'Brien*. The long day's worst hour—more casualties, heavier damage, and the most tragic circumstances—waited again for dusk when inshore units were withdrawing to open water. Three of the final victims were from a bombardment group: battleship *California* and cruisers *Australia* and *Louisville*. Their combined casualties, all in a fifteen-minute span, exceeded 300, including nearly 50 dead. During the worst of the melee, *California* caught friendly fire; for both *Australia* and *Louisville*, the suicide crashes were their second in as many days.

Lingayen Gulf skies had quieted by sunrise on the 7th, though not before *Hovey* took an aerial torpedo to her starboard side near the engine room. *Hovey* immediately lost power and headway and rapid flooding swamped and sank her within minutes. Dying with *Hovey* were 22 of her own crew and 24 as well who'd been rescued from *Long* just hours before. With S-Day still two days off, the Japanese were marshaling *kamikaze* raids of heretofore unseen scale and destructive power.

At twilight on 8 January, escort carrier *Kitkun Bay*, one of two CVEs providing air cover for the Lingayen Attack Force, rounded the tip of Cape Bolinao in company with other Task Force 77 ships heading into Lingayen Gulf. It was, wrote historian Samuel Morison aboard MacArthur's flagship *Boise*, "one of those sunsets that poets wrote about in happier times."

On the 7th, hewing to their routine, *kamikazes* had broken the day's tranquility at dusk with the quick sinking of *Palmer* (DD-161/DMS-5). They followed this day with a diminished round of morning hits: two glancing (to cruiser *Australia,* her third and fourth) and three more damaging (to escort carrier *Kadashan Bay,* a transport and an LST). Then, once more, quiet—as if somehow respectful of the weather or the next day's planned landings or (U.S. sailors hoped) running out of planes

A cool wind greeted sailors coming topside to relieve watch for dinner, but the wind also carried six *kamikaze* aircraft who swooped in a half hour before sunset. C.A.P. splashed four of the would-be crashers while triple A seemed to discourage the remaining two momentarily. Then one of them, an Oscar, worked its way back into the formation. It climbed to about six thousand feet and then nosed over, heading for *Kitkun Bay,* a victim of one of the *kamikaze* debuts off Samar in October.

Last-second maneuvering almost brought *Kitkun Bay* clear, but the pilot crashed the water so close on the port side that his plane's explosion ripped a huge underwater gash in *Kitkun Bay*'s hull near the after engine room. Water flooded fire rooms and engine rooms, blacking out all power except for steering and tilting the ship thirteen degrees to port.

Many if not most of *Kitkun Bay*'s more than 50 casualties were victims of friendly fire—proximity rounds shot by other ships. With flooding so bad and *Kitkun Bay*'s fate uncertain, only a skeleton crew stayed aboard as the carrier was towed north to open water. Alfred White, 19, a seaman assigned to *Kitkun Bay*'s flight deck, jumped to the bow of destroyer *Stembel* (DD-644) where he spent the night sleeping in a passageway, as did many of his Kitkun Bay shipmates.

There was just one more *kamikaze* try—a near miss to an Australian transport—before attack group ships reached their position for S-Day landings. It had been a grueling day during which the U.S. and Australian ships had been badly mauled by the suiciders. It was an experience that never escaped the memories of those who survived it. They had been battered, but not turned back.

Get to Manila!

On S-Day morning, the weather in Lingayen Gulf was cool with barely a breeze. The invasion fleet rode a gentle ocean groundswell under a partial overcast of cumulus and cirrus clouds. Anticipating the arrival of early morning *kamikazes,* sailors now experienced the same pre-landing jitters as GIs. Ships rode at close quarters, making it difficult to either maneuver or fire guns without injuring friends.

As it turned out, only a few bogeys turned up to oppose the landings. At 0700, one *kamikaze* pilot took poor aim at *Hodges* (DE-231) just as the shore bombardment guns opened fire. One of his plane's wings barely clipped the DE's mainmast, and he nosed into Lingayen Gulf, taking no lives but his own.

Forty-five minutes later a second *kamikaze* had better luck against cruiser *Columbia* then hemmed in by landing craft on all sides. It made *Columbia*'s third suicide crash in four days, this time to the ship's forward main battery director that was uprooted and carried over the side. With 92 new casualties, fully 15 percent of Columbia's crew had been killed or wounded in the Lingayen operation.

S-Day saw just two more suicide crashes, both in early afternoon when two Vals from a flight made wave-top runs on battleship *Mississippi* and cruiser *Australia,* both on call-fire stations off San Fabian landing beaches. *Mississippi*'s attacker came in on the bow and slammed the superstructure before caroming into an AA gun mount and over the port side. It took just an instant, but casualties cost was steep: 86, including 23 dead. *Australia,* much battered after four crashes but much more fortunate on this fifth, took just a glancing blow to a stack.

And that was it for the day—after the ordeal of 6 January and dreading what S-Day had in store. It was cause for relief, but also some grumbling as news about the troop landings reached the ships. At 0930, when the first GIs stepped ashore on the beaches, they faced virtually no opposition and soon learned why. The Japanese had bugged out, leaving beach defenses all but deserted.

This was good news for the GIs of course, and who could begrudge them an unopposed landing? Still, after so much damage and so many shipmate casualties, it must have seemed to many sailors that the trip to Lingayen actually had as much to do with fighting *kamikazes* as it did with landing troops.

The Luzon Plain that lay before MacArthur's GIs was a forty-mile-wide amphitheater bounded by rugged mountain ranges—the Ilocos and Zambales. Maneuvering by tank and on foot, one Army corps hewing to the right and the other to the left, the Lieutenant General Walter Krueger's GIs had to travel 110 miles south to reach Manila.

At first, troops and ground intelligence officers worried about being lured into a trap; but the first day without significant opposition led to a second day. By dusk on 10 January, advance units had already pushed eight miles inland with only a handful of casualties.

Sizing up his opponent's options, MacArthur was convinced he knew what was happening. Recalling his own last ditch stand in the Philippines, MacArthur assumed the Japanese were withdrawing to a more defensible site—if not to Bataan and Corregidor as he had three years before, then into the mountains east of Manila. Wherever the final stand, it would not be in Manila.

And so MacArthur urged Krueger to race south. "Go to Manila!" MacArthur implored field commanders at every opportunity. "Go around the Japs, bounce off the Japs, save your men but get to Manila!"

Each night at sunset, a chemical smoke screen was spread by gunboats stationed to westward and seaward of the battleships, cruisers, and transports in Lingayen Gulf. It gave no cover to invasion tin cans, and they were kept busy throughout S-Day's dusk, fighting intruders—and sidestepping friendly fire. That same night nearly seventy Japanese "suicide boats"—high-speed plywood craft equipped with two depth charges and a machine gun—left concealment to attack the formation. The boats with their two-man crews caused damage to a few small ships, but most paid for it with the loss of their lives.

Dawn and dusk on 10 January each claimed a lone suicide casualty—a destroyer escort in the morning and a transport at sunset. But that night, and then through all of 11 January, not one *kamikaze* showed over Lingayen or elsewhere. Once again, there was the hope that the Philippine *kamikazes* had run their course.

By 12 January all but a handful of Japanese planes were gone from the Philippines, including the several hundred replacements sent to Luzon in December. A day before the Americans troops landed on Luzon, Vice Admiral Shigeru Fukudome ordered the remnants of his Second

Air Fleet flown to Formosa,* and Rear Admiral Takajiro Onishi (the inspiration for *Tokkotai* operations in the Philippines) left that same day. Air Fleet ground crews were sent to join Luzon's infantry. Some pilots ordered to fly aircraft to Formosa instead detoured for impromptu *tokkō* strikes on American resupply convoys spotted heading toward or leaving Lingayen.

Among the Philippine ground crew units reassigned to fight with the Japanese Army was an advance unit of technicians and ground personnel sent to prepare for the Thunder Gods deployment. Now, the total unraveling of that plan stirred widespread disillusion throughout the corps. After training so hard only to face postponement after postponement, many pilots began to question their resolve.

Disillusion only deepened with the influx of hundreds of new Thunder God recruits. Many were young naval reserve officers fresh from basic flight training and nowhere near ready to qualify as *Ōka* pilots. The additions doubled the pilot ranks to nearly four hundred while creating two hostile camps of roughly equal size—older experienced pilot petty officers and younger inexperienced reserve officers. To Thunder Gods veterans, the new arrivals cheapened the corps's prestige.

A near riot erupted on 9 January, sparked by a drunken confrontation between petty officers and reserve officers. The uprising threatened traditions of structure, authority, and unquestioning obedience. Two petty officers were court-martialed, with both being expelled from the corps and one sentenced to a prison term.

The turmoil coincided with new deployment plans for the Thunder Gods Corps. With the Philippines no longer a possibility, operations would instead shift to Kanoya, a base in southern Kyushu.

With the Philippines skies virtually cleared of Japanese planes, there was opportunity to step back and assess its impact. Not just the loss of ships and lives—but the odds and means for surviving attacks.

There was much talk about tactics. Some extolled evasive maneu-

---

*Toshu Yoshitake was among the IJA pilots evacuated to Formosa. There he awaited orders for another *tokkō* mission. The orders never came and he eventually returned to Japan in 1946.

vering, while others argued that no ship at 30 knots could hope to outmaneuver an aircraft at 300 knots. No one disputed that accurate and rapid gunfire was crucial.

As to the objective odds (beyond ship handling and marksmanship), they seemed to be roughly this: In the skies above the Philippines, 27 percent of *kamikazes* managed to survive C.A.P. and AA to hit a ship. Once hit, 3 percent of the ships sank.

To a sailor it meant this: if your ship was jumped by four or more *kamikazes,* it was going to be hit. But what, then, were your odds of surviving that crash and returning home in one piece?

In his 9 January letter, Orvill Raines described the odds-setting mindset of *Howorth*'s crew: "We still haven't found another 'can' that escaped two suicide divers. Incidentally, that is now the only thing we fear from them."

Chapter 18

From Hot Rocks, February 1945

*Now indeed is the time for us, the one hundred million, to give
vent to our flaming ardor . . . in the footsteps of the valiant men
of the Special Attack Corps.*

— JAPANESE PRIME MINISTER KUNIAKI KOISO

The New "Old Breed"

In two months' time, Eugene Sledge, a mortarman with K Company of
the 3rd Battalion, 5th Regiment (K/3/5), part of the 1st Marine Division, would land on Okinawa. Sledge was now a blooded U.S. Marine,
veteran of the September 1944 invasion of Peleliu, where his company was tested in more than a month of the Pacific War's most brutal
combat.

Little understood at the time was Japan's use of Peleliu as a full-
fledged proving ground of its revised strategy for island defense—at
first "permitting" Marines and GIs to land, then decimating their
ranks from concealed, enfiladed positions on high ground and finally
fighting to the last man by falling back through a series of nearly im-
pregnable inland defense lines. The concept—later mounted on a large
scale on Luzon and envisioned as the strategy for defending the home
islands—precipitated a drawn-out struggle claiming more than 6,500
1st Marine Division casualties, including 1,200 killed. Afterward, all
who survived Peleliu had unquestionably earned their place in the
ranks of the "Old Breed."

Sledge himself emerged unwounded, but forever changed by Peleliu.
As K Company Marines withdrew from the slopes of Bloody Nose

Ridge, the Japanese defenders' last stand on the island, and boarded Higgins boats bound for waiting Navy transports, Sledge was plagued by the thought he might never get away, as if "Bloody Nose Ridge was pulling us back like some giant, inexorable magnet. It had soaked up the blood of our division like a great sponge. I believed it would get us yet."

The worn-out remnants of the 1st Marine Division were transported from Peleliu to Pavuvu, a Southwest Pacific island and part of the Russell Chain. The Marines had trained on Pavuvu in preparation for Peleliu and at the time quickly came to loathe its isolation, intense heat, pervasive smell of rotten coconuts, and infestation with tiny land crabs. Returning from combat, however, they were surprised to see how welcoming Pavuvu now looked when compared with the desolation and carnage of Peleliu. During the voyage to Pavuvu, Sledge learned in detail the stories of those who had survived Peleliu and those who hadn't. "I began to feel that I hadn't been just lucky," he wrote later, "but was the survivor of a major tragedy."

The Marines rested until year's end as new replacements filled out their depleted ranks. As 1945 began, however, the intensity of training picked up, generating a flurry of rumors about the new "blitz"—where it would be and when it would happen. No one would tell the troops about their specific destination, but the training emphasized street fighting and working with tanks in open country. In other words, the objective would not be a small island, and this would mean fighting alongside the U.S. Army, a prospect Sledge and his buddies did not relish.

While they weren't revealing the exact destination, Marine leaders were not pulling punches about what to expect. It was as though, after Saipan and Peleliu, no one dared again underestimate the Japanese. The Marines were told to expect heavy casualties—maybe as high as 85 percent. The prevailing mood was reinforced by news reports coming through in late February about the terrible fighting encountered by the 3rd, 4th and 5th Marine Divisions on Iwo Jima, a place already being called "Hot Rocks." The men of the 1st and 6th fully expected the same reception when they reached their next objective—whatever it was.

Soon enough, the cumulative weight of small clues and scuttlebutt pointed to the big island of Okinawa as their destination. Seeing the island's size and proximity to the Japanese mainland (Sledge first learned of Okinawa's existence from a *National Geographic* map of the Northern Pacific), K/3/5's men approached the remainder of the training with a heightened mix of focus and dread. It looked to be a hard place.

Hot Rocks for Flying Castles

Iwo Jima is part of the Bonins, an island archipelago (*Nanpo Shoto* to the Japanese) stretching from its northernmost point not far off Tokyo Bay south some seven hundred miles. Iwo Jima (*Jima* or *Shima* means island), among the southernmost islands in the chain, is a plot of terrain shaped like an inverted pear roughly four and a half miles long and two and a half miles wide. At its southern tip (the pear's stem) is Mount Suribachi, a 550-foot-high crater-capped volcanic cone. Suribachi's deep molten core remained inactive throughout the war; but the surface of its island outcropping was so layered with dark volcanic ash and its surface spat such high-pressured bursts of sulfurous steam, an eruption at any moment seemed likely.

Iwo Jima had little to recommend it other than its combination of relative size and location. Among many small islands in the archipelago, only Iwo Jima and Chichi Jima—a near and larger neighbor island to the north—had enough real estate to accommodate large airstrips. Both islands lay roughly equidistant between the Marianas and Japan's Honshu, making them ideal locales to support the B-29 air strikes from the Marianas. Either could be used as an emergency landing strip for crippled Superfortresses and double as an operational base for fighter aircraft to protect the B-29s over Japanese-defended air space.

In the choice between taking Iwo Jima or Chichi Jima, Iwo won out because it seemed, according to aerial reconnaissance, an easier, less-defended target. Scant intelligence estimates of the two islands held that Chichi Jima had been the center of Japan's naval operations in the archipelago for decades. Iwo Jima, by contrast, was estimated to have a single small airstrip and a garrison of just 1,500 troops. The thinking that chose Iwo Jima also prevailed in the choice of invasion forces. Before settling on the Bonins, a good deal of thought had been given to invading Formosa, an island comparable in size to Luzon. Iwo Jima was a much smaller piece of real estate: precisely the sort of target the Alligator and the U.S. Marines were best organized, equipped, and prepared to take on.

After the long diversion of resources and attention to the Philippines, the move to take Iwo Jima was like the opening of a new front—in some ways like beginning a new war. After the dreadful December news coming out of the European front, the Allies were again on the move and racing toward Germany. Not surprisingly, the sense of approaching the "end of the end" in Europe played havoc with the minds of men in the Pacific. Expectations and moods fluctuated based on the latest scrap of news or scuttlebutt. In a 2 February letter to his wife Ray Ellen, *Howorth*'s Orvill Raines expressed one shade of the mood: "How long before we can go home? It's something we don't discuss very often because some guy always says 'Three more years' or something and we chase him off the bridge."

Aboard ships with long Pacific tours, speculative rumors about going home were especially epidemic, built on seemingly irrefutable (but usually hollow) trains of logic. Writing in his personal diary in early February, destroyer *Dashiell*'s engineering officer Fred Wright rejoiced at orders sending ship and crew to Manus because, he reasoned, "Manus is usually the Stateside route." Three days later Wright's hopes still rode the crest: "Stevens [*Stevens* (DD-479)], Pennsy [*Pennsylvania* (BB-38)], and we are headed out for Manus—that much we know for sure. Then Pearl we think. But then—oh please!—let it be the States." Only to evaporate on the 17th: "Well it's no go." Instead of heading home, Wright wrote resignedly, *Dashiell* was "off for the next operation, probably the Bonins and Iwo Jima."

In mid-February, just before the Iwo Jima invasion, Army pilot Ryuji Nagatsuka began advanced fighter training. During several months attached to a squadron trying to repel B-29 raids on Kyushu, Nagatsuka never managed to shoot down a flying castle. Whenever Nagatsuka flew within sight of a B-29 cockpit, it drove him to a murderous fury seeing the pilots with their bloated faces and ruddy cheeks sitting calm and unblinking, like inanimate dummies. But Nagatsuka also knew his squadron's slow, lightly armed *Ki-27*s had no more impact on the B-29 (flying then without fighter escort) than "gadflies on the back of a large, impassive cow." Most often he simply ran out of ammunition before inflicting any damage.

"For a moment," Nagatsuka wrote in his diary following one of his first, hapless missions, "I wanted to beat the enemy, even at the cost of my own life." Nagatsuka realized that fighting in the air demanded absolute contempt for death—even for those, like himself, who were atheists with no belief in an afterlife.

Nagatsuka's fighter training base was forty miles northwest of Tokyo near a remote village. When he first arrived, Nagatsuka was surprised to find the base hangars empty; he soon learned that, due to frequent air raids, the airplanes were stowed in tunnels burrowed in the woods surrounding the airfield.

The aircraft—single-engine Nakajima *Ki-43 Hayabusa* (Peregrine Falcon, American code name Oscar)—were a step up in speed, climb, maneuverability, and firepower from the *Ki-27*. Still, while Japanese pilots touted them as worthy competitors to American Grumman Hellcats, the *Ki-43*s were no match for the Americans' newer land-based fighters.

Of course, the *Ki-43*s were of no use whatsoever without fuel; this was the other surprise that greeted Nagatsuka's arrival. The base had no fuel and, until new supplies arrived, he and other pilot trainees would, between lectures, assist the beetles in fabricating *Ki-43* mockups and placing them on the airfields to deceive the Americans.

Nobody Can Live Through This

Watching the predawn bombardment of Iwo Jima from the deck of attack transport *Bayfield* (APA-33), *Time* reporter Robert Sherrod thought it more terrifying than any similar spectacle he'd ever seen. He wrote in his notebook: "Though I've seen this many times, I can't help thinking, 'nobody can live through this.' " Then he added: "But I know better." Watching the impact of the shells, Sherrod and other spectators could see they seemed to set nothing afire. Each burst with a fierce twinkle but seldom with a secondary explosion. "We could see very early the Japanese were deep underground on Iwo."

In truth, despite all the practice and tactical refinements (including, early on, the diversion of outdated battlewagons with their huge guns for invasion use), the effectiveness of the Navy's island bombardment fire continued to disappoint. Sometimes—as at Luzon—the disappointment came from faulty intelligence, wasting Navy artillery fire on imagined targets. But there were also more fundamental problems.

Though aided by radar, sophisticated optics and even rudimentary computers, ships' main battery guns—including the DD 5-inchers—were relatively blunt instruments. In the crucial moments before and after the actual landings, the naval guns had to cease fire or risk dropping "friendly fire" on GIs and Marines. During these unavoidable lulls, the Japanese defenders invariably scrambled out of hiding to deliver murderously effective machine gun and mortar fire.

This enemy's tactic was better countered by smaller caliber automatic weapons. While most ships were equipped with such weapons, the shallow reefs encircling virtually every Central Pacific island made it all but impossible for deep draft ships to get in close enough to use them effectively. The obvious need was to bring floating fire power still closer to the beaches. The solutions were ever more heavily armed and versatile amphibious craft.

Dragons and Fire Trucks

Perhaps the oddest looking, but, pound for pound, most lethal of these craft was the LCS [the complete designation was LCS(L)3, for Landing Craft Support (Large) Mark 3], a subtle evolution of a landing craft (the LCI, for Landing Craft Infantry) first used during the invasion of Sicily. From the beginning, "Elsie items" had been "field modified" to install .50-caliber, 20- and 40-mm guns—even rockets and mortars.* The LCS design incorporated these features while adding some

*The LCI also became the platform for a range of other gunboat modifications, designated according to the primary weapons onboard: LCI-(G) for Gunboat; LCI-(R) for Rocket; and LCI-(M) for mortar.

protective armament and—equally important—storage magazines to hold the ammunition. The flat-bottomed, diesel-powered LCSs, each roughly 160 feet long, were also equipped with two high-capacity Hale pumps. To compensate for its ungainly lines (including a superstructure resembling a medieval castle turret), the LCS was, in effect, a practical (if somewhat contradictory) blend of fire-breathing dragon and fire truck.

The LCSs were built at such volume and pace (65 in Boston, another 65 in Portland, Oregon, each in an average thirty days from keel to launch) that it created a manpower crunch. Because of all the armament—five 40-mm, four 20-mms, six lesser-caliber machine guns, and ten rocket launchers—each LCS required a seventy-man crew: roughly ten thousand newly trained officers and enlisted.

To meet this need, cores of experienced amphibious sailors were sprinkled into mobs of recruits fresh from boot camps for three months' training at special facilities, including one constructed in Maryland's tidal flats—aptly named Solomons. Typical of the enlistees was Virgil Branch, a Texan from the oil boomtown of Refugio. Branch, 19, had enlisted just shy of his 18th birthday and been assigned to Solomons right after boot training.

Getting officers—experienced or otherwise—was another challenge. Most were 90-day wonders fresh from Midshipman School. Just about all the roughly two thousand ensigns graduating in June 1944 from the school in Plattsburgh, New York, for example, got amphibious duty. This was the route for Charlie Towers, a 20-year-old Princeton undergraduate originally from Gainesville, Florida. Towers' first assignment was to Higgins boat training at Fort Pierce, Florida. The base proved so miserably hot, humid, and mosquito infested (even to a native Floridian) that when volunteers were requested for LCS duty, Towers jumped at the chance. After four weeks of gunnery training (still at Fort Pierce), Towers transferred to Solomons and eventual assignment to *LCS-118* as gunnery officer.

Most prospective LCS skippers were drawn from junior officer billets on other small ships and amphibious craft. But there were occasional instances of near simultaneous emersion in shipboard command and in the Navy itself. At the Navy's prompting, for example, about fifty 1944 Annapolis graduates volunteered for LCS duty, lured by the prospect of getting a seagoing command right out of the gate—a giant first stride in any "Ring Knocker's" career.

One of these volunteers was Ensign Richard McCool, a 22-year-old Oklahoman whose father was active in Democratic state politics. Although McCool understood that qualifying for command would be a long shot, he at least had a slight edge in maturity. Prior to beginning Annapolis, McCool had already, at 19 years of age, received an undergraduate degree from the University of Oklahoma. Because the Academy's wartime curriculum had been accelerated for all Middies, many of McCool's classmates were raw 20-year-olds. This small but important element of gravitas apparently played out during McCool's three months' experience at Solomons where he demonstrated both ship-handling skills and at least a glimmer of command acumen. In November 1944, when *LCS-122* was commissioned at a shipyard in Neponset, Massachusetts, a Boston suburb, Ensign Dick McCool was assigned as its skipper.

As crews were taking the Boston-built *LCS-118* and *LCS-122* through the paces of shakedown and operational training on the East Coast, other crews crossed the continent to reach LCSs being readied at the Albina Shipyard in Portland, Oregon. In early August 1944, Virgil Branch, along with the rest of a pickup crew for *LCS-51* left DC's Pennsylvania Station for the five-day trip west. There was inevitably some slippage en route, not least because of temptations at train junctions along the way. In the boomtown of Pasco, Washington, for example (railhead for Hanford, Washington, where, unknown to any of the transients, atomic bomb research was pushing ahead), liquor was served nonstop at impromptu bars fashioned from rough boards stretched between empty beer barrels. Fortunately for *51*'s young skipper Howell D. Chickering, his crew arrived in Portland short just two strays.

The LCSs left for the Pacific in stages, usually in groups of four or five. After its West Coast shakedown, *51* left Portland bound for Pearl Harbor on 12 November 1944. About a month later, *LCS-118* and *LCS-122* left Solomons for the much longer trip, first south hugging the Atlantic seaboard and, when at all possible, its inland waterways and then through the Panama Canal into the Pacific.

Many LCSs would make their Central Pacific debut at Iwo Jima, but, by then, a handful were already at work in the Philippines. It was there, on 16 February, barely three days before Detachment's kickoff, an LCS flotilla was caught off guard in a sudden, bloody, and humbling introduction to suicide warfare.

Poised for a landing on Corregidor, six LCSs anchored across the mile-wide channel into Mariveles Harbor at the tip of the Bataan Peninsula were pounced on by a swarm of twenty Japanese suicide boats—Ocean Shakers—launched from caves hidden in the coastal cliffs of Corregidor. The attack came without warning, and in the confusion, the green LCS crews were scarcely able to defend themselves.

David Demeter, *LCS-7*'s 25-year-old communication officer on watch that night, managed to fire his handgun and carbine at a suicide boat just before it rammed *7*, exploded, and peppered him with shrapnel. Seaman Robert Alexander, 19, was blown over the side of *LCS-49* as he climbed a ladder to reach his gun station.

When Harry Meister, 23, *LCS-27*'s engineering officer, woke to the GQ alarm, he raced to his battle station—the stern anchor winch—to find *27* already being reeled in and its 20-mm gunners firing wildly into the surrounding water. Meister then headed up the port side. When he reached the deckhouse, Meister glimpsed one of the boats just about to ram. He dove to the deck ahead of a booming explosion and its shrapnel broadside, which killed two *27* crewmen, wounded others, and left *27*'s port-side hull riddled with holes.

During the melee, three *LCSs*, including *7* and *49*, were sunk by the combined work of six suicide boats. Meister's skipper kept *27* from sinking only by alertly running it aground. The remaining LCSs fled the harbor in such haste that some wounded survivors were run over or left stranded in the waters of Mariveles Harbor. Alexander, with no life jacket, and with burns and a wounded leg, was eventually hauled aboard an LCT. In all, 73 LCS sailors died. It was, to say the least, a costly, inauspicious debut for what came to be called the Mighty Midgets.

Twelve LCSs* idled off Iwo Jima's landing beaches when the sun rose just after 7 A.M. on 19 February. Although smoke and haze from the

---

*These included *LCS(L)-31, -33, -51, -52, -53, -54*.

predawn bombardment lingered over the island, the sky above was sunny and clear and the invasion craft rode a calm sea, with light winds and slight swells.

Two miles offshore, Marines climbed from troop ships into landing craft. At 0730, ninety minutes before the scheduled H-hour, the midgets began the first of two rocket-firing runs on the beach, the initial assault wave of troops trailing six hundred yards behind.

Though the LCS crews may well not have known about the LCS fiasco in the Philippines on 16 February, they were all too aware of the severe pounding taken by a flotilla of LCI gunboats covering UDT operations two days before. The twelve craft had been chewed up by Japanese mortar, machine-gun fire, and small-arms fire, some of it coming from Mount Suribachi. Nine gunboats were damaged and one was sunk.

When heavier ships squared off to take out the batteries, they took punishment as well. Artillery hits to destroyer *Leutze* sprayed shrapnel that badly wounded CO B. A. Robbins and killed 7 sailors. When the smoke cleared from the morning catastrophe, more than two hundred Navy sailors lay dead or wounded. Few on the LCSs doubted the same sort of treatment could be in store for them.

Twenty-five hundred yards out, the midgets opened fire with bow-mounted 40-mm guns. At 1,600 yards, harassing fire from 20-mm and .50-caliber machine guns was added and, at 1,000 yards, a first salvo of 120 rockets aimed to explode in a fanlike pattern across the beach. After these first salvoes, the midgets withdrew for a second run timed to begin as landing craft crossed the line of departure. After firing another pattern of rockets, the midgets turned on the oblique, unmasking beam and stern 40s and 20s to rake the shore.

By now, assault craft passed through the midgets' line, bearing down on the beach. Just before 0900, when the first Marines reached Hot Rocks' sands, final rocket spreads flew from seven hundred yards offshore. LCS casualties, it turned out, were light: 2 wounded and minor damage from mortar and artillery fragments to *LCS-33* and an antitank gun hit to Virgil Branch's *LCS-51*.

A half hour later, the first waves of Marines reported being several hundred yards inland, fighting through light machine-gun and mortar fire. This was a good pace, but by 1030, it had slowed as successive waves of amphtracs began taking heavy fire.

Harold Scott, destroyer *Bennion*'s gunnery officer who, en route to Iwo Jima, had practiced feverishly with different powder charges and firing trajectories so *Bennion*'s gunfire wouldn't hit advancing Marines, now witnessed a problem he hadn't anticipated. While *Bennion*'s rounds landed comfortably ahead of friendly lines, they didn't seem to be achieving much. The Marines were meanwhile catching hell from concealed Japanese artillery, mortar and machine-gun fire from inland but also, and especially, on their flanks.

The fields of fire must have been precisely registered before the landings. Amphtracs and tanks churned helplessly on the slopes of volcanic sand and became sitting ducks. Some of the mortar rounds hitting the beaches proved to be enormous "ash can" projectiles—each 320 millimeters in diameter and weighing 675 pounds. Even when pinpointed, the guns retracted into caves or behind steel doors too quickly and too securely for seaborne guns of any caliber at any range to take them out. It was hard to fight back against what you couldn't spot or draw a bead on.

In the afternoon, some of the LCSs moved close to shore. Using stern anchors as leverage, crews hitched heavy winch-powered chains to some demolished vehicles in an effort to pull them clear. It didn't work very well. When Robert Wells, 24, pharmacist's mate, on *LCS-31,* reached the beach, its sands looked to be covered with a sprawling carpet of Marine corpses.

As night settled, the *Bennion* and other ships began to fire star shells, brilliant yellow lights that burst high in the air and then floated down under small parachutes. The illumination prevented Japanese infiltration. Meanwhile, 5-, 6-, and 8-inch-high explosive rounds from other ships were fired to the north of the island in hopes of doing damage and warding off a counterattack.

In contrast to the preinvasion decimation of the LCIs, the blue-water Navy had gotten off lightly—for now, at least, they seemed out of *kamikaze* range. Without its carriers, Japan lacked mobile air-strike capabilities. This and the distance between Iwo Jima and air bases on Japan, Formosa and the Ryukyus, made a concerted air offensive against Detachment out of the question.

In a letter written that night, *Howorth*'s Orvill Raines had a reassuring prediction for Ray Ellen: "I don't believe it will take more than a week to clean out the whole place of Japs."

Detachment Days

The next day, in a morning that was typical of destroyer duty off Iwo Jima, *Mannert L. Abele* (DD-733) lay off the western slope of Mount Suribachi to provide artillery support to the Marine 28th Regimental Combat Team (RCT). Before the 28th jumped off on its assault, *Mannert L. Abele* had fired nearly one thousand rounds, standing barely 1,500 yards from shore. But it was slow, murderous going against a line of hidden pillboxes and cave mouths. The Marines' assault gained them barely 50 yards during the balance of that morning and barely 150 yards more during the entire afternoon. It was soon painfully clear that Iwo Jima would be a long, hard go.

On D+3, destroyer *Bush*'s Coit Butler got an even closer sense of the Marines' struggle on Hot Rocks. Dressed in his shipboard khakis, with only his gray-painted GQ helmet for outward protection, Butler was met at the waterline by three Marines in full battle dress, one equipped with backpack radio gear.

Butler, who'd started flight training then switched to fighter director training, was in the FIDO team newly attached to *Bush*. Butler's first assignment in the Pacific had been in command ship *Eldorado*'s CIC in the Marianas and at Peleliu. Vice Admiral Richmond Kelly Turner himself had spent a lot of time in CIC (enough time to know Butler by sight and called him Coit) and was, in Butler's estimation, a cordial but hardworking, hands-on, no-nonsense commander.

Butler was ashore to help direct *Bush*'s call-fire missions on Mount Suribachi, where Japanese gun placements were racking up Marine casualties. Butler followed his Marine escort through ankle-deep black sand to a position about one hundred yards inland. From there the two men climbed a 20-foot-high embankment—the only cover from enemy fire—and then sprinted another seventy-five yards to a dug-out artillery-spotting shelter. The "shelter" was little more than a shallow scooped-out indentation, and Butler had to hug the ground to keep from being hit. But it was from there that Butler relayed coordinates to *Bush*'s gunners.

While Detachment was immune to concentrated *kamikaze* initiatives, opportunistic strikes staged through airstrips elsewhere in the Bonins were still feasible. Several hours before dusk on 21 February, six Japanese aircraft on just such a mission stumbled across an isolated detachment from Task Force 58—carrier *Saratoga* (CV-3) with three destroyers—positioned thirty-five miles northwest of Iwo Jima.

The planes attacked through low overcast skies. C.A.P. and ships' gunners quickly splashed two, but bombs from each exploded against *Saratoga*'s starboard side. Two more bombs and two separate suicide crashes halted flight operations. A break in the attacks followed, during which crews managed to contain hangar deck fires. Then, at dusk, parachute flares signaled the arrival of more *kamikazes*. The AA fire claimed four well clear of the carrier. But the crash of a fifth plane and the explosion of its bomb tore a 25-foot hole in *Saratoga*'s flight deck.

Moments later, this time east of Iwo Jima, another *kamikaze* aircraft, already hit and aflame, rammed low into the starboard side of *Bismarck Sea* (CVE-95). The impact dislodged *Bismarck Sea*'s after flight deck elevator, toppling it to the hangar deck. One explosion there ignited a chain of gasoline fires. Then a second, bigger explosion all but demolished the after portion of the hangar. The crew abandoned ship and, as they waited for rescue, watched *Bismarck Sea* shudder through three more hours of explosions before rolling and sinking.

This one night's attack delivered the sort of exponential destruction and casualties (nearly 500 *Saratoga* and *Bismarck Sea* sailors killed, missing, or wounded) special attack proponents dreamed of. Ten planes and as many men, in addition to killing or wounding fifty times their number, had sunk one carrier and dealt crippling damage to a second. It was a reminder—if one were needed—of the renewed peril waiting closer to Japanese shores.

* * *

By 25 February, Marines were making slow but certain progress toward cornering the surviving Japanese in the north. Three Marine divisions advanced along one continuous shore-to-shore front—the 4th on the right, the 3rd in the center, and the 5th (the conquerors of Mount Suribachi) on the left flank—that expanded as the island widened. By 1 March troops controlled the northern village of Motoyama, along with its airfield.

On 9 March, destroyer *Bennion* with two Marine spotters aboard took up a position just off Iwo Jima's northern coast. The Marines sat atop the main battery director and pointed out some caves that needed to be taken out. *Bennion* steamed slow and close to shore and occasionally saw splashes of mortar fire. But using director optics, gunnery officer Harold Scott was able to lock on the cave entrances and put 5-inch salvos dead on target.

The next day, *Bennion* was on its way to Ulithi.

★ Chapter 19 ★

To the Great Loochoo, March 1945

*There were many times in World War II when the men who man
the ships rose to unbelievable heights.*

—Robert Sherrod

May You Walk in the Ashes of Tokyo

In March, General Douglas MacArthur's 6th Army GIs continued the
protracted conquest of the Philippines. Japanese defenders were finally
cleared from Manila on 4 March, but only after the city itself was
all but leveled. Manila's capture left 170,000 Japanese troops dug in
elsewhere on Luzon and still others in garrisons on bypassed islands
throughout the central and southern Philippines. MacArthur's already
extended "return" would stretch into August.

Though Iwo Jima would be declared "secured" in mid-March, Japanese resistance was still fierce. By 26 March, when Detachment was
stamped "operation completed," Iwo Jima had extracted Marine casualties disproportionate to its size—and maybe even (some thought)
to its importance for the strategic air war on Japan. Not until month's
end did the actual "mop-up phase" begin. At its conclusion, estimates
revealed the combined land, air, and naval offense had killed 20,000
Japanese while inducing the surrender of just 200. Detachment's U.S.
casualties would reach nearly 5,000 killed and 20,000 wounded.

Meanwhile, if the GIs on Luzon and the Marines on Iwo Jima had
paused to look out to sea, they might have noticed the winnowing
of the huge fleets that had transported, landed, and supplied them.
Answering to plans begun fully six months earlier, hundreds of ships

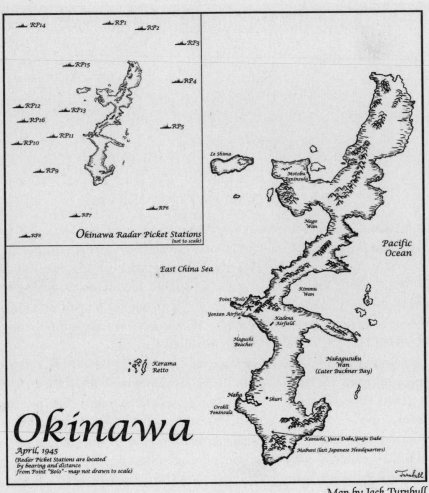

RP14   RP1   RP2

RP3

RP15

RP4

RP12   RP13

RP16

RP11   RP5

RP10

RP9

RP7   RP6

RP8

Okinawa Radar Picket Stations
(not to scale)

East China Sea

Le Shima

Motobu
Peninsula

Nago
Wan

Pacific
Ocean

Point "Bolo"

Kimmu
Wan

Yontan Airfield

Kadena
Airfield

Hagushi
Beaches

Nakagusuku
Wan
(Later Buckner Bay)

Kerama
Retto

Naha   Shuri

Orokú
Peninsula

Kunishi, Yuza Dake, Yaeju Dake

Mabuni (last Japanese Headquarters)

Okinawa

April, 1945
*(Redar Picket Stations are located
by bearing and distance
from Point "Bolo" - map not drawn to scale)*

Turnbull

Map by Jack Turnbull

like *Bennion* were pulling out to reprovision and reassemble at staging points on Ulithi, Leyte, and Saipan in preparation for the conquest of Okinawa.

In the process, the strategic road maps of the Southwest and Central Pacific were converging. Using Okinawa as the arsenal, Admiral Nimitz would command the fleet and MacArthur would lead GIs and Marines ashore for Operation Downfall, the massive two-stage invasion of Japan. But even if Okinawa fell quickly, the target date for just the first stage—landings on Kyushu, code name Operation Olympic—was not until 1 November. Olympic called for three quarters of a million troops—fourteen full combat divisions—and the next stage (code-named Operation Coronet and projected for March 1946) even more.

Until preparation for Downfall began and while MacArthur was still fighting his way through the Philippines, Okinawa would be a Central Pacific show. Overall command for its capture went to Admiral Raymond A. Spruance who'd relieved Halsey at the end of January, once more transforming 3rd Fleet to 5th Fleet. Spruance—Lord of himself—seemed an ideal choice for a campaign of the scale and intricacy (and code name) of Iceberg. In Vice Admiral Richmond Kelly Turner—the Alligator—Spruance also had the ideal subordinate to orchestrate all the complex minutia of the amphibious landing. As usual, Turner had written a plan in such explicit detail that there was little for on-site commanders to second-guess, misinterpret, or improvise. In Samuel Morison's eyes, Turner was "still the same driving, swearing, sweating 'Kelly' whose head could conceive more new ideas and retain more details than any flag officer in the Navy."

Iceberg, however, would not be another reprise of the Turner-Smith team. Though Howlin' Mad had put in a prominent appearance at Iwo, he was there largely in his capacity as Commander Fleet Marine Forces Pacific, essentially a desk job. A younger Marine general commanded Detachment's ground assault corps, and now an Army lieutenant general named Simon Bolivar Buckner, Jr., would lead Iceberg's 183,000 ground troops: Marines organized as III Corps and GIs as XXIV Corps joined under the umbrella of 10th Army.

Buckner's father was a nineteenth-century Kentucky aristocrat, an early convert to the secessionist cause turned cautious and unimaginative Confederate field general. Buckner Sr.'s hasty capitulation of Tennessee's Fort Donelson early in the War Between the States, earned his Union opponent the enduring sobriquet "Unconditional Surrender" Grant. Described by *Time*'s Robert Sherrod as "the ruddy-faced, white-haired 'old man of the mountain,' " to some it seemed that Buckner, Jr., now 59, pursued his Spartan idiosyncrasies in places and ways designed to erase the vestiges of his heritage—and perhaps the blot of Fort Donelson's fall.

During four years commanding troops in Alaska (where he owned a farm), for example, Buckner slept on a thin mattress with just a single sheet to cover him. He had also willed himself to read without glasses by squinting. In the days leading up to the landings, Buckner's outward demeanor was fearsome. "May you walk in the ashes of Tokyo" was his toast to his staff as he raised a glass of Kentucky bourbon. Once the war was over, however, he looked forward to retirement to Alaska. "I expect it will take me a solid year to catch up with my hunting and fishing," he confided to Sherrod. "And I'll be so far away from things, I won't be able to exercise a retired general's prerogative of swearing that the new Army has gone to hell since he got out of it."

Tale of Two *Franklins*

Iceberg groundwork called for air strikes against bases on Kyushu designed to preempt or at least substantially diminish air attacks on the invasion fleet. Marc Mitscher, once again at Task Force 58's helm and embarked on *Bunker Hill*, left Ulithi on 14 March with two carrier task groups. Three days before, *Randolph* (CV-15), one of Task Force 58's newest carriers, had been crashed by a suicide aircraft while at anchor in the supposed sanctuary of the atoll. The crash had killed 25 sailors and put *Randolph* out of action for at least a few weeks. As with the November sinking of oiler *Mississinewa (Miss),* it was another sign of how far-reaching and audacious Japan's aerial suicide capabilities could be—and how vital it was to destroy them.

By 18 March, Mitscher's task groups were stationed ninety miles southeast of Kyushu and were launching air strikes whose timing was flawed—and nearly disastrous. When Navy pilots reached target air-fields, they found few Japanese planes left on the ground to destroy. About fifty enemy planes, it turned out, were just then on their way to Mitscher's carriers.

Though these Japanese attacks caught Task Force 58 off guard, luckily most proved ineffective: *Enterprise* took a bomb hit, but it was a dud; 2 *Intrepid* crewmen were killed (and scores more wounded) by a diving Betty's near miss crash; and *Yorktown* (CV-10) fended off attacks by two Judys while sustaining a bomb hit and explosion from a third.

Luck that held that day turned the next, first against carrier *Wasp* just after sunrise when an undetected attacker placed a bomb on her flight deck. As so often before, the bomb pierced the deck timbers, eventually detonating in the crew's mess galley two levels below the hangar. One hundred sailors were killed outright or mortally stricken by the explosion, fires, and smoke, and close to 300 were wounded. Most were cooks and mess attendants. This was bad, but even worse lay over the horizon and just minutes away.

Task group flag carrier *Franklin*—Big Ben to her crew—was launching her second strike of the morning when an unseen bogey dropped two well-placed bombs, the first exploding in the hangar deck forward, the next above the hangar deck aft. Each explosion destroyed a flight deck elevator, and both ignited aircraft and hangar deck stores of fuel and ammunition. Within minutes, *Franklin* was all but consumed by flame and blinding smoke.

One of the sailors trapped below decks was 23-year-old Louis Casserino, a gunner in one of *Franklin*'s starboard side 20-mm gun tubs. Casserino, a veteran of the *kamikaze* crash to Big Ben the previous October, would normally have been topside, but this morning he had a pass for early chow. He'd gone to the mess deck, prepared himself a scrambled egg sandwich, and detoured to his berthing space before going topside. Casserino's compartment, starboard side aft below the hangar deck, adjoined the Marine contingent's compartment, and Casserino was there, chatting with some Marine buddies, when explosions erupted.

Another sailor assigned the same berthing space as Casserino was

Bill Albrecht, an 18-year-old from Patterson, New Jersey, whose father, a State Police investigator, had been assigned to the 1932 Lindbergh kidnapping case. Albrecht joined *Franklin* in January during her state-side repairs, was assigned to the 40-mm gunnery division, and stood GQ as a loader on a 40-mm gun sponson located just aft of the island.

Big Ben's crew had been at GQ on and off for much of the previous night—extra vigilance prompted by the surprise attacks on the 18th—and Albrecht had watched as occasional parachute flares lit up the darkness. His gun crew eventually decided to rack out in the ready ammunition locker adjacent to the gun sponson. Sitting on the locker deck, his back propped against a bulkhead, Albrecht got little sleep that night; when dawn broke he went below to get a shower.

After dressing, Albrecht tried to reach the mess hall, but found the closest access hatch blocked and guarded by an unyielding Marine. When he set off to find a different route, Albrecht heard and felt a heavy explosion above him. More explosions seemed to follow him as he reached the mess compartment and found it already crowded with hundreds of panicky sailors.

The first explosion knocked *Franklin*'s CO, Captain Leslie H. Gehres, off his feet. Seeing the damage forward, Gehres ordered full right rudder, thinking to push smoke and flames clear of planes aft. Learning *Franklin* was also hit aft, Gehres reversed the turn and slowed the ship.

As *Franklin*'s forward damage control parties battled flight deck fires, they became the targets of "Tiny Tim" air-to-ground rockets attached to the wings of *Franklin* fighter-bombers on the afterdeck. The ten-foot-long rockets, triggered by the fires, zoomed unpredictably in every direction. Sailors instinctively dived each time they heard a rocket's whistle or the pops and bangs of ammunition cooking off in the storage lockers aft of the island. Meanwhile, below decks, Casserino, Albrecht, and hundreds of other *Franklin* men were trapped with seemingly no means of escape.

Casserino had been knocked unconscious and came to in the middle of a pile of bodies. When he finally extricated himself, Casserino crawled from the Marines' compartment to his own berthing space, where he saw two buddies sitting upright in their bunks. He approached the sailors only to realize both were dead with eyes wide open. Both compartments were thick with smoke. Casserino knew the closest exit was the fantail, so he crawled out of the compartment and continued moving aft.

The crowded messing compartment where Bill Albrecht took refuge also filled with smoke, even though the access hatch was dogged down and the ventilators closed. Albrecht had located two sailors from his gun crew and stuck close to them. The men thought they heard commands to abandon ship, but realized conditions would only be worse in the passageways outside. By then, Albrecht noticed, one of the messing compartment bulkheads had begun to glow cherry red.

Conditions were still desperate topside, but both aboard and in surrounding waters, men and ships were rallying to *Franklin*'s crisis. CO Gehres had directed all but a skeleton crew of key officers and men to abandon ship as best they could. Destroyers were circling to drop life rafts and pick up survivors. By 0930, despite the continued explosion of ready ammunition stores, cruiser *Santa Fe* (CL-60) had pulled alongside where she stayed for three hours fighting fires and evacuating more than 800 survivors.

Smoke had forced the evacuation of *Franklin*'s engineering spaces, leaving the ship dead in the water, but a second cruiser, *Pittsburgh* (CA-72), was getting into position to pass a towing line. Rigging the towline was made easier by the containment of fires forward on the flight deck—as was use of portions of the deck as a battle dressing station.

One of *Franklin*'s heroes that day was a damage control officer named Donald A. Gary. In the process of searching the ship for survivors, Gary found his way to the hot, smoke-filled after mess compartment where three hundred sailors, including Albrecht, were trapped. Gary also found them an exit route and returned through smoke three times to lead all the men to safety. Albrecht was in the second group Gary brought topside, emerging to the miracle of fresh air on a starboard-side catwalk just forward of *Franklin*'s island.

By then, Louis Casserino, on his own, exhausted and suffering from smoke inhalation, had finally reached *Franklin*'s fantail. From there Casserino somehow made it into the water, reached one of the survival rafts thrown overboard by screening ships and was eventually rescued by the crew of destroyer *Hunt* (DD-674).

With the rest of *Franklin*'s fires controlled and her starboard list stabilized at thirteen degrees, the ship was towed south by *Pittsburgh*, destined for Ulithi under the protection of *Santa Fe* and several destroyers. By the next day, steering and enough power were restored for *Franklin* to drop the tow and maintain a speed of 15 knots the rest of the voyage.

Franklin's staggering damage and casualties (724 dead or missing, 265 wounded) made her without question the most heavily damaged carrier in the war to survive. Robert Sherrod (then getting ready to cover Iceberg for *Time*) saw *Franklin*, *Enterprise*, and *Wasp* when they reached Ulithi. "It seemed to us beyond human belief that the shattered *Franklin* could have made port," Sherrod wrote, "but there were many times in World War II when the men who man the ships rose to unbelievable heights."

And times, perhaps, when their leaders sunk to heartless depths. Bill Albrecht remained aboard *Franklin* after his rescue from the messing compartment. He joined the firefighting efforts aft and eventually was assigned to a still-functioning 40-mm gun mount atop the bridge for the voyage to Ulithi. The battle to save *Franklin*'s life—and his own—would be a defining episode in a still young life.

For Casserino and many other *Franklin* survivors who had no choice but to jump over the side, however, the episode turned to enduring tragedy. When *Franklin* reached Pearl Harbor and sailors like Casserino tried to return, they were only allowed aboard to retrieve personal effects. Gehres, it turned out, considered them little better than deserters, refused their returns and forced their transfers. It was a stain on men and ship that lasted decades.

Spring Blossoms

Thunder God pilots at Kanoya Naval Air Station on Kyushu were placed on heightened alert when the Task Force 38 carriers were spotted. Combined Fleet leaders were uncertain of the Americans' strength or intentions—whether this signaled air raids or a full-scale invasion of Japan. To Ōka pilots who'd sat idle through February and March it seemed just one more in a series of false alarms. Finally, on the afternoon of 17 March, Vice Admiral Matome Ugaki, commander of Fifth Naval Aviation Fleet to which Thunder Gods Corps was now attached, ordered a coordinated attack for the next day. Attacks would combine torpedo and Special Attack units with a massed Thunder God strike.

The fifty planes that were to hit *Enterprise, Intrepid,* and *Yorktown,* took off at 0330 on 18 March. When word the dawn attacks had sunk at least a carrier, a battleship, and cruiser, Ugaki ordered the Ōkas sent in. Preparations began, but American raids that afternoon destroyed many Ōka escort planes, forcing cancellation.

By 21 March there were fewer American air strikes and American carriers, including several that were clearly damaged and spotted steaming south under clear skies without air cover. Hearing this, Ugaki decided to roll the dice and again ordered a Thunder Gods strike.

Fifteen Ōka-laden bombers escorted by thirty-two covering fighters took off late in the morning. Before the mission, the Ōka pilots and mother plane crews placed nail clippings and locks of hair in plain wooden boxes for delivery to their families. They burned their old uniforms and put on new ones. Then they sat down to write brief death statements. Outside the base headquarters building, the personnel not assigned to the mission waited anxiously with those who were. Finally, Vice Admiral Ugaki arrived for the official send-off: a round of salutes, bows, and final toasts.

On Tuesday, 20 March, Task Group 58.2, still covering the damaged *Franklin,* retired slowly away from Kyushu. After two days of raids and the crippling hit to *Franklin,* a quiet Tuesday morning turned into chaotic afternoon. Destroyer screen *Halsey Powell* was refueling to carrier *Hancock*'s starboard side as the afternoon began and was nearing completion at 1454, when a *kamikaze* Zeke off *Hancock*'s port beam suddenly dove for the carrier's flight deck. Ken Courteau, a loader on the forward starboard twin 40-mm just heard the roar of a plane. Jack Barrett, 21, a sonarman watching from *Halsey Powell*'s port bridge wing, saw the Zeke get hit by AA and burst into flame as its left wing collapsed.

Halsey Powell's deck crews cast off lines and her skipper tried to maneuver his ship clear, but the flaming wreckage overshot *Hancock* and instead crashed the destroyer's main deck astern. The impact lifted the fantail clear out of the water. The blow also jammed *Halsey Powell*'s steering, and she barely avoided a disastrous collision with *Hancock* by inches. Spared this calamity, *Halsey Powell*'s crew was spared another when the Zeke's 550-pound bomb failed to explode and instead passed straight through the tin can's hull.

What *Halsey Powell* couldn't avoid were the flat trajectories of several 40-mm projectiles from other ships close by trying to bring down the Zeke. Twelve *Halsey Powell* sailors were killed and 29 wounded. Bridge quartermaster Casey Kraft saw one dead sailor missing a leg sprawled in a pool of blood on the port side main deck.

During twilight, attacks by twenty or so aircraft kept crews alert and on edge, but the busy day turned into a bloodless night and quiet morning. The Japanese, though, were back that afternoon—now 21 March—this time in the form of a large formation of bogeys approaching unusually slowly from the northwest. Nearly 150 carrier fighters were launched, and sixty miles out they found the bogeys: 48 aircraft, 18 of them Bettys, each with what appeared to be a large winged torpedo strapped to their belly. Whatever the contraption was, it slowed the aircraft and made it difficult to maneuver. The Bettys—and the escorts that stayed with them—were fat targets for the Navy Hellcats, and not one Japanese aircraft got through.

It was Spring on Honshu, but pilots at the fighter base northwest of Tokyo had yet to see cherry blossoms on trees lining the avenue between their barracks and bathhouse. Ryuji Nagatsuka now believed this would be his last spring and last opportunity to see the blossoms. Several nights before, Nagatsuka and twenty-two fellow trainees—half the squadron—were called to muster in the CO's office and told the squadron had been ordered to form its own Special Attack Corps tasked with sinking American carriers off Japan's shores.

Even though they'd long been anticipating this moment, both the CO and his men were momentarily stunned. The obviously distressed CO took pains to emphasize he was "asking," not "ordering" them to undertake the mission. They would have twenty-four hours to decide.

Despite the CO's formal disclaimer, Nagatsuka and the others knew they had little choice. Uncomplaining obedience to superiors, whether to orders or requests, was an inviolable cornerstone of Japanese army tradition. Added to this—at least for Nagatsuka—was news of the indiscriminate destruction to Japan's cities and slaughter of its civilians caused by the flying castles' incendiary bombs. Low-level fire-bombing raids had begun in early March and already had devastated Tokyo, Nagoya, Osaka, and Kobe.

Now the increasingly constant presence of American carriers off Japan's shores promised only more slaughter. In the end, reasoned Nagatsuka, it mattered little "whether they volunteered or acted under strict orders." They had no choice except to defend the homeland.

Lieutenant General Mitsuru Ushijima, the quiet, competent commander of Japanese defense forces on Okinawa realized that any chance of repelling the American invasion was lost with the removal of his 32nd Army's crack 9th Division. The 9th, a unit with high morale and lengthy combat experience, represented more than half of the 32nd's fighting strength. For that reason, the 9th had been strategically positioned on high ground protecting both Shuri and Naha, gateways to Okinawa's south. But in December, still intent on salvaging the Philippines, Imperial Japanese Headquarters had shipped the 9th south via Formosa. Its surviving remnants were now being mopped up by American GIs on Luzon.

Loss of the 9th shifted Ushijima's plans. He would have to make do with the mix of forces left to him: 31,000 army troops (including several thousand local conscripts), 15,000 navy personnel organized for ground fighting, a tank regiment, and a handful of artillery units. These regular forces were augmented by the 20,000 members of a loosely organized but fanatical home guard unit. An additional 4,000 civilians were pressed into labor battalions, and 600 students became messengers and orderlies.

In all, Ushijima had more than 100,000 men, women, and children to deploy for defense. But given the uneven quality of his forces, Ushijima knew that in place of a decisive battle, he would be forced to substitute a long and costly war of attrition. Ushijima had his forces secretively reposition themselves to new and deeper fortifications on higher ground well back from the island's beaches and airfields. If the Americans failed to detect and counter Ushijima's strategy, they would be in for a long and painful struggle. If Ushijima's plans succeeded, he understood he was no less likely to die along with all his forces. But by then, the Americans might finally have lost the taste for trying to invade Japan and the will to exact its unconditional surrender.

Ping and Picket

In the days leading up to L-Day, Turner worried a good deal about the Japanese air threat to Okinawa. Intelligence estimated Japan's remaining air strength at 2,000 to 3,000 aircraft, but he suspected there were more. Whatever the actual number, they would all be positioned within range of Okinawa and many—if not most—would be deployed as *kamikazes*.

The air threat influenced the choice of Okinawa's southwestern beaches as the primary landing sectors. Coming ashore here, the Marines would be close to Yontan Airfield and the GIs close to Kadena. Although experience suggested the Japanese would fight tooth and nail to hold the fields, their early capture would permit the use of Army fighter aircraft to cover the invasion fleet and troops ashore.

The air threat also influenced the depth and comprehensiveness of Turner's Iceberg screening plan. In addition to close-in layers, including two antisubmarine screening lines and a "skunk" screen to intercept suicide boats, there would be a dedicated deep-sea Radar Picket line of the sort first conceived by John McCain and perfected by Halsey's fast carrier groups.

* * *

It would be the work of these screening lines—both close-in and re-mote—that defined the routines (and jargon) of U.S. ships and sailors off Okinawa. The "Outer Screen," for example, a chain of thirty-nine patrol stations, was soon known as the "ping line" because its ships (many of them smaller DEs) used surface radar and sonar to detect submarines.

For most of the day, ping line patrol routine was numbingly repeti-tive: keeping a 15-knot speed along 7,000-yard station tracks; passing through track midpoint each quarter hour; making turns synchronized to reduce collision risk and sonar interference. Only at dusk and dawn (or when air attack was imminent) would the routine change. Each ship then closed to within 1,000 yards of its neighbor, affording mu-tual protection and concentrating fire power.

Edward Stafford, an officer aboard ping line ship *Abercrombie* (DE-343), later recalled a day-to-day grind suggesting the life of a trench sentry: "No ship left the line unless it was relieved on station, sunk, or incapacitated by damage—and in the last two cases it was immedi-ately replaced. Every third or fourth day a tanker came down the line, refueling each ship in turn. On different days but with about the same frequency, an LCI made the same run, delivering and picking up mail. Mail service off bloody Okinawa was the best afloat in the Pacific—a major blessing in the accursed place. Every couple of weeks, on a rota-tional schedule, each ship went into the anchorage at Kerama Retto or Hagushi for dry and fresh provisions, ammunition, and repairs beyond the capabilities of the crew."

RP1, an imaginary parcel of ocean real estate fifty miles almost due north of Zampa Misaki (designated as "Point Bolo"), the westernmost outcrop of land on Okinawa's central coast, was one of a necklace of fifteen blue water outposts circling Okinawa and its adjacent islands. The others, numbered in ascending order clockwise, also took ranges and bearings from Point Bolo. Under Turner's plan, RP (Radar Picket) spacing and manning balanced two realities: the proximity and direc-tion of the Japanese air threat, and competing claims for the employ-ment of combat ships.

Without aircraft carriers and (once Iwo Jima fell) little access to bases in the Bonins, Japan's air forces (except for Ryukyus-based sorties) posed little threat from the east. Accordingly, only three picket stations—RP4, RP5, and RP6—were set up to guard that direction. Of the twelve RPs spaced along an arc from southwest to northeast of Okinawa, six (RP7 through RP12) guarded flyways from Formosa and China's mainland. The rest (RP13 through RP15 and RP1 through RP4) faced Kyushu.*

Formosa, China, and Kyushu were each roughly equidistant from Okinawa, but Kyushu posed the biggest threat because the essential operational resources—aircraft, fuel, parts, munitions, and pilots—were still most readily at hand. In all, looking southwest to Formosa, west to China, and north to Kyushu, at least one hundred Japanese bases were within one-way flying range.

Picket ship availability, meanwhile, stacked the needs of the ground invasion against the special requirements of the RPs. Picket ships had to be combat ships with enough antiaircraft firepower, enough radar tracking capability, enough maneuverability to fight back, and (perhaps unsaid, but nonetheless crucial) enough expendability to be easily replaced.

The outer screen's core pieces would be destroyers or equivalents such as DMs. These destroyer types were equipped with the most advanced radar capable of spotting aircraft more than a hundred miles out. Each was also well armed, fast, nimble, and expendable.

The choice for supporting craft settled primarily on LCS and LSM gunboats. While these amphibious craft had only surface search radar and were relatively slow, each possessed enough onboard firepower to defend itself. Each was small enough—just a speck to aircraft at high altitude—to avoid detection. Even if spotted, there was good reason to suspect *kamikaze* pilots would judge them "unworthy" targets.

Of course, if deemed "worthy" by the enemy, each craft was unquestionably expendable. And there was one more consideration. No one doubted there would be RP casualties and damage and even sinkings. Survivors deserved the possibility of rescue or, failing that, someone nearby to pick up the pieces. In time, tin can sailors took to calling the LCSs and LSMs "pallbearers." It was a name the midgets' crews

---

*RP6, RP8, RP11, and RP13 were never used.

didn't much appreciate because they did much more than "pick up the pieces." Still, the name had the ring of sardonic truth.

Destroyer sailors and gunboat sailors occupied two different strata. Though tin cans were called "little boys" by carriers, battleships, and cruisers, destroyermen were still blue water sailors. The LCSs belonged to the burgeoning, vital, but less glamorous, green water navy. Relationships between destroyer and gunboat sailors on the picket lines would often prove awkward and sometimes disdainful, but their fortunes and fates would become tightly entwined.

The RPs, designed as early warning posts, on occasion became "last-stand" garrisons. The blue water and green water sailors who manned them in the weeks ahead would endure the same monotony, confront the same enemy, risk the same triumphs and losses, sustain the same casualties, and die the same deaths.

FIDO Spells Trouble, DELEGATE Is God

When things got hot—as they inevitably would—no one expected the picket ships to defend the RPs alone. Protective air cover—RP C.A.P.— would go to the rescue. RP C.A.P. control was its own subset of RP operations, with teams of specialists such as *Bush*'s Coit Butler detailed to destroyers designated as fighter director ships. These Fighter Director Officer (FIDO) teams—also called "Freddies"—had a vital function, but a usually uneasy relationship with the ships they rode.

Though crews were courteous and cooperative, FIDO teams were not necessarily welcome additions. During his time at Okinawa, FIDO officer Joseph Masters served short tours on three picket destroyers, and each time sensed the crew's unspoken dread: a FIDO team on board—like red skies in the morning—meant trouble ahead.

The Freddies huddled over radar screens and plot boards in CIC, communicating with flagship *Eldorado* (call sign DELEGATE) to dispatch and coordinate the C.A.P. aircraft. The C.A.P. fighters were crucial resources, and therefore scarce.

When it came to RP C.A.P. protection, DELEGATE was God. Without notice, DELEGATE could pull C.A.P. from one RP and vector it to another RP under attack. While C.A.P. sped to the rescue, the naked

RP might suddenly be jumped. Though you might sympathize with the guys on another RP about to catch hell, you also could very soon end up feeling sorry for yourself.

To reach their targets, Japanese suicide pilots had to contend with RP C.A.P. pilots like John Wesolowski and Willis E. (Bill) Hardy. Wesolowski, 25, was a fighter ace whose first carrier deployment was with VF-5 aboard *Saratoga*. When *Sara* was disabled by a torpedo, VF-5's remnants joined the Cactus Air Force on Guadalcanal. Flying Wildcats from Henderson Field, Wesolowski shot down seven Japanese aircraft.

Wesolowski was now deployed on *Yorktown* with VBF-9, one of the new fighter-bomber squadrons. In contrast to Wesolowski, VF-17's Hardy, was a rookie. Not only was Hardy on his first Pacific deployment (aboard *Hornet),* he had not yet experienced life or death aerial combat. In fact, Hardy had not yet even gotten within shooting range of a Japanese aircraft.

Both pilots had one thing in common. Both flew the exquisite F6F Hellcat. Compared to the Spartan Wildcat, the Hellcat's cockpit made Wesolowski feel as if he were sitting in a plush living room chair. Well armed and armored, the Hellcat could outclimb and outmaneuver anything the Japanese put in the air.

Some of the Japanese Wesolowski encountered might still be good pilots, but they were also predictable, especially the ones sent out to crash the ships. The *kamikazes* were single-minded, diving directly for ships with no thought to what might be chasing them. They were easy to shoot down. Still, you couldn't get all of them, and Wesolowski felt sorry for the poor bastards on the tin cans he tried to protect.

RP tactics were worked out over time. The destroyer's RP routine was to cruise (at 15 knots so as not to kick up a large wake or outpace the small boys) the same roughly 10,000-yard-diameter piece of ocean, alerted by lookout, radar, and sonar to intruders. All contacts were to be reported to DELEGATE; all enemy air contacts closing within 12,000 yards drew fire. Equipped only with surface search radar, the RP LCSs and LSMs depended on the RP destroyer to alert them to bogeys. At first, their modest goals were to stay within surface radar range of the picket destroyers and keep radio contact. Initially, RPs were so thinly occupied, the LCSs settled on patrol spots more or less midway between RPs.

Days were dangerous—and dawn and dusk especially so. At night on the picket stations, darkness moved in like something you could feel, something that wrapped around you. As the last daylight left the sky, the horizon disappeared and the sea, which might have been gray or cobalt, turned to infinite black. The black pressed at the eyeballs of watch standers topside, at first challenging them to try to see what couldn't be seen. If there was no overcast, stars eventually emerged to dangle above the sea. First came the navigator stars—Canopus, Capella, Vega, Sirius—but then, as the night deepened, the lesser stars in numberless precision across the sky.

Chapter 20

Far from Ordinary Skies, 1 April–6 April 1945

I've already lived longer than I thought I would.

—7TH DIVISION INFANTRYMAN

Kerama Retto

Kelly Turner had seen in the Kerama Retto, a cluster of mountainous islands fifteen miles west of Okinawa, possibilities for convenient fueling and replenishment close to Okinawa. Kerama Strait, a long north–south channel separating the largest island in the cluster from five smaller ones to the west, looked ideal for ship anchorages. Openings at either end could be easily defended and Aka Channel, a second, intersecting roadstead, was ideal for a seaplane runway and anchorage.

At first, few agreed with Turner, believing that should a protracted siege result, the invasion fleet risked being trapped. But then two considerations intervened: Japanese use of depth-charge-equipped suicide boats in Lingayen Gulf pointed to Kerama Retto as an ideal setting to conceal such craft near Okinawa. Second, and more important, the tough struggle for Iwo showed the value of having a sheltered anchorage nearby. The Alligator again got his way.

Though hindsight would show the islands could have been captured by a single battalion, plans called for a coordinated assault (by what was called the Western Islands Attack Group) on the five islands adjoining Kerama Strait and Aka Channel. This prelude operation officially commenced on Palm Sunday, 25 March, a day before the scheduled landings (and just a week before Iceberg's Easter Sunday

L-Day) when Kerama Retto island beaches and potential strong points were bombarded by a cruiser-destroyer detachment. But, even before that, mine-clearing units—minesweepers teamed with gunboats to explode floating mines—were at work in surrounding approaches and channels.

The minesweeping ships were a mix: some designed and built from scratch, others (designated DMS) converted from older destroyers. For Iceberg, stepped-up protection for each minesweeping group was provided by high-speed minelayers. These ships (designated DMs) were actually new destroyer retrofits—bigger, more agile, and even faster than workhorse Fletchers. Stripped of torpedo tubes but armed with more 5-inch and 40-mm firepower, DMs afforded the minesweeping groups potent (and undistracted) antiaircraft defense.

As destroyer minelayer *Harry F. Bauer* did its screening work for units sweeping Kerama Retto's channels, XO Robert Morgenthau absorbed the islands' terrain—for the most part steep, craggy cliffs dotted with sparse vegetation. White sand beaches fronted some islands, but coral reefs also blocked easy access.

The combination of landscape and bracing weather made Kerama Retto seem more Icelandic or Scandinavian than the Western Pacific. It seemed evident (as Morgenthau reflected later) that *Bauer* and surrounding ships had assembled under "far from ordinary skies."

GIs caught the Japanese by surprise and easily captured their Kerama Retto objectives. Most enemy troops in the island garrisons fled to higher ground—but not before convincing a dozen or more island natives to commit suicide. They staged two nighttime counterattacks and made a series of futile last stands, but by afternoon on 28 March, the entire eight-island group was in American hands. The Navy seaplane base began operation the next day.

As suspected, one of the operation's harvests were caches of the 18-foot-long, depth-charge-equipped speedboats, some 250 in all, hidden in well-camouflaged hangars and caves on the four biggest islands. The presence of these boats (Who knew how many more were hidden on Okinawa itself?) added to the list of Okinawa's anticipated dangers—and underscored the need for the skunk patrols Turner had incorporated into the Iceberg screening plan. The most anticipated danger—aerial *kamikazes*—had already snooped the Kerama Retto preliminaries. They staged their first attacks at dawn on the 26th.

Iceberg's first *kamikaze* targeted high-speed transport *Gilmer* (DD-233/APD-11), the underwater demolition teams' (UDT) flag ship. The plane—a Val with its distinctive "pants-down" fixed landing gear—crashed through *Gilmer*'s galley deckhouse, killing one sailor and wounding several before hitting the water. About the same time, in a stiffer blow, another suicide plane crashed destroyer *Kimberly* (DD-521), a picket ship southwest of Kerama Retto.

This plane, another Val, circled *Kimberly* before making a slow, low-level run at her stern. *Kimberly*'s CO maneuvered to keep his gun batteries aimed broadside, but the pilot kept turning to stay inside her wake and finally crashed the 40-mm mount perched atop the after deckhouse. Henry Fuller, 19, gunner on a starboard 20-mm, was standing just yards away as the Val crashed and exploded, carrying away the mount and its crew as though they'd never existed.

Within seconds of the hit, two 17-year-old *Kimberly* sailors, Arthur McArthur, stationed in the No. 4 gunhouse just aft of the impact, and Robert Gacke, stationed in the No. 5 handling room, stumbled on deck to behold an abattoir of burns, wounds, and death neither could have conceived. It was the first glimpse of battle for either boy: McArthur had joined *Kimberly,* his first ship, barely a week before.

Henry Fuller, meanwhile, though dazed by the explosion, got to his feet and tried to help victims. Fuller, it turned out, was himself badly wounded with a three-inch piece of shrapnel embedded in one knee. He didn't feel it at first, but when another sailor pointed to blood on his shoe, Fuller collapsed to the deck, regaining consciousness only as he was later being transferred to a hospital ship.

If sailors exposed to the *kamikazes*' new airborne mode of death somehow forgot the dangers of more standard seaborne perils, one crystallized when destroyer *Halligan* (DD-584), passing near sunset through shallow waters east of the Kerama Retto, struck a mine. The blast triggered *Halligan*'s two forward magazines into explosions that eviscerated the ship from the bow all the way aft to No. 1 stack.

PC-1128, skippered by 25-year-old Jim Gilbert (who'd been playing cards at a shipmate's house on Oahu when the Japanese attacked Pearl Harbor), was patrolling 10,000 yards southeast with two other craft looking for floating mines and was surprised to see *Halligan* straying alone through treacherous waters. While *1128*'s companion ships approached *Halligan* to take off wounded, Gilbert searched for castaways until well after sunset through waters he was certain still contained derelict mines.

Only six men were rescued by *PC-1128*. Meanwhile, *Halligan*'s abandoned remains drifted several hours before grounding stern high on a reef. In all, 153 of her 325-man crew perished, including all but one of her ship's officers. Barely two days later, Gilbert and his crew were called on to rescue survivors of yet another mine sinking, this time in daylight while clearing mines off Hagushi beaches, and this time from one of their own: minesweeper *Skylark* (AM-63).

The dawn *kamikazes* were at it again on 27 March, though this time many shunned the screens and went straight for the heavies. Their pilots got little to show for their sacrifices: *Nevada* (BB-36) suffered casualties and damage when the flaming wreckage of one plane tumbled from the sky; another splashed close to *Tennessee;* and a third holed cruiser *Biloxi* (CL-80). Destroyer *O'Brien,* detached to fire night illumination off Kerama Retto, was not so lucky.

O'Brien and her crew had taken punishment before—a *kamikaze* hit at Lingayen Gulf and, worse, a direct hit from German shore battery fire off Cherbourg in June 1944 that killed 13—but this morning's blow nearly destroyed her. *O'Brien* gunners were able to knock down one *kamikaze.* But a second, a Val, crashed port side amidships, and its 550 pound bomb detonated explosive rounds in *O'Brien*'s forward magazine. The blast wreaked havoc forward, demolishing much of the superstructure, including *O'Brien*'s radio shack and CIC. Avon Blevins, a radioman who survived only because his GQ station was on the after 40-mm and not in radio, was blown clear of the gun tub by the concussion. Syd Schafman, a 28-year-old quartermaster, got a face full of shrapnel wounds, but was one of the few lucky ones to escape from CIC alive. The morning cost *O'Brien* the lives of 50 sailors; after surviving Cherbourg and Lingayen, Okinawa had at last put her out of the war.

Dawn attacks on each of the next three days were either missing or ineffective, raising more wistful hopes that the Japanese might be running out of aircraft or suicidal fervor. The invasion fleet's final preinvasion *kamikaze* casualty occurred on L-1 when flagship *Indianapolis* absorbed a crash and bomb blast to her stern, killing 9. Damage to *Indianapolis* was not crippling—a bent propeller shaft—but the damaged shaft sank after slipping the grasp of emergency repair crews. With L-Day imminent, Admiral Raymond A. Spruance transferred his flag to *New Mexico*. Meanwhile, *Indianapolis* (minus the deep-sixed shaft) set sail for stateside repair. It was the first in a string of sad ironies leading to one of the U.S. Navy's worst maritime tragedies.

"Hadn't Even Gotten Our Feet Wet"

Iceberg's main amphibious assault began at 0837 on a cool, overcast Easter Sunday, with 10th Army's lead elements bounding ashore on Hagushi Beaches, a swath of western shoreline guarded by coral reefs just south of Okinawa's narrow waist. *Time* reporter Robert Sherrod, watching the progress of the first waves from the vantage of transport *Cambria* (APA-36), was stunned and delighted to see troops step ashore facing only "slightly more opposition than they would have had in maneuvers off the coast of California."

No one was more bewildered about this than the troops themselves. Hours earlier, waiting at a different transport rail with other K Company Marines, Eugene Sledge, the 1st Division mortarman, was nearly overwhelmed with dread. It was all he could do to remind himself he was a Peleliu veteran who'd already survived the worst the Japanese could throw at him. Then, when the Higgins boat carrying Sledge reached the transfer point, the amphtrac drivers returning from the beach gave the Marines incredible news: despite some light mortar fire, the landings seem to be unopposed.

As K/3/5's amphtracs neared the beach drop point, the Marines saw the troops from preceding waves moving unhurriedly up the rising landscape with no explosions erupting around them. When the amphtrac climbed out of the water, slowed, and opened its tailgate,

Sledge and his buddies calmly picked up their gear and stepped onto the beach.

It was the same story for the Army troops landing farther south. One GI battalion landed by stepping directly from amphtracs onto an exposed seawall. "I've already lived longer than I thought I would," one disbelieving 7th Division infantryman told a reporter.

After knocking out a lone machine-gun position, 7th Division GIs captured Kadena, one of the two strategic airfields. During a search of one of its concealed underground bunkers, troops uncovered four unusual-looking pieces of weaponry: what looked like large bombs with stubby wings, a cockpit, and canopy.

Yontan, the second airfield, fell so quickly that an unsuspecting Japanese fighter plane pilot landed and taxied his aircraft to a stop, only to have it shot up by every Marine in firing range. Startled, the pilot scrambled from the cockpit, gun drawn, only to be mowed down. Marine casualties were 2 killed and 9 wounded. Newspaper correspondent Ernie Pyle accompanying the Marines told his Scripps Howard readers: "We were on Okinawa an hour and a half after H-hour, without being shot at, and hadn't even gotten our feet wet."

When Sherrod finally landed on Okinawa, he noted how the beaches were steep and how the land beyond was little more than a thin topsoil layer above a hard coral base. Built into the surrounding hillsides, Sherrod saw hundreds of keystone-shaped burial vaults, each fashioned from coral blocks and standing about six feet high. Fronting each vault was a porch and inside were ceramic urns or small caskets said to contain the skulls and bones of departed family members.

As the main landings at Hagushi progressed, other units and ships were conducting a demonstration landing on the southern beaches—a feint to distract the Japanese and, it was hoped, draw some resistance away from Hagushi. The operation deployed all the elements for a real landing: shore bombardment, transports, and even landing craft filled with troops.

To enhance the deception, nearly a score of LCSs were set to parade toward the beaches ahead of the phony landing. When first told of the operation the night before, many amphib sailors were keyed up at the prospect of their first landing under fire. When Charlie Towers, *118*'s gunnery officer, got word the next morning that the "landing" was only a ruse, he, for one, was more relieved than disappointed.

While the elaborate sideshow roused no more Japanese response than did the real landings, the crowd of large ships lured *kamikaze* aircraft, one of which crashed transport *Hinsdale* (APA-120) while a second slammed the *LST-884*'s port quarter. *884* embarked a company of Marines complete with equipment, weapons, and ammunition, and the explosion set off a firestorm that quickly claimed lives and threatened *884*'s ammunition stores. As destroyer *Van Valkenburgh* (DD-656) rushed from a screening station to assist, *884*'s skipper ordered abandon ship, and survivors jumped directly over the side or into *884*'s own waiting Higgins boats.

By the time *118* and three other LCSs reached the scene, its crew had topside salvage pumps running and pressure to fire hoses on the bow. The groundswell and *884*'s exploding ammunition made it risky for deepwater ships like *Van Valkenburgh* to stay close. The LCSs were better able to ride the swells. Their skippers moved in, each from a different quadrant, determined to douse the fires.

As *LCS-118* stood off *884*'s starboard quarter, Charlie Towers could see water wasn't reaching the fire's core—the LST's main hold. Towers urged *LST-118*'s skipper Peter Gilmore to hold the bow against *LST-884*'s stern while Towers took a fire and rescue party aboard. Gilmore agreed and Towers made for the bow to assemble the party. Once *LCS-118*'s bow and *LST-884*'s stern were lined up, Towers stepped across with his four-man salvage team close behind.

LST-884's deck was too hot for crawling and the air around too filled with explosive pops and ricochet pings to risk standing up. So the men ended up duckwalking single file, pulling the hose and its fog nozzle closer to the hold. As they moved, they could hear ammunition popping and feel the ricochet impact of some rounds hitting the underside of the deck at their feet. It seemed an eternity before Towers and his party could get close enough to put a good stream on the fire, but once they did, it took just minutes to get the blaze under control.

Sailors from other LCSs were now aboard *LST-884* as well, bringing more hoses and manpower for salvage work that steadily changed from dangerous to grimy and gruesome. Men who tried to get belowdecks occasionally had to retreat as small ammunition caches continued to cook off and explode. *LCS-116*'s Ray Davis, who was wearing elbow-length asbestos gauntlets, worked in a line of sailors passing smoldering (and sometimes flaming) ammunition boxes and heaving them over the side.

Men who'd comported themselves bravely amidst fires and explosions were abruptly stunned and shaken at the sight of its human detritus: the charred remains of dead Marines and sailors. For the moment, Towers was the senior officer aboard *884*, responsible for deciding what to do with the corpses. Fires and explosions still seemed huge threats, so Towers instructed a few sailors to remove dog tags, weight the corpses with spare 20-mm gun barrels, and drop them over the side. Almost at once he regretted his choice—and, even more, his audacity in presuming he had the right to make it. It was too much like playing God. Several bodies were already over the side, but Towers had the remains of others moved to a piece of deck away from the salvage work. Let someone else more qualified decide.

A second demonstration landing was staged the next day, but already the invasion fleet's focus had turned to providing artillery support and moving cargo ashore. Combatant ships that had already lobbed over twenty-seven thousand explosive rounds on Okinawa began rotating call-fire shifts, coordinating with radio-equipped forward spotter teams to pinpoint and take out suspected Japanese strong points.

Cargo unloading, particularly during the first Pacific assaults, routinely backed up while Marines and GIs cleared fierce beachhead resistance. Now it was Iceberg's uncontested landings that fouled things up. The bulk of L-Day's vanguard of sixty thousand troops was already well inland and outrunning supply lines. Cargo stacked up on the beach and delivery turnaround times ballooned as supply trucks went looking for their customers. The situation improved on 3 April, only to worsen again as high winds and seas kicked up and curtailed unloading on the 4th and 5th.

Iceberg's cargo and troop transports loitering off the beaches made particularly inviting targets, so most were sent to open water as darkness set in. Even this precaution wasn't foolproof. Two transports took suicide hits the evening of L-Day, and the next night at least ten *kamikazes* staged attacks on transports retiring south from Kerama Retto invasion anchorages.

In one duel, fast transport *Dickerson* (DD-157/APD-21) lost her CO and XO along with 52 other crewmen when a *kamikaze* wiped out her bridge. Other planes staged coordinated attacks on transports *Telfair* (APA-210), *Goodhue* (APA-107), and *Henrico*. All three ships were hit, *Telfair* the least seriously. *Goodhue*'s attacker crashed a cargo boom and plowed through an after gun tub before toppling over the side. *Henrico* took the worst of it.

Glenn Grant, standing watch on a talker station a level above *Henrico*'s bridge, saw the *kamikaze,* a twin-engine Frances, in the instant before it rammed the bridge on the starboard side. Communications officer Gradus L. Shoemaker saw it as well from a sheltered spot on the port side. Had he been in the coding room—his normal duty station—he would surely have been killed, as many of his men were.

The impact unleashed a gasoline fireball that enveloped the superstructure. The plane's two bombs penetrated the superstructure to explode at the main deck, killing *Henrico*'s CO, the transport division commander, and the CO and XO of the Army regiment embarked on the ship.

The blasts touched off fuel oil fires. They also destroyed the radio shack aft of the bridge, where just moments before, radioman Tom Love had been relieved from watch. Duke DeLuca had also been in the shack but was on his way to get ice cream for the watch detail. The explosion knocked him off a ladder and slammed him into a vent.

Henrico sailors Calvin Carl and Ray LePage were both belowdecks playing poker—and losing—when they heard the big bang. To get topside they had to fight though knots of GIs blocking the ladders. Motor machinist mate John Brooks (the sailor had survived an impromptu "frogman" mission during the Normandy landings a year before), on watch in the boiler room two levels down, was knocked unconscious. Brooks, the boiler room watch officer and another machinist mate were finally pulled clear by ship's electricians.

On the main deck, Carl saw *Henrico*'s XO looking for a route through the fire to get to the superstructure. LePage tried to reach a 20-mm gun station on the stern but had to work his way past the wreckage and fires. He saw three more planes trying to attack and being taken under fire by the screening destroyers. By the time he reached the 20-mm, the planes were too far away.

The smoke and fires took hours to quell and the ship had to be towed to Kerama Retto's roadstead. Top and bottom, *Henrico*'s casualty toll was heavy. In addition to the four senior officer casualties, 45 GIs and sailors died and 125 more were wounded.

Suicide Is Not the Objective

Ryuji Nagatsuka's Special Attack unit was officially titled the "*Kikusui* (floating chrysanthemums) group of the *Jun-no* (sacrifice to the Emperor) Special Attack Corps." On 2 April its pilots began a training and practice period scheduled to last thirty days. Training began with takeoffs, no easy maneuver with the bomb loads (twice as heavy as those used in the Philippines) they would carry. For these practice runs, heavy logs instead of bombs were strapped to plane undercarriages.

Their instructor cautioned them that a successful suicide crash was no sure thing. Some body crashers missed their targets by diving at full throttle. Failing to compensate for their aircraft's lift characteristics caused them to overshoot the target.

With a large canvas awning used for a target, the trainees practiced both high-and-low-altitude approaches. The high approach tactic—hiding in the clouds at sixteen- to twenty-thousand feet then diving suddenly—improved the odds of evading American fighter pilots. The low approach—skimming in just above the water, picking a target then "zoom" climbing to ten thousand feet before diving—was better for evading radar detection. But there was also risk: American ships, they were told, sometimes aimed long-range salvos into the water, creating huge water spouts to bring down low flyers.

The targets for either approach were carriers' flight deck elevators. The instructions for impact were also the same: at the last instant, the trainee should lift the plane's nose at a forty-five- to fifty-five-degree angle. Above all, they should keep their eyes wide open all the way.

On 2 April, Combined Fleet Chief Soemu Toyoda gave the final go ahead for Second Fleet, including its centerpiece battleship *Yamato*, to contest the Okinawa invasion. It was a desperate move made necessary by the devastating scale and pace of the American invasion. If a concerted strategic effort to counter the invasion were to be made, it would have to begin in the next few days and would have to use the arsenal at hand.

Second Fleet, now moored in Japan's Inland Sea, was down to just a handful of ships. In addition to *Yamato,* there were eight destroyers and a single cruiser, *Yahagi,* commanded by Captain Tameichi Hara.

Yamato remained the world's largest battleship and the symbolic pride of the IJN. Launched in 1941, *Yamato* displaced 72,800 tons fully loaded. Her nine 18.1-inch main battery guns—the biggest shipboard guns on earth—were each capable of firing 3,200 pound projectiles. Formidably armed, *Yamato* was also thickly armored. Her engine rooms were encased in sixteen inches of vertical and eight inches of horizontal armor plate. Yet, despite this heft, *Yamato* was also remarkably fast. Her four turbine engines developed a combined 150,000 horsepower and delivered a 27.5 knot flank speed.

Yamato had been built for showdowns that never happened. At Midway, *Yamato* lingered at the fringe of the action and failed to play a decisive part. Off Samar, *Yamato* anchored the task group that threatened the U.S. Leyte Gulf invasion fleet before abruptly turning back. On both occasions *Yamato*'s vaunted firepower and impregnability went mostly untested. After Leyte, *Yamato* withdrew to the safety of the Inland Sea, a pristine, silvery gray bull elephant surrounded by a small pack of greyhounds.

Second Fleet's go-for-broke sortie would be coordinated by a second operation designated *Ten-Go* (Operation Heaven One)—a campaign of massed air attack against the invasion fleet composed of both conventional and suicide aircraft *(Kikusui)*. The two operations would be mutually supportive; launching them simultaneously would, planners hoped, make it hard for the Americans to concentrate their forces against either thrust.

Heaven One

Even after five days on Okinawa's southern plains, the Marines were still meeting only light resistance. "So far" *New Yorker* correspondent John Lardner explained to his readers, "the Okinawa invasion was like a fierce, bold rush by cops, hunting gunmen, into a house that suddenly turned out to be only haunted."

After securing Yontan Airfield, Marines of the 1st and 6th Divisions, organized under the title of III Amphibious Corps, sprinted east at a breathless 7,000-yard daily clip across fresh, cool, scenic, but mostly empty terrain to occupy Katchin Peninsula and the deserted coastal village of Ishikawa. The advance was speeded by the use of vehicles on loan from the Army, an astonishing luxury for Marines used to traveling exclusively on foot.

There'd been a few encounters with the enemy during the cross-country blitz; in the worst, infiltrating Japanese slipped into a Marine encampment during the first night to bayonet thirteen men sleeping in foxholes. There'd also been thousands of bewildered women, children, or elderly men, whom the Marines, reported Lardner, "firmly ignored and tried to avoid shooting."

By early afternoon on 4 April, twenty days ahead of schedule, 6th Marine Division troops had scaled the high coral cliffs above Ishikawa Isthmus, the narrow waist of the island and gateway to the north. From this vantage they could see scattered groups of Japanese straggling toward Motobu Peninsula, a rugged, easily defensible enclave on the island's northwest coast.

Two narrow roads, one along each coast, wound from the Ishikawa Isthmus to the base of the peninsula. The roads threatened to be more obstacle than conduit. Stretches hugged sea walls or wound around steep hills, and aerial reconnaissance indicated many bridges were out. Between these coastal roads was a rugged mountain range, covered with brush and grass.

Things were not as easy in the south. Below the Bisha River, the rough demarcation between the III Amphibious Corps and Army XXIV Corps sectors, 96th Division GIs had faced stiff resistance since their second day ashore. On 4 April, the GIs finally broke through. On

5 April, a cold and rain-soaked day, they slogged south toward Shuri, Okinawa's ancient capital east of Naha.

On the morning of 6 April, when he first stepped out on the deck of cruiser *Yahagi,* her skipper Tameichi Hara felt a soft breeze blowing across the quiet waters of the Inland Sea. The shoreline just a few thousand yards away was dotted with cherry blossoms, and the backdrop of distant mountains stood bold under a deep blue sky.

When the order to sortie came at 1600, Hara's *Yahagi* took the lead, followed by three destroyers, then *Yamato,* and then five more destroyers. The formation steamed at 12 knots and kept a close watch for mines in narrow Bungo Channel. Two hours later, the ships cleared the channel, entered the Pacific, and steered south.

Yamato, Yahagi, and the eight escorts carried only enough fuel to reach Okinawa. Before departure, nonessential supplies and nonessential personnel were offloaded. *Yamato*'s magazines, however, were filled to capacity with ammunition for every weapon she carried. The operation plan spread across the chart table on *Yamato*'s bridge contained a detailed map of the waters surrounding Okinawa. An arc was drawn on the map whose focal point was the Hagushi beaches. The radius of the arc was 40 kilometers, the firing range of *Yamato*'s big guns.

By 6 April the rain had moved through, but the skies above Okinawa and the East China Sea remained overcast. The winds still raised white caps while the air temperature—60 degrees—was cool enough to cast a chill on the ships' lookouts, bridge personnel, signalmen, and gun crews. After months in the tropics, the climate change was just as welcome to the sailors as it had been to Marines and GIs. In a letter to Ray Ellen a day after L-Day, *Howorth*'s Orvill Raines described the weather as "good and comfortable. The air is so pure and clean and refreshing."

The scattering of suicide aircraft appearing off the beaches during L-Day and the day after were thought to fly from Okinawa itself and other spots in the *Nansei Shoto.* Meanwhile the outer picket line was mostly quiet—always a good thing, but especially now when so many LCIs, LCSs, and LSMs destined for the line were still needed at the beaches.

Pritchett (DD-561), well north on RP1, had two LCSs—62 and

64—on station with her when bogeys appeared during midwatch on 3 April. Intermittent skirmishes, during which each ship splashed a plane, flared until dawn. In a lull between raids, a search of one crash site turned up the corpse of a pilot along with some charts and navigation material. Next morning *LCS-62* left RP1 to deliver these items to intelligence teams at Hagushi. *Pritchett,* having taken some bomb damage to her fantail during the night, also departed, bound for Kerama Retto, with *Bush* coming out to replace her.

Bush, in company with *LCS-64* was still on RP1 when dawn broke on 6 April. *Bush's* crew, as usual, stood at GQ for most of the morning. At 0800 she steamed north to check out a report of a surfaced submarine, a search which came up empty. *Bush* finally secured from GQ at 1300 and went to condition One-Easy.

During the afternoon watch, Ed Cregut, a radar striker at the air-search console in *Bush's* CIC, spotted a huge, fast-moving radar blip ninety miles northwest. He knew air-search radar sometimes displayed storm clouds as big blips, but this seemed different. Cregut alerted the watch officer, and a sailor at the air-plotting table began to track it. A few minutes of marking ranges and bearings confirmed it was no cloud. It was traveling about 145 knots and heading straight for them.

The blip had to be aircraft. "There must be hundreds," the watch officer said, with a look of wonder and disbelief Cregut never forgot. The officer passed the sighting up to the bridge and, within seconds, *Bush's* crew was called back to GQ.

Cregut gave his seat to the GQ operator and rushed to his own GQ station, the 40-mm amidships on the port side. The gun's captain Mario Petroni was already there when Cregut arrived. "What's up?" Petroni shouted, knowing Cregut had come from CIC. "Big raid coming," Cregut hollered in response.

At 1745 that same day, submarines *USS Threadfin* (SS-410) and *Hackleback* (SS-295) patrolling the Bungo Strait entrance to Japan's Inland Sea, spotted a group of ten surface contacts—two clearly larger than the other eight—steaming southwest at 25 knots, hugging Kyushu's eastern coastline. Though the targets were tempting, both submarine skippers passed up the chance to attack and instead sent contact reports to Task Force 58.

Chapter 21

A Perfect Day for What Happened, 6 April 1945

Today was a perfect day for what happened
—Dwight Donnewald, USS *Ellyson*

Something Bad Coming

When *Bush***'s XO Tom Owen reached CIC,** he established sound powered phone contact with gunnery officer Harry Stanley in the fire control director—the basket. Close on the heels of the first bogey formation a second formation popped up on air-search radar, then another, and then a fourth. Owen designated them as raids, and this last became Raid 4. Around 1430, the first of fifty or so Japanese aircraft orbiting above *Bush* attacked.

Across from Owen, the FIDO team's Coit Butler vectored four C.A.P. aircraft to intercept Raid 1. All of *Bush*'s gun batteries seemed to open fire at once. Bogeys must be everywhere, Butler realized, and he was relieved moments later to hear a "Tally-ho" from the C.A.P. leader: confirmation pilots at last had the bogeys in sight and were attacking. Moments later, C.A.P. leader radioed even better news: all the bogeys—maybe five or six—were splashed. And then good news at home: *Bush*'s own guns claimed two bogeys—both to port.

Then, all at once, Owen was calling out a new bogey to starboard. Stanley swung the basket and main battery guns to engage. The target, a low-flying Jill carrying a bomb or maybe a torpedo, was already close—less than four miles. *Bush* CO Westholm had his ship at 27 knots and midway through a turn to port. Realizing this masked his forward batteries, Westholm ordered the rudder hard left, an effort to bring the target full on the starboard beam.

As they locked on the Jill, *Bush*'s guns began a steady and apparently accurate fire. Al Blakely, a 40-mm gun captain saw the plane's wing surfaces being chewed off, making it look more like a torpedo than an aircraft. But it still kept coming, and everyone who could see, hear, or sense what was happening braced for impact.

On the boat deck, Ray Mayhugh, *Bush*'s chief torpedoman, who normally would have sought cover under the forward torpedo mount, instead dashed to the port side and leaped to the main deck. In No. 5 gunhouse, Ralph Carver saw his gun captain duck and close the hatch, a sure sign of something bad coming.

Westholm now fully expected *Bush* would be hit. He tried one last maneuver—a hard right rudder to swing the stern clear—but the plane's pilot matched the turn and hit *Bush* hard at main deck starboard side. A near simultaneous explosion—the plane's bomb—shook the ship, ripping out starboard plating from the forward fireroom back to the forward engine room. It was 1515.

To 20-year-old Gilmer Thomas, forward in No. 2 handling room, the impact seemed to lift *Bush* clear out of the water and abruptly drop her. It catapulted Bob Carney, 22, *Bush*'s supply officer, from his GQ station on the boat deck down to the main deck, where he landed in such pain that he was sure his back was broken. He tried to move, but the pain was unbearable.

Three levels down, water was pouring into the after fire room from the starboard side rupture, and sailors made for a starboard exit ladder. Water tender Frank Grigsby was the first to begin scaling the ladder to the second level when he ran into a layer of superheated steam. Unable to see or breathe, Grigsby had to wait for the rising water to cool the steam above him before he could keep climbing. When he reached the main deck, Grigsby realized there was no one following him.

At 1530, after picking up *Bush*'s distress signal, RP2 destroyer *Colhoun* bent on speed and headed west. Rocket Three (the radio call name for *Colhoun*'s four-plane C.A.P.) led the way. *Colhoun* drew a slew of attackers as she approached RP1; Rocket Three downed six of them, but then ran low on fuel and ammunition and had to leave. *Colhoun* reached RP1 at 1610: *Bush* was already dead in the water, listing to port and down by the stern, with the wing of the crashed Jill draped across her starboard bulwark. *Bush* was also being circled by twelve to fifteen Japanese aircraft with no replacement RP C.A.P. in sight.

Colhoun skipper G. R. Wilson signaled *LCS-64*, then approaching from the south, to maneuver alongside *Bush*'s port quarter and remove the wounded. Wilson then positioned *Colhoun* between *Bush* and the Japanese planes lining up for new attacks.

Before 1600, other groups of *kamikazes* were already south of the Radar Picket line and entering skies just north of Okinawa. Planes from one flight spotted *Emmons* (DD-457/DMS-22) and *Rodman* (DD-456/DMS-21) screening six sweepers in the waters between Iheya Shima and Okinawa's northwest coast.

Without warning, one plane sliced into *Rodman*'s bow. Its bomb exploded at the base of the superstructure, killing 16 sailors and wounding another 20. *Emmons* immediately picked up speed and circled the stricken ship, throwing up a thick curtain of AA that would eventually splash twelve Japanese planes. Marine Corsairs flying C.A.P. would take down twenty more bandits, but could not prevent four *kamikaze* hits that severed *Emmons*'s fantail and demolished her No. 1 gun, CIC, and bridge.

Even farther south, while en route to a skunk screening station near Ie Shima, destroyer *Hyman* (DD-732) squared off in the first of a series of *kamikaze* duels. In the space of ten minutes (beginning, her log would show, at 1615), *Hyman* gunners took out three planes—a Zeke more than a mile distant, a second Zeke at one thousand yards, and then a twin-engine Nick, which roared past (on its back and in flames) to a crash just yards off the starboard beam. Next a Hamp (a newer model Zeke) approached from the same direction, its pilot angling for *Hyman*'s bridge against intense 40- and 20-mm fire. AA sheared off one wing and the Hamp veered between *Hyman*'s stacks and finally crashed in flames into the No. 1 torpedo mount.

Momentum carried the plane's engine all the way to *Hyman*'s port side where it punched a hole in the main deck and exploded in the forward engine room, killing two men. Damage forced evacuation of the space and, with propulsion power halved, *Hyman* slowed from 28 knots to 15 knots. Meanwhile, repair parties worked their way across the torpedo deck intent on jettisoning ready rack ammunition dangerously close to the gasoline fires.

John Jones, an electrician's mate stationed on a searchlight platform attached to the after stack, ducked just before the plane hit and then dropped to the deck and fled aft to escape flames and smoke. The crash also chased 19-year-old radioman Don Milbrandt out of the emergency radio shack forward of the torpedo mount. Milbrandt escaped to the forecastle only to see another *kamikaze* approaching low on the starboard beam. It looked certain to crash the bow but, at the last instant, climbed, carried over No. 2 gun, and splashed off the port side. Milbrandt thought the worst might be over until a terrific explosion erupted amidships.

At 1700, north on RP1, another plane—*Bush*'s sixth attacker of the afternoon—began a run for the destroyer. Damage control parties working on the forecastle had dangled knotted lines from the railings; now, from the bridge, Westholm shouted them onto the lines and over the side to avoid strafing.

On *Bush*'s port quarter, casualties were being transferred to *LCS-64* and lines were thrown across to lash the ships. Joe McLendon, an 18-year-old fire controlman on 64, had almost cried with joy earlier to see *Colhoun* charging over the horizon like a cavalry column to rescue RP1. Now *Colhoun* was in bad shape too, and McClendon could see another Japanese plane peeling off for a dive toward *Bush*. Through a charthouse porthole, *LCS-64*'s XO John Littleton saw one of *Bush*'s chief petty officers shouting frantically and waving them off—*Bush* gunners needed a clear field of fire. Deck hands chopped lines and *LCS-64* pulled clear as *Bush*'s 40s opened up and tracers bracketed the attacking plane. On the way out, Littleton took a range and bearing on Iheya Shima, the nearest point of land he could find on surface radar—information they might need should *LCS-64* have to find its way back here.

Nearby, *Colhoun* was under attack as well, shooting first at a Zeke that dropped a bomb wide before crashing midway between *Colhoun*

and *Bush*. *Colhoun* gun crews' next targets were a Val on the starboard bow and a Zeke on the starboard quarter. One 5-inch shot at
four thousand yards hit the Zeke, setting a wing on fire. Guns No. 1
and 3 then swung toward the bow to lock on the Val, hitting it with
the first salvo and sending it into the water fifty yards off *Colhoun*'s
starboard beam. It was good shooting, but against too many targets.
The Zeke with the flaming wing was now barreling in unopposed on
the ship's port side.

Too late, *Colhoun*'s Wilson ordered full left rudder. Jim Pollock, the
6-foot 6-inch gun captain on *Colhoun*'s after twin 40-mm gun, saw
what happened next: the Zeke wiped out the port amidships 40-mm
and its crew, slid across the boat deck and sideswiped the after stack
before demolishing the starboard 40-mm and its crew as well.

A belowdecks explosion quickly followed: the Zeke's bomb, after
piercing decks and bulkheads, had detonated in the engineering spaces,
killing the after engine room crew and cutting the main steam line to
the forward room. Joe Orabona, a 23-year-old machinist's mate in the
forward room, escaped the superheated steam only by diving for the
bilges. It was 1710, and though *Colhoun* still had steering, propulsion,
and power to operate her guns, the ship was now in bad trouble.

The amidships crash to destroyer *Hyman*, which demolished the forward torpedo mount, had scattered sections of tubes and torpedoes
across the deck. Within minutes, heat from gasoline fires cooked off
one or more of the warheads. The thunderous explosion that resulted
blew out *Hyman*'s amidships passageway, sickbay, and sections of the
deckhouse over the forward engine room. It also killed most of the
men in the midships repair party.

A flood of acrid smoke streamed into the shipboard ventilation
ducts. *Hyman* lost power to guns, to emergency fire pumps, and to
steering, until electrician's mate Ray Novotny, located a switch in the
I.C. room to re-route the ship's electrical power. Back came the lights,
steering, and, most important, guns.

So Far from You . . .

At 1700, when destroyer *Howorth*'s CO E. S. Burns received word *Hyman* was hit, damaged badly, and needed help, he ordered a turn toward Ie Shima from *Howorth*'s submarine screening station north of Point Bolo. *Howorth* gathered speed, crossed the wake of a mine-sweeper, and maneuvered to keep clear of other ships churning through the waters off Motobu Peninsula.

Howorth's gun crews had already fired at two planes and brought one down in flames, but not before it passed between the stacks, snapping stays and radio wires. Larry Nelson, a seaman gunner stationed on the port side 20-mm near the after stack, hit the deck and felt the plane's heat ripple up the backs of his legs as the low-flyer went by and crashed into the sea off the port beam.

Now *Howorth*'s air-search radar was tracking new bogeys and port bridge wing lookout Russ Bramble—known as Radar for his uncanny ability to visually spot distant targets ahead of CIC—was craning his neck to ID four bogeys off the starboard bow. They were Zekes, and they converged off *Howorth*'s starboard quarter before splitting and approaching in two groups. Burns ordered course changes to keep *Howorth*'s guns unmasked and rang up full speed. The aircraft were at 5,000 feet, 6,500 yards out when gunnery officer Henry Hamner opened 5-inch fire on the closest target.

The Zeke was in a shallow dive and fishtailing when the starboard 40-mm opened fire at four thousand yards. Watching from the bridge, Burns was almost glad *Howorth* had the chance to fight off nuisance attacks earlier. The crews had shed their "kick-off" nervousness, settling down and getting more hits. Sure enough, the first Zeke exploded in a ball of flames two hundred yards short on *Howorth*'s starboard quarter.

A second Zeke—now the fourth *kamikaze* taking aim at *Howorth* in little more than an hour—came in at a steeper glide. Hit several times by *Howorth*'s main batteries, the smoking *kamikaze* veered toward the fantail where its left wing scraped the deck and cut port side lifelines and, before nosing into the water, knocked off the battle helmet of Ozzie Schwiesow, the gunner's mate in charge of the fantail 20s.

The splash of the third Zeke followed, though at a more comfortable distance. Despite close calls, the ship seemed poised to outlast all four Zekes.

Bob Lyons, 20, a fire controlman at the 40-mm gun director on *Howorth*'s flying bridge, could see the fourth *kamikaze* way out but heading in. The 40-mm guns Lyons controlled were by now either jammed or without ammunition, but all the 5-inch guns were still firing. The Zeke was wobbling—or maybe it just seemed so because *Howorth* was turning and bucking so wildly.

At 1717, two Vals and a Zeke began the latest round of attacks on *Colhoun* and *Bush* at RP1. *Colhoun* gunners splashed one Val and combined fire from *Bush* and *LCS-64* downed the second, but the Zeke splintered *Colhoun*'s starboard whaleboat on its way to an explosion in the forward fireroom. The blast ruptured both boilers, tore a 4- by-20-foot underwater gash in the starboard side and broke *Colhoun*'s keel. Joe Orabona somehow survived this latest blast. After swathing his hands with rags so he could grab the escape ladders' hot steel rungs, Orabona scrambled his way topside where, just then, *Colhoun* was being stalked by four new *kamikazes*.

Three of the planes made flanking runs at *Colhoun*'s bow while a fourth hovered teasingly off the port quarter. *Colhoun* was now without power, so guns could only be controlled and fired in manual. It was sweat-heavy work, but gunners forward somehow splashed one of the three planes off the bow. Jim Pollock, meanwhile, had raised his after twin-40s to forty-five degrees and gave his pointer voice commands to lob rounds at the decoy plane astern.

The two remaining bow *kamikazes,* both slightly damaged, kept coming. The pilot of one hooked his wing on *Colhoun*'s after stack and his plane spun in a cue shot to hit No. 3 gun. The impact tore lose, ruptured, and ignited the plane's belly gas tank. The plane itself bounced into the sea where its bomb exploded close aboard, ripping another hole in *Colhoun* below the waterline, but also throwing so much water back over the ship that all gasoline fires were instantly extinguished.

Oscar Blank, *Howorth*'s CIC officer, was leaning over the plot board when, at 1708, the *kamikaze* crashed the face plate of the main battery director, killing "gun boss" Henry Hamner and all but one of his crew. Despite the big impact that he and everyone else in CIC had felt at that instant, Blank at first thought gunners had shot down the plane. Hamner's last transmission from the basket had been "target angle zero," meaning the bogey was right on them. The range reading from the director optics was low—seven hundred yards—but then opened to eight hundred yards, and the 40-mm guns bearing on the target had stopped firing. But Blank could also smell gasoline and, even in CIC's dim light, could sense the horror in people's faces.

Larry Nelson, the midships 20-mm gunner, could tell the plane had hit the director basket squarely, lifting up its bulk and dangling it over the side like a large uprooted steel tooth. The flying bridge itself was on fire and pieces of the plane and its engine were scattered and still bouncing across the deck.

Nelson spotted three men in the ocean as *Howorth* swept by. Someone threw a life jacket over the side, but Nelson doubted they'd be stopping to pick up any castaways. Just then another plane was astern: flying low, in flames, and an instant away from crashing. The plane's wreckage, when it hit the water, skipped like a flat stone, leaving a patch of flame behind at each bounce point.

Meanwhile, in the waters off Hagushi, daylight was fading as a formation of nine battleships and cruisers with seven screening destroyers departed the increasing chaos bound for the safety of open sea. At 1753, air-search radar on *Leutze,* one of the destroyer screens, detected a bogey, which soon materialized as a dozen-strong group of low-flying Kates and Oscars. *Leutze* CO Leon Grabowski (promoted from XO after Leutze's CO was badly wounded at Iwo) maneuvered his ship broadside to the targets, and at 1800 ordered his new gun boss, a 23-year-old ensign named Malcolm Fortson, to fire when ready.

Fortson, controlling main batteries from the basket, immediately narrowed his sights on four aircraft closest to *Leutze.* With guns broadside to port, using director optics to set range, bearing, and elevation, Fortson triggered shots that nailed the first bogey at six thousand yards and two more at four thousand yards. C.A.P., meanwhile, took down the fourth—it was all over in less than three minutes. At one point, Fortson had shifted his aim to avoid hitting *Newcomb,* the destroyer screen closest off *Leutze*'s port bow. Now, with his own targets dispatched, Fortson saw more Japanese planes angling toward *Newcomb*.

Newcomb's gunners had already shot down a *kamikaze* diving in high off the starboard quarter, when these new attackers approached—both to port. One crashed *Newcomb*'s after stack, scattering wreckage and splashing aviation gasoline across the decks. John Bennard, part of the midships repair party, got soaked by gasoline and his clothes caught fire, but several sailors quickly doused the flames. Bennard was badly burned but still able to make his way to the aid station in the after crews head. No sooner had he reached the aid station, however, than the second plane hit amidships with an impact and explosions that demolished *Newcomb*'s two engine rooms and the after fire room.

After a third crash, this time to *Newcomb*'s forward stack, gasoline fires raged out of control from the bridge all the way aft to No. 3 gun. *Newcomb* went dead in the water, with no power except that supplied by the forward emergency diesel engine. When Bill Smith, the *Newcomb* Fire Control Chief, realized the diesel supplied power to No. 1 and No. 2 guns, he ran forward to act as a spotter for their crews.

As soon as *Leutze* CO Grabowski saw *Newcomb* go dead in the water, he turned back to help. By 1810, *Leutze* was at *Newcomb*'s starboard side and Grabowski was sending across a repair party and the ship's doctor. *Leutze* sailor John Perkins, stationed at a 40-mm gun director on the after stack, thought the skipper was crazy doing this. Perkins could see *Newcomb* was in an awful way: decks and bulkheads hot as stoves, sailors lying on the decks, their clothes smoldering. Now, with *Leutze* so close to this crippled ship, they might be in for it too.

Lew Campbell, a *Leutze* assistant gunnery officer stationed on the flying bridge, was also staring awestruck at the damage when he saw another Japanese plane lining up for a run at *Newcomb*'s bridge. Out the corner of one eye he saw someone on *Newcomb*'s bow as well: a ship's officer or chief using a megaphone to shout firing instructions to the crew in *Newcomb*'s No. 1 gun.

Shortly before 1800, at RP1, destroyer *Bush*'s bow began to settle. *Colhoun*, itself dead in the water, was in no position to help, and *LCS-64* had long since departed with a load of *Bush* wounded. CO Westholm was expecting *Bush* to split in half, but nursed hope of somehow salvaging both pieces. Crewmen were still jettisoning topside gear thirty minutes later when a heavy ocean swell smacked *Bush,* and the ship caved in amidships.

There was little time to abandon ship. Gilmer Thomas, the No. 2 handling room captain, jumped from *Bush*'s rising bow and, as he swam clear, could hear *Bush* creaking and groaning like the hinges of a haunted house door. Thomas swam first for a flat-bottomed punt used when painting the ship's hull. Seeing it overloaded with survivors and about to be swamped, Thomas moved on, eventually to reach the side of one of the ship's large rafts. The raft's interior was packed with injured crewmen including *Bush*'s supply officer Bob Carney, who'd been shot up with morphine and strapped to a wire stretcher before being deposited inside.

Some crewmen, including FIDO officer Coit Butler, gunnery officer Harry Stanley, and Ray Mayhugh, attached themselves to the perimeter of a floater net, while others relied on even more perilous flotation devices. Frank Grigsby, for example, jumped into the water grasping two 5-inch powder casings lashed together. Boatswain's mate Wesley Northey, who'd fractured both legs, had been lowered into the water wearing a life jacket, his legs splinted with pieces of damage control shoring.

Just then, VF-17's Willis (Bill) Hardy, a VF-17 fighter pilot off *Hornet* was flying north of Okinawa when he picked up a distress call from a picket destroyer FIDO. Hardy and his wingman Lt. H. G. "Crash" Morgan went looking for the destroyer.

The two Hellcat pilots had trouble finding the ship but soon intercepted Japanese aircraft rigged for suicide. Hardy quickly splashed three—his very first air combat and very first kills. Daylight was fading, and Hardy and Morgan were about to return to *Hornet* when they finally spied the burning ship. The FIDO spotted them as well and was back on the circuit, giving them headings and altitude (angels) for two bogeys.

Low on fuel and a long way from the carrier, Hardy tried to beg off. "It sure would be appreciated," the FIDO said, almost offhandedly.

"We're burning amidships. Those guys are just stalking us. When the sun goes down they're going to clobber us. Just come fifteen degrees right and, you'll be on their tails."

Hardy thought to himself: this guy's a pretty good salesman. He made it sound like he was asking them to pick up milk and eggs on the way home from the office. But to Hardy it quickly became a challenge within a challenge. He'd started out as an enlisted aviation machinist, built on those skills in his pilot training and prided himself in knowing how to coax the maximum flight time from his Hellcat's engine. Despite the low fuel and gathering darkness, Hardy and Morgan followed the FIDO's vector.

The directions were perfect. Within moments Hardy and Morgan pulled in behind a Judy with a big explosive charge bolted to its undercarriage. With his wingman on the outside herding the Judy toward him, Hardy got him with a beam shot. To his surprise, the Judy had a rear-seat gunner, and Hardy was forced to drop down to escape the gunner's line of sight. When Hardy pulled back alongside the Judy moments later, the back of the aircraft was swallowed in flames and the rear gunner sat curled up, burned to a cadaverous cinder. The doomed Japanese pilot was looking directly his way as Hardy pulled up, and the Judy nosed over and hurtled down.

"Okay," the FIDO radioed Hardy in the same offhanded voice, "if you just head south now on the way back to your ship, you're going to run right into the other bogey." Hardy looked down at the destroyer as he went by and saw it was listing, its midsection on fire. Sure enough, there was the second plane, another Judy. Pumping his gun charger with his foot, Hardy fired a series of single shots. One round hit the Judy's centerline tank and the aircraft abruptly exploded.

The FIDO thanked the pilots, gave them a surface radar vector back to *Hornet*, and then was off the circuit. Using the vector and flying low on the water, Hardy and Morgan picked up a phosphorescent trail that led them right to *Hornet* where both pilots landed just before nightfall.

The second Judy, it turned out, was Hardy's fifth kill of the day—qualifying him as an "ace-in-a-day." Hardy never learned the FIDO's name or the name of his ship, but timing and circumstance suggest it might have been the *Colhoun*.

. . . and Yet So Close

The *kamikaze* that crashed *Howorth*'s director basket hit just ten feet aft of where Bob Lyons was standing. He was knocked out, and when he came to, all the flying bridge canvas had been burned away, his battle helmet was gone, and his pant legs were on fire. The flying bridge deck was murderously hot. Trying to escape it, Lyons dove for the bridge level below, only to get trapped in a web of wires.

Bridge wing lookout Russ Bramble's clothes also caught fire. Bramble batted at the flames and tried to get clear by climbing down a ladder, but there was just too much smoke and he had no choice but to jump over the side. When he hit the water, Bramble removed his big talker's helmet, his shoes, and the binoculars still draped around his neck.

Bramble's first thoughts were about his mom who passed away when he was just 13. There was an explosion in the water—a Japanese plane crashing in flames—and showers of metal fell around him. Then Bramble heard a plaintive voice and looked over to see Orvill Raines floating nearby. Raines also recognized Bramble and cried out "Radar, help me!"

The water was cold and choppy, and Bramble could see Raines wasn't wearing a life jacket. When he finally reached him, Bramble did his best to keep Raines afloat. Raines was in rough shape: badly burned and vomiting and breathing with great difficulty. After some minutes, Raines began to convulse, as if something was throttling the life out of him. "This is a hell of a way to die" were the last words Russ Bramble heard from Raines. If he was going to be picked up before darkness set in, Bramble knew he had to be alert and busy himself with his own survival. There was no choice but to let Raines' limp body drift away and sink.

After the second hit to *Newcomb* knocked out power to No. 4 gun, its crew exited the gunhouse. Royce Holyfield, No. 4's pointer, suddenly heard someone shout, "Let's go!" On instinct, Royce jumped into the water and, as he did, caught sight of a plane coming in low off the deck right at *Newcomb*.

From his vantage on *Leutze*, John Perkins saw the *kamikaze* staggered by a round from one of *Newcomb*'s bow guns. The stricken plane abruptly veered left: its port wing hit the elevated barrel of *Newcomb*'s No. 3 gun, deflecting the plane to a final collision with *Leutze*'s stern.

Leutze's No. 5 gunhouse bore the brunt of the impact. Its after bulkhead ripped open, and its gun crew was tossed over the side. As gunhouse and airplane wreckage blossomed in flame, the *kamikaze*'s bomb detonated at the waterline. The explosion warped one of *Leutze*'s propeller shafts, demolished the after handling room, and peeled back the fantail deck plates. By the time *Leutze* pulled clear of *Newcomb,* its stern was underwater, and many burned and wounded crewmen from both ships were adrift. It was no longer possible to tell whether *Newcomb* or *Leutze* was in worse condition.

By 1900, time was running out for destroyer *Colhoun*. *Cassin Young* (DD-793) was on the scene as were two LCSs: *84* and *87*, both over from RP2, where *Colhoun* had begun the morning. Most of *Colhoun*'s crew had already crossed to *Cassin Young*'s decks, when, at 2045, *LCS-87* was ordered alongside to take off the rest.

Colhoun was listing ever more to starboard when *LCS-87* tied up to her port quarter. Once the lines were over, a young *Colhoun* ensign bounded across to *87*'s stern and cheerfully asked Rosse Long, 19, a motor machinist's mate stationed at *LCS-87*'s stern anchor winch, what help *87* needed for the transfer of personnel.

Long was startled by the officer's exuberance and noticed he was maybe only a year or two older than Long himself. Long gave the ensign directions where *Colhoun*'s sailors should gather once they were aboard. The ensign smiled, thanked Long, and hopped back aboard *Colhoun* to get the process started.

As the officer bounded off, Long could see by the light of the fires still burning amidships that one leg of the ensign's khaki trousers was split open. Underneath was a deep blood-fringed laceration extending from the ensign's upper thigh all the way down to his shoe top.

The transfer of personnel was quick, and among the last *Colhoun* sailors to cross over to *LCS-87* were Jim Pollock and his 40-mm gun crew. With *Cassin Young* standing by to sink *Colhoun* with 5-inch gunfire, *LCS-87*'s deckhands ensured a quick getaway by chopping the lines connecting them to the destroyer.

* * *

When *LCS-64* returned to the vicinity of RP1, XO John Littleton established contact with destroyer *Cassin Young*, whose skipper at first ordered *LCS-64* north to look for *Bush* survivors. For several hours the effort yielded no sign of *Bush* survivors for any of the flotilla of craft combing the water. Finally, *LCS-64* returned south to pick up the radar bearing Littleton had marked when *64* pulled away from *Bush* that afternoon. Moving slowly northwest along the reciprocal of that bearing, *LCS-64*'s crew finally found *Bush*'s gig a little after 2000.

During the next hours, *LCS-64* pulled in 95 sailors, and other craft, an estimated 150 more. Most were alive, but some were dead—or soon to die. A number remained missing. Some of these, though otherwise unhurt, had surrendered to the siren call of lost hope—quietly slipping from life jackets or releasing holds to a raft, gig, punt, or floater net. Others, like Wesley Northey with his two fractured legs, were simply unable to hold on any longer. Perhaps the most tragic ends of all came to a handful of sailors killed by rescue craft propellers or by fumes from their exhaust manifolds.

To a man, the survivors were cold, wet, and tired, stretched to the limits of exhaustion—or beyond. Many were wounded, burned, or, like supply officer Bob Carney, crippled by fractures. Some had outlasted simple conditions that under the circumstances might have killed them. (Coit Butler, for example, who was rescued by *LCS-40* at 0200, fought painful leg cramps the ship's doctor helped him massage.)

Each rescue was a moment to savor (either then or in the days, weeks, months, and years ahead) in ways specific to each sailor. To Ralph Carver (picked up by a fleet tug) it was the noise of the crew and the throbbing of the ship's engines; to Coit Butler it was a cigarette and a slug of brandy; to XO Tom Owen, dry clothes; to Bob Carney, coffee with cream. To a man, it was undisturbed sleep.

At 0300 on 7 April, *Ellyson* radioman Dwight Donnewald was in his bunk ("clothes and all," as he wrote later in his journal) when he heard a GQ call for *Ellyson* 5-inch gun crews. "We are going to sink the *Emmons*."

About 1800 the report came in that the *Rodman* was abandoning ship, later the *Emmons* was doing the same. The small minesweeps were out picking up the survivors, and the last total I heard was 250 from both ships. Later in the evening *Rodman* was reported underway and *Emmons* was still afloat but drifting toward an enemy beach. I don't know how many ships got hit but I counted seven for sure, and I'm really sure there were more."

A fifth *kamikaze* had crashed *Emmons* at 1633 and two hours later an explosion in the after magazine finally forced the few remaining crewmen aboard over the side. Dwight Donnewald was on radio watch when *Ellyson* closed with *Emmons* and sank her with gunfire. "We go within 100 yards of it and turned a light on her. The boys on the bridge say she had been hit on the port side of CIC by a suicide plane because it was all smashed up and they had been bombed again and again. The whole fantail was missing because the after magazine blew up."

Donnewald was not that far off in his estimate of 6 April losses. In addition to three destroyer types—*Bush, Colhoun,* and *Emmons*—there'd been the outright loss of two ammunition ships and an LST (each caught in or near Kerama Retto). Destroyers *Leutze, Newcomb,* and *Morris* (DD-417) (crashed head-on between No. 1 and No. 2 guns while patrolling the ping line) were so badly mangled they would eventually be scrapped. While *Howorth* and *Hyman* would return to service before war's end, others, like *Rodman* and *Mullany* (DD-528), would still be laid up. The day's casualties at sea—367 dead (including 88 from *Bush*, 64 from *Emmons*, 40 from *Newcomb*, and 30 from *Mullany*) and 408 wounded—outpaced casualties ashore, both in numbers, and (due to burn injuries) crippling horror. When *Howorth*'s Bob Lyons was finally pulled from the web of wires above the bridge and carried down to the wardroom aid station, the ship's doctor looked him over (he was badly burned and temporarily blinded), injected him with morphine, and voiced a sentiment that doubtless spoke for all the day's survivors: "Now's the time to break out the whisky," he told Lyons, pouring them both a tumbler full.

In truth, the day's U.S. Navy losses paled only when compared to Radio Tokyo's exaggerated claims—60 American ships sunk and 61 crippled. If these boasts made any sense, they did so in light of the results fervently hoped for from seven hundred aircraft and air crews (half of them *kamikazes*) tossed into the cauldron—and what *bushido* justice demanded for the roughly 350 men who never returned.

At 0415 Dwight Donnewald closed his journal entry with his own deck-level take on the meaning of 6 April. "Today was a perfect day for what happened because the clouds were real low and the planes were on you in no time at all. I hope tomorrow is a nice sunny day."

★ Chapter 22 ★

"Delete All After 'Crazy,'"
7 April–13 April 1945

Our mission appears suicidal and it is. But I wish to emphasize that suicide is not the objective. It is victory.

—Captain Tameichi Hara

Get Yamato

Just before midnight on 6 April, word reached *Bunker Hill,* one of thirteen Task Force 58 carriers steaming northeast of Okinawa, that *Yamato* had left Japan's Inland Sea accompanied by a cruiser and eight destroyers. The next morning, strike planes sat warmed on *Bunker Hill's* flight deck and flight crews waited in ready rooms while scout seaplanes shadowed *Yamato's* every move.

For the first time since Air Group 84's February deployment with *Bunker Hill,* its Avengers would be armed with aerial torpedoes. In dozens of strikes against factories, airfields, and coastal shipping, VT-84 aircraft had flown armed only with bomb payloads. Not that its pilots lacked torpedo practice or savvy.

For some, like flight section leader Al Turnbull, 26, this was their second tour on *Bunker Hill.* And every pilot, including Turnbull, received plenty of practice during pre-cruise training at Naval Air Station (NAS) North Island near San Diego. While at North Island, VT-84 was housed adjacent to the Pacific Fleet Test Unit, and squadron pilots eagerly tried out torpedo modifications before they were approved for fleet use. In the process, they'd launched nearly five hundred torpedoes during test runs.

* * *

Yamato, VT-84's target objective, and the centerpiece of Japan's Second Fleet, reached the southern tip of Kyushu at daybreak on 7 April. Second Fleet's ships at first turned southwest, a feint to make it appear they were bound for Sasebo in the northwestern corner of Kyushu. During the course change, the escorts established a ring formation around *Yamato* with cruiser *Yahagi* still in the lead. Compared to the previous day's glorious weather, 7 April's morning conditions were dismal, with dark, low-hanging clouds threatening rain. After its modest try at deception, Second Fleet turned due south into the East China Sea. With visibility so poor, Kyushu's coast and its familiar mountain backdrop quickly disappeared astern.

Two of *Yamato*'s and *Yahagi*'s remaining catapult scout planes flew off at this time, bound for Kyushu, where aircraft and pilots would be put to other use. The escort planes overhead at the start of the voyage were gone as well, leaving the Fleet no air cover whatsoever. When a formation of twenty Zeros briefly roared by, it raised hopes the sortie might receive air fleet protection after all. But the Zeros turned out to be on a training flight and had winged overhead merely to bid Second Fleet farewell. Once they disappeared, the only aircraft visible was a U.S. reconnaissance seaplane lurking just outside AA range.

The captain of destroyer *Asashimo* signaled he was dropping back to repair engine problems. This left a breach in the screening circle, and other ships maneuvered to close the gap. Ahead were several two-thousand-ton cargo ships who signaled: "Good luck! Wish you success!" Someone on *Yahagi*'s bridge expressed surprise that Japan had ships of such size still afloat.

Earlier, Tameichi Hara had ordered *Yahagi*'s one thousand crewmen assembled on the forecastle, where he addressed them, first reading a formal message from Combined Fleet's Soemu Toyoda. Then Hara shared his own thoughts. "Our mission appears suicidal and it is," Hara began and then added, "but suicide is not the objective. The objective is victory. Once this ship is crippled or sunk, do not hesitate to save yourselves for the next fight. *Bushido* says that a warrior lives in such a way that he is always prepared to die. It means that we live so that we will have no regrets when we die. We can commit suicide at any time. But we are going on this mission not to commit suicide but to win, and turn the tide of war."

* * *

Pilots left the *Bunker Hill* ready room at 0948, stepped onto the catwalk, and climbed to the flight deck. Bomber and torpedo pilots like Turnbull and Francis Guttenberger huddled briefly with their crews before climbing into cockpits. VT-84 and its torpedoes would go in as part of the second wave. The weather reports were grim: ceiling varied from 2,000 to 3,000 feet and was unlikely to improve en route to the targets.

Earlier, Admiral Raymond Spruance had instructed Task Force 58's Marc Mitscher to allow the Japanese to continue south to face the guns of task force battleships and cruisers, but Mitscher preferred to use what he considered Task Force 58's best weapons. After sending off his planes, Mitscher turned to his chief of staff, Arleigh Burke and instructed Burke to inform Spruance that Mitscher proposed to attack *Yamato* "unless otherwise directed." Mitscher then scribbled out a personal postscript: "Will you take them or shall I?" Soon after, on his own message blank, Spruance dashed off a reply to Mitscher: "You take them."

Following the launch, fighters, bombers, and torpedo planes joined up over *Bunker Hill*, then headed for the target coordinates: bombers in the lead, TBMs behind, and fighters on the flanks. Seventy-five miles from the target area, the ceiling lifted, but only briefly. By then, though, the Japanese ships were within radar range. VT-84's Avengers stayed close to VB-84's bombers until, unexpectedly, the bombers pushed over through an opportune hole in the cloud cover and set off after *Yamato*'s escorts. The Avengers continued their methodical approach straight and level at five thousand feet. Finally, at about 1210, they pushed over through heavy clouds, aiming to break through the base of the overcast five miles from *Yamato*.

On *Yamato*, junior radar officer Ensign Mitsuru Yoshida spent the morning in the upper radar room where men were smoking His Majesty's brand cigarettes and sipping liquor from pocket flasks. A little after noon, *Yamato*'s radar detected aircraft. At 1220, alerts went out to the other ships, only two of which had antiaircraft radar. Soon, the Grummans were in visual range—first 10, then 30, then easily more than 100 aircraft. To brace for the coming attacks, *Yahagi* and the destroyers opened up range between each other and *Yamato*—all at full speed ahead.

Ships passed briefly through a heavy squall. It gave them momentary cover, but without radar to aim their guns, it also robbed gun crews of precious time to pick out targets and aim. At 1232, as the rain clouds passed, planes were spotted close off *Yahagi*'s port bow. It seemed to Mitsuru Yoshida on *Yamato* that his ship's 24 antiaircraft guns and 150 machine guns opened fire all at once.

From his vantage in *Yahagi*'s antiaircraft command post, Tameichi Hara saw two groups of U.S. aircraft circling clockwise, a third group counterclockwise. Gun crews who were expecting the planes to swoop in directly at first seemed baffled and indecisive about choosing targets and opening fire.

The first planes to lunge at *Yahagi* were four bomb-equipped Avengers. Bombs curved down toward the cruiser's port side, but all missed by a wide margin. Hara ordered hard right rudder to evade a group of strafing Hellcats that came in next. Machine-gun bullets whined and thudded into *Yahagi*'s decks and bulkheads, but no one was wounded. One plane pulled out of its dive so close Hara could make out the pilot's face. Bombs from this group missed *Yahagi* as well, as did bombs from the next two groups of planes.

When word reached *Yahagi* that destroyer *Asashimo* was under attack, it amazed Hara how, in the midst of this huge battle, Americans could spare aircraft to go after a lone straggler. Still, he was pleased at his own crew's bravery and how nimbly *Yahagi* maneuvered to keep them from being hit.

VT-84's 14 Avengers broke through the cloud cover at two thousand feet. As hoped, *Yamato* was five miles away, stern-to but midway through a sweeping turn to starboard that would position the huge ship bow-on to the Avengers. The planes began circling. At the command "break" from Squadron CO Chandler Swanson, the VT-84 formation split into two divisions: eight planes led by Swanson banking right to attack *Yamato*'s port side, and six, including Al Turnbull, to the left for starboard runs.

Earlier that morning, Ed Duffy and Tom Kelly's pilot "Guts" Guttenberger had strode to the front of the Ready Room, picked up a piece of chalk and scrawled GET THE YAMATO in huge letters across the blackboard. Now, Guttenberger followed Swanson for the runs on *Yamato*'s port side. From his seat (little more than a bench) in the TBM's radio compartment, Kelly caught piecemeal glances at *Yamato* through his starboard "window"—a small square of Plexiglas in the side of the fuselage.

The AA fire from *Yamato* and the escort ring was already thick as the two divisions of VT-84 Avengers split once more, first into three-plane sections and then into individual units for separate runs. The sky was filled with puffs of purple, red, yellow, and green flak. Al Turnbull saw his wingman Dick Walsh's Avenger explode just as Walsh turned into his run and watched helplessly as the airplane plowed nose first into the sea.

Turnbull was by then at the start of his own run, flying just fifty feet off the deck. He was low, but also slow: the shallow drop from the low cloud deck held air speed to barely 180 knots. Perhaps the "low-slow" combination disrupted the accuracy of the ships' AA or perhaps it was luck or just bad shooting by the Japanese. With so many planes crisscrossing from so many directions, collisions seemed just as much a risk as the flak. After dropping his fish and climbing clear of *Yamato*'s forward superstructure, Turnbull found he was on the exact bearing needed for the return trip to *Bunker Hill*.

As soon as Guttenberger pulled up from launching his torpedo at *Yamato*'s port beam, Duffy unhooked his harness and raised himself up to have a look. In that instant, the plane caught flak and the jolt pounded Duffy's head into the canopy. Meanwhile, AA shrapnel pierced the radio compartment fuselage to Kelly's right, and although most was absorbed by Kelly's parachute pack hanging from the bulkhead, a few shards caught his shoulder and arm. Kelly noticed flame sprouting from a hydraulic line and reached over with one gloved hand to smother the fire, meanwhile reaching up with his other to steady Duffy.

At 1241 *Yamato* sustained two bomb hits, both near the main mast, and at 1245, the first torpedo hit. Almost simultaneously, destroyer *Hamakaze* was sunk by separate blasts from a bomb and a torpedo.

Yahagi was still untouched, but suddenly Hara heard a port side lookout scream "Torpedoes!" He immediately ordered an evasive turn, but it was already too late. As the Avengers that launched them thundered overhead, the lead edges of three torpedo wakes were only a few hundred yards away. *Yahagi* staggered into a turn, but a torpedo hit the hull amidships below the waterline. Momentum carried the ship forward for a time, but then it slowed and went dead in the water.

It was 1246, less than fifteen minutes since the battle began. Already Hara knew *Yahagi* was doomed. He tried getting a damage report from the engine room, but got no response. He assumed that was where the ship had been hit. Soon he had confirmation from a messenger: every sailor in the engine room was dead.

Other groups of planes attacked: a bomb exploded on the forecastle, followed by two heavier explosions on the stern, and then a second torpedo hit, this one to the starboard bow. *Yahagi,* already listing to starboard, sagged even farther.

The Very Breath of the Hostile Planes

American torpedo planes had scored three direct hits on *Yamato*'s port side near the after mast. At 1335, with more waves of American planes approaching, *Yamato* was still pressing south toward Okinawa, but her speed had slowed to 18 knots, her sides were buckled, her decks were covered with dead, and those still alive had few operable weapons with which to fight back.

Positioned amidst the chaos of *Yamato*'s bridge, Mitsuru Yoshida was awed by the effectiveness of the American planes and pilots. They swooped in, dropped their payloads, turned to avoid antiaircraft fire, and then strafed *Yamato*'s bridge. It was if the very breath of the hostile planes was being puffed against them.

Between 1337 and 1344 five more direct torpedo hits on *Yamato*'s port sent the ship listing even more dangerously to port. To correct the list, starboard engine and boiler rooms—*Yamato*'s largest and lowest compartments—were ordered flooded, a decision dooming hundreds of sailors in those spaces.

* * *

After taking a ninety-minute pounding during which, by Tameichi Hara's count, his ship had absorbed thirteen bombs and seven torpedoes, *Yahagi* was listing thirty degrees to port with waves lapping her main deck. Standing next to Hara on *Yahagi*'s bridge was Rear Admiral Keizo Komura, *Yamato*'s escort force commander. Komura was unhurt, but Hara was bleeding from a wound to his left arm. "Bodies and debris were everywhere in *Yahagi*," Hara later recalled in a memoir. "Hardly anything remained intact." *Yamato* lay six thousand yards ahead, still battling, but two of the eight escort destroyers were already gone and three more were dead in the water and burning.

Komura at last glanced at Hara and said simply: "Let's go." It was 1405. The two men removed their shoes and jumped into the sea. As they did, *Yahagi* sank, creating an immense whirlpool that at first grabbed Hara "like a mighty fist" and held him for what seemed minutes. When Hara, gasping, finally bobbed to the surface, he could see that *Yamato* was still afloat but plagued by swarming enemy aircraft. Hara clung to a floating piece of debris and watched as a pillar of fire and smoke completely enveloped *Yamato*. When the smoke lifted, there was nothing left but empty sea where *Yamato* had once been.

Counter flooding had no impact on *Yamato*'s list, and the loss of the starboard engine halved *Yamato*'s speed. At 1415 a twelfth torpedo struck *Yamato*. The list had reached thirty degrees, and the portside deck, normally twenty-five feet above the water, was awash. After making the decision to abandon ship, Second Fleet Commander, Vice Admiral Seiichi Ito shook hands with his staff officers, walked resolutely into his cabin and closed the door.

When they saw *Yamato*'s CO, navigator, and other senior officers lashing themselves to the bridge to avoid the disgrace of surviving the sinking, Mitsuru Yoshida and other young officers began to do likewise. The older officers angrily admonished them to stop and to leave the ship.

Yamato had heeled to an unsustainable eighty degrees by the time Yoshida climbed through a lookout port and reached the nearly vertical deck. *Yamato* soon lay flat on her beam ends with gun projectiles caroming like pinballs into stanchions and bulkheads and exploding.

The ship began to slide down, at first pulling Yoshida and other struggling survivors with her.

As *Yamato* plunged deeper, compartments imploded under the pressure, while magazine ammunition exploded, sending tendrils of flame and smoke so high above the water's surface they were seen from Kyushu. One of these explosions blasted Yoshida back to the surface.

None of VT-84's thirteen surviving Avengers flew in formation on the return to *Bunker Hill*. Several planes, including the one crewed by Guttenberger, Duffy, and Kelly, were limping. Every pilot was trying to conserve fuel, in some cases jettisoning excess gear, including ammunition, guns, radar gear, and armor plate—"everything," one pilot later remarked, "except my crewmen."

Guttenberger's Avenger had enough fuel, but because of the loss of his hydraulics, he was one of two VT-84 pilots who had to lower his wheels manually and land without flaps. Guttenberger lined up as squadron CO Swanson touched down. His approach was good, the landing hard, but the Avenger's talehook grabbed a wire and jerked to a stop abreast of the island. Seeing the tattoo of shrapnel holes in the plane's starboard side, plane crews got ready to carry Tom Kelly out on a stretcher. When Kelly climbed out of the side hatch, some thought they beheld a ghost, others a miracle.

Meanwhile, the squadron's second division of aircraft were lining up for approaches. Al Turnbull's was the final VT-84 TBM to return safely to *Bunker Hill*'s flight deck.

The surviving crewmen of Second Fleet's Okinawa sortie were rescued by three destroyers who somehow weathered the American attacks. Mitsuru Yoshida was one of only 269 *Yamato* sailors rescued—less than 10 percent of her crew. Cruiser *Yahagi* lost half its crew, but among the survivors were Tameichi Hara and Rear Admiral Keizo Komura, both recovered by destroyer *Hatsushimo*.

On the war's first day, Komura had commanded cruiser *Chikuma*, the ship catapulting the first float planes to scout ship locations at Pearl Harbor before dawn. Now, after cleaning fuel oil off his face and putting on a borrowed uniform, Komura wrote a message for Combined Fleet headquarters advising them Second Fleet's two destroyers were continuing the advance toward Okinawa. Before Komura's message could be sent, however, Combined Fleet canceled the mission and ordered the ships to return. "I've had enough," Komura was heard to mutter.

One for the Fool

Combined Fleet's coordination of Heaven One's air and surface resources was, at least from hard evidence, a failure. Reeling from the huge aircraft losses on 6 April, Japan's air forces were able to sortie relatively few aircraft the next day—nowhere enough to divert American aircraft from swarming Second Fleet. Just twenty *kamikazes* threatened Hagushi Roadstead in the morning and twelve were splashed. One crashed battleship *Maryland*; another *Wesson* (DE-184), a tin can on the ping line north of Ie Shima; and, at midday, carrier *Hancock* (which launched 53 aircraft against Second Fleet, none of which located their targets).

En route from Kyushu, six *kamikazes* detoured over RP1 (6 April's hunting reserve) now patrolled by destroyer *Bennett*. RP1 had become a sort of hand-me-down assignment: *Bennett* inherited RP1 after "moving up the line"—beginning at RP4 on 6 April and then shifting counterclockwise to RP3 and finally RP2 as the day wore on. Today was her turn on RP1.

RP1 C.A.P. aircraft shot down five of the bogeys and were on the tail of the sixth high off *Bennett*'s port beam. *Bennett* yeoman Larry Finn saw the twin-engine plane trailing smoke as it looped in a wide turn around *Bennett*'s fantail, curled back on the starboard beam, and plowed into the water just yards from the ship. The plane's bomb ruptured *Bennett*'s hull under No. 1 stack, demolished a boiler drum, tore out the forward engine room's bulkhead, and ruptured steam lines. Three men were killed instantly, and most stationed in the forward fire and engine rooms, including *Bennett*'s chief engineer Don Sheridan, were scorched by steam. A water tender in the forward boiler room instinctively cut the burners before diving into the bilges—an alert move that probably saved the ship but couldn't prevent major damage. In just a day, suicide attacks on RP1 ships had sunk or crippled three destroyers and taken nearly 150 lives.

Though disquieted by the concentrated and seemingly unremitting *kamikaze* attacks, Vice Admiral Kelly Turner was resolute. "If this is the best the enemy can throw against us," he signaled his command at noon on the 7th, "we shall move forward." The following day, brimming with confidence after *Yamato*'s sinking and the Marine progress on land, the Alligator cabled Nimitz: "I may be crazy," he began his assessment, "but it looks like the Japs have quit the war, at least in this section." "Delete all after 'crazy' " was Nimitz's immediate, succinct, and prescient response.

Meanwhile, from their own assessments, Japan's military leaders were firmly convinced *Kikusui* No. 1 had dealt the Americans a staggering blow. Wanting to believe, they failed to question exaggerated claims of blows dealt to American ships. But they also relied on other compelling "evidence": the dramatic downturn in American raids on Kyushu and the interceptions of clearly panic-stricken voice communications from the American invasion fleet.

If *Kikusui* No. 1 had failed, Vice Admiral Matome Ugaki (now in charge of all IJN *Tokkotai* forces) believed it would have been senseless to launch further attacks. Now, however, with *Tokkotai* mobilized in defense of the homeland and showing such dramatic results, the *Kikusui* would continue until or unless every last pilot and plane was expended.

On 9 April, Combined Fleet's Admiral Soemu Toyoda ordered the launch of *Kikusui* No. 2, and on 11 April when the dismal weather blanketing Second Fleet's tragic sortie finally lifted, a vanguard of *Tokkotai* fighter-bombers sortied to take on American ships off the southern tip of Kyushu. The main attacks of *Kikusui* No. 2, however, began the next day.

At midday on the 12th, a flight of 129 planes, including nine *Ōka*-laden Mitsubishi medium bombers (Bettys) sortied from Kanoya, the Thunder Gods' Kyushu air base. *Ōka* pilot Saburo Dohi was on the second Betty to take off. When his flight was called, Dohi, the would-be schoolteacher, was busy setting up bamboo cots in officers' quarters at the base. Dohi was expecting the delivery of more cots, so as he left, he asked another officer to be sure to receive the shipment when it arrived.

The flight of Bettys was over the East China Sea when it was intercepted by American fighters. Several Bettys were shot down, but others, including the plane carrying Dohi, escaped into the clouds and continued on toward Okinawa.

At 1445, a lookout finally spotted American ships in the distance. Dohi, who looked to be napping, woke up when he heard the alert, removed his leather helmet, life jacket, and pistol, and tied his Thunder Gods ceremonial band across his forehead. When someone removed the floorboard access hatch to the Ōka, Dohi, silent and pale looking, lowered himself into the cockpit behind the Ōka's warhead nose. Dohi soon signaled he was ready, but when the release button was pushed, the detonating charge malfunctioned and nothing happened. Finally, someone yanked a manual tripwire, the lightened Betty abruptly lifted, and Dohi's Ōka was spotted, plummeting at first, but then, once Dohi ignited his booster rockets, racing in a straight line toward the target ships, now 18,000 meters in the distance.

Kelly Turner was not entirely naïve about Japan's will to fight. He suspected—as did most of his sailors—that worsening weather alone accounted for the decline in attacks from 8 to 11 April. Sunday, 8 April and then Monday each brought a single serious attack, though the locales for both were radar picket stations athwart the Kyushu-Okinawa flyway.

Sunday's happened at dusk, when RP3 destroyer *Gregory* (DD-802) took on three *kamikazes*. The first, an IJA Sonia, crashed *Gregory*'s hull port side, cutting power to the forward engine room and wounding two men. Gene Leganza, 20, a machinist's mate and sound-powered talker in the after engine room, heard a bang and a hiss. The line abruptly went dead (a mere hiccup of chaos, it seemed to him later) but soon things were back under control. When Howard Tomlin, a ship's coxswain and trainer on No. 4 gun, saw the plane's wing splinter the CO's gig—his boat—he was so distraught he almost missed the command to swing No. 4 gun starboard to fire at two new incomings.

Both these planes were splashed close aboard, but *Gregory*'s damage was enough to take her out of the war.

Monday, destroyer *Sterett* (DD-407), covering RP4 with two LCSs, battled a formation of Vals. One exploded and splashed on the ship's starboard bow, while a second, though hit, crashed *Sterett* at the waterline. Forty-mm gunfire severed the wing of a third Val, but carried the one-winged wreck over *Sterett*'s flying bridge before dropping it in the water—a splash that tossed the pilot's body back over No. 2 gun.

Tuesday brought flying weather unsuitable for either side, but on the 11th there was both clearing weather and a rough afternoon for Task Force 58 picket destroyers south of Kyushu. *Kidd* (DD-661) took the worst punishment: A *kamikaze* poised to crash nearby *Bullard* (DD-660), instead pulled off at the last instant, skimmed the water between the ships (thus masking batteries on both), and careened into *Kidd*'s forward fire room, claiming nearly 40 lives and wounding another 60.

Within sight of flames and smoke towering above *Kidd*, destroyer *Hank* (DD-702) next squared off against a strafing low flyer barreling in to port. Quartermaster Ted Teagle (a 17-year-old who'd enlisted at age 15), stationed on a 40-mm gun director platform, tracked the plane but never got the command to fire. When the aircraft was virtually on top of him, Teagle finally closed the firing key and hit the deck. The guns squeezed off just a few rounds and, when Teagle got to his feet, he found the director platform riddled with bullet holes and his director console reduced to little more than glass and cogs. Behind Teagle, two *Hank* sailors sprawled dead; the body of another had been thrown head over heels to starboard as though drop kicked out to sea. The Japanese plane, meanwhile, hooked by its tail over *Hank*'s starboard lifeline, trailed a wake of oil and gasoline until the ocean at last pulled it under.

When Thursday's dawn broke clear and cool, Turner immediately warned his ships to expect heavy attacks, and added, "Don't let any return." Turner also ordered the beach gunfire ships—ten battleships, seven cruisers, and twelve tin cans—to deploy for antiaircraft protection in "*kamikaze* gulch" the rough triangle of water bounded by Ie Shima, Kerama Retto, and Okinawa's west coast.

Early that afternoon a flight of Vals reached RP1—now called the "coffin corner" to picket line veterans—whose latest occupants were *Cassin Young*, *Purdy* (DD-734), and four LCSs. *Cassin Young* splashed two Vals but was crashed by a third that knocked out her radar and a fireroom and claimed 60 casualties.

At 1445, with damaged *Cassin Young* no longer on station, a second raid appeared. After *kamikaze* planes sank *LCS-33* and badly damaged *LCS-57*, a Val pursued by three C.A.P. aircraft crashed twenty feet from *Purdy* and skidded into her side. The bomb explosion knocked out all but emergency power and steering, sending *Purdy*, like *Cassin Young*, in retreat to Hagushi Roadstead. Destroyers *Stanly* and *Lang* (DD-399), the latest in RP1's line of succession, were at that moment on their way over from RP2.

As the second *kamikaze* raid reached RP1, on RP14 destroyer *Mannert L. Abele* sat dead in the water and without power, the victim of a Zeke crash and bomb explosion that demolished an engine room, broke her keel, and snapped both propeller shafts. Though 40s and 20s were still firing, some *Abele* sailors were already standing by to abandon ship when Jim Morris, a seaman stationed topside, saw something quite unlike anything he'd ever seen before. It looked to be a torpedo zipping through the air off the starboard quarter and heading directly toward *Abele*. Whatever it was, within seconds it smashed *Abele*'s hull below No. 1 stack, split her in two, and sent both pieces—and nearly 80 men—to the bottom.

Abele survivors like Morris had just a few minutes to escape. One sailor, pharmacist's mate Nick Korompilas, 21, cut his getaway margin especially close. Korompilas had escaped the wardroom aid station with the ship's doctor and was about to step from the bow but instead went back to retrieve *Abele*'s chief steward who lay injured on the wardroom galley deck after being scalded by a vat of soup. With just seconds to spare, both men got clear.

Among the survivors from CIC were Coit Butler and his FIDO team—transferred by verbal orders from Kelly Turner to *Abele* barely three days after surviving *Bush*'s sinking. Radarman Gordon Chambers, meanwhile, was already at the starboard side near CIC, life jacket on, when the impact knocked him overboard. The next thing Chambers knew he was in the water with a sinking ship to either side. Only later did Chambers realize that they were the two halves of Abele.

Off to the southwest, destroyer *Stanly* was still en route to RP1 when radarman Irv Brewer caught a brief, incredulous glimpse of a second Ōka (what Americans would soon call *baka,* meaning "crazy" or "fool"). Brewer had briefly stepped outside CIC when he spotted something small and fast skimming at wave-top height toward *Stanly*'s starboard bow. Brewer hit the deck just before the object pierced both sides of *Stanly*'s thin shell plating and finally exploded off the port side.

Stanly's bow was holed and rumpled, but serviceable. Minutes later, as *Stanly* evaded more air attacks, a second mystery bullet zoomed in.* This one missed *Stanly* completely, instead camelbacking over the forward part of the ship, banking to the left, and bouncing out of control into the sea. All hands were amazed, but the time to ponder all this had to wait. *Stanly* was being recalled from RP1 to help ships being attacked in *kamikaze* gulch.

Bogeys arrived an hour after the first picket sightings, and for a riotous ten minutes, the waters of *kamikaze* gulch became, as *Montpelier* sailor James Fahey had put it five months before, "suicide at its best": a pageant of destruction (the finale for *Kikusui* No. 2) played out by ships, *kamikaze,* aircraft and Navy Corsairs beneath a canopy of AA fire.

Richard Graves, an officer on ping line DE *Rall* (DE-304), counted seven bogeys circling his ship, then patrolling within sight of *Tennessee.* Two peeled off and streamed past off *Rall*'s bow. One crashed a destroyer off the port beam—most likely *Zellars* (DD-777)—while *Tennessee* gunners splashed the second. *Rall*'s gunners, firing outmoded 3- and 1.1-inch guns as well as short range 20s, accounted for three planes, but then a fourth, a low-flying Nate, bounced first off the water and then crashed *Rall*'s starboard beam. Its bomb—a jury-rigged artillery shell—passed clear through the ship and exploded ten yards off

*Minutes later, farther south on RP12, a fourth *baka* splashed fifty yards from destroyer minesweeper *Jeffers* (DD-621/DMS-27). *Jeffers* then raced to RP14 to assist *LSM(R)-189* and *LSM(R)-190* rescue survivors from *Mannert L. Abele.*

to port. The collision, combined with gasoline fires and shrapnel from the bomb, left a trail of casualties and damage that stunned Graves. He remembered being told in Midshipman school there might come a time "when the decks were slippery with blood." And now, starboard side amidships on *Rall*, the time had indeed arrived: blood-red water streaming from overhead gun tubs ran down bulkheads, crossed the main deck, and spilled into the scuppers and over the side.

Rall, with 21 dead and nearly 40 wounded was hard hit, but there were others, including *Zellars* and *Tennessee*. Two ping line ships in waters south of Kerama Retto—*Whitehurst* (DE-634) and destroyer minelayer *Lindsey*—also caught it. *Lindsey* took a crash that all but severed her bow and looked like a total loss.

Fatality in Chief

News of President Franklin Roosevelt's 12 April death in Warm Springs, Georgia, first reached the Northern Pacific at dawn the next day, Friday, 13 April.

ALNAV 69, FROM SECNAV TO ALNAV was the heading of the coded dispatch received by duty radiomen in thousands of ships' radio shacks.

It began:

I HAVE THE SAD DUTY OF ANNOUNCING TO THE NAVAL SERVICE THE DEATH OF FRANKLIN DELANO ROOSEVELT, THE PRESIDENT OF THE UNITED STATES, WHICH OCCURRED ON TWELVE APRIL.

Though the typewriters clacked on in each shack, someone invariably was already out the door spreading the word. Minutes later, when ships' speakers barked the message's substance, it was fresh news to no one: "Attention! Attention! All hands! President Roosevelt is dead. Repeat, our Supreme Commander, President Roosevelt is dead."

Many listeners were boys still years shy of voting age. For them, and even for older sailors, Franklin Roosevelt was the only president remembered or imagined. Few knew Harry Truman's name—or just how it was he stood in line to be president.

Reactions and emotions ran the gamut. To 18-year-old Rolland Floch, duty radioman on destroyer *Ammen*, it seemed the world was falling apart. Roosevelt was gone and who was this Truman? In radioman Dwight Donnewald's diary, however, the news got passing mention and second billing: "GQ at 0100—enemy aircraft near us. We opened fire but saw no results. Bergy, another radioman was on the skeds [radio traffic duty] when we got the message telling of President Roosevelt's death. I don't like it. I think Dewey is a better man than Truman. But what can I say?" For Donnewald and thousands of others, the news was a distant event, like the war in Europe—important, but also abstract, and unlikely to change their lives today, tomorrow, or next week.

Meanwhile, for Commander Wilfrid Walker, the skipper of destroyer *William D. Porter* (DD-579), Roosevelt's passing exposed a disquieting memory. In November 1943, while serving as a screening destroyer for battleship *Iowa* (BB-61) carrying Roosevelt to a war summit with Churchill and Stalin in Tehran, the newly activated "Willie Dee" had misfired a torpedo that came perilously close to hitting *Iowa*.

Though it had been an accident during a routine practice drill, fear of sabotage sent *Porter* to Bermuda, where she was met by armed Marines. Her crew was arrested en masse and each sailor was subjected to a lengthy grilling. The accident's perpetrator, a 22-year-old torpedoman who neglected to remove a firing primer and then ditched the evidence overboard, was sentenced to fourteen years hard labor*—and the "Willie Dee's" reputation as a bad-luck ship was sealed. Though official information about the incident was not released until well after the war, "Don't shoot, we're Republicans" became a well-worn greeting whenever Walker's ship joined a formation or the crew pulled liberty.

News about Roosevelt also was reaching the troops ashore. *New Yorker* correspondent John Lardner learned about it as he breakfasted with the Army's 7th Division on the southern front. The word spread quickly but quietly, almost like a secret. "Now and then," he told his readers, "when two men met, they would stop to speak of what had

---

*Roosevelt later ordered the sentence commuted.

happened, but they spoke slowly, with long pauses between their sentences, and when at last a pause grew into a silence, they would part and move on, as though it were impossible to understand the event and therefore discuss it."

Farther north, Marines like Eugene Sledge were saddened but also curious and apprehensive about Harry Truman and concerned about how he would handle the war. "We surely didn't want someone in the White House who would prolong it one day longer than necessary."

Things were still going extremely well for both 1st and 6th Division Marines. Soon after hearing about Roosevelt, Sledge's 5th Regiment set off by truck and amphtrac for landings on small islands off Okinawa's east coast. K Company scoured Taka Shima but found no Japanese and just a handful of civilians. The company set up defensive positions on a rocky hill overlooking a beach from where Sledge could see a DE bobbing offshore. "It had been standing by during our landing and remained with us for the several days we stayed on Taka Shima. We felt important, as though we had our own private navy."

Over on the mainland, the lead battalion of 1st Division's 4th Regiment was moving with textbook precision as it raced up the eastern coast. There was slightly more resistance on the west coast, where 6th Division Marines cornered two Japanese troop battalions on Motobu Peninsula—the first fighting of any consequence in the north. Even so, Marines managed to send advanced patrols all the way to Hedo Saki, the island's northern tip. Progress was so encouraging, in fact, that Admiral Turner and 10th Army commander Simon Bolivar Buckner, Jr., agreed to advance the date set for the Army assault on Ie Shima, an island just west of the Peninsula.

★ Chapter 23 ★

Wiseman's Cove, 13 April–30 April 1945

(To the tune of "Home on the Range")
Oh, give me a home, far away from the foam,
Far away from the smoke and this bay,
Where seldom is seen, FLASH RED, CONTROL GREEN,
And the GQ alarm is silent all day.

Bone Yard

The TBS voice call for Kerama Retto's task group commander was "Wiseman," and his repair facility's was "Wiseman's Cove," but it didn't take long for sailors aboard Wiseman's expanding collection of damaged ships to come up with their own names. One was "Wiseman's Junkyard." Another was "Bone Yard."

When wounded ships arrived in the Bone Yard, their wounded sailors were transferred either to hospital ships or to battle casualty ships—transports and other vessels converted for the purpose. Storekeeper Wally Dickerman and gunner's mate Charles Serey were both able to leave *Cassin Young* more or less under their own power. Dickerman, who had multiple shrapnel wounds, was so shot up with morphine it seemed to him he was moving in a dream. Serey, with shrapnel in his left foot, limped painfully in the same shoes he'd been wearing when wounded. Blood that had pooled and partially congealed along the shoe's insole squished with each step.

Some of the most horrible and disfiguring wounds were burns, from either gasoline fires or steam-line ruptures. Destroyer *Bennett*'s medical officer treated chief engineer Don Sheridan's burns by smearing them with a white cream. The cream soon hardened to a chalky glaze that further stiffened Sheridan's painful limbs. Still wearing his asbestos-caked khakis and with a skin pallor to match, Sheridan lurched down *Bennett*'s gangway looking as though he'd just stepped out of a mummy's casket. When Russ Bramble's clothes caught fire on *Howorth*'s bridge, he dove over the side. By the time Bramble was pulled from the water, he was suffering from exposure as well as burns and had to be transferred by stretcher.

Although Sheridan's and Bramble's burns required weeks to heal, theirs were relatively mild cases. In addition to second- and third-degree burns across his hands, face, and legs, Bob Lyons, another *Howorth* casualty, was temporarily blinded. Worse yet was *Newcomb*'s John Bennard with second- and third-degree burns across two thirds of his body. Bennard was carried off *Newcomb* completely swathed in bandages—medical gauze augmented by strips of bed linen—and his head covered by a pillowcase with cutouts for eyes and mouth.

Even for injured sailors certain to recover, the wounds and burns represented inescapable brushes with mortality—the first for most. In that one regard, the impact was just as real for uninjured sailors. Many of these men, after all, had helped—maybe even saved—the wounded and looked after the remains of the dead.

For men who escaped alive and intact, there were also jarring lessons in how circumstance (or fate) took some lives but not others. They were reminded, for example, that deaths came in clusters, and medical personnel, black gangs, and damage control parties were as likely victims as gunners or bridge personnel. The suicide hit to *Zellars* demolished its wardroom, killing *Zellars*' doctor, a pharmacist's mate, and many damage control personnel stationed there. *Hyman*'s dead included most of a damage control party wiped out by a secondary explosion of the ship's torpedoes. Destroyer *Mullany* lost every sailor in its after damage control party except one. The survivor was its officer John Wiessler, who'd been delayed on the bridge when GQ sounded. Wiessler, it might be said, had arrived too late for his own death.

The flood of casualties and crippled ships was a telling reminder of Kelly Turner's foresight in securing Kerama Retto. Without Wiseman's sheltered roadstead, its repair facilities and the moorages for battle casualty ships, matters would only be more staggering: both in lost lives and lost ships.

When possible, damaged ships anchored in the roadstead, waiting for availability along tenders, LSTs, and other repair vessels. Although limited and overburdened, there were even floating dry docks to accommodate ships with hull or steering damage. The work ranged from minor to mind-boggling, but the patch ups began as soon as possible, with priority for ships that either could be put back on the lines or made seaworthy enough for the voyage to the States. Destroyers *Sterett, Howorth, Cassin Young*, and *Purdy* fit these categories while others, like *Leutze, Lindsey* and *Newcomb,* had to wait weeks and sometimes months for repair work.

Life aboard Bone Yard ships was never pleasant and held its own dangers. The atmosphere was spooky—all the sights, sounds, and smells of carnage framed by Kerama Retto's spectral backdrop. For crews on ships not going anywhere soon, there were unpleasant work parties: sometimes to cannibalize their ships for parts and equipment needed by others, other times to help clear the debris from the decks of new arrivals. Medical personnel, of course, were kept busy all across the roadstead.

Japanese planes, mindful of Kerama Retto and busily tallying its wrecks, circled, scouted, probed, and occasionally attacked. As a precaution, special watches were set to guard against enemy swimmers and suicide boats. The gun-toting guards tended to be jumpy and trigger happy, especially at night. And when one fired, others usually joined in.

Worries about such attacks, while often overblown, were not totally unfounded. One night, two Japanese swimmers climbed a cargo net onto the hulk of *LST-884,* shot a deck sentry and escaped. Another time a lone swimmer climbed onto a damaged destroyer through the gaping hole in its bow. Nevertheless, by any measure, the risks were greater outside Kerama Retto than in.

As Fast as You Can

On Friday, 13 April, destroyer *Laffey* sailed into Wiseman's Cove after being detached from the bombardment screen and slated for picket line duty on RP1. *Laffey* tied up alongside destroyer *Cassin Young,* then just beginning repairs, to transfer *Cassin Young*'s FIDO team.

Under different circumstances, *Laffey*'s skipper Julian Becton might have paid a courtesy call on J. W. Ailes, his counterpart on *Cassin Young.* Both were Annapolis graduates—Ailes a year ahead of Becton. However, because of the quick turnaround (barely an hour) and the constant air threat, each skipper stuck close to his ship. The main job was getting the FIDO team and its gear aboard and setting out for RP1.

Purdy was also nested nearby, and a few *Laffey* sailors got the scoop on RP1 from a *Purdy* gun captain. "You guys have a fighting chance," he told them. "But they'll keep on coming till they get you. You'll knock a lot of them down, and you'll think you're doing fine. But in the end there'll be this one bastard with your name on his ticket."

Refueled, rearmed, and loaded down with mail—the first received in seven weeks—*Laffey* prepared to shove off. As Becton backed his ship, Ailes came up on *Cassin Young*'s bridge and called over: "Go as fast as you can, shoot as fast as you can."

"Will do," Becton called back.

The Okinawa RP line had generally remained quiet after 12 April. Destroyer *Pringle,* which took over RP14 following the sinking of *Mannert L. Abele,* spent its first days on station without engaging a single bogey.

Life aboard the Task Force 58 pickets had been just as quiet, but that changed abruptly on 14 April when an afternoon raid struck Task Group 58.1. Destroyer *Hunt* (DD-674) lost her mainmast to a *kamikaze* before it splashed alongside. A crash to *Sigsbee*'s fantail did worse, severing a propeller shaft and leaving *Sigsbee*'s main decks awash. Explosion and fires killed or wounded nearly 100 sailors. Without steering and propulsion, Gordon P. Chung-Hoon's ship had to be towed all the way to Guam. Once again, a sign that more trouble was in store for the Okinawa ships: *Kikusui* No. 3 had begun.

* * *

When *Laffey* reached RP1 on the 14th, she was joined by two midgets, *LCS-51* and *LCS-116*, both transfers from adjacent stations. Turning over RP1 to Becton and *Laffey,* the skipper of *J. William Ditter* (DM-31) reported an uneventful stay—few snoopers and no raids. Although bogeys did show on *Laffey*'s radar Saturday night, conditions continued unremarkable until Sunday night, when the sky all at once seemed to fill with snoopers. It put everyone on edge. When GQ finally secured at 0300, and bridge quartermaster Aristides (Ari) Phoutrides, 19, crawled exhausted into his rack, he and most of the crew were convinced *Laffey* was in for it when the sun came up.

Dawn Monday arrived bogey free both on the picket line and outside Nago Wan where, at 0800, GIs would be assaulting Ie Shima, the volcanic island slab just west of Motobu Peninsula. Gunners on *Bowers* (DE-636), the ping line ship patrolling closest to Ie Shima, had shot down a lone intruder at 0550, but then secured GQ at 0700.

Laffey, meanwhile, had also secured from her dawn GQ, and the breakfast chow line was backed up all the way to the main deck when, at 0744, *Laffy*'s radar operators picked up a single bogey, what turned out to be a Val snooper off the port bow. *Laffy*'s crew returned to GQ and forward 5-inch guns opened fire, but the Val retreated. As a precaution, *Laffey*'s crew stayed at battle stations, and sure enough at 0829 CIC officer Lloyd Hull's radar operators detected a swarm of bogeys to the north—this time perhaps as many as fifty. Lookouts soon were calling out reports of Val, Judys, Kates, and Oscars, all gathering and circling in the skies over *Laffey.*

First to peel off from the swarm were four Vals—two on the starboard bow, two angling for the stern. CO Becton ordered hard left rudder to stay broadside. Paul Smith, *Laffy*'s gun boss, controlling the three 5-inch twin mounts from the basket, promptly splashed the two bow Vals. Flying at wave-top level, one of the stern Vals caught a landing gear, stumbled, and nosed into the water. Converging gunfire from the 20s and 40s on *Laffey* and nearby *LCS-51* destroyed the other.

The next targets were two Judys, the first flying in low and straight on the starboard beam—a sitting-duck target for *Laffey*'s starboard 40s. To engage the second plane, Becton again swung *Laffey* sharply, this time to starboard. The forward guns traversed, locked on the Judy and knocked it down, but not before its bomb dropped, exploded close aboard, and threw shrapnel across *Laffey*'s weather decks. Bob Robertson, 19, a port side 20-mm gunner caught pieces all along his right side. The wounds would cost Robertson his right eye, but gun captain Fred Burgess saved Robertson's life with a timely shove to the deck. (Burgess's instinctive bravery cost him a leg and, a few days later, his life.)

Then two more flankers (the seventh and eighth *kamikazes):* a Val to port and a Judy to starboard. *Laffey* gunners splashed these two as well, though the Val, closing in dead astern, clipped the after deckhouse, drenched it with gasoline, and touched off fires topside and in No. 3 handling room before finally hitting the water.

These first fires were out quickly, and No. 3 mount was switched from director to local control. It was 0842. Phoutrides had counted eight planes and eight kills. Going fast and shooting fast, everyone aboard *Laffey*—and especially the gunners—had held their own. But Phoutrides, checking his watch and keeping the bridge log, also realized *Laffey* had been under siege just twelve minutes.

Names on the Tickets

Laffey's ninth *kamikaze,* a Val on the port side, was the first to actually crash the ship, demolishing a 20-mm gun tub atop the after deckhouse and killing 3 men. The deckhouse again burst into flames, this time more fierce and throwing off plumes of black smoke so thick they obscured the approach of a Val dead astern. This Val crashed the main deck starboard side, spilling fire and damage belowdecks as well as topside and chasing several men over the side trailing flames.

Firing in local control and using proximity fuses, the gunners in No. 3 mount had already splashed a *kamikaze* when, at 0847, mount captain Lawrence "Ski" Delewski spotted a Val off the starboard quarter. The plane was so low and already so close only the gunners on the fantail 20s had a shot. They opened fire, and their rounds broke off pieces of fuselage and wing. But the Val's momentum easily carried it into the fantail where it skidded past the 20s before bulldozing Delewski's mount. Six men inside were killed as the Val's engine wedged in the gunhouse. The impact also slewed the gunhouse to starboard, wrenched the port gun skyward, and peeled back the gunhouse top deck. Delewski, who'd been leaning out the gunhouse port hatch, flew clear, landing on the port side main deck fifteen feet forward of the remains of No. 3 mount.

All this time, *LCS-51*'s skipper Howell Chickering had somehow managed to stay within range of *Laffey*'s port quarter while his gunners, including Virgil Branch, a loader on the after 40s, had split their efforts between helping *Laffey* and avoiding being hit themselves. After teaming to splash one of the first set of Vals twenty minutes earlier, *LCS-51*'s gunners shot down a Val on their own at 0850.

During one close call, a handful of *LCS-51*'s sailors had jumped over the side. At first, Chickering slowed, thinking to pick them up. "If you stop," warned one of his chief petty officers, "I'm jumping off too!" Chickering heeded the warning and resumed full speed.

LCS-116, meanwhile, with neither *Laffey* nor *LCS-51* in sight, had its own hands full of *kamikazes*. Ray Davis, pointer on *LCS-116*'s forward 40-mm, got his sights on one aircraft when a Corsair suddenly swooped in and splashed it. Cheers went up across *LCS-116*'s decks. With C.A.P. swarming to the scene, *LCS-116* seemed to be out of the woods.

Off to the west of *116*, embattled *Laffey*'s stern was now engulfed in flames. At flank speed the fires raged even more, so Becton was forced into trade-offs between defense and damage control: go fast at the height of an attack and ease up between. Becton could still maneuver and soon did—a hard swing to port—to throw off the aim of a dive-bombing Val on the starboard quarter. But the turn came too late: the explosion of the Val's 550-pound bomb jammed both rudders to port, locking *Laffey* into a predictable twenty-six-degree port turn.

The combination of uncontrolled fires and crippled steering put *Laffey* on the ropes. Her FIDO team had pleaded with DELEGATE to vector C.A.P., and now some finally arrived: four FM2 Wildcats dispatched from *Shamrock Bay* (CVE-84). The Wildcats helped—downing six of *Laffey*'s tormentors before running out of ammunition and then fuel. But even as they disrupted attacks, two more planes and one more bomb struck *Laffey*. With bridge communications out, Becton sent Phoutrides aft to survey the damage. When Phoutrides saw the extent of the fires and human carnage, it stunned him: "My God, will this ever end?" was Phoutrides' desperate thought as he went back to the bridge. And as he returned to *Shamrock Bay*, Carl Rieman, leader of the Wildcat formation, was convinced *Laffey* was a goner.

LCS-116's respite from the *kamikazes* was shattered by a crash to its after 40-mm gun tub. The crash and explosions of the plane's bomb demolished the gun and its splinter shield, killing 3 of its crew. Others were wounded, and ready ammunition tumbled forward, exploding over the heads of Davis and the rest of the forward 40 gun crew.

Just then a second aircraft zoomed in; its approach angle was outside the stops of the forward 40. Davis saw a sailor at a rail-mounted .50-caliber machine gun open fire and stitch a line of tracer rounds straight into the plane's cockpit. Davis could see the pilot's torso slump as the plane's nose abruptly jumped up. The plane and its dead pilot cleared *LCS-116*, rolled, sliced into the water, and exploded.

It was now 0910 and *Laffey*, *LCS-51*, and *LCS-116* were not the only ships being hard pressed. To the west on RP14, *Pringle* and *Hobson* (DD-464/DMS-26) were also under siege. After *Pringle* scored a direct hit on a Zeke, three low-flying Vals edged into view off *Pringle*'s starboard bow. *Pringle* opened fire at ten thousand yards and brought down one Val when its wing clipped a shell splash. The two others stayed low, weaving in and out of range, apparently content to draw fire.

But then, during a check fire, one finally turned toward *Pringle*. Skipper George DeMetropolis swung the ship to starboard and rang up flank speed as the main batteries opened fire. The Val continued to turn and twist, while smoke from the forward guns obscured DeMetropolis' view from the bridge.

The smoke also obscured Milton Mapou's view from the flying bridge. Mapou, the sailor who began the war aboard cruiser *Detroit* at Pearl Harbor, was at the director controlling the starboard 40-mm. He was still trying to pick up the incoming Val when it finally emerged from the smoke and crashed at the base of *Pringle*'s forward stack.

The impact and the huge explosion that followed snapped *Pringle*'s keel. Thrown to the deck by the concussion, Mapou suffered a compound fracture to his leg. Someone inflated Mapou's lifebelt and helped him get into the water, but a not a minute too soon. After breaking in half, *Pringle* sank within five minutes of being hit, taking 65 of the crew down with her.

Compounding problems with casualties, raging fires, crippled steering, and loss of communication, *Laffey* had also lost power to her main batteries, reducing her AA defense to just four 20-mm guns. Conditions were so desperate that when CO Becton vowed he'd not abandon ship as long as one gun fired, at least one man on the bridge wondered aloud whether they might run out of gunners first.

Then, with thirty *kamikazes* still poised for a turn at *Laffey*, a dozen Corsairs, part of the same C.A.P. that came to the aid of *LCS-116*, finally reached the destroyer's position. The Corsairs screamed in, most of their pilots flying dangerously low through *Laffey*'s remaining AA fire to pick off targets. Trying to deflect an attack by an Oscar, one Corsair even sheared off one of *Laffey*'s radar antennas and absorbed such damage its pilot was forced to bail out. Still, the remaining Corsairs were making quick work of the Japanese, and damage control personnel at last got a chance to gain ground on the fires.

Laffey's sailors could now breathe a little easier. With power long gone to the main batteries, Glenn Radder, the gunner's mate in the forward magazine, was finally told to secure his space. After sending his crew topside, Radder followed, shutting watertight hatches on his way to the main deck. On the bridge, Phoutrides began to believe he'd be coming out of this alive.

Though RP14 was itself in need of help, ships from other stations were converging on RP1 to assist *Laffey*—or at least trying to. At 0934, destroyer *Bryant* was on the way from RP2 when she faced attacks by six *kamikazes*. With *Bryant* maneuvering at flank speed, gunners splashed several planes, but then a *kamikaze* crashed the base of her superstructure, demolishing CIC, communications, and I.C. rooms. *Bryant* took heavy casualties, including 34 killed and 30 more wounded—among them *Bryant*'s operations officer Al Gallin, who was on the bridge.

Gallin's injuries were so severe he was twice left for dead: first when the bridge was abandoned right after the crash and then after being hauled from the bridge, when he was triaged to the forecastle with the other terminal cases during *Bryant*'s retreat to the Bone Yard.

Meanwhile, at 0940, south of Ie Shima, one of two Vals targeting *Bowers* had just been splashed by her gunners, and a second Val was approaching to port, strafing *Bowers'* boat deck as it closed. All *Bowers'* gunners (including her CO Charles F. Highfield, armed with a Thompson submachine gun) concentrated fire on the Val, but despite taking repeated hits, the pilot just kept coming, his own guns still blazing. Before being wounded himself, Tony Natale, 20, loader on a port side 20-mm, saw his gunner John McCardle catch a bullet to the skull and slump lifeless in his harness.

Then, at the last instant, the Val, instead of crashing, angled up over *Bowers'* boat deck, crossed to starboard, banked, and raced forward of *Bowers'* bow. A mile out and still off the bow, it banked again, this time left, and pointed in for another approach. Highfield ordered a hard port turn to get the Val on the beam, but the pilot used speed and his own maneuvering skill to stay on the bow. His machine guns were still firing as his aircraft crashed just below *Bowers'* flying bridge. The Val's undercarriage bomb pierced both pilothouse bulkheads before landing and exploding just forward of the boat deck. Shrapnel killed most boat deck personnel, including a gunner standing near Tony Natale. Natale, meanwhile, lay unconscious, with shrapnel peppered into his feet, legs, neck and face.

When he finally reached *Laffey*'s main deck on the port side, Glenn Radder could see Corsairs still battling Japanese planes. As Radder moved toward the forecastle to get a closer look, he saw a Val diving in unopposed on the starboard bow. Ed Samp, 26, the AGO in charge of *Laffey*'s forward 20s, also stepped forward, balancing his weight on a floater net basket suspended from the starboard bulwark as he barked directions to his gunners.

It was nearing 0947. In an after action diagram, this particular Val would be labeled number 21: the next to last of twenty-two aircraft to dive at *Laffey* during an unbroken and unprecedented eighty minutes—

and the last to inflict damage. Number 21 was not a suicide plane, not one of the six wrecks that still littered and fueled fires on *Laffey*'s decks. Number 21 instead made a conventional bomb run, dropping a 550-pound bomb that became the last of four such bombs to explode on *Laffey*. Radder saw number 21's bomb land at the feet of a starboard 20-mm gun crew. The explosion wiped out the gun and its crew. It also tore through the starboard bulwark and the floater net basket on which Samp was standing.

D-Day for Ernie

After being hit, *Bowers* still sped across the bows and wakes of other ships entering and leaving Nago Wan. His clothes on fire, *Bowers*' skipper Highfield had jumped over the side, and the XO, his legs torn up by shrapnel, had fled the fire-ravaged bridge and collapsed unconscious on the boat deck. With nearly all bridge, communications and CIC personnel either dead or wounded, *Bowers* lacked sight, hearing, voice, and command.

In the first minutes after the crash, belowdecks crewmen like throttleman Bob Graves and water tender Frank Martinez were still trying to keep *Bowers* at full speed. Until Truman Hinkle, *Bowers*' damage control officer, at last stepped in to take command, it appeared other ships might have to resort to gunfire to stop the runaway DE. Finally, at 1010, ping line DE *Swearer* (DE-186), was able to approach *Bowers*, remove nearly 60 wounded sailors and assist with damage control. At noon, *Swearer* was bound for the transport anchorage off Hagushi.

At 1035, crews on *LCS-34* and *LCS-121* reached the edge of the debris field and spotted the first of the rafts, floater nets, and swimmers that were the last remnants of *Pringle*'s presence on RP14. On the way to the scene, *LCS-34* had squared off with three Vals, in the process exhausting their ready supplies of 20- and 40-mm ammunition. During the worst of the fighting, when his gun crews were struggling through knee-deep drifts of expended shell casings, *LCS-34*'s XO Ed Hathaway called extra men topside to help clear away the piles and keep the guns in action.

At 1045, the LCSs pulled in the first *Pringle* survivors. Eighty-seven sailors, including Mapou, were rescued by *LCS-34*, another twenty-eight by *121*.

At 1100, *LCS-51* pulled alongside *Laffey*'s starboard quarter to help douse fires in the after magazine and crew spaces. Virgil Branch was awestruck by the deckhouse and fantail damage. *Laffey* was down by the stern, and crewmen were busy jettisoning everything they could from the fantail, including depth charges. One depth charge that wasn't disarmed exploded, momentarily lifting both ships' sterns.

LCS-51 guns had splashed six Japanese aircraft during the morning action. The fifth plane, a Val, exploded within feet of *LCS-51*'s port beam, impaling the plane's engine into the hull plates inches above the waterline.

Once the fires on *Laffey* were out, intake hoses from *LCS-51*'s salvage pump were passed over to the fantail and wormed down into the after crew compartment. On his way aft on the port side, Radder passed the ruins of the boat deck. In the debris of the crew's after head, Radder saw an aircraft engine and, atop it, what looked to be the incinerated corpse of its pilot.

At the fantail Radder saw the three demolished 20-mm guns (they were the guns Radder was responsible for maintaining) and briefly peered into the burned-out carcass of the No. 3 mount. Then Radder and other sailors took turns working in the flooded after crew compartment, searching for bodies (*Laffey*'s survival had cost 103 casualties, including 31 dead) and periodically freeing up the intake hose when it clogged with crew clothing.

Bowers spent the night of 16 April tied up alongside *Biscayne* (AGC-18). After breakfast on *Biscayne*, Truman Hinkle mustered the remaining crewmen and, after offering each sailor a swig of "medicinal" whiskey, had them begin locating and tagging the bodies of what would eventually total 48 *Bowers* fatalities.

It was such agonizing work that it left electrician Henry Seeba convinced it would have been better to switch places with the crew of another wrecked ship. Let them handle *Bowers'* dead while *Bowers'* survivors handled theirs. One body Seeba identified belonged to a sailor who bunked near him. Seeba remembered the man most for the Aqua Velva he always wore. The dead sailor was in two parts: his legs and hips still sat in the trainer's seat of the ruined No. 2 mount's 3-inch gun, his torso lay facedown on the deck. Picking through the ruins on the bridge, *Bowers'* water tender Frank Martinez found the body of the ship's first class radioman. He was cooked, but Martinez was able to remove a ring from one finger and tag it with the dead man's name.

On 18 April, as crewmen on *Laffey*, *Pringle*, *Bowers*, and the other ships mourned their dead shipmates, Iceberg's soldiers and sailors alike were stunned by news of another fatality. Accompanying GIs for the assault on Ie Shima, Ernie Pyle was killed by Japanese gunfire. For many, the news was at least as earth shattering as Roosevelt's death a week before; without a doubt, it was also a loss more personal and relevant to their own lives and fates. *Time* reporter Robert Sherrod had last seen Pyle in the berthing compartment they shared on *Panamint* (AGC-13). "I'm getting too old to stay in combat with these kids," Pyle had confided to Sherrod at the time. When Sherrod left Okinawa on 11 April, both he and Pyle believed that though there was stiff fighting ahead, the battle to capture Okinawa was well in hand.

No Haven on *Comfort*

When *Aaron Ward* arrived in Kerama Retto on 27 April to replenish ammunition, Iceberg's fleet had mostly been spared *kamikaze* damage and sinkings since the 16th. The only raid over coastal waters had come at dusk on 22 April when two small ping line ships (minesweeper *Swallow* and *LCS-15*) were sunk and destroyer *Isherwood* damaged. *Isherwood*—with heavy damage and casualties from the secondary explosions of her depth charges—was the only new admission to Wiseman's Cove since 16 April.

Aaron Ward tied up alongside *Mayfield Victory* (AK-232) in the afternoon of the 27th. Toward dusk on the 28th, as ammunition loading continued, several Navy patrol seaplanes (PBMs) approached for landings in the anchorage. Suddenly, alarms whooped. A Japanese plane, tailing the PBMs to escape radar detection, was on the loose and headed for *Mayfield Victory*. Ships in the roadstead held fire momentarily, but (much like the guards they posted for suicide swimmers) when one finally opened up, others joined in. Kerama Strait lit up with tracers and echoed with the booms of ships' cannons.

Aaron Ward's CO W. H. Sanders screamed at his deck gang to cut mooring lines and ordered all ahead full. Ward's engineers wasted no time pouring on steam, and *Ward* began to move even as a cry came from *Mayfield Victory* that her CO had been hit. Like barroom gunfighters, other ships were firing as they made for the exits. The lone *kamikaze* aircraft that was the cause for all the mayhem, by now had been hit and was trailing smoke. At the last moment, the pilot seemed to give up on reaching *Mayfield Victory*, instead smashing into *Pinkney* (APH-2), a battle casualty ship.

There was a flat WOOMPH of an explosion as *Pinkney*'s superstructure erupted in flames that raged for hours. There were ruptures to water lines, electrical conduits, and steam pipes, plus explosions of ready ammunition stores. When it was over, *Pinkney* was left smoldering and listing heavily to port. Sixteen *Pinkney* patients who perished in the initial blast were joined by 18 crew fatalities.

There were more bad days ahead for wounded evacuees. *Pinkney*, although it carried wounded, was not classed as a noncombatant as was hospital ship *Comfort* (AH-6). *Comfort*, with its distinctive white paint scheme set off by prominent red crosses, left Okinawa on 28 April. *Comfort* was bound for Saipan, and as usual for such voyages, its wards and surgical suites were filled with Okinawa wounded, including a number of *Isherwood*'s casualties.

At 2241, fifty miles southeast of Okinawa, fully lit and in company with other ships (among them destroyer *Purdy*), *Comfort* was struck by a single *kamikaze*, a crash to the superstructure that killed 30, including 6 Army nurses. Elvan Hall, a wounded electrician's mate from *Isherwood*, was assigned to a ward near the point of impact but escaped the crash. Moments before the plane hit, Hall had been helped into a wheelchair by another ward patient and gone aft to visit a wounded buddy.

* * *

When the threat to *Mayfield Victory* ended on the 27th, *Aaron Ward* was one of the ships that evacuated *Pinkney*'s wounded. As *Aaron Ward* readied to leave Kerama Retto on 29 April, the wounded still aboard were transferred, this time to minesweeper *Terror* (CM-5). At 0400 on 1 May, while still at anchor in Kerama Retto, *Terror* was crashed by a predawn *kamikaze*, leaving 48 dead and 123 wounded, including some of those offloaded by *Aaron Ward*.

★ Chapter 24 ★

The Same Tooth, May 1945

RADAR PICKET LINE

WHY STOP HERE?

MAIN BODY TASK FORCE 38

→

25 MILES SOUTH

Wording on a placard displayed on the superstructure of a Task Force 38 picket line destroyer.

Elephants Fall

On Saturday, 5 May, five children from the Christian and Missionary Alliance Church in Bly, Oregon, went on a fishing trip to nearby Gearhart Mountain accompanied by Reverend Archie Mitchell and his pregnant wife Elsie. After picking out a shaded spot for lunch about sixteen miles into the mountains, Reverend Mitchell drove the car around by a road, while Elsie Mitchell and the children hiked through the woods.

"As I got out of my car to bring the lunch," Reverend Mitchell explained to reporters (though not until June, when War Department officials finally cleared the story), "the others were not far away and called to me they had found something that looked like a balloon. I had heard of Japanese balloons, so I shouted a warning not to touch it. But just then there was a big explosion. I ran up there—and they were all dead."

When two forest service employees who heard the explosion reached Mitchell, he was dazed from the blast and the shock of seeing the dead. The foresters covered the six bodies (Elsie Mitchell plus the children, all aged 11 to 13, including a brother and sister) and took Mitchell to Bly. The foresters told police it appeared that before the explosion the victims had clustered around the balloon and, out of curiosity, someone tugged it. The blast plowed up the ground and virtually destroyed the balloon.

It turned out the Central Oregon tragedy was hardly the first incident involving the mysterious (and now deadly) balloons. There had been sightings since the previous December all across the Pacific Northwest and Central Plains.

A Wyoming sheriff received perhaps the first confirmed reports: four explosions and what was believed to be a parachute dropping from the sky. Several days after the Wyoming sightings, Montana woodsmen discovered an actual balloon. In January, when a news item on the Montana discovery appeared in *Newsweek* and *Time*, the U.S. Office of Censorship asked journalists not to report further on balloon bomb incidents.

Balloon bomb activity finally peaked in March, when officials recovered 74 balloons and received reports of 89 other sightings. By then, having found radio transmitters on a few downed balloons, authorities managed to intercept transmissions from several others still aloft. The signals were enough to confirm the balloons were actually coming from the direction of Japan and from a great distance, ending speculation they were either released by offshore submarines, by Japanese frogmen, or even German POW camps inside the United States.

Two weeks after the Oregon deaths, the government finally issued a statement warning of the danger of tampering with the big balloons, but officials continued to puzzle over their purpose. Were their bombs meant to kill people? Were they being used for germ warfare or something even more diabolical? Of one thing they were reasonably certain: if Japan's intent was to start forest fires, the balloons were doomed to fail. They were only able to cross the Pacific because of the jet stream—and the jet stream was only strong enough to carry them that distance when it also brought heavy rains.*

*Fragments of 285 balloons have since been found all over North America; the majority turned up in Washington and Oregon, but some made it as far south as Mexico, as far north as Alaska, and as far east as Michigan.

Calling All Destroyers

Meanwhile on the frontlines in the Pacific, there was equal bewilderment and speculation about Iceberg's steep April picket line toll. Why did Japanese suicide pilots swarm around destroyers instead of larger, higher value targets? Was it just because the picket targets were closer and more convenient? Had Japan's top brass decided to wipe out pickets first (along with the early warnings they provided) and then go after bigger fish? Or were the suiciders just inexperienced and over-eager to die?

During one early May exchange overheard by Samuel Morison, Fleet Admiral Chester Nimitz asked Rear Admiral Forrest Sherman, one of his staff planners, whether the Japanese might eventually abandon picket line attacks and concentrate on more strategic targets—the fast carriers and the supply ships off Okinawa.

Sherman pondered a moment then replied: "You could get a man down quicker by hitting him on the same tooth than by punching him all over."

"Anyway," the still perplexed Nimitz concluded, "we can produce new destroyers faster than they can build planes."

If, as this exchange by top brass suggested, the long-term outcome boiled down to such harsh, straightforward math, it offered no comfort to picket line sailors. Tin can production was a meaningless solution for any one ship's survival—or any one sailor's. Sailors and ships lived and died in the short term and had to rely on applying practical lessons.

A mimeographed pamphlet with the hand-lettered cover title *Calling All Destroyers* compressed fundamental lessons in terms that spoke to the average sailor. *Calling All Destroyers'* origins were snippets and cartoons from the ship's newspaper for destroyer *Wadsworth* (DD-516), which joined the picket line in mid-April and survived a twelve-plane standoff at month's end. The illustrated material (complete with a cartoon dog—*Wadsworth*'s mongrel mascot Willie) circulated unofficially before getting the imprimatur of Pacific Fleet Cruiser and Destroyer Command.

" 'So long Frisco' must be the saddest words in the book these days," the pamphlet began, "when the bucktoothed Banzai boys are waiting out here to mess up that new paint job. But remember this . . . the Japs have sent out hundreds of these guys with their one-way ticket, but only a relative few have gotten hits. What's happened to the rest? Well . . . the same old ground rules still apply—perhaps more than ever before." The "ground rules" (tidbits of information, encouragement, and caution culled from *Wadsworth* sailors' three years of shooting down Japanese aircraft) were addressed to men stationed at different posts.

To lookouts, for example: "Watch the clouds . . . watch the low haze over the water . . . watch the 20 degrees either side of the sun. Radar doesn't always pick them up, so if a plane suddenly pops in on you, be able to tell in a split second whether it's a Zeke or an F6F."

To the fighter director teams: "Let the C.A.P. take care of them. It's easier on the nerves, and the planes are built for it. . . . Get out the bearing, course, speed, and angels [altitude] in a hurry."

But foremost to the gunners: "The more shrapnel you give him to come through, the less chance he has of making it. Fire early and save your ship. . . . Keep shooting until his prop brushes your whiskers. In the last thousand yards, he still has a lot of smart flying to do to hit you. Work on the pilot. Aim for the cockpit with the 20s and 40s. . . . A dead Jap can't fly a plane, and instead of making those last-minute corrections on his stick, he'll flop in the drink out of control."

Japan launched four more *Kikusui* (Nos. 5–8) during May. Month's end postmortems would reveal downward trends in attack volume and frequency, if not ferocity and, as with April, a mid-month lull. Still, there were plenty of opportunities to apply *Calling All Destroyers'* key pointers.

May Day, May Day

RP flotillas had expanded since April, as more LCSs and LSMs became available. RP 10s contingent on 4 May included destroyers *Aaron Ward* and *Little*, plus three LCSs and one LSM. Minutes after an 1822 call to GQ, *Aaron Ward* gunners splashed two attackers: the first close aboard to starboard, the second farther to port. But a third attacker, a Zeke, dropped a bomb near *Ward*'s stern, cutting off steering and power to No. 3 mount.

By then, action was spreading all across RP10. Within sight of *Aaron Ward, Little*'s crew waged a separate, hopeless battle with nearly two dozen planes. Gunners shot down two, but the suicide crash of a third to *Little*'s port side at 1843 was quickly followed by two more to the hull and a final crash—the terminus of a near vertical dive—to *Little*'s torpedo mount. Seven minutes later, *Little*'s keel snapped and water covered her decks. Crewmen like Franklin Wahl, 21, a gun captain on the starboard 40-mm mount just forward of the bridge, could do little but wait for *Little* to settle and the water to rise to the level of his post so that he could step away from the ship. *Little* sank at 1855.

Meanwhile, after escaping a close call—a *kamikaze* aiming for the bridge instead snapped wires and antennas—*Aaron Ward* absorbed a chain of jarring collisions: to the hull, amidships' deckhouse, superstructure aft, and No. 2 stack. With steering already gone, fires raging, and ready ammunition stores exploding, *Ward* went all but dead in the water.

RP10 pallbearers rushed to help the big ships but fared little better. When one plane crashed *LSM-195*, the impact ignited onboard rockets, shut down pumps, and cut water pressure, leaving the crew little choice but to go over the side.

At 1920, scarcely twenty minutes after *Little*'s sinking, the remnants of *LSM-195* exploded and sank. Nearby, *LCS-83*'s gunners fired at both *LSM-195*'s attacker and at a second suicide plane that sliced off *LCS-25*'s mast. They then swung their guns to defend themselves, splashing a plane a few short feet from the bow. Two of the three LCSs, first *LCS-14* and then *LCS-83*, finally made it alongside *Aaron Ward* to remove wounded, fight fires, and pump flooded spaces. *LCS-25*, though damaged and with her own wounded, combed the night waters to locate survivors.

Two hours later, *Aaron Ward* was under tow and heading for Wiseman's Cove. By that time, battle damage and its casualties had spilled over to adjacent RP9—a *kamikaze* crash to minesweeper *Macomb* (DD-458/DMS-23)'s after mount. The hit blasted out the back of the gunhouse, hurling dead and wounded gun crewmen into the water and across the decks.

With *Macomb*'s 7 killed, the combined 3 May casualty toll for RPs 9 and 10 rose just shy of 250. But next morning things only got worse. On RP12, destroyer *Luce* (DD-522) lost radar and power to her guns from a *kamikaze* near miss and then quickly flooded and sank from the crash of a second. Beginning at 0715 on RP1, *Morrison* (DD-560) and *Ingraham* (DD-694) battled a seemingly unending procession of *kamikaze* and conventional raids. C.A.P. Corsairs were quickly on the scene to help, but *Ingraham* absorbed a *kamikaze* crash forward of the bridge while *Morrison* withstood close brushes by four *kamikazes* and a direct hit by a fifth.

Morrison might have survived, had it not been for what came next: a raid by seven twin-float biplanes coming in from the west. In a way, the ancient Japanese planes were ideal *kamikaze* weapons: Their slow speed often confounded radar- and computer-controlled gunfire and their wood-and-fabric construction made them virtually immune to proximity-fused projectiles. If need be, they could even land in the water close by and wait for the ideal time to strike. Indeed, this was exactly what a second float plane did after another crashed and ignited ammunition in one of *Morrison*'s handling rooms. Taxiing, lifting off, and crashing No. 4 gun, the antique finally sent *Morrison* and 159 of her crew to the bottom.

The 4 May casualties—over 1,000 dead and wounded along with two destroyers and two LSMs—included nearly 130 casualties from DM *Shea*. Ironically, *Shea*'s morning attacker was a *baka* whose pilot scored a bulls-eye to the bridge. The impact killed 27, but once again the *baka*'s warhead exploded only after zooming clear through the ship. *Shea*, though badly damaged, made it on her own back to Hagushi Roadstead.

"It's Hell up There, Marine"

As Nimitz pondered the *kamikazes*' mindset, Tenth Army Commander Simon Bolivar Buckner, Jr., pondered ways to unlock the stalemate chewing up GI ranks and stalemating the conquest of Okinawa. While sentiment soon grew among Navy and Marine leaders for an end-around landing to break the stalemate, Buckner's immediate counter was to shift more Marines into front lines in the south. He would continue to grind it out with his GI—and now Marine—pawns.

Already, since mid-April, the 1st Marine Division's artillery regiment had been in the south helping out. Then, after a score of tanks were lost in a failed 27th Division offensive at Kakazu Ridge, Buckner ordered in the 1st Marine Division's tank battalion as well. When III Amphibious Corps commander Major General Roy Geiger USMC took exception to this piecemeal approach, Buckner countered by ordering the entire 1st Marine Division to relieve the 27th.

So it was, at April's close, a handful of Marine 1st Division officers and NCOs visited the 27th's lines to inspect the position they would inherit: the far right of the American front lines just north of Machinato Airfield. The situation, Eugene Sledge, and his K/3/5 buddies were told, was not good.

K Company's Marines were issued ammo and rations, rolled up their shelter halves, and, in the chill of a dismal 1 May morning, climbed aboard trucks for the trip south. To get there they rode over the dusty roads of central Okinawa, now transformed into the rear lines of their own triumphant northern offensive. They passed artillery positions piled high with brass shell casings and, farther on, tidy rear echelon bivouacs adjacent to vast camouflage-netted supply depots.

When Sledge and his buddies disembarked from the trucks, they walked south in single file—each man separated by five paces from the next to avoid being hit by mortar or artillery rounds—on the right lane of a coral surfaced road. Already they could hear incoming enemy mortar and artillery fire in front of them and their own outgoing artillery rounds whistling overhead.

Soon another column of men approached them heading north— what turned out to be a regiment of the Army's much maligned 27th Division. To Sledge the GIs looked "dead beat, dirty and grisly, hollow-eyed and tight-faced."

As he passed Sledge, one GI said in a weary voice, "It's hell up there, Marine." Sledge, though filled with dread, wanted to let the GI know he was no boot. "Yeah, I know. I was at Peleliu." The GI gave Sledge a blank stare and just moved on.

Late in the evening on 7 May, a message sent by flashing light from the yardarm blinkers of *Mount McKinley* (AGC-7) went out to the ships anchored off Hagushi beaches. It began:

TO TASK FORCE 51: FROM COMMANDER, TASK FORCE 51. NEWS BULLETIN. COMMUNIQUÉ. RADIO NEWS. GERMANY HAS SURRENDERED UNCONDITION-ALLY TO WESTERN ALLIES AND RUSSIA.

It was great news, but in the same way Roosevelt's death less than a month before was horrible news.

"So what?" was the typical reaction of Okinawa's Marines who, after nearly a week in the south, were fighting knee-deep mud as well as the Japanese. K Company Marines were resigned to the fact that the Japanese would fight to total extinction on Okinawa—and eventually on their homeland. As far as Eugene Sledge was concerned, "Nazi Germany might as well have been on the moon."

Meanwhile, 1st Division Marines had run into a pocket of heavy Japanese resistance near Awacha and Dakeshi, two towns in the shadow of main ridges of Shuri farther south. The Marines dug in for a 9 May attack that achieved little but claimed heavy casualties in Sledge's K Company. K/3/5 was pulled into reserve while another regiment took its place in the line.

Even though they remained in reserve for much of the stalemate that developed at Shuri, K/3/5's casualties mounted. The Marines were under nearly constant artillery shelling and, consequently, took wounds from shell fragments and blast concussions. The rain was unrelenting and disease swept through flooded foxholes—immersion foot, malaria, and pneumonia. Sleep was impossible and Marines ate, Sledge remembered, only when instinctive hunger forced them to.

Face to Face

Kyushu's skies were overcast at dawn on 11 May but, despite the threat of rain, *Kikusui* No. 6 was officially under way. Day one's sorties were airborne a little after 0500; IJA and IJN aircraft were bound both for Okinawa and for U.S. carriers east of Kyushu. Many of Okinawa-bound aircraft were intercepted by American fighter-bombers well north of Okinawa, but, for once, the carrier-bound group had better luck getting through.

Carriers like *Bunker Hill* and *Enterprise* had managed to sidestep the best efforts of *Kikusui* No. 4 and No. 5. Indeed, since a mid-April hit to *Intrepid* (her third), all Task Force 58 carriers (though not all the picket destroyers) were untouched.* That was about to change as two carrier-bound *tokkō* eluded both American C.A.P. and the ring of radar detection surrounding Vice Admiral Marc Mitscher's flagship *Bunker Hill.*

VT-84 pilot Al Turnbull was in the squadron ready room that morning filling out a post-mission Intel form when a squabble broke out over who should taxi several Avengers that needed re-spotting on the flight deck. Tired of listening to the argument and anxious for some fresh air, Turnbull volunteered to help out, grabbed his flight helmet, and headed for the flight deck

The midmorning sky above *Bunker Hill* was filled with broken clouds when Turnbull reached the flight deck's starboard quarter and climbed into the cockpit of one of the Avengers. Turnbull shouted a greeting to a pilot friend nearby and was just starting to buckle in when, off to starboard, he heard the *rat-ta-tat* of a strafing plane. Turnbull looked up just in time to see a *kamikaze* Zeke drop a bomb, crash astern No. 3 elevator, and plow into a cluster of parked aircraft just re-armed and refueled for launch. After piercing the flight deck, the *kamikaze*'s bomb exploded at gallery level, hurling shrapnel into hangar bays and catwalks.

Within seconds, Turnbull spotted another plane, a Judy, falling in

---

*Haggard (DD-555) and *Halligan* (DD-531) were both badly hit on 29 April.

a vertical dive to a crash at the base of *Bunker Hill*'s superstructure. The *kamikaze*'s fuel ignited, sending back drafts of flame into narrow passageways and up superstructure access ladders. The Judy's bomb, released an instant before the crash, exploded—as had the Zeke's moments before—at the gallery level.

Bunker Hill's CO Gene A. Seitz* swung the ship in a hard turn, clearing some of the worst patches of burning fuel and debris. But beneath the flight deck, fire and smoke consumed *Bunker Hill* spaces from amidships all the way astern and down three levels. Some of the spaces hit hardest were Air Group 84's ready rooms, including the one Al Turnbull had just left.

Avenger pilot Frances "Guts" Guttenberger and his crewmen Tom Kelly and Ed Duffy had 11 May off after flying a strike the day before. Kelly, fighting a fever, had gone down for sick call when *Bunker Hill*'s sick bay started to fill with smoke. Wounded were already being carried in, but the space was in no condition to receive them. When Kelly asked how he could help, one of the pharmacist's mates just told him to hit the deck and cover up. Duffy, meanwhile, was on the hangar deck, already manning one of the fire hoses being used to wet down planes and keep them from exploding.

Bunker Hill's crew battled the hangar deck fires for hours. Cruiser *Wilkes Barre* (CL-103) and several destroyers closed to pour on water and remove crewmen trapped on *Bunker Hill*'s catwalks. Damage control personnel fought through smoke to reach trapped sailors like Kelly and lead them topside. Kelly, Duffy, and Guttenberger were all able to stay aboard *Bunker Hill* although hundreds jumped into the water or onto the decks of *Wilkes Barre* and other ships standing by to assist. Al Turnbull, cornered by fire and explosions on the starboard catwalk, jumped over the side, but not before first tossing over a survival pack and inflatable raft. Turnbull was rescued near sunset by destroyer *Cushing* (DD-729).

The worst of *Bunker Hill*'s fire and damage was contained by 1530, but at a staggering cost—396 dead and 264 wounded. The worst of

---

*No relation to Gene Seitz, VC-10 Wildcat pilot aboard *Gambier Bay*.

the aftermath for Kelly, Duffy, and other Air Group 84 personnel, however, came next day when they had to locate, tag, and remove squadron-mate bodies—many killed by smoke inhalation and piled high in gangways or jammed into ready room hatchways.

After the fires were extinguished, Robert Schock, a *Bunker Hill* salvage diver, volunteered to go down where the remnants of the Zeke (the first attacker) had finally settled. Schock found the wreckage still half submerged in water. Moving carefully to avoid live wires, Schock climbed to where he could see into the cockpit and found himself face-to-face with the dead Japanese pilot.

Searching inside the man's flight jacket, Schock removed some papers and other items and put them in his pockets. After he returned topside, he laid the items out on his bunk to dry. The papers included photographs and what appeared to be a letter. Schock had also retrieved a blood-soaked name tag from the dead pilot's flight jacket, the buckle from his parachute harness, and a smashed pocket watch imbedded in his chest. To avoid having them confiscated, Schock stashed the souvenirs in his locker.

Until His Prop Brushes Your Whiskers

The 11 May *kamikazes* bound for Okinawa reached the skies over RP15 as early as 0750. Five minutes later, radar operators on *Hugh W. Hadley* (DD-774), RP15's command ship, had plots on as many as 150 bogeys. After frantically acknowledging so many sightings, John Rooney, duty radioman on *LCS-82* (one of three RP15 LCSs), was almost grateful when GQ sounded and he had to go topside.

Hadley's FIDO sorted the bogeys into four raids and vectored a twelve-plane Corsair and Hellcat C.A.P. to intercept. By the time of C.A.P. tally-ho, RP15's two destroyers—*Robley D. Evans* (DD-552) in addition to *Hadley*—were already in the sights of dozens of *kamikazes*.

During the next one hundred minutes, both ships registered many kills—15 by *Evans* and 12 by *Hadley*—but also crippling crashes. Four separate hits to *Evans* exploded two boilers and flooded all engineering spaces, leaving her dead in the water. After a crash by a *baka* and two solid hits aft (one a *kamikaze* crash, the other a bomb), *Hadley*'s engineering spaces were also flooded, and exploding ammunition threatened to capsize her. Keeping a fifty-man skeleton crew aboard, *Hadley* CO Baron Mullaney ordered the rest of his sailors over the side.

As *LCS-83* and *LSM-193* pulled in men from *Hadley*, *LCS-82* and *LCS-84* went alongside. While some of *LCS-82*'s sailors rigged pumps to control flooding, others cut a hole in *Evans'* forecastle to free a dozen badly burned crewmen trapped below.

Including this dozen, *Evans'* casualties would total near 60, half of them fatalities. *Hadley* would tally 100 more. Both had survived the fleet's third worst day in a month that might yet outdo April.

During the course of the Okinawa invasion, Navy battleships, cruisers, and destroyers fired nearly a half-million rounds of 5-inch ammunition. Two thirds of these rounds were fired by ships on the picket lines, but the rest were aimed at Japanese shore targets, usually called in by GI and Marine spotters. Seaborne artillery was always active supplying night illumination to prevent Japanese infiltration and night counterattacks. It was particularly intense during mid-May as the 10th Army struggled to bust through stiff Japanese resistance along the defensive line at Shuri.

While some destroyers rotated between radar picket and call-fire assignments, destroyer *Longshaw* (DD-559), which had problems with faulty air-search radar, was assigned to call-fire full time. This condemned *Longshaw*'s crew to an operating routine rivaling the RPs for exhaustion, if not danger: a grind of call-fire and night illumination missions plus daytime screening duties. On 18 May, the effects of the grind finally caught up with them.

After firing night illumination missions on 17 May, *Longshaw* was dispatched to a daytime screening assignment just west of Naha. At 0700, close to station, *Longshaw*'s bow ran up hard on a reef, her port side exposed to the beach. *Longshaw* broached but was unmolested for several hours, as *Picking* (DD-685) and then fleet tug *Arikara* (ATF-98) tried to haul the bow clear.

Just when it looked like *Longshaw* might finally escape, a Japanese shore battery opened up, first with a ranging shot, but then with four salvos directly on target. As abandon ship was called, the fourth shore battery round ignited the forward magazine into a huge explosion, demolishing *Longshaw*'s bow all the way aft to the bridge.

Machinist's mate John Schneider, 18, had fled the forward fire room carrying a badly wounded sailor named Pete Okson and both were in the water on the port side when the magazine blew. Schneider, who was still grasping Okson's collar, suddenly went blind. Jim Macomber and Harry Leonard, both on a work detail shifting projectiles aft to lighten the bow, jumped from the fantail without life jackets and were picked up by a gig sent by cruiser *Salt Lake City* (CA-25). Schneider, still blind, was one of *Longshaw*'s 97 wounded. Pete Okson, the sailor Schneider tried to save, was among the 85 sailors killed. The unsalvageable remains of *Longshaw* were later destroyed by naval torpedoes and gunfire.

Well before dawn on 25 May, Thunder Gods Flight Petty Officer Keisuke Yamamura climbed aboard a mother plane for an *Ōka* mission. He had survived an aborted April mission that ended in a forced water landing. In the weeks since, his squadron mates noted that Yamamura had lost much of his fire. He was no longer "Earnest"—perhaps not even "Eager."

The Thunder Gods mission was part of *Kikusui* No. 7, which numbered 165 *Tokkotai* aircraft and was timed to support 32nd Army's withdrawal from Shuri. After takeoff, the weather quickly worsened until torrential rains forced nine Bettys—including the one carrying Yamamura to return to base. Three others disappeared without a trace.

Early that same morning, Destroyer escort *O'Neill* (DE-188) was anchored south of Hagushi beaches aligned so its sonar could detect any skunks or submersibles that might try to sneak north from Naha. *O'Neill* had been pulled from the ping line for a few days of rest, a reflection of the much-reduced *kamikaze* activity after 11 May.

During this interval of nearly two weeks—aside from the shore battery destruction of *Longshaw*—there'd been only two suicide crashes. The more serious was to destroyer *Bache*, hit at sunset, 13 May by one of three low flyers.* The crash and bomb explosion killed 41 sailors, including 5 of the Indiana boys who often gathered on *Bache*'s fantail. A sixth, 40-mm gunner John Vaught, survived but was one of 32 wounded.

By now, after experiencing six organized and concerted onslaughts since April, ships' crews were wary of the lulls—each seemed to up the level of anxiety. *O'Neill*'s chief engineer Jim Creighton, 26, prepared for deck watch that night by outfitting himself with every piece of fireproof apparel (face mask, goggles, gauntlets, and leggings) he could find.

At 0025, a lone *kamikaze,* masking its presence by approaching over the rocky outcropping of Point Bolo, crossed *O'Neill*'s stern and crashed at deck level forward of the bridge. Topside personnel, including Creighton, were doused with gasoline, but even after an explosion above the main deck, there were no fires. Despite the death of two gunners, *O'Neill*'s crew had been lucky.

The hit to *O'Neill* was the opening round in four days of attacks broken by a one-day lull. Later that morning there were crashes to *Stormes* (DD-780) on RP15 and to minesweeper *Spectacle* (AM-305) and the sinking of fast transport *Bates* (DE-68/APD-47), in each case with heavy casualties.

That same night, American ships patrolling near Point Bolo witnessed antiaircraft fire, explosions, and enormous fires near Yontan Field. The Japanese had tried to belly-land five Sally bombers. Four were shot down, but one landed successfully and disembarked a cargo of ten airborne attack commandos. Before being killed, the grenade-wielding suicide team destroyed several planes and an aviation gasoline storage tank.

Attacks resumed the next day under an early morning overcast, this time targeting RP5 pickets east of Okinawa. Destroyer *Braine* (DD-630), on station with *Anthony* (DD-515), took crippling suicide crashes at No. 2 mount and No. 2 stack. Fires erupted on *Braine*, ready supplies of ammunition exploded, and the ship briefly lost steering command and communications. RP15's four LCSs, unable to keep pace

*Destroyer *Douglas H. Fox* (DD-779) was hit and damaged with casualties on 17 May.

with *Braine,* instead traveled in her wake as *Braine* sailors clustered on the fantail upwind of the fires before jumping in. There were sharks in the water, and while *LCS-82*'s crew rescued several survivors, they also retrieved one dead sailor with an arm and leg torn loose by the predators.

That same day Admiral Raymond A. Spruance turned over Pacific Fleet Command to Admiral William Halsey—transforming 5th Fleet once again into 3rd Fleet. With just three days left in the month, and because of the *kamikaze* boys' nearly two-week hiatus, May would not after all exceed April's deaths, wounds, sinkings, and busted ships.

There was some consolation in that, though not much. The two-month total, once tallied, would add up to 90 ships sunk or out of action, already the most costly naval campaign of this and perhaps any war.

Spruance had presided over it all, fulfilling his reputation of dogged persistence in taking an island objective. He had simply done it—as had the men and ships under his command. Even in his most contemplative moment, Spruance had probably never questioned whether Okinawa was worth capturing. As he handed over the reigns to Halsey, neither man had reason to believe circumstances were about to change.

In fact the next day saw the early morning sinking of destroyer *Drexler* with dead and wounded on a scale with the sinkings of *Luce* and *Morrison* in the awful first days of May. Fred Mitchell, one of two survivors of a *Drexler* 40-mm mount, lived only because he applied the practical pointer he'd picked up from a 6th Division Marine he'd befriended during the voyage to Okinawa.

It was the sort of tip that might well have been included in *Calling All Destroyers* under What to do when the *kamikaze* gets closer than your whiskers.

"Hit the deck," the Marine had told Mitchell, "and make yourself as small a target as possible."

★ Chapter 25 ★

Short of Home, June and July 1945

It is as if our leaders had broken off the writing of a novel they had started and which, for lack of inspiration, they are incapable of finishing.

—Letter received by Flying Officer Ryuji Nagatsuka
from another Special Attack pilot

Past the Meat Grinder

By dawn on 30 May, outflanked by GI units on the east and Marine units on the west, the last of Vice Admiral Mitsuru Ushijima's 32nd Army troops withdrew from their defensive positions at Shuri, leaving behind only a rear guard to cover the retreat. Army Intelligence was still predicting a prolonged siege, but when 1st Division Marines stormed Shuri Ridge on 29 May, they found it lightly defended and swept on through to the ruins of Shuri Castle, a building that had taken ten thousand laborers eight years to construct.

As they pushed farther south, the Marines at first stuck to the better cover afforded by the muddy low ground, but they nonetheless moved so fast that supply, communication and casualty evacuation personnel were hard put to keep up. Though the rain slackened, it never entirely stopped.

When it felt safe enough, K Company's CO ordered his Marines to high ground—what turned out to be a road surfaced with coral overlooking a wide grass and tree-covered ridge. The wind blew fresh and the scent reminded mortarman Eugene Sledge of Alabama pines.

Burial vaults and trench emplacements lined the ridge, but with little hint the Japanese had recently occupied them.

By 4 June, 7th Regiment Marines (operating to the right of 5th Regiment) sealed off the thumb-like Oroku Peninsula. The 6th Marine Division was assigned to clear out Oroku, and 4 June launched a ten-day battle of attrition that cost 1,600 Marine casualties and in turn killed 5,000 Japanese. Just 200 prisoners were captured. That same day, K/3/5 got word their regiment was once more pulling back into reserve. This meant a small, welcome but brief step back from the firing line. The 5th Marines would soon be back in the worst of it.

They dug in near the ruins of some abandoned houses; below them a valley stretched south as far as they could see. The next day the rain finally stopped, and that night Sledge felt settled enough to remove his soaked, muddy boondockers for the first time in two weeks.

The Formidable Power of One-Hit Sinking

On 28 May, Japan's Navy Ministry for the first time made public the operations of the Thunder Gods, extolling them for their fighting spirit and "the formidable power of one-hit sinking." Newspaper accounts also carried the names of 332 Thunder God pilots who had already sacrificed their lives. Despite the public adulation, most *Ōka* pilots now went about their duties under a cloud of despondency, often ignoring the frequent air raid alarms, instead staying in their quarters. Increasingly, petty officers were even sneaking off base to carouse at local inns.

For Ryuji Nagatsuka, meanwhile, May's end marked the completion of suicide tactical training for *Jun-no* Special Attack Corps. Nagatsuka received his promotion to flying officer and now was in line for a posthumous promotion. Credible war news was sparse, but conditions were undoubtedly desperate. Each time flights of American Grummans headed for their base northwest of Tokyo, the pilots flew to safer airspace. Machine guns had been removed from their planes and the primary objective was to preserve them for *tokkō* missions.

The rainy season was in full swing, and the only possible bright spot was a brief visit from his mother and two of his sisters. But even this reunion was awkward. Candor about the future went unspoken in the presence of the young girls. When Nagatsuka left the three of them at a nearby train station, he knew he was seeing them for the last time.

The horrid weather, while it curtailed American air attacks, also delayed launch of *Kikusui* No. 9. An announcement trumpeting the assault went out each morning only to be rescinded by afternoon. Finally, on 3 June, a break in the weather set *Kikusui* No. 9 in motion. The operation's buildup vastly overshadowed its substance: in a scattered series of sorties, barely fifty suicide aircraft flew south toward Okinawa, most without escorts.

These handfuls of *kamikazes* were having a harder time sneaking through, and their attacks seemed to be odd sideshows. Though not any less chaotic or dangerous, the air-sea duels involved many fewer planes and ships.

On 6 June, eight bogeys set upon DMs *J. William Ditter* and *Harry F. Bauer* on patrol southeast of Nakagusuku Wan. One attacker's wing clipped *Ditter*'s after stack and tore open a long strip of shell plating on the port side, flooding the after fire room and forward engine room.

A plane also crashed close to *Bauer*'s starboard beam, tearing a twelve-foot gash in her side. *Bauer*'s damage seemed to be limited to flooding, but crewmen also spotted a large hunk of metal submerged near the forward fireroom and worried it might be a bomb. After taking a look, a bomb disposal expert dispatched from Wiseman's Cove assured *Bauer*'s XO Robert Morgenthau it might be the plane's engine or its landing gear, but was no bomb.

Destroyer *William D. Porter*'s time off Okinawa did much to erase the stigma that plagued her CO and crew since the accidental but near disastrous torpedo shot at battleship *Iowa*. But then, on 10 June, bad luck caught up with *Porter* on RP15 when an undetected *kamikaze* Val dove at her through a low overcast. The plane struck only a glancing blow to *Porter*'s radar mast, but when its bomb exploded in the water nearby, the blast tore up the after half of *Porter*'s hull and unleashed uncontrollable flooding. Even the pumps on LCSs dispatched to help *Porter* could not stay ahead of the rising water, made worse by the explosion of several jettisoned depth charges. *Porter*'s sailors were finally evacuated to CO Richard McCool's *LCS-122*. Lined up along *LCS-122*'s railings, *Porter*'s men watched their hard-luck ship sink at 1119.

On RP15 at dusk the next day, it was *LCS-122*'s turn, but almost a different kind of turn. After escaping a near miss crash by one Val, *LCS-122* took a direct hit to its conning tower by a second Val. The crash and explosion killed 11 men and seriously wounded another 29, including McCool. Despite his wounds, with *122* on fire and at risk of sinking, McCool somehow managed to exit the conning tower, jumping first to the gun deck and finally the main deck. McCool rallied his crew to fight fires, hauled one man to safety, and helped rescue several others before *122* had to be abandoned.

This was to be the last *kamikaze* blow for a week—though by no means the last off Okinawa or the last of the war. Still it was almost a showcase—an attack that occurred in focus and isolation, instead of the thudding, relentless blur of April's and May's attacks (and, earlier, the attacks in the Philippines). The *LCS-122*'s casualties (over half the crew) and the actions of the survivors and the rookie CO somehow symbolized all the suffering, determination, and instinctive heroism displayed by thousands of men through the seemingly unending days of eight long months.

The End of the Island and the End of Our Agony

By mid-June, after two and a half months of combat, there remained few familiar faces in K/3/5's ranks. Counting replacements, K/3/5 was down to about one hundred men and several officers—just half the full-strength company that landed at Hagushi 1 April.

Though still in reserve, 5th Regiment Marines heard rumors they'd be sent into action to help 1st and 7th Regiment Marines attack Kanushi Ridge, the defensive line the Japanese withdrew to after Shuri. Kanushi, westernmost of three adjacent ridges (the other two were Yuza-Dake and Yaeju-Dake) was a steep coral escarpment with heavily fortified caves on both slopes. Kanushi's only approaches were across exposed grasslands and rice paddies. Some 1st and 7th Regiment Marines had already attacked across those fields at great cost and even briefly reached Kanushi's crest, but Japanese defenders were still there—and dug deep.

* * *

The tin cans' support for Iceberg's land campaign by now was mostly limited to call-fire missions in the south. Throughout the invasion, though, as some destroyers rotated between the picket line and gunfire support, their sailors learned only too well how brutal and painfully slow the going was for Okinawa's Marines and GIs. In a way, the sailors were more attuned to the soldiers' agony than the soldiers were to the sailors'.

On the night of 16 June, destroyer *Twiggs* was stationed near Okinawa's western fire support area. Scuttlebutt had it that the ship was heading stateside. *Twiggs'* luck had largely held through three months off Okinawa, though a *kamikaze* near miss on 28 April nearly killed her XO and sent *Twiggs* to Wiseman's Junkyard for weeks of hull repairs. *Twiggs'* sailors were now more eager than ever for call-fire assignments—the surest and quickest way of dispensing ammunition before heading for the States.

Evening watch had just begun when a low flyer hugging the shore launched a torpedo aimed for *Twiggs*. Torpedoman Don Witmer had just reached the bridge and settled in for his watch on the port bridge wing when someone shouted: "He dropped something!" Within moments an aerial torpedo hit *Twiggs'* port side, touching off *Twiggs'* No. 2 magazine into an explosion visible for miles.

The impact tossed Bob Melville, a quartermaster sitting in the chart house, to the deck. By the time Melville reached the main deck, *Twiggs'* bow was bent skyward and consumed in flame. Melville helped several other sailors heave a life raft overboard and then leaped after it. Melville and Witmer were two of 188 oil-soaked *Twiggs'* sailors eventually rescued by destroyer *Putnam* (DD-757). Melville, with multiple injuries including a badly broken leg, was one of *Twiggs'* 34 wounded. The toll of dead and missing reached 152 and included *Twiggs'* skipper George Philip. Their tally did not include six undocumented missing: the ship's mascot, a dog named Jeannie, along with a brood of five pups she'd delivered right after the Battle of Leyte Gulf.

That same night—within ear shot of *Twiggs'* destruction—K/3/5 Marines were dug in atop Yuza-Dake, the ridge next to Kanushi. They'd reached Yuza-Dake (its terrain reminded Sledge of Peleliu's Bloody Nose Ridge) on 15 June and sat tight while U.S. tanks hammered

Japanese positions on Kanushi. The tanks were equipped with sirens whose nonstop wailing was intended to unnerve the Japanese. However, Sledge and his buddies doubted the noise could possibly rattle an enemy who'd taken so much, yet never seemed to surrender.

·The Marines left their positions on Yuza-Dake well before dawn on the 18th in order to cross the exposed terrain leading to Kanushi. The veterans knew this would probably be the last big fight before the Japanese were wiped out and the Okinawa campaign ended. Sledge worried about the finality—convinced that after making it this far through the war, his luck would surely run out.

As K Company reached the foot of the ridge, its riflemen began moving up its slope while mortarmen stayed back to guard against infiltrators. From the start, K/3/5's lines took heavy casualties, from Japanese grenades and rifle fire atop the ridge but also from "short rounds"—poorly aimed salvos of "friendly" artillery fire. When daylight broke, Sledge saw the poncho-covered bodies of about 30 dead Marines.

Unable to fire mortars at such close range, the mortarmen worked instead as stretcher bearers, carrying wounded from the ridges and loading them onto the decks of waiting Marine tanks for transport to aid stations. Once, while Sledge was helping a wounded Marine off the ridge, he took a chance, stood up, and looked south. There, beyond the carnage that still lay all around, beyond the explosions of artillery, mortars, and grenades, and beyond the mud, filth, and stench "lay the end of the island and the end of our agony."

By day's end, K/3/5 Marines had fought their way to the eastern edge of Kanushi and made contact with Army units on the heights of the Yuza-Dake and Yaeju-Dake. The Marines received rations, water, ammo, and mail, which was best of all. Sledge learned from his sergeant that K/3/5 had taken 50 casualties, half of its strength just a few days before. He also heard Army General Simon Bolivar Buckner, Jr., had been killed by a Japanese artillery round that same morning.

"Hurry up! Kill Me! Get it over with!" Ōka pilot Keisuke Yamamura finally shouted as he stood with five other Ōka pilots waiting to climb aboard mother planes and set off on a 22 June mission. This was now Yamamura's third Ōka mission. After aborted missions in April and then in May, Yamamura was beside himself with fear. It was all he could do to keep from screaming that he just couldn't go through with it.

The mission itself—fourteen mother planes carrying Ōkas—was part of *Kikusui* No. 10, the latest (and last) of a string of *Tokkotai* blitzes that began with great fanfare the first week of April. In retrospect, and by all measures (numbers of aircraft, enthusiasm, and results) the effort had been downhill ever since. Yet at first, despite Yamamura's disconsolation, this particular mission started off with promise. When the mother planes took off, they were surrounded by fighter escorts. But it was only a comforting illusion and soon changed: many fighters turned back with mechanical problems and the rest were scattered by American fighter aircraft. In the end, Yamamura's plane had no escort as it approached Okinawa, and its pilot spotted the wake of an American warship.

Like a cowed and subdued animal, Yamamura once more climbed into the Ōka cockpit. He still wore his long *hachimaki,* but it now felt more like a leash than a defiant symbol, and its message ("I shall now take revenge for 100 million people!") was more mocking than inspirational. He waited for the sequence of ready lights, and this time they flashed. This was it. Yamamura's mouth went dry and he felt a sharp pain in his stomach. Still, he instinctively grabbed the control bar and got ready.

But then nothing happened. The Ōka was locked to the Betty. Nothing, not even the backup tripwire, could dislodge it. Now, screaming in hysteria and desperate to shake it loose, Yamamura rocked the craft side to side. It was as though, at the end of these months of passion, frustration, and failure, neither living nor dying could now give him peace.

In the end it was no use, and there was only one place Yamamura could go—out of his coffin and back into the cabin of the Betty for the return flight. Yamamura's mother plane was the only one to return to base, and the day's mission was the last ever operational sortie for the Ōka. On Okinawa that same day, Japanese troops making their final stand with Ushijima began committing suicide. At dawn on 23 June, both Ushijima and his chief of staff committed hara-kiri. The battle for Okinawa was over.

During the three-month campaign, nearly 4,000 Japanese navy and army air crewmen perished in organized *Tokkotai* missions. They took with them the lives of nearly 5,000 U.S. sailors and wounded another 4,800. In the process they had sunk thirty-two U.S. ships and craft and damaged nearly four hundred more. But by the standard of the campaign's goal ("one life—one ship"), the effort, while spectacular, bloody, and unnerving, had also been futile. It had taken an average of 125 Japanese lives to sink each U.S. ship. Moreover, its inexplicable terror had only had steeled the conviction of virually every American political and military leader, every airman, GI, Marine, and sailor, that no measure was beyond the pale when it came to forcing Japan's unconditional surrender.

Essence of Their Mission

Weather grounded *Jun-no* Special Attack Corps through much of June, and it was not until the 29th, when conditions seemed to be improving, that an attack was scheduled. As he prepared for the sortie, Ryuji Nagatsuka believed he had finally come to terms with what he was about to do—and why. He reasoned the terms of his death were at least preferable to those of a bed-bound terminally ill man waiting helplessly for the end. Nagatsuka, by contrast, would be fit at the height of his manhood and acting "with absolute lucidity" to the very last instant.

Next morning, after gathering around makeshift tables to share a toast of *sake*, a formal salute, and a ceremonial bow to the Emperor, eighteen pilots flying *Ki*-27 Type 97s (Anns) and *Ki*-43 Peregrine Falcons (Oscars) rigged with 500 kilogram bombs, took off at 0600 into overcast skies bound for carrier targets 300 miles distant. They carried just enough gas to fly 330 miles.

Skies were expected to clear to the east, but an hour later and near the point of no return, clouds were denser than ever and there was no trace of the American carriers. Twelve of the pilots, including Nagatsuka, reluctantly turned back.

Nagatsuka took no joy in returning alive—he was simply following his flight leader's instructions. But when they assembled before the squadron CO, he raged at the young pilots. The true exemplars of courage, he insisted, were the six older N.C.O. pilots who didn't return (and whose fate was never learned): "Those N.C.O.s were imbued with ardent military spirit," he shouted, "but you have remained students. You have dishonored our squadron and I am ashamed of you. You have wasted our remaining fuel."

Nagatsuka fought the urge to speak up. Hadn't they been ordered to turn around by their flight leader? Weren't they obliged to obey his order? Wasn't the essence of their mission to sink enemy ships, not just to die? He knew it was of no use and he kept silent. The CO ordered the shamed pilots to a schoolboy task—copying out the "sacred words of the Emperor" until further orders.

There would be no more flying until fuel supplies arrived at the end of July. After three days copying and recopying the Emperor's words, the disgraced pilots joined the ground crews for infantry training.

Destroyer *Callaghan,* which took up RP9 picket duties on 28 July, had gotten this far with no damage. Indeed, *Callaghan*'s only casualty was an 18-year-old baker caught topside during a strafing run, and no one seemed sure whether he'd been delivering sandwiches or passing ammunition. Back in June, *Callaghan*'s sailors had retrieved the pilot and navigator of a Frances bomber that crashed near them on 25 May. The pilot died later that night, but the navigator survived. Before being turned in as a prisoner of war, the young Japanese officer pleaded with his *Callaghan* guards to shoot him so that he could avoid the shame of imprisonment.

Attacks were down dramatically, but RP9 was well stocked with defenders—in addition to *Callaghan,* destroyers *Cassin Young* and *Pritchett* with four LCSs. A measure of ease had begun to settle in the minds of picket crews. Since mid-July, to relieve the strain on equipment and manpower, some picket COs were given the option of securing two boilers between sunset and sunrise. During the first afternoon of this tour, one LCS was released to return to Hagushi with an emergency hospital case.

The measure of ease was especially high for *Callaghan*'s crew. *Callaghan* was due to arrive in Nagagusuku Wan (now renamed Buckner Bay) at daylight, off-load ammunition, refuel, and begin the six-thousand-mile journey to the West Coast and overhaul. Destroyer

Laws (DD-558), *Callaghan*'s relief, had left Hagushi before midnight and was already en route.

Just after midnight, RP radars picked up a single bogey, thirteen miles southwest. It was moving slowly—one plot tracked it at barely 60 knots. Some questioned whether it was an aircraft, but others suspected what it turned out to be: another ancient twin-float biplane like the one that sank destroyer *Morrison* in May.

GQ was called while ships held courses and speeds, waiting to see what the snooper was up to. Bridge watch stander Bill Benton, 19, had the helm. When he was relieved by the GQ helmsman, the target was closing on the port quarter and *Callaghan* was in a starboard turn to unmask guns. As Benton left the bridge, headed for his own GQ station on a forward 40-mm, the TBS barked: "Any ship having a good solution open up." In other words, thought Benton, if anyone can hit this plane, please do.

When Benton reached his gun, *Callaghan*'s after 5-inch guns were already firing. An instant later, Benton heard an explosion and knew *Callaghan* had been hit. Soon he could see flames climbing high amidships. The crash and explosion to *Callaghan*'s after fire room and No. 3 handling room tossed E. C. "Woody" Woodward, a radar technician manning a starboard side 20-mm, into the midships passageway. Woodward could barely breathe and hardly move, but managed somehow to crawl under a ladder to avoid being stepped on.

After the crash, RP station control passed from *Callaghan* to *Cassin Young* whose skipper J. W. Ailes ordered *Prichett* to stand by *Callaghan* while *Cassin Young* watched for other bogeys. *Callaghan*'s fires were already visible for miles when ammunition in the No. 3 handling room erupted into a second colossal blast.

Jehu Frasheur, a gunner on a fantail 20-mm, survived the explosion, but the stern was settling and, with smoke everywhere, Frasheur couldn't locate Sam Elrod—the Oklahoma schoolteacher and torpedo petty officer manning the fantail phones. Frasheur tried shouting Elrod's name above the din, but got no answer.

When radioman Marland Moreau left the radio shack and made his way toward the forecastle, *Callaghan*'s bow was rising. Moreau took off his shoes and arranged them at one end of a long, orderly line of other pairs before going to the railing. Crewmen were already standing outside the lifeline. Even when word finally came to abandon ship, everyone clung momentarily to the railing, waiting it seemed for someone else to move first. When one sailor finally let go, few wasted any time in following.

Back on the fantail, Frasheur continued to search for Elrod. With the stern decks awash and *Callaghan* listing badly, the few remaining sailors were stepping overboard. Frasheur felt his way along the deckhouse bulkhead until he located the jack outlet for the sound-powered phone line. The phone jack was still connected and Frasheur felt resistance at the other end. Keeping low, he followed the line aft until, near the railing, Frasheur finally reached out his hand and touched Elrod's lifeless body.

Recoveries

Anticipating the needs of Operation Downfall, the Navy fast-tracked the repair of the ships damaged by *kamikaze* attacks. A lot of it was accomplished in the Pacific. After being hit on 16 April, for example, *LCS-116* was sent to Pearl Harbor to undergo its repairs. Minelayer *Harry F. Bauer,* with flooding damage to the bow, went no farther than a destroyer tender at Leyte (where further inspection revealed that *Bauer* indeed had an unexploded bomb lodged near its fire room).

While DE *Bowers* waited in Kerama Retto for temporary repairs of damage from a 16 April attack, one of her officers was already being flown to the Camden Naval Shipyard in New Jersey with photographs of the damage. Using these photographs plus information obtained from the facility in Ulithi where *Bowers* had gone for additional repairs, a new deckhouse was completed and ready for installation four days before the ship's arrival in Camden.

Damaged ships were even being used to motivate shipyard work crews and spur shipyard recruiting. When destroyer *Laffey* reached Seattle 24 May and entered dry dock at Todd Shipyard Corp., her external damage was still plainly visible and still dramatic. To attract new shipyard job applicants, *Laffey* was opened to the public and thousands took tours.

While round-the-clock efforts to repair *Laffey* continued, the crew got the opportunity to go on leave. Ari Phoutrides, whose own home was in Seattle, took a couple days leave to travel to Portland, Oregon, where he looked up Ensign Robert Thomsen's family. Thomsen had been *Laffey*'s navigator and Phoutrides' division officer. He was a tall, affable young man who rarely mentioned his Annapolis schooling.

During the 16 April attack, with radars out of commission, Thomsen had volunteered to help with damage control efforts in the after part of the ship and was killed in an explosion. Phoutrides had seen Thomsen's body when it was carried out on a stretcher. Killed by a concussion, Thomsen was intact, in sharp contrast to the burned and mutilated remains of other *Laffey* fatalities.

The brief meeting with Thomsen's parents Jens and Dagmar in their North Portland home was as wrenching as Phoutrides anticipated. But when he mentioned seeing their son after his death, Dagmar Thomsen seized the opportunity, insisting Phoutrides describe the moment. Close to tears, Phoutrides was at least able to tell her truthfully: "Mrs. Thomsen, your son looked peaceful, like he was asleep."

Recoveries for wounded sailors weren't always on the same fast track as their ships; sometimes recovery began just a step short of death or despair. After *Callaghan*'s sinking on 29 July, radar tech Woody Woodward was transferred to a battle casualty ship. Still strapped to a stretcher, Woodward was at first triaged to a spot on an open deck— not a good sign. When he was finally taken to a compartment and stretched out on a table, a doctor examined him briefly and then made a quick incision in his chest. Woodward could hear and feel air rushing in to fill a lung and soon got his first full breath since being wounded. Having pretty much assumed he would die, Woodward suddenly felt he might live.

Following *Longshaw*'s 18 May loss to Japanese shore batteries off Naha, John Schneider was transferred to hospital ship *Relief* (AH-1) where he lay in utter darkness, not knowing what would happen next. Then, almost as suddenly as it left, Schneider's vision returned. The first person Schneider beheld was a *Longshaw* gunner's mate nicknamed "Cisco" because of his suave Hispanic features and his pencil-thin moustache. It was, Schneider recalled, a true joy to see him.

Don Witmer, whose leg was broken in the 16 June sinking of

Twiggs, began his recovery strapped to a wire stretcher being transferred to a small patrol craft rigged as a hospital ship. There Witmer got his first medical care, a splint, which seemed inadequate even in his "naïve estimation." It turned out that the new doctors in a succession of facilities, including hospital ship *Rescue,* the Army hospital on Guam, and Navy hospitals in Seattle and Oakland—thought little of the previous facility's work. Meanwhile, as each facility focused attention (and criticism) on cast making, no one seemed concerned about Witmer's hair, which was still slick with bunker oil from the sinking. Not until Witmer reached Oakland did a nurse finally and thoroughly scrub his head. Only then did Witmer finally feel like a survivor.

The recovery path for Don Sheridan, destroyer *Bennett*'s engineering officer, required more time and patience than effort. It began aboard battle casualty ship *Crescent City* (APA-21), and then moved to hospital ship *Hope,* which transported Sheridan to Saipan and its Army hospital. He'd received quick—and effective—first aid treatment aboard *Bennett.* He really just had to wait for his skin to heal, a slow and ugly process: Sheridan couldn't be shaved and when his scalp and beard grew out, the hair easily fell out in greasy swatches. At Guam's Army hospital, Sheridan was voted the second ugliest man on his ward. The top prize went to a man who had lost part of his face. It pained Sheridan more than anything to see the long and agonizing treatment the really bad burn cases had to endure.

Some recoveries took much longer than Sheridan's, with many stops—and hurdles—along the way. After being rescued by *Hobson,* for example, *Pringle*'s Milton Mapou was transferred to hospital ship *Hope* and placed in a full body cast. Mapou's hospitalization continued in Saipan, then Hawaii, and finally Oakland, where his sister was an Army nurse. Mapou was not discharged until 1946, even then still wearing a leg brace (and facing years more of intermittent hospitalization).

Bush's Robert Carney had his broken pelvis encased in a plaster "pants cast" aboard *Comfort* and wore the cast during the shipboard journey to Guam, evacuation flights to Hawaii and Oakland, and a long train ride to the Naval hospital in Seattle. The cast finally came off at a recuperation facility in Sun Valley, Idaho.

After a week aboard hospital ship *Solace, Bowers*' Tony Natale began what would be an eighteen-month odyssey through military hospitals in Saipan, Pearl Harbor, Oakland, Oceanside (where he got a bedside visit from Bing Crosby), and Bainbridge, Maryland. Twice doctors considered amputating Natale's foot but each time held off. Doctors aboard *Hope* repaired one of Natale's ears, which had nearly been severed. In contrast to Witmer's experience, during each of Natale's hospital stays local doctors had nothing but praise for the suture work performed on *Hope*.

For Ed Samp, the AGO wounded by the last bomb blast on *Laffey,* recovery was a particularly long and difficult journey. His inventory of wounds was extensive, including shrapnel and a compound fracture to his right arm. But his most devastating injuries were the loss of a portion of his skull and collateral impairment to his motor and memory skills. Samp's hospitalization began in Guam, continued in Hawaii, and stretched a full fifteen months in San Diego. During these protracted stays, Samp worked tirelessly to retool his brain: flexing its storage capacity by memorizing Shakespeare's sonnets and plays. Samp had interrupted Harvard Law School to join the Navy, but when he reached Chelsea Naval Hospital near Boston, he re-enrolled at Harvard and completed his law degree. He was finally released from Chelsea in July 1946.

Since January 1945, *Hull* sonarman Pat Douhan had been working at the Fleet Post Office in San Francisco. When Douhan first reached San Pedro following the typhoon sinking of *Hull,* he was pressured to report to San Francisco as soon as possible: the mail addressed to *Hull* crewmen was piling up and someone needed to get it processed. So, instead of going on survivor's leave for thirty days, Douhan arranged to go to Fresno first and have his pregnant wife accompany him to the new duty station.

Douhan was assigned to the Inoperative Ship Section (ISS). Like Douhan, each of the other sailors in the section was the survivor of a ship sunk in the Pacific. On any given day there were about fifteen of them assigned to ISS, each sailor responsible for disposing of the mail destined for his ship.

By the time each of these sailors reached the Fleet Post Office, the first telegrams to next of kin had already been sent out, and the mail was piled up in huge bins. Each man had a roster with names and, in the case of survivors, forwarding addresses of his shipmates. Survivor mail was forwarded; mail for the dead was stamped and returned to sender.

Depending on the circumstances—the size of the ship, for example, and the number and disposition of survivors—the temporary assignment might take weeks or months. A backlog needed to be cleared and the survivor forwarding addresses needed to be verified and updated. Eventually, the mountainous piles would shrink and the influx of new mail would slow to a trickle. And, eventually, this would mean the end of another aspect of the ships' existence—the webs of relationships and communications that fleshed out the lives and deaths of their sailors.

★ Epilogue ★

Movies on Topside,
August 1945–Present

Farewell to Victory! Farewell to the Efforts for Victory! Farewell to the Achievement of Defeat!
—Higher Flight Petty Officer Motoji Ichikawa, surviving Ōka pilot

The Last

During late July and early August, reconnaissance missions flown by Task Force 38 pilots over Honshu and Kyushu increased in frequency and impunity. After wrapping up one photo sortie over Tokyo's Kanto Plain (where U.S. planners believed Operation Coronet's decisive battle would be fought), VF-16's Art Whiteway landed his Hellcat on a deserted airstrip and watched from a distance by Japanese children, scooped up a pocketful of soil and returned with it to *Lexington*.

Photo intelligence missions continued to reveal hidden aircraft caches. When tactical strikes resumed several days after the first atomic bomb fell on Hiroshima 6 August, Hellcats and Corsairs swooped in at treetop level to blast camouflaged aircraft revetments. Action reports claimed 251 planes destroyed and another 141 damaged; postwar analysis revealed that 200 of these were to be used to transport commandos on a raid to destroy B-29 airfields in the Marianas.

No Japanese aircraft rose to contest the 9 August air sweeps and none came close to Task Force 38 carriers, but five planes drew fire from tin cans on picket station fifty miles southwest.* One attacker, a

---

*On 13 August, however, six Navy Hellcats off carrier *Yorktown* on a mission over Honshu were attacked by a group of Japanese fighters. Just moments before, the Hellcat pilots had received word to abort the air strike because of the cessation of hostilities. In the untimely melee that followed—reportedly the last significant aerial battle of World War II—the U.S. Navy pilots shot down nine Japanese aircraft but lost four of their own.

Val, flew up the wake of destroyer *Borie* (DD-704) and crashed near *Borie*'s bridge.

The Val's bomb broke loose on impact and exploded between No. 1 and No. 2 mounts, demolishing the 5-inch guns, disabling the forward 40s, and silencing internal communications circuits. Robert White, 22, a CIC radarman, was sure at first *Borie* was hit by torpedo. White's job was to destroy radar equipment when this happened, but gasoline was leaking through the overhead, sparking fires that quickly chased everybody out.

Borie's skipper Noah Adair survived the explosion, but the impact blew him clear out of his shoes. Wounded and unsteady on his feet, Adair dispatched a messenger to engineering to slow the ship. Two men then helped Adair reach secondary control amidships where he could control *Borie* through voice commands to after steering.

When Jerry Harvey, an electrician's mate on the after damage control party reached the blazing superstructure, he faced a solid wall of heat. Harvey saw one sailor step out of the inferno: shirtless, his torso, arms, and head cinder black. The sailor stood for a moment, balanced on his toes, punching his fist in rage at the vacant sky. As one or two men finally approached to help him, the sailor's body started shaking and then dropped in a charred heap. He died soon after.

Stuart White, 20, part of the midships repair party, dodged the blast by diving into the midships passageway. Later, while carrying a fire hose to the bridge, White saw blackened, still-smoking corpses in the 40-mm gun tubs.

Borie's fires were soon contained and, once communications circuits were repaired, control passed back to bridge. Destroyer *Abbot* (DD-629), dispatched from the main force, came alongside with a doctor and additional medical supplies to help with *Borie*'s more than 60 wounded. That night *Borie*'s dead, nearly 50 in all, were put in weighted mattress covers for burial at sea the next day.

Borie's casualties and damage, it turned out, were the last from U.S. Navy engagements with *kamikaze* aircraft—though not yet Japan's final attempts to strike. By the time *Borie* reached the hospital ship *Rescue* (AH-18), transferred its wounded, and set off for repairs in Saipan, the war was all but over. The second atomic bomb fell on Nagasaki the same day as the attack on *Borie*.

* * *

Following the *Jun-no* Special Attack Corps abortive mission in late June, priorities shifted. Precious fuel couldn't be wasted trying to hunt down carriers offshore. Instead, missions were limited to confronting American aircraft—and only when they were actually overhead.

On 12 August, when American fighters were spotted heading toward the city of Kumagaya near Tokyo, Ryuji Nagatsuka and five other pilots sortied in the squadron's six remaining Oscars. Flying south of Kumagaya, Nagatsuka spotted five specks in the skies below him: Grummans. But just as Nagatsuka's flight leader ordered his pilots to fan out and get ready to dive, more enemy planes suddenly burst through the clouds above them.

Nagatsuka turned left and into a series of barrel rolls trying to shake a Grumman close on his tail, but it was too late: ice candies grazed the Oscar's fuselage and Nagatsuka felt a violent shock, as if his right shoulder had been hit with a hammer. Blood stained his flight suit, his arm went limp, and Nagatsuka drifted into unconsciousness.

When he awoke seconds later, the Grumman was gone, but Nagatsuka's Oscar was spiraling out of control. His altimeter read three thousand feet and was dropping fast. Nagatsuka grabbed the stick with his left arm. He knew his only hope was to prepare for a crash landing. He tried to lower his landing gear but the control wouldn't work. The Oscar's descent had slowed, but Nagatsuka was at six hundred feet and then just three hundred. The aircraft nose was pointed west and the setting sun blinded him. Nagatsuka saw just enough to know he was heading toward a paddy field. He felt the jolt of the plane hitting the ground and then once more plunged into unconsciousness.

Enduring the Unendurable

Nagatsuka awoke the next day lying in a bed at a tiny village hospital. It was hot and his mind was dulled by pain, but Nagatsuka learned it was now a day after the crash. Two days later Nagatsuka's condition had improved, and he was alert enough to listen to Emperor Hirohito addressing the Japanese people.

The Emperor's language was elaborate and formal—in stark contrast to the thin, reedy voice coming over the radio:

The hardships and sufferings to which Our nation is to be subjected hereafter will certainly be great. We are keenly aware of the inmost feelings of all ye, Our subjects. However, it is according to the dictate of time and fate that We have resolved to pave the way for a grand peace for all the generations to come by enduring the unendurable and suffering what is insufferable.

The speech was actually a recording, but his audience didn't know this and it probably wouldn't have been less earth shattering if they had. It marked the first time the Japanese public had ever heard the Emperor speak, and so people paid as much attention to the messenger as his message. Hirohito's language and voice were disconcerting, and poor radio reception made the broadcast unintelligible to many. Still, whatever the precise details, it could only signify a catastrophe. Most understood it to be the Emperor's admission of total defeat. He was commanding his subjects to submit to their barbaric enemies.

As Japan's public tried to decipher the full meaning of what the Emperor was asking them to do, some of Japan's senior military officers, including Vice Admiral Matome Ugaki and Vice Admiral Takijiro Onishi, were acting out dramas in the uncertain space between the official surrender and its actual implementation.

When commanding 5th Naval Air Fleet, Ugaki (though himself not an aviator) had presided over the training, deployment, and deaths of upward of 2,500 IJN Special Attack fliers. Now he was at an airbase on Kyushu, preparing for one final *Tokkotai* mission—his own. Ugaki's suicide attack plan (unquestionably a violation of Hirohito's surrender decision) called for a three-plane strike, but when he arrived at the flight line wearing a uniform stripped of all insignia, Ugaki instead found eleven small bombers waiting, with flight crews for each ready to go.

After climbing atop a small platform to address the cheering fliers, Ugaki strode up to the lead plane and climbed into the cockpit behind its pilot. In doing so, Ugaki displaced a young warrant officer already in the seat. At first, the warrant officer surrendered his seat, but then, emboldened, jumped back in and wedged himself next to Ugaki. Good naturedly, Ugaki made room.

As Ugaki's flight lifted off from the Kyushu airfield on a mission in which Ugaki was offering his life as penance for his insubordination, Takijiro Onishi, *Tokkotai*'s prime instigator and strategist, lay near death in his Tokyo home. Onishi sent for a close associate, who found Onishi lying in a pool of blood, his throat, chest, and abdomen slit by his own hand using a borrowed sword. The associate offered to join Onishi in death, but Onishi implored him instead to deliver a letter propped up on the desk nearby.

Even after the atomic bombs were unleashed on Hiroshima and Nagazaki, Onishi had implored Combined Fleet Commander Soemu Toyoda and Japan's foreign minister to reject surrender and instead prepare to sacrifice 20 million or more lives in defense of the homeland. Now, in his letter, Onishi reversed himself and pleaded for a diametrically opposite course: "You must abide by the spirit of the Emperor's decision with utmost perseverance. Do not forget your rightful pride in being Japanese. With all the fervor of spirit of the Special Attackers, strive for the welfare of Japan and for peace throughout the world."

Thus, two competing messages were aloft on the day Japan's citizenry had first heard the "Crane" (the Imperial symbol) speak. One message flew with Ugaki's bombers, seven of which reached the skies over Okinawa after sundown. Though Ugaki sent a last defiant signal before his planes dove on the enemy, no *tokkō* attacks were listed in U.S. battle records for that date.

In the end, it was the second message (Onishi's and others like it) that ultimately took wing. Throughout the rest of August, reckless attempts at mutiny—some real, others symbolic—flared sporadically as Japan and its edgy citizens awaited the arrival of its conquerors' first emissaries.

In one instance, a plan circulated among pilots in a few special attack squadrons to sortie against battleship *Missouri* (BB-63) as it entered Tokyo Bay. A smaller, more public incident occurred on 22 August, when ten young men armed with pistols and grenades made a stand on a Tokyo hill within sight of what was to become the American embassy. After three *banzai* shouts, the demonstrators (like the groups of cornered Japanese soldiers *Time* reporter Robert Sherrod had seen the previous summer on Saipan) pulled grenade pins to blow themselves up. Still, as these and other defiant acts sputtered and played out, the passions for a suicidal fight to the finish dissipated as if carried away by the wind.

Sagami Wan

Dawn broke cool and gray over Tokyo Bay 2 September 1945, the day set for the formal surrender. The site chosen for the ceremony, the deck of the battleship *Missouri*, greatly pleased President Truman of the United States: his home state was the ship's namesake, and it had been christened by his daughter, Margaret.

In the weeks and hours before this event, the Americans had prepared with a combination of pomp and precaution. Because of its ships, the U.S. Navy would be the most visible—and endangered—participant. Having access to message traffic, *Ellyson* radioman Dwight Donnewald could update his journal with some of the details.

On 23 August: "I found out the OP PLAN for the occupation of Japan goes into effect at 1400 today. We are going to fuel this morning and will probably leave for Tokyo tonight and early tomorrow morning. Com 3rd Fleet [Halsey] expects trouble and is running this business like any other landing. The first troops will land Sept 1st and more on the 6th and 13th."

On 27 August, when *Ellyson* first approached Japan: "About 1300, sighted the main island of Honshu. About supper we dropped the hook. We are near the shore, about a mile away. It doesn't look so bad; the grass is green, plenty of trees."

And then 28 August, as ships moved in to clear channels of mines: "Entered Tokyo Bay! Got underway at 0900 and streamed our sweep gear. Met the *San Diego* [(CL-53)] and *Hambleton* [(DD-455/DMS-20)] plus some destroyers and proceeded toward the entrance to Tokyo. We swept the channel." And that night: "They are showing movies on topside in Sagami Wan."

Ellyson and the other ships continued their sweeps for two more days, and then, in company with 250 other U.S. and Allied ships anchored on the sidelines to await Japan's ceremonial surrender.

At 0855, the eleven member Japanese delegation arrived from Yokohama aboard destroyer *Lansdowne* (DD-486). Though Japan's delegation was led by Imperial Army Chief of Staff Yoshijuro Umezu and included Japan's new foreign minister Mamoru Shigemitsu, most important Japanese officials were conspicuous by their absence. Newly installed prime minister Toshihiko Higashikuni (a member of the royal family), for example, was missing, as was Navy Chief of Staff Toyoda, who sent a despised subordinate as a delegate.

Foreign Minister Shigemitsu, who wore an ill-fitting prosthetic leg (he'd been the target of an assassin's bomb in Shanghai), lurched painfully up the gangway. All but ignored by Umezu, who considered him a diplomatic weakling, Shigemitsu was finally given a hand by one of the escorting U.S. Navy officers.

Once the Japanese delegates were in place, there followed an invocation and the playing of a record of "The Star-Spangled Banner." Then General Douglas MacArthur, flanked by Admiral Chester Nimitz and Admiral William Halsey strode briskly to the signing desk—a table from the crew's mess on the *Missouri* covered by a green cloth with coffee stains artfully hidden under the official documents. MacArthur's words (once translated) impressed at least one of the Japanese delegation with their lack of rancor and retribution. First, Shigemitsu and then Umezu approached the table to sign the instruments of Japan's unconditional surrender. Then it was MacArthur's turn, followed by Nimitz, and finally by representatives from eight Allied nations: China, the United Kingdom, the Soviet Union, Australia, Canada, France, the Netherlands, and New Zealand.

After MacArthur's closing words, there was a rumble in the distance followed by the appearance overhead of wave after wave of U.S. B-29's and carrier-based aircraft.

During Ryuji Nagatsuka's months of recuperation, he was almost overwhelmed by feelings of frustration, shame, rage, and despair. When he finally returned to his family's home, he wasn't sure what to expect. When the door opened and he saw his parents and sisters, they seemed to be staring at him fixedly. One young sister, obviously upset at the sight of Nagatsuka's wounds, rushed away in tears. Soon, however, the others warmly embraced Nagatsuka. His father in particular greeted him with a voice swelling with emotion. "At last the war is behind us," he said. "The important thing is we're alive."

Full Circles

Veterans of the *kamikaze* attacks of 1944 and 1945 returned, as did most World War II veterans, to homes, families, careers, and personal lives that ranged from the ordinary to the unusually accomplished. *Bennett* sailor Larry Finn, for example, was an NYPD detective for thirty years. *Intrepid*'s Sal Maschio, worked as a longshoreman for forty-three years. Robert M. Morgenthau, XO of *Harry M. Bauer* has been Manhattan District Attorney since 1975. Oscar Blank, *Howorth*'s CIC officer, retired from an academic career as an economist, now volunteers for a university-oriented organization promoting world peace. *Bache* veteran Kit Hall retired as a construction carpenter (a trade he picked up from *Bache* as a carpenter fashioning plywood trunks to return the effects of sailors killed in action). *Laffey*'s Ari Phoutrides, who left MIT to join the Navy, finished schooling at the University of Washington and later retired from a career as a chemical engineer for Crown Zellerbach. *Franklin*'s Bill Albrecht became an FBI agent and later a New Jersey State Judge. The list and its variety go on.

Too frequently they returned disabled. Some wounded veterans of the *kamikaze* attacks, and especially some burn victims, bore lasting visible scars. Others returned with less visible, but equally disabling psychological afflictions, what today is called Post-Traumatic Stress Disorder (PTSD). Joseph Masters, for example, a picket destroyer FIDO decorated for bravery, for years dreaded situations where he felt trapped, even activities as benign as riding the Swan Boats in Boston's Public Garden. Another, Fred Mitchell, the only survivor of a *Drexler* 40-mm gun crew, sleepwalked through nightmares in which he looked endlessly for an escape route.

Time resolved these afflictions for some, while for others time served only to pospone the anguish. John Vaught, a wounded *Bache* gunner decorated for heroism, was first diagnosed with PTSD at 40 years old and still continues counseling. And Kenneth Courteau received his diagnosis fully sixty-two years after his ship, destroyer *Halsey Powell*, was hit by a *kamikaze*.

The special, almost personal terror of *kamikaze* warfare left even the healthiest Navy veterans perplexed and embittered at a nation, culture, and people capable of devising such attacks, and these feelings have been particularly tenacious. Few doubted the necessity and inevitability of using the atomic bomb to bring about Japan's surrender. The experience shattered innocence at a young age and has shaped memories, beliefs, and biases ever since. Inevitably though, with years, the deepening of experience, the knowing of the horrors routinely visited on humans in war, and the passing of generations, the "War with the Wind" has, for some at least, found context, connection, and closure.

Context began for *Drexler* shipmates Fred Mitchell and Eugene Brick in 2006, when Japanese-American film director Risa Morimoto interviewed them for her documentary about the *kamikaze* phenomenon. After viewing the completed version of *Wings of Defeat,* Mitchell and Brick asked Morimoto about the possibility of meeting with former *kamikaze* pilots. The result, in the summer of 2007, was their visit to Japan in conjunction with the film's theatrical release. While in Japan, the two *Drexler* veterans met with several of the Japanese pilot veterans profiled in Morimoto's film. For Mitchell (who still struggles with PTSD), it was a chance to confront what he knew to be a lingering hatred and to move a bit closer to a sense of peace.

For the veterans of destroyer *Callaghan*, meanwhile, there has been the connection with Kaoru Hasegawa. Hasegawa, the IJN bomber navigator rescued by *Callaghan* crewmen in May 1945, was later transferred to battleship *New Mexico* and eventually sent to Hawaii as a POW. Returning to Japan after the war, Hasegawa pursued a business career culminating as CEO of a worldwide paper conglomerate. Enduring gratitude and curiosity about the ship and men who saved his life (and ignored his pleas to be shot) spurred Hasegawa along a trail of research and networking that eventually connected him to *Callaghan*'s reunion association. In 1999, Hasegawa attended his first

Callaghan veterans' reunion in Pigeon Fork, Tennessee, and remained, until his death, an honorary member of *Callaghan*'s crew.

As to closure, there is the story of Robert Schock, his grandson Dax Berg, and the family of Ensign Kiyoshi Ogawa.

Robert Schock, the salvage diver who first discovered the body of a Japanese suicide pilot in the depths of carrier *Bunker Hill,* remained in the Navy for a few years after the war, but finally returned to his hometown of Haysville, Kansas. Schock worked for many years as an aircraft engineer and eventually became town mayor. Although he seldom talked about the war, Schock did tell his grandson Dax Berg the story about finding the dead pilot. He also alluded to the souvenirs, but never actually showed them to Berg.

By the time Schock died in November 2000 at 72 years of age, his grandson had moved to Northern California and begun a career as a software designer. Berg returned for Schock's funeral and afterward went through Schock's personal effects. It was then that he came across a cardboard box containing the items Schock had retrieved so many years before.

His grandfather's passing inevitably turned Berg's thoughts to the dead Japanese pilot and what were, after all, *his* last remains. It turned out that Paul Grace, Berg's boss in California, was married to a Japanese native, Miyuki (Mickie) Grace. Mickie Grace was also a professional translator, one of whose clients was Japan's Ministry of Defense. Like Dax Berg, Mickie Grace was intrigued by the puzzle and its human possibilities. She also had the skills—and the possible connections—to find the dead pilot's family.

Mickie Grace's trail began with only one solid piece of information: 11 May 1945, the date of the *Bunker Hill* attack. From a fragment of the dead pilot's identification tag, Grace deciphered his rank and service (ensign in the IJN) as well as small portions of the characters in his last name. She also noticed that the blood-stained letter Robert Schock found on the pilot included a poem by a traditional poet from the Japanese prefecture of Gumna. Armed with the bits of information she'd gleaned, Mickie Grace contacted a representative from the Ministry of Defense, who in turn pointed her to a research institute then compiling a database of Special Attack Force missions and personnel. Remarkably, a long-lost name and even a 1945 address popped up: IJN Ensign Kiyoshi Ogawa in Takasaki, a town north of Tokyo.

Using the old address, Grace wrote a letter to the family. Address schemes had changed radically since the war, but a savvy Japanese postal worker finally got the letter through to Ogawa's grandniece. Until Grace's letter arrived, Ogawa's family never knew what happened to Kiyoshi Ogawa. Still, they had not forgotten him: he had both a gravestone and a shrine.

It had all happened with amazing speed: a mystery buried for fifty-six years unearthed in a matter of months. When Berg learned its answer, he quickly decided to return Ogawa's last remains. It was one of those times when a decision "seemed so right."

Ogawa's family, represented by Ogawa's niece, grandniece, great grandnephew, and one of Ogawa's old college friends, flew to San Francisco to receive the items in person. By now, media on both sides of the Pacific were on to the event and its symbolism. Berg worked to keep it low key, permitting only two print media representatives to sit in on a luncheon arranged at the San Francisco Hilton.

During the get together, Ogawa's family received the small pieces of Kiyoshi Ogawa's life with deep bows and tears. Mickie Grace read aloud from Ogawa's last letter, and pictures of the pilot were passed around. When Ogawa's college friend talked about what they were like when they were young men, he began to weep.

★ Notes ★

Portents: *Cole* and *Lindsey*

Author interviews with *Leutze* crewman: Malcolm Fortson, Jr.; *Lindsey* crewmen: Leonard (Pete) Petersen, Walter L. Gau.
Books: *9/11 Commission Report;* Morison, *Victory in the Pacific.*
Articles: Burns, "A Maimed Destroyer Cole Starts for Home."
Other: *Lindsey* (DM-32), Battle Damage Report of 12 April 1945; Letter dated 12 May 1945, and Letter to Erin Hayles, dated 25 September 1945, both supplied by a surviving *Lindsey* crewmember.

The Alligator and the Bull

Books: Beschloss, *Conquerors;* Halsey, *Admiral Halsey's Story;* Manchester, *American Caesar* and *Goodbye, Darkness;* Morison, *Victory in the Pacific;* Sherrod, *On to Westward.*
Articles: Kennedy, "Victory at Sea."

Dark Waters

Author interviews with *Bache* crewmen: John Vaught, Hugo P. Cipriani; *Bennett* crewman: Lawrence C. Finn; *Bryant* crewman: Alvin L. Gallin; *Cooper* crewman: James W. Villiers; *Cowell* crewman: Donald E. Roller; *Daly* crewman: William J. Wyatt; *Drexler* crewman: Fred W. Mitchell; *Lansdale* XO Robert M. Morgenthau; *Macdonough* crewman: James Gilbert; *Pringle* crewman: Milton Mapou; *Richard P. Leary* crewman: Leon Wolper; *Stack* crewman: P. A. (Tony) Lilly.
Books: Friedman, *U.S. Destroyers;* Morison, *Victory in the Pacific;* Prang, *At Dawn We Slept;* Raines, *Good Night Officially;* Sherrod, *On to Westward.*

Articles: Kennedy, "Victory at Sea"; Lardner, "A Reporter on Okinawa."

Other: *Callaghan:* Correspondence of Samuel T. Elrod; *Ellyson:* Wartime diary of Dwight Dean Donnewald; *Dashiell* (DD-659): Wartime journal of Fred M. Wright; *Ward:* Richard E. Farwell Internet narrative: hometown.aol.com/worddd139/richard2_story11.html

Green Hells

Author interviews with *Bennion* crewman: Harold M. Scott, Jr.; *Drexler* crewman: Fred W. Mitchell; *Henrico* crewmen: John Brooks, Robert G. (Duke) DeLuca; *Nashville* crewmen: Ben Limbaugh, Rufus B. Thompson, Jr.

Books: Morison, *Victory in the Pacific;* Sledge, *With the Old Breed at Peleliu and Okinawa;* Toland, *Rising Sun.*

Forager, June and July 1944

Author interviews with *Halsey Powell* crewmen: Jack Barrett, Kenneth F. Courteau, Casey Kraft; Lorin Nelson (sailor, formerly on *Dewey,* attached to Acorn 38, a Navy detachment landed on Saipan to construct a seaplane base).

Books: Morison, *New Guinea and the Marianas;* Sherrod, *On to Westward;* Sledge, *With the Old Breed at Peleliu and Okinawa;* Toland, *Rising Sun.*

The Big Blue Blanket

Author interviews with *Bunker Hill* VT-84 squadron crewmen: Edward Duffy, Thomas F. Kelly; *Hornet* VF-17 pilots: Willis E. (Bill) Hardy, Ted Crosby; *Lexington* crewman: Richard J. Fullam; *Lexington* VF-16 pilot: Arthur P. Whiteway; *Lexington* VF-19 pilot: Bruce Williams; *Lexington* VT-16 pilot: Warren E. McLellan.

Books: Drury and Clavin, *Halsey's Typhoon;* Morison, *Coral Sea, Midway and Submarine Actions* and *New Guinea and the Marianas;* Nagatsuka, *I Was a Kamikaze;* Sherrod, *On to Westward;* Toland, *The Rising Sun;* Wooldridge, *Carrier Warfare in the Pacific.*

Clearing Skies, July 1944

Author interviews with *Lexington* VF-16 pilot: Arthur P. Whiteway; *Lexington* VF-16 pilot: Bruce Williams; *Lexington* VT-16 pilot: Warren E. McLellan.

Books: Bryan and Reed, *Mission Beyond Darkness;* Morison, *Leyte* and *New Guinea and the Marianas;* Toland, *The Rising Sun;* Wooldridge, *Carrier Warfare in the Pacific.*

Other: *Lexington:* Wartime diary of Robert R. Davis.

Returning

Author interviews with *Drexler* crewman: Dudley Gallup; *Harry F. Bauer:* XO Robert M. Morgenthau; *Mississinewa* crewmen: Herb Daitch, Charles Scott; *Walke* crewman: Benjamin Edward Hall, Jr.

Books: Cutler, *The Battle of Leyte Gulf;* Drury and Clavin, *Halsey's Typhoon;* Friedman, *U.S. Destroyers;* Hara, *Japanese Destroyer Captain;* Hoyt, *The Battle of Leyte Gulf;* Jones, *Destroyer Squadron 23;* Mair, *Oil, Fire and Fate;* Manchester, *American Caesar;* Morison, *Leyte;* Raines, *Good Night Officially;* Sears, *The Last Epic Naval Battle;* Toland, *The Rising Sun.*

Articles: Boyd, "My Father's Band of Brothers"; Kennedy, "Victory at Sea."

Narrow Straits, October 1944

Author interviews with *Bache* crewman: Kittridge G. Hall; *Daly* crewman: James E. Kelly; *Leutze* crewman: John Perkins; *Melvin* CO: Barry K. Atkins; *Newcomb* crewmen: Raymond (Hoffer) Hoffman, Robert Reid; *PT-127* crewman: Don Bujold; *Richard P. Leary* crewman: Robert J. (Bob) Durand.

Books: Cutler, *Battle of Leyte Gulf;* Friedman, *U.S. Destroyers;* Hara, *Japanese Destroyer Captain;* Hoyt, *The Battle of Leyte Gulf;* Manchester, *American Caesar;* Morison, *Leyte;* Raines, *Good Night Officially;* Sears, *Last Epic Naval Battle;* Sheftall, *Blossoms in the Wind;* Toland, *Rising Sun.*

Becoming Young Gods, October 1944

Author interviews with *Gambier Bay* VC-10 pilots: Burt Bassett, Joseph D. McGraw, Richard W. Roby, Gene Seitz; *Kitkun Bay* crewmen:

Ronald Vaughn, Alfred Porter White; *St. Lo* VC-65 pilot: Thomas Van Brundt; *St. Lo* crewmen: Lawrence Rodman Collins, Evan H. Crawforth, Joseph A. Lehans, Bill Pumphrey, Brock Short; *Suwannee* crewmen: Charles P. Casello, Paul K. (Cactus) Walters.

Books: Cutler, *Battle of Leyte Gulf;* Friedman, *U.S. Destroyers;* Hara, *Japanese Destroyer Captain;* Hoyt, *The Battle of Leyte Gulf;* Manchester, *American Caesar;* Morison, *Leyte;* Raines, *Good Night Officially;* Sears, *Last Epic Naval Battle;* Sheftall, *Blossoms in the Wind;* Toland, *Rising Sun.*

To Get In and Get Aboard, November 1944

Author interviews with *Abner Read* crewmen: Lee P. Chase, Paul (Sam) McQueen; *Ammen* crewmen: Leon Darrow Carver, Giles Nelson Chancellor, Jr., Charles Francis Corgiat, Rolland Floch, Herbert James Garcia, William Earl Hart, Hubert Hunzeker, Joseph Isaac Masters, John Henry Moynahan, Warren E. Sandidge; *Bush* crewmen: Robert M. Aguilar, Edmond B. Bennett, Franklin Coit Butler, Robert R. Carney, James A. Collinson, Robert Melvin Cowherd, Edward D. Cregut, John E. Lavelle, P. A. (Tony) Lilly, Hilliard L. Lubin, Gilmer Haydon Thomas; *Claxton* crewmen: Tom Clyce, William E. Monfort, Robert W. Proudfoot, Charles Wilke; *Killen* crewmen: Raymond E. Cloud, Donice Copeland, Harold Johnson; *Richard P. Leary* crewman: Francis E. Gauthier.

Books: Manchester, *American Caesar;* Morison, *Leyte;* Raines, *Good Night Officially;* Sheftall, *Blossoms in the Wind;* Toland, *Rising Sun;* Warner and Warner, *Sacred Warriors.*

Other: *Abner Read* Action Report; *Claxton* War Diary, 1 November 1944.

HI-RI-HO-KEN-TEN, November 1944

Books: Hara, *Japanese Destroyer Captain;* Hoyt, *Kamikazes;* Lamont-Brown, *Kamikaze;* Mair, *Oil, Fire and Fate;* Manchester, *American Caesar;* Morison, *Leyte and Liberation of the Philippines;* Naito, *Thunder Gods;* Nagatsuka, *I Was a Kamikaze;* Sheftall, *Blossoms in the Wind;* Toland, *Rising Sun;* Warner and Warner, *Sacred Warriors.*

Target Paradise, November 1944

Author interviews with *Lexington* crewman: Robert R. Davis, Raymond E. Dora, John R. Edenfield, Richard J. Fullam, James T. Harper, Morris (Bud) King, Charles F. Ryberg, Ralph Truax; *Lexington* pilot: Bruce Williams (VF-19); *Mississinewa* crewmen: Fernando Cuevas, Herb Daitch, Charles Scott, Winston Whitten.

Books: Mair, *Oil, Fire and Fate;* Manchester, *American Caesar;* Morison, *Leyte;* Nagatsuka, *I Was a Kamikaze;* Sheftall, *Blossoms in the Wind;* Toland, *Rising Sun;* Warner and Warner, *Sacred Warriors.*

Other: Wartime diary of *Lexington* crewman Robert R. Davis.

Suicide at Its Best, November–December 1944

Author interviews with *Aulick* crewmen: J. R. Croker, Brian Masterson, Arthur Rhodes, Horace Wright; *Claxton* crewman: Tom Clyce; *Hull* crewman: Patrick H. Douhan; *Intrepid* crewmen and squadron personnel: J. Arthur Bohn, Edward T. Coyne, George B. DuBois, Warren J. Fegely, Lee Galbraith, Donald A. Lorimer, Salvatore Maschio, Wallace Russell (VT-18); *Reid* crewmen: Leonard L. Olson, Jesse N. Pickeral.

Books: Fahey, *Pacific War Diary;* Manchester, *American Caesar;* Morison, *Leyte;* Nagatsuka, *I Was a Kamikaze;* Raines, *Good Night Officially;* Sheftall, *Blossoms in the Wind;* Toland, *Rising Sun;* Warner and Warner, *Sacred Warriors.*

Other: *Dashiell:* Wartime journal of Fred M. Wright; *Hull:* E-mail correspondence with Liz Strannigan, Robert (Scotty) Wilson's niece; *Spence:* personal correspondence of Roy Merritt.

The Far Side of Leyte, December 1944

Author interviews with *Caldwell* crewmen: Vaughn Adjemian, Wesley F. Wadsworth; *Cooper* crewmen: Clarence Brinker, Thomas J. Hogan, Harvey K. Huff, James W. Villiers; *Hughes* crewmen: Oliver Jones, Gordon Sayner; *Mahan* crewman: George Pendergast; *Mugford* crewmen: James R. Cofer, George R. Garmon, Jr.

Books: Manchester, *American Caesar;* Morison, *Leyte;* Nagatsuka, *I Was a Kamikaze;* Raines, *Good Night Officially;* Sheftall, *Blossoms in the Wind;* Toland, *Rising Sun;* Warner and Warner, *Sacred Warriors.*

Other: *Caldwell* (DD-605): Action Report, 15 December 1944; *Cooper:*

Personal correspondence of Marvin H. Davis, dated 1 April 1945; *Liddle:* Harold S. Deal's journal, part 1, 12/6/43–1/17/45; *Ward:* Richard E. Farwell Internet narrative: hometown.aol.com/warddd139/richard2_storyll.html

The Shadow of Lingayen, December 1944

Author interviews with *Caldwell* crewmen: Vaughn Adjemian, Wesley F. Wadsworth; *Haraden* crewmen: John B. DiBella, Thomas J. Inman, Carl D. Spiron; *Nashville* crewmen: Ben Limbaugh, Rufus B. Thompson, Jr.; *Twiggs* crewman: Robert Melville.

Books: Drury and Clavin, *Halsey's Typhoon;* Morison, *Liberation of the Philippines;* Nagatsuka, *I Was a Kamikaze;* Raines, *Good Night Officially;* Sheftall, *Blossoms in the Wind;* Toland, *Rising Sun;* Warner and Warner, *Sacred Warriors.*

Other: *Dashiell:* E-mail correspondence from Fred M. Wright; *Haraden:* Written account by Thomas J. Inman, dated 30 March 2006.

Uncompensated Losses, December 1944

Author interviews with *Hull* crewman: Patrick H. Douhan; Liz Strannigan, niece of *Hull* crewman Robert Wilson; *Spence* crewman: Albert Rosley; Richard Strand, brother of *Spence* crewman Robert Louis Strand.

Books: Adamson and Kosko, *Halsey's Typhoons;* Drury and Clavin, *Halsey's Typhoon;* Jones, *Destroyer Squadron 23;* Morison, *Liberation of the Philippines;* Naito, *Thunder Gods;* Parkin, *Blood on the Sea;* Raines, *Good Night Officially;* Toland, *Rising Sun;* Warner and Warner, *Sacred Warriors.*

Other: *Hull:* Written account by Patrick H. Douhan; Text of letter dated 24 April 1945 provided by Liz Strannigan, niece of *Hull* crewman Robert Wilson; *Spence:* Telegram texts from Jeannette S. Marshbanks, Roy Louis Merritt's niece; Text of letter dated 28 February 1945, provided by Richard Strand, Robert Louis Strand's brother; Strand, *Naval History of the USS* Spence.

Corpses That Challenge the Clouds, January 1945

Author interviews with *Kitkun Bay* crewmen: Ronald Vaughn, Alfred Porter White; *O'Brien* crewmen: Avon R. Blevins, Thomas Roger Joseph, Jr., Sydney (Syd) Schafman, Ray Woods; *Ommaney Bay* crewman: Clifford Grant; *Richard P. Leary* crewmen: Roy Crawford, Lee Dawdy, Robert J. (Bob) Durand, Francis E. Gauthier, A. Robert Read, Leon Wolper; *Walke* crewmen: Benjamin Edward Hall, Jr., William (Bill) Rugh.

Books: Manchester, *American Caesar;* Morrison, *Liberation of the Philippines;* Raines, *Good Night Officially;* Sherrod, *On to Westward;* Toland, *Rising Sun.*

From Hot Rocks, February 1945

Author interviews with *Bennion* crewmen: Jesse C. Frazier, Robert (Bob) Pitts, and Harold M. Scott, Jr.; *Bush* crewman: Franklin Coit Butler; *Dashiell* crewman: Fred M. Wright; *LCS(L)-7* crewman: David Demeter; *LCS(L)-31* crewman: Robert A. Wells; *LCS(L)-49* crewman: Robert E. Alexander; *LCS(L)-51* crewman: Virgil C. Branch; *LCS(L)-118* crewman: Charles D. Towers; *LCS(L)-122* CO: Richard M. McCool; *Mannert L. Abele* crewmen: Gordon E. Chambers, Nick J. Korompilas, Jim Morris.

Books: Manchester, *American Caesar;* Morrison, *Liberation of the Philippines;* Nagatsuka, *I Was a Kamikaze;* Raines, *Good Night Officially;* Rielly, *Mighty Midgets at War;* Sherrod, *On to Westward;* Sledge, *With the Old Breed at Peleliu and Okinawa;* Toland, *Rising Sun.*
Articles: Gault, "The Mighty Midgets of Mindanao."
Other: *The Story of the* Bennion.

To the Great Loochoo, March 1945

Author interviews with *Franklin* crewmen: Bill Albrecht, Louis Casserino; *Halsey Powell* crewmen: Jack Barrett, Kenneth F. Courteau, Casey Kraft; *Hornet* VF-17 pilots: Ted Crosby, Willis E. (Bill) Hardy; *Randolph* crewman: Alan J. Sanderson; *Yorktown* VBF-9 pilot: John Wesolowski.

Books: Manchester, *American Caesar;* Morison, *Victory in the Pacific;* Nagatsuka, *I Was a Kamikaze;* Naito, *Thunder Gods;* Raines, *Good Night Officially;* Rielly, *Mighty Midgets at War;* Sherrod, *On to Westward;* Sledge, *With the Old Breed at Peleliu and Okinawa;* Stafford, *Little Ship, Big War;* Thompson, *Empires on the Pacific;* Toland, *Rising Sun.*
Other: Herod, *Gangway.*

Far from Ordinary Skies, 1 April–6 April 1945

Author interviews with *Bush* crewmen: Robert M. Aguilar, Edmond B. Bennett, Franklin Coit Butler, Robert R. Carney, James A. Collinson, Robert Melvin Cowherd, Edward D. Cregut, John E. Lavelle, Hilliard L. Lubin, Gilmer Haydon Thomas; *Harry F. Bauer* XO: Robert M. Morgenthau; *Henrico* crewmen: John Brooks, Calvin Carl, Robert G. (Duke) DeLuca, Glenn Grant, Leonard D. Howell, Tom Love, Gradus L. Shoemaker; *Kimberly* crewmen: Henry W. Fuller, Robert Gacke, Arthur McArthur; *LCS(L)-116* crewman: Ray B. Davis; *LCS(L)-118* crewman: Charles D. Towers; *O'Brien* crewmen: Avon R. Blevins, Thomas Roger Joseph, Jr., Sydney (Syd) Schafman, Ray Woods; *St. Mary's* crewman: Joe Crain.

Books: Manchester, *American Caesar;* Morison, *Victory in the Pacific;* Nagatsuka, *I Was a Kamikaze;* Naito, *Thunder Gods;* Raines, *Good Night Officially;* Reilly, *Mighty Midgets at War;* Sherrod, *On to Westward;* Sledge, *With the Old Breed at Peleliu and Okinawa;* Stafford, *Little Ship, Big War;* Toland, *Rising Sun.*

Articles: Baldwin, "Greatest Sea-Air Battle," Lardner, "A Reporter on Okinawa," Yoshida, "The End of Yamato."

Other: *LCS(L)-118:* Blanton, *Boston to Jacksonville;* Personal correspondence of Randall Lathrop.

A Perfect Day for What Happened, 6 April 1945

Author interviews with *Bush* crewmen: Robert M. Aguilar, Edmond B. Bennett, Franklin Coit Butler, Robert R. Carney, James A. Collinson, Robert Melvin Cowherd, Edward D. Cregut, John E. Lavelle, Hilliard L. Lubin, Gilmer Haydon Thomas; *Cassin Young* crewmen: Wallace M. Dickerman, Charles E. Serey; *Colhoun* crewmen: Edward E. Mueller, Joseph F. Orabona, James Monroe Pollock, Jr.; *Howorth* crewmen: Oscar Blank, Russell A. Bramble, Robert B. Lyons, Larry Nelson, Osmand (Ozzie) Schwiesow: *Hyman* crewmen: R. J. Acheson, John Warren Jones, Jr., Donald N. Milbrandt, Robert F. Moldenhauer, Raymond Novotny; *Leutze* crewmen: Eugene Balinski, Lewis W. Campbell, Jr., Malcolm Fortson, Jr., DeVal Gillette, Dr. John R. Goff, John Perkins; *Morris* crewman: David M. Aronsohn; *Mullany* crewmen: Matt Caulfield, Harlan Johnson, Gerald Lundgren, John C. Wiessler; *Newcomb* crewmen: John Bennard, Sr., Raymond (Hoffer) Hoffman, Royce W. Holyfield, Robert Reid, William R. (Bill) Smith.

Books: Morison, *Victory in the Pacific;* Nagatsuka, *I Was a Kamikaze;* Naito, *Thunder Gods;* Rielly, *Mighty Midgets at War;* Sheftall, *Blossoms in the Wind;* Stafford, *Little Ship, Big War;* Toland, *Rising Sun;* Warner and Warner, *Sacred Warriors.*

Other: *Ellyson:* Wartime journal of Dwight Donnewald.

"Delete All After 'Crazy,' " 7 April–13 April 1945

Author interviews: *Ammen* crewman: Rolland Floch; *Bennett* crewmen: Robert N. Boyd, Michael A. Capuano, Lawrence C. Finn, Charlie Greco, Edwin Hamilton, Frank Hanratty, Roland G. Laliberte, Donald Reese, Don Sheridan, John E. Syrek, Stanton J. Taylor; *Black* crewmen: Maurice (Mike) Couwenhoven, Fred Muth; *Bullard* crewman: Arthur R. Brown; *Bunker Hill*/VT-84 squadron crewmen: Edward Duffy, Thomas F. Kelly, Al Turnbull; *Cassin Young:* Wallace M. Dickerman, Charles E. Serey; *Gregory* crewmen: Eugene W. Leganza, Howard Tomlin; *Hand* crewmen: Herman C. Martin, Henry S. Smith, Theron (Ted) Teagle; *Lindsey* crewmen: Walter L. Gau, Leonard (Pete) Petersen; *LSM(R)-189* CO: James M. Stewart; *Mannert L. ABele* crewmen: Gordon E. Chambers, Nick J. Korompilas, Jim Morris; *Purdy* crewmen: Robert F. Grose, Kenneth E. Vogel; *Rall* crewman: Richard W. Graves; *Stanly* crewmen: Irvin D. Brewer, John C. Lott, Jr.

Books: Fahey, *Pacific War Diary;* Graves, *Men of Poseidon;* Hara, *Japanese Destroyer Captain;* Morison, *Victory in the Pacific;* Naito, *Thunder Gods;* Rielly, *Mighty Midgets at War;* Sheftall, *Blossoms in the Wind;* Sledge, *With the Old Breed at Peleliu and Okinawa;* Toland, *Rising Sun.*

Articles: Freeman, "Don't Shoot, We're Republicans!"; Newell, "Bunker Hill 9; Yamato 0!"; Yoshida, "The End of Yamato."

Other: *Ellyson:* Dwight Dean Donnewald, wartime diary; *LSM(R)-189:* Stewart, *90-Day Naval Wonder;* Rice, *Stanly: Diary of the Stanly and Its Actions.*

Wiseman's Cove, 13 April–30 April 1945

Author interviews with *Bennett* crewman: Don Sheridan; *Bowers* crewmen: Robert Graves, Frank Martinez, Anthony Natale, Henry Seeba; *Cassin Young* crewmen: Wallace M. Dickerman, Charles Serey; *Howorth* crewman: Russell A. Bramble; *Laffey* crewmen: Lawrence R. Delewski, Lloyd N. Hull, Aristides S. Phoutrides, O. Glen Radder, Shirley Dalton (Bob) Robertson, Edward Samp, Jr., Oliver J. Spriggs; *LCS(L)-34* XO: Edward V. Hathaway; *LCS(L)-51* crewman: Virgil C. Branch; *LCS(L)-116* crewman: Ray B. Davis; *Pringle* crewmen: Mike Goettina, William L. Herman, Milton Mapou; *Purdy* crewman: Robert F. Grose.

Books: Friedman, *U.S. Destroyers;* Morison, *Victory in the Pacific;* Stafford, *Little Ship, Big War.*

Articles: Harper, "USS Laffey's Pacific Ordeal"; Rooney, *Sailor* (interview with Julian Becton, Commanding Officer of the *USS Laffey*).

Other: Rogers, *Foote: Days in the Life of the* Foote; *Isherwood:* written account of crewman Elvan M. Hall supplied by son Marshall A. Hall.

The Same Tooth, May 1945

Author interviews with *Bache* crewmen: Hugo P. Cipriani, Kittridge G. Hall, John I. Vaught, Wade T. Winstead; *Braine* crewman: George Cintron; *Drexler* crewmen: Eugene Brick, Dudley Gallup, Fred W. Mitchell; *Evans* crewman: Martin M. Fleischer; *Hugh W. Hadley* crewmen: Robert I. Eaton, Jr., Douglas A. Eggen; *Little* crewman: Franklyn A. Whall; *Longshaw* crewmen: Harry Leonard, James R. Macomber, Joseph G. Schneider; *Macomb* crewman: James R. Tankersley; *Melvin* crewmen: William R. Campbell, Jr., Dr. Edgar A. (Ed) Hawk, William A. Robie; *O'Neill* crewman: James Creighton; *Wadsworth* crewman: Richard M. Lowe.

Books: Morison, *Victory in the Pacific;* Nagatsuka, *I Was a Kamikaze;* Naito, *Thunder Gods;* Rielly, *Mighty Midgets at War;* Rooney, *Mighty Midget U.S.S. LCS 82;* Sheftall, *Blossoms in the Wind;* Sledge, *With the Old Breed at Peleliu and Okinawa;* Stafford, *Little Ship, Big War;* Staton, *Fighting Bob;* Toland, *Rising Sun;* Warner and Warner, *Sacred Warriors.*

Articles: *Saturday Evening Post,* "Road Sign on the High Seas" (undetermined postwar date); *Seattle Times,* "Saw Wife and Five Children Killed by Jap Balloon Bomb"; Taglan, "Terror Floated over Montana."

Other: *LCS(L)-82:* Rooney, *Mighty Midget U.S.S. LCS-82;* O'Neill: Creighton, *No More War Stories; Robley D. Evans:* Staton, *The Fighting Bob; Wadsworth: Calling All Destroyers.*

Short of Home, June and July 1945

Author interviews with *Bush* crewman: Robert R. Carney; *Callaghan* crewmen: William Benton, Marland Moreau, Joe Sprouse, Woody Woodward; *Harry F. Bauer* XO: Robert M. Morgenthau; *Hull* crewman: Patrick H. Douhan; *Laffey* crewmen: Aristides S. Phoutrides, Edward Samp, Jr.; *LCS(L)-66* crewman: Robert P. Grimes; *LCS(L)-122* CO Richard M. McCool; *Longshaw* crewman: Joseph G. Schneider; *Pringle* crewman: Milton Mapou; *Twiggs* crewmen: Joe McDonough, Robert Melville, Leo L. Preston, Joseph L. Sanchez, Donald R. Witmer.

Books: Manchester, *American Caesar;* Morison, *Victory in the Pacific;* Nagatsuka, *I Was a Kamikaze;* Naito, *Thunder Gods;* Sheftall, *Blossoms in the Wind;* Sherrod, *On to Westward;* Sledge, *With the Old Breed at Peleliu and Okinawa;* Stafford, *Little Ship, Big War;* Toland, *Rising Sun;* Warner and Warner, *Sacred Warriors.*

Articles: *Camden Courier-Post,* "Camden Man's Life Saved by Shipmate"; Freeman, "Don't Shoot, We're Republicans!"; *Philadelphia Inquirer,* "New Bridge for Blasted Warship."

Other: *Callaghan:* September 1995 letter from *Callaghan* crewmember Bill Benton to Rich Cunningham, nephew of Samuel T. Elrod, killed in action; Rielly, *Mighty Midgets at War; Twiggs:* Personal written account by Don Witmer.

★ Glossary ★

U.S. and Allied Historical Names, Aircraft, and Acronyms and Terminology

Historical Names

Rear Admiral William H. P. Blandy, USN (1890–1954) Commander, Group I Amphibious Force, during the assault on Kerama Retto.

Rear Admiral Gerald F. Bogan, USN (1894–1973) Task Group 38.2.

Lieutenant General Simon Bolivar Buckner, Jr., USA (1886–1945) Commander Tenth Army for Operation Iceberg.

Captain Arleigh A. ("31-knot") Burke, USN (1901–1996) Chief of Staff to Vice Admiral Marc Mitscher; earlier, Commander Destroyer Squadron 23.

Lieutenant Colonel James (Jimmy) Doolittle, USAAF (1896–1993) Commander of the 1942 aerial bombing raid against Japan's home islands.

Brigadier General William C. Dunckel, USA Commanded Western Visayen Task Force for Mindoro invasion.

Vice Admiral Frank Jack Fletcher, USN (1885–1973) Task force commander during the invasion of Guadalcanal and Tulagi.

Major General Roy S. Geiger, USMC (1885–1947) Commanded III Amphibious Corps in the Battle of Okinawa; assumed command of the Tenth Army upon the combat death of Lt. General Simon Bolivar Buckner, Jr.

Vice Admiral Robert L. Ghormley, USN (1883–1958) Commander

South Pacific Area and South Pacific Force during the early stages of the campaign to seize Guadalcanal and Tulagi.

Admiral William F. Halsey, Jr. USN (1882–1959) Commander U.S. 3rd Fleet.

Andrew Jackson Higgins (1886–1952) Founder and owner of Higgins Industries, the New Orleans-based manufacturer of Higgins boats during World War II.

Lieutenant General George C. Kenney, USAAF (1889–1977) U.S. Army Air Forces general and commander of the Allied air forces in the Southwest Pacific.

Fleet Admiral Ernest J. King, USN (1878–1956) Commander in Chief, U.S. Fleet and Chief of Naval Operations.

Admiral Thomas C. Kinkaid, USN (1888–1972) Commander Allied Naval Forces in the South West Pacific Area and concurrently commander U.S. 7th Fleet

William Franklin "Frank" Knox (1874–1944) Secretary of the Navy under Franklin D. Roosevelt during most of World War II.

Lieutenant General Walter Krueger, USA (1881–1967) General commanding the U.S. 6th Army in the South West Pacific Area.

General Douglas MacArthur, USA (1880–1964) Commander, South Pacific Forces in June–October 1942, during the early stages of the campaign to seize Guadalcanal and Tulagi; later Commander, South Pacific Area.

Vice Admiral John Sidney (Jock) McCain, USN (1884–1945) Commanded Task Force 38, part of the U.S. 3rd Fleet.

Vice Admiral Marc (Pete) Mitscher, USN (1887–1947) Commander Task Force 58, part of the U.S. 5th Fleet

Fleet Admiral Chester W. Nimitz, USN (1885–1966) Commander of Pacific Naval Forces

Vice Admiral Jesse B. Oldendorf, USN (1887–1974) Commanded U.S. Navy's Bombardment and Fire Support Group during the Battle of Leyte Gulf.

Major General Harry Schmidt, USMC (1886–1968) Commanding General of the Fifth Amphibious Corps during the battle of Iwo Jima.

Rear Admiral Forrest P. Sherman, USN (1896–1951) Deputy Chief of Staff to Admiral Chester W. Nimitz.

Lieutenant General Holland M. Smith, USMC (1882–1967), U.S. Marine Corps general led the V Amphibious Corps during major amphibious assaults in the Central Pacific.

Major General Ralph C. Smith, USA (1894–1998) Commanded the U.S. Army's 27th Infantry Division during the battle of Saipan.

Rear Admiral Clifton A. F. Sprague, USN (1896–1955) Commanded Task Unit 77.4.3—Taffy 3—during the action off Samar, part of the Battle of Leyte Gulf ; (not related to Thomas L. Sprague).

Rear Admiral Thomas L. Sprague, USN (1894–1972) Commanded Task Group 77.4 and Task Unit 77.4.1—Taffy 1—during the action off Samar, part of the Battle of Leyte Gulf (not related to Clifton Sprague).

Admiral Raymond A. Spruance, USN (1886–1969) Commander U.S. 5th Fleet.

Rear Admiral Arthur D. Struble, USN (1894–1983) Commanded a 7th Fleet amphibious group during landing operations in the Philippines.

Vice Admiral Richmond K. Turner, USN (1885–1961) Commander, Task Force 51, Joint Expeditionary Force for the invasion of Okinawa.

Major General Alexander "Archie" Vandegrift, USMC (1887–1973) United States Marine Corps general who commanded 1st Marine Division on Guadalcanal; later Marine Corps Commandant.

Aircraft

Avenger   Grumman carrier-based torpedo bomber. Alphanumeric designations include TBF and TBM.

Black Cat   U.S. patrol bomber/float plane equipped for night operations. Alphanumeric designations include PBY-5.

Corsair   Chance Vought land- and carrier-based fighter aircraft Alphanumeric designations include F4U.

Dauntless   Douglas carrier-based dive-bomber Alphanumeric designations include SBD-5.

Hellcat   Grumman carrier-based fighter-bomber. Alphanumeric designations include F6F.

Helldiver   Curtiss carrier-based dive-bomber. Alphanumeric designations include SB2C.

Lightning   Lockheed-built twin-engine, twin-tail Army Air Force fighter aircraft. Alphanumeric designations include P-38.

Mustang The North American Aviation-built, long-range, single-seat fighter aircraft. Alphanumeric designations include P-51.

Superfortress U.S. Army Air Force four-engine strategic bomber used in aerial bombing raids on Japan. Alphanumeric designation B-29.

Wildcat U.S. Navy fighter (predecessor of Hellcat). Alphanumeric designations include F4F and FM-2.

Acronyms and Terminology

AA or **AAA** Antiaircraft (AA) or antiaircraft artillery (AAA Also called flak or Triple-A).

AA Special Antiaircraft projectiles equipped with VT fuses.

AAF Army Air Forces.

AGC Alphabetic designation for U.S. Navy amphibious force command ships.

AGO Assistant gunnery officer.

amphtracs (amtracs) Amphibious tractors; vehicles for landing troops during Pacific island invasions; Navy designation LVT.

AP Armor piercing.

APA Alphabetic designation for U.S. Navy attack transport ships.

APD Alphabetic designation for U.S. Navy high-speed transport ships (converted destroyers).

Big Blue Blanket (B.B.B.) Tactic of keeping fighter aircraft over Japanese air bases to prevent planes from taking off.

Binnacle list Ship's sick list.

Breeches buoy Canvas or metal rig suspended by lines used to transfer personnel or supplies between ships at sea.

Buck Rogers shells Nickname for antiaircraft projectiles equipped with VT fuses.

bulkhead Wall—Navy (and Marine) terminology.

CA Alphabetic designation for U.S. Navy heavy cruiser.

Cactus Air Force Name given aircraft squadrons flying from Henderson Field during the Battle for Guadalcanal.

'Canal Guadalcanal; nickname used by veterans of the Solomons invasion.

C.A.P. Combat air patrol.

CIC Combat Information Center.

CL   Alphabetic designation for U.S. Navy light cruiser.

CO   Ship, squadron, or unit commanding officer.

crossing the line   Shipboard hazing ceremonies during equatorial crossing to "induct" sailors who had not yet "crossed the line."

crossing the T   During a surface sea battle, maneuvering ships into position to bear all guns on an advancing column of ships while in turn masking—blocking—the aim of guns on ships of the advancing column.

CV   Alphabetic designation for U.S. Navy fleet aircraft carrier.

CVE   Alphabetic designation for U.S. Navy escort aircraft carrier.

CVL   Alphabetic designation for U.S. Navy light aircraft carrier.

DD   Alphabetic designation for U.S. Navy destroyer.

DE   Alphabetic designation for U.S. Navy destroyer escorts.

Desron   Destroyer squadron.

DM   Alphabetic designation for U.S. Navy destroyer minelayer.

DMS   Alphabetic designation for U.S. Navy destroyer minesweeper.

dogged down   secured or made watertight (e.g. shipboard hatches) by use of mechanical latches.

Elsie Items   Nickname for LCI (Landing Craft, Infantry).

FIDO   Fighter director officer.

fireman   Navy enlisted occupational specialty working with propulsion and propulsion-related equipment.

flag plot   shipboard command and control (flag) space used by task force or task unit admiral and staff.

flattops   informal name for aircraft carriers.

Forager   Operational code name for the invasion of Saipan.

GQ   General quarters, a U.S. Navy ship's highest degree of readiness with all crewmembers assigned to specific battle stations.

Great Loochoo   Okinawa.

gunner's mate   Navy petty officer occupational specialty performing duties related to naval guns and explosives.

handy billy   Portable gas-engine-powered water pump.

H-hour   Precise time for scheduled invasion landing or other offensive action.

Higgins boat   Barge-like troop and small vehicle amphibious landing craft, usually with a full width bow ramp; official designation LCVP.

Hose Nose   Nickname for Corsair fighter aircraft.

I.C. Internal Communications.

Iceberg Code name for the U.S. invasion of Okinawa.

IFF Identification, Friend or Foe—an electronic transmitter/receiver device to detect the "friend or foe" identity of approaching aircraft.

King II Operational Code name for the U.S. invasion of Leyte in the Philippines.

knot A unit of speed used for maritime and aviation purposes. One knot is roughly equivalent to 1.5 mph.

LCI Letter designation for U.S. Navy Landing Craft, Infantry.

LCT Letter designation for U.S. Navy Landing Craft, Tank.

LCVP Letter designation for U.S. Navy Landing Craft Vehicle, Personnel—the official designation for the Higgins Boat.

L-Day 1 April 1945, the date for the American troop landings on Okinawa.

left-arm rates U.S. Navy Deck and engineering occupational specialists who wore their petty officer insignias on their left sleeves.

Little Beavers Nickname for Destroyer Squadron 23.

LORAN Acronym for "long-range navigation" technology.

LSO Landing Signal Officer.

LST Letter designation for U.S. Navy Landing Ship, Tank.

LVT Letter designation for U.S. Navy Landing Vehicle, Tracked (Amphtrac).

MacArthur's Navy Nickname for the U.S. 7th Fleet, which primarily supported General Douglas MacArthur's offensive operations in the Southwest Pacific.

machinist's mate Navy petty officer occupational specialty responsible for operation, maintenance, and repair of ship propulsion machinery and auxiliary equipment.

Mae West Common nickname of an inflatable life jacket made of cotton with inflatable rubber bladders.

Marianas Turkey Shoot Name given the first phase of the June 1944 Battle of the Philippine Sea.

Marsden Matting Standardized, perforated steel matting material used for the rapid construction of temporary runways and landing strips.

murder hole Term given bow ramp opening on the Higgins boat.

N.C.O. Noncommissioned officer; also NCO.

Navy Cross   The second highest medal awarded by the Department of the Navy and the second highest award given for valor.

Old Breed   Term of respect for Marine Corps veterans of early World War II battles in the Solomon and Gilbert Islands.

Omaha Beach   Code name for one of the landing beaches during the 6 June 1944 invasion of Europe at Normandy.

overhead   Ceiling—Navy (and U.S. Marine Corps) terminology.

polliwogs   Sailors who have not yet crossed the equator on board a ship.

PT   Patrol torpedo boat.

quartermaster   Navy petty officer occupational specialty performing navigation duties.

repeater   Radar visual display console.

right-arm rates   Technical, communications, radar, radio, and signaling occupational specialists who wore their petty officer insignias on their right sleeves.

scuttlebutt   Nautical term for a shipboard water fountain or water cask; more commonly used as slang for "information" or "gossip."

SG radar   Letter designation for surface search radar installed on U.S. Navy ships.

shellbacks   Sailors who have crossed the equator on board a ship.

shipfitter   Navy petty officer occupational specialty performing sheet-metal and plumbing duties.

Shoestring   Informal name for Operation Watchtower.

single purpose   Artillery capable of being used for surface-to-aerial or surface-to-surface warfare, but not both.

SK radar   Letter designation for aerial search radar installed on U.S. Navy ships.

striker   An enlisted sailor qualified for an occupational specialty (rate), but has not yet become a petty officer (e.g., radar striker).

Task Force 38   Main component of the Navy's 5th Fleet (when commanded by William Halsey).

Task Force 58   Main component of the Navy's 5th Fleet (when commanded by Raymond Spruance).

TBS   Talk between ships: a wireless voice circuit for short-range communications between ships.

Thach Weave   Combat flight maneuver originally credited to U.S. Navy fighter pilot John S. "Jimmy" Thach.

tin cans   Widely used informal designation for destroyers, destroyer escorts, and ships converted from destroyers for specialized purposes.

Tokyo Express   Name given to IJN night supply convoys delivering personnel, supplies, and equipment to Japanese forces operating in the Solomon Islands (and later in the Philippines).

torpedo juice   Illicit shipboard alcoholic drink, often distilled from a combination of high-proof, alcohol-based torpedo fuel and citrus juice.

Trade School   Informal name for the U.S. Naval Academy.

Triple A   See AAA.

unrep   Underway replenishment.

UDT   Underwater demolition team.

VT   Variable-time fuses used on U.S. Navy antiaircraft guns.

Watchtower   Code name for the invasion of Guadalcanal and Tulagi; also nicknamed "Shoestring."

XO   Ship, squadron, or unit executive officer; second in command.

yeoman   Navy petty officer occupational specialty performing administrative and clerical duties.

Japanese Historical Names, Aircraft, and Terminology

Historical Names

Vice Admiral Shigeru Fukudome (1891–1971), Commander of 2nd Naval Air Fleet.

Admiral Mineichi Koga (1885–1944) Commander, Japanese Combined Fleet, successor to Yamamoto.

Kuniaki Koiso (1880–1950) Army general and 41st prime minister of Japan from July 1944 to April 1945.

Lieutenant General Tadamichi Kuribayashi (1891–1945) Overall commander of the Japanese garrison during the Battle of Iwo Jima.

Vice Admiral Takeo Kurita (1889–1977) Commander in Chief, Japanese Second Fleet during the Battle of Leyte Gulf.

Vice Admiral Teiji Nishimura (1889–1944) Commanded battleships, a heavy cruiser, and several destroyers during the Battle of Leyte Gulf.

Rear Admiral Sueo Obayashi Commander, Carrier Division 3, part of Japan's Mobile Fleet.

Vice Admiral Takijiro Onishi (1891–1945) Commander of 1st Naval Air Fleet (became chief of staff to Shigeru Fukudome when Naval Air Fleets were consolidated).

Vice Admiral Jisaburo Ozawa (1886–1966) Commander, Japanese Mobile Fleet.

Vice Admiral Kiyohide Shima (1878–1973) Commanded the "Second Striking Force" of three cruisers and seven destroyers in the Battle of Surigao Strait.

Admiral Shigetaro Shimada (1883–1976) Appointed Naval Chief in February 1944, but removed in July 1944, after the fall of Saipan.

Lieutenant General Sosaku Suzuki (1891–1945) General in charge of the defense of the Central Philippines in 1944.

Prime Minister Hideki Tojo (1884–1948) The Prime Minister of Japan during much of World War II, from October 1941 to July 1944.

General Kyoji Tominaga Fourth Air Army commander.

Admiral Soemu Toyoda (1885–1957) Commander, Japanese Combined Fleet following the deaths of Yamamoto and Koga.

Vice Admiral Matome Ugaki (1890–1945) Japanese admiral in charge of IJN *kamikaze* forces during the last stages of the war. Flew a self-appointed—and apparently unsuccessful—*kamikaze* mission on 15 August 1945 in the hours following Japan's capitulation.

Lieutenant General Mitsuru Ushijima (1887–1945) Japanese general defending against American invasion of Okinawa.

Admiral Isoroku Yamamoto (1884–1943) Commander, Japanese Combined Fleet, predecessor to Koga.

Lieutenant General Tomoyuki Yamashita (1885–1946) General in overall command of Japanese Imperial Army forces in the Philippines.

*Aircraft**

Ann   Mitsubishi *Ki*-30 Type 97 light bomber.
Betty   Mitsubishi G4M medium bomber designed and built for IJN.

*Japanese aircraft are listed alphabetically by the U.S.-assigned designation.

Frances   Yokosuka P1Y *Ginga* (Milky Way) IJN land-based, twin-engine fighter-bomber.

Hamp   Mitsubishi *Zero-Sen* A6M (model 32 variant) carrier-based fighter-bomber.

Jill   Nakajima B6N *Tenzan* (Heavenly Mountain); IJN's standard torpedo bomber for the final years of World War II.

Judy   Yokosuka D4Y *Suisei* shipborne torpedo bomber.

Kate   Nakajima B5N; IJN's standard torpedo bomber for the first years of World War II.

Lily   Kawasaki *Ki*-48; Japanese Army twin-engine light bomber.

Nate   Nakajima *Ki*-27 Japanese Army fighter aircraft.

Nick   Kawasaki *Ki*-45 *Toryu* (Dragon Slayer); Japanese Army twin-engine fighter aircraft.

Oscar   Nakajima *Ki*-43 *Hayabusa* (Peregrine Falcon); IJA single-engine land-based fighter.

Sonia   Mitsubishi *Ki*-51 Type 99; assault aircraft used primarily in the China-Burma-India theater, but later adapted for suicide use.

Val   Aichi D3A; Primary IJN carrier-borne dive-bomber.

Zeke   Mitsubishi *Zero-Sen* A6M carrier-based fighter-bomber.

Terminology

A-Go   Operation A, the operational plan to attack American naval forces in a decisive battle close to Japan's interior supply lines.

Bushido   "Way of the Warrior," a Japanese code of conduct and a way of life.

hachimaki   Stylized headband, usually made of red or white cloth, worn as a symbol of perseverance or effort by the wearer; famously worn by *kamikaze* pilots.

IJA   Imperial Japanese Army.

IJN   Imperial Japanese Navy.

IMA   Imperial Military Academy—Japan's West Point.

kesshi   "Dare to die"; applied to combat tactics that, while not expressly suicidal, very likely would result in death.

Kikusui   "Floating chrysanthemums"; symbolic designation for the series of concentrated aerial suicide raids conducted by the Japanese against the U.S. Navy ships off Okinawa between 1 April and 22 June 1945. The aerial suicide component of Operation *Ten-Go.*

Long Lance American designation for Japanese surface-to-surface torpedo.

Marudai A name for the project to design, develop, test, and deploy the *Ōka* suicide rocket-assisted glide bomber.

Ōka Cherry Blossom; the official name eventually given the Project *Marudai* special attack craft.

Senjin Kun Ethics in Battle: code of battle ethics distributed to every member of the Japanese armed forces.

Shinpu **Special Attack Unit** First IJN aerial *kamikaze* unit, organized in the Philippines.

taiatari seishin Body crashing spirit.

Ten-Go "Operation Heaven One"; designation for the massed air attacks (both suicide and conventional) and surface naval attacks launched against the U.S. invasion fleet at Okinawa. The surface component involved the deployment of battleship *Yamato.*

Tokkotai (tokkō) Special attack corps.

Yamato damashi Japanese fighting spirit.

★ Sources and Acknowledgments ★

Personal Interviews

In researching and writing this book, I interviewed literally hundreds of surviving veterans who (as young officers and enlisted sailors and soldiers) directly experienced the *kamikaze* attacks beginning late in 1944 through to August 1945, the end of the war in the Pacific. If the sample I spoke with is any indication, nearly all continue to lead vital lives—a circumstance for which they have themselves to thank. Their accomplishments made possible an unprecedented era of prosperity in which dramatically fuller and longer lives became possible.

As I talked with these remarkable men about events now more than sixty years past, the emphasis was not primarily on dates, times, or the "big picture." There are many other sources for such details. Instead the focus was on what each man (to the best of his recollection) "saw, heard, said, felt, or experienced" during moments of battle. When integrated with additional interviews and tempered with research into personal writings, source documents, and other histories, the accounts build into what I hope is a unique, poignant, and compelling mosaic.

In crediting the indispensable interview sources listed here I must also apologize to some who are not named—and add a disclaimer for those who are.

First the apology: I simply underestimated the response I would get as I identified and established contact with eyewitnesses to these attacks. Although I interviewed hundreds, I was not able to interview everyone I might have. If there are instances where their unique accounts would have added new insights and perspectives, I am truly sorry that time and deadline did not permit interviews. Their names are found in "Roll Call" (as are the names of the interviewees), and I sincerely hope that this book validates their experiences, achievements, and legacies.

At the same time, I also want to absolve the many veterans I did interview of any responsibility for what in the end are my own editorial choices, conclusions, interpretations, and errors. The choices, emphasis, inclusions, and exclusions of this book are mine. To the extent I got things right, I have these many men, collectively and individually, to thank. To the extent I got things wrong, or incomplete, I alone am responsible.

USS *Abner Read* (DD-526): Lee P. Chase, Paul (Sam) McQueen
USS *Ammen* (DD-527): Leon Darrow Carver, Giles Nelson Chancellor, Jr., Charles Francis Corgiat, Rolland Floch, Herbert James Garcia, William Earl Hart, Hubert Hunzeker, Joseph Isaac Masters, John Henry Moynahan, Warren E. Sandidge
USS *Aulick* (DD-569): J. R. Croker, Brian Masterson, Arthur Rhodes, Horace Wright
USS *Bache* (DD-470): Hugo P. Cipriani, Kittridge G. Hall, John I. Vaught, Wade T. Winstead
USS *Bennett* (DD-473): Robert N. Boyd, Michael A. Capuano, Lawrence C. Finn, Charlie Greco, Edwin Hamilton, Frank Hanratty, Roland G. Laliberte, Donald Reese, Don Sheridan, John E. Syrek, Stanton J. Taylor
USS *Bennion* (DD-662): Jesse C. Frazier, Robert (Bob) Pitts, Harold M. Scott, Jr.
USS *Black* (DD-666): Maurice (Mike) Couwenhoven, Fred Muth
USS *Borie* (DD-704): Charles A. Besse, Jerome A. Harvey, Robert E. White, Stuart K. White, Sr.
USS *Bowers* (DE-637): Robert Graves, Frank Martinez, Anthony Natale, Henry Seeba
USS *Boyd* (DD-544): Edward Shaffer, Julius Warzybok
USS *Braine* (DD-630): George Cintron
USS *Bryant* (DD-665): Daniel J. DeRoch, Jr., Alvin L. Gallin, Dale B. Hanson
USS *Bullard* (DD-660): Arthur R. Brown

USS *Bunker Hill* (CV-17): Edward Duffy (VT-84), Thomas F. Kelly (VT-84), Al Turnbull (VT-84)

USS *Bush* (DD-529): Robert M. Aguilar, Edmond B. Bennett, Franklin Coit Butler, Robert R. Carney, James A. Collinson, Robert Melvin Cowherd, Edward D. Cregut, John E. Lavelle, P. A. (Tony) Lilly, Hilliard L. Lubin, Gilmer Haydon Thomas

USS *Caldwell* (DD-605): Vaughn Adjemian, Wesley F. Wadsworth

USS *Callaghan* (DD-792): William Benton, Marland Moreau, Joe Sprouse, E. C. Woody Woodward

USS *Cassin Young* (DD-793): Wallace M. Dickerman, Charles E. Serey

USS *Clarence K. Bronson* (DD-668): Gil Girdauskas

USS *Claxton* (DD-571): Tom Clyce, William E. Monfort, Robert W. Proudfoot, Charles Wilke

USS *Colhoun* (DD-801): Edward E. Mueller, Joseph F. Orabona, James Monroe Pollock, Jr.

USS *Cooper* (DD-695): Clarence Brinker, Thomas J. Hogan, Harvey K. Huff, James W. Villiers

USS *Cowell* (DD-547): Donald E. Roller, Dean E. Scully, Chester Trojanowski

USS *Daly* (DD-519): Charles L. Dunn, James E. Kelly, William J. Wyatt

USS *Dashiell* (DD-659): Fred M. Wright

USS *Dewey* (DD-349): Lorin J. Nelson

USS *Drexler* (DD-741): Eugene Brick, Dudley Gallup, Fred W. Mitchell

USS *Evans* (DD-552): Martin M. Fleischer

USS *Franklin* (CV-13): Bill Albrecht, Louis Casserino

USS *Gambier Bay* (CVE-73): Burt Bassett (VC-10), Joseph D. McGraw (VC-10), Richard W. Roby (VC-10), Gene Seitz (VC-10)

USS *Gregory* (DD-802): Eugene W. Leganza, Howard Tomlin

USS *Halsey Powell* (DD-686): Jack Barrett, Kenneth F. Courteau, Casey Kraft

USS *Hank* (DD-702): Herman C. Martin, Henry S. Smith, Theron (Ted) Teagle

USS *Haraden* (DD-585): John B. DiBella, Thomas J. Inman, Carl D. Spiron

USS *Harry F. Bauer* (DD-738/DM-26): Robert M. Morgenthau

USS *Henrico* (APA-45): John Brooks, Calvin Carl, Robert G. (Duke) DeLuca, Glenn Grant, Leonard D. Howell, Joseph J. Javaruski, Raymond J. LePage, Tom G. Love, Gradus L. Shoemaker

USS *Hornet* (CV-12): Ted Crosby (VF-17), Willis E. (Bill) Hardy (VF-17)

USS *Howorth* (DD-592): Oscar Blank, Russell A. Bramble, Robert B. Lyons, Larry Nelson, Osmand (Ozzie) Schwiesow

USS *Hughes* (DD-410): Oliver Jones, Gordon Sayner

USS *Hugh W. Hadley* (DD-774): Robert I. Eaton, Jr., Douglas A. Eggen

USS *Hull* (DD-350): Patrick H. Douhan

USS *Hyman* (DD-732): R. J. Acheson, John Warren Jones, Jr., Donald N. Milbrandt, Robert F. Moldenhauer, Raymond Novotny

USS *Intrepid* (CV-11): J. Arthur Bohn, Edward T. Coyne, George B. DuBois, Warren J. Fegely, Lee Galbraith, Donald A. Lorimer, Salvatore Maschio, Wallace Russell (VT-18)

USS *Killen* (DD-593): Raymond E. Cloud, Donice Copeland, Harold Johnson

USS *Kimberly* (DD-521): Henry W. Fuller, Robert Gacke, Arthur McArthur

USS *Kitkun Bay* (CVE-71): Ronald Vaughn, Alfred Porter White

USS *Laffey* (DD-724): Lawrence R. Delewski, Lloyd N. Hull, Aristides S. Phoutrides, O. Glen Radder, Shirley Dalton (Bob) Robertson, Edward Samp, Jr., Oliver J. Spriggs

LCS(L)-7: David Demeter; *LCS(L)-27:* Harry G. Meister; *LCS(L)-31:* Robert A. Wells; *LCS(L)-34:* Edward V. Hathaway; *LCS(L)-49:* Robert E. Alexander; *LCS(L)-51:* Virgil C. Branch; *LCS(L)-61:* A. P. (Pete) Jensen, Walter Longhurst, Mark V. Sellis; *LCS(L)-64:* John E. Littleton, Reverend Joseph C. McLendon; *LCS(L)-66:* Robert P. Grimes; *LCS(L)-82:* John A. Rooney; *LCS(L)-86:* Maurice T. Jenson; *LCS(L)-87:* Rosse V. Long, William John Mason; *LCS(L)-116:* Ray B. Davis; *LCS(L)-118:* Charles D. Towers; *LCS(L)-122:* Richard M. McCool

USS *Leutze* (DD-481): Eugene Balinski, Lewis W. Campbell, Jr., Malcolm Fortson, Jr., DeVal Gillette, Dr. John R. Goff, John Perkins

USS *Lexington* (CV-16): Robert R. Davis, Raymond E. Dora, John R. Edenfield, Richard J. Fullam, James T. Harper, Morris (Bud) King,

Warren E. McLellan (VT-16), Charles F. Ryberg, Ralph Truax, Arthur P. Whiteway (VF-16), Bruce Williams (VF-19)

USS *Lindsey* (DD-771/DM-32): Walter L. Gau, Leonard (Pete) Petersen

USS *Little* (DD-803): Franklyn A. Whall

USS *Longshaw* (DD-559): Harry Leonard, James R. Macomber, Joseph G. Schneider

LSM(R)-189: James M. Stewart

USS *Macomb* (DD-458/DMS-23): James R. Tankersley

USS *Mahan* (DD-364): George Pendergast

USS *Mannert L. Abele* (DD-733): Gordon E. Chambers, Nick J. Korompilas, Jim Morris

USS *Melvin* (DD-680): Barry K. Atkins, William R. Campbell, Jr., Dr. Edgar A. (Ed) Hawk, William A. Robie

USS *Mississinewa* (AO-59): Fernando Cuevas, Herb Daitch, Charles Scott, Winston Whitten

USS *Monssen* (DD-798): Virgil Melvin

USS *Morris* (DD-417): David M. Aronsohn

USS *Mugford* (DD-389): James R. Cofer, George R. Garmon, Jr.

USS *Mullany* (DD-528): Matt Caulfield, Harlan Johnson, Gerald Lundgren, John C. Wiessler

USS *Nashville* (CL-43): Ben Limbaugh, Rufus B. Thompson, Jr.

USS *Newcomb* (DD-586): John Bennard, Sr., Raymond (Hoffer) Hoffman, Royce W. Holyfield, Robert Reid, William R. (Bill) Smith

USS *New Orleans* (CA-32): James Montgomery

USS *O'Brien* (DD-725): Avon R. Blevins, Thomas Roger Joseph, Jr., Sydney (Syd) Schafman, Ray Woods

USS *Ommaney Bay* (CVE-79): Clifford Grant

USS *O'Neill* (DE-188): James Creighton

USS *PC-1128:* James E. Gilbert

USS *Pringle* (DD-477): Mike Goettina, William L. Herman, Milton Mapou

PT-127: Donald Bujold

USS *Purdy* (DD-734): Robert F. Grose, Kenneth E. Vogel

USS *Putnam* (DD-757): William Harrison

USS *Rall* (DE-304): Richard W. Graves

USS *Randolph* (CV-15): Alan J. Sanderson

USS *Reid* (DD-369): Leonard L. Olson, Jesse N. Pickeral

USS *Richard P. Leary* (DD-664): Roy Crawford, Lee Dawdy, Robert J. (Bob) Durand, Francis E. Gauthier, A. Robert Read, Leon Wolper

USS *Spence* (DD-512): Albert Rosley

USS *Stanly* (DD-478): Irvin D. Brewer, John C. Lott, Jr.

USS *St. Lo* (CVE-63): Lawrence Rodman Collins, Evan H. (Holly) Crawforth, Joseph A. Lehans, Bill Pumphrey, Brock Short, Thomas B. Van Brunt (VC-65)

USS *St. Mary's* (APA-126): Joe Crain

USS *Suwannee* (CVE-27): Charles P. Casello, Paul K. (Cactus) Walters

USS *Twiggs* (DD-591): Joe McDonough, Robert Melville, Leo L. Preston, Joseph L. Sanchez, Donald R. Witmer

USS *Wadsworth* (DD-516): Richard M. Lowe

USS *Walke* (DD-723): Benjamin Edward Hall, Jr., William (Bill) Rugh

USS *Yorktown* (CV-10): John Wesolowski (VBF-9)

USS *Zellars* (DD-777): Arthur H. Barnes

In addition to these eyewitness sources, there are a number of family members and friends of veterans (living and deceased) who were especially helpful in making introductions, arranging interviews, and providing access to source materials such as diaries and letters. A list of these people includes USS *Bennett* (DD-473): Patricia Caler and Tom Greco, children of Charlie Greco; USS *Bunker Hill* (CV-17): Dax Berg (grandson of crewman Robert Schock), Miyuki (Mickie) Grace (translator); USS *Bush* (DD-529): Ted Mayhugh, son of crewman S. R. (Ray) Mayhugh; USS *Caldwell* (DD-605): Roger James Cratsley, son of Frank Melvin Cratsley; USS *Callaghan* (DD-792): Rich Cunningham whose uncle Samuel T. Elrod was a crewman killed in action; USS *Dickerson* (DD-157/ADP-21): Edward Geleski, whose uncle Edward J. Young was a crewman killed in action; USS *Drexler* (DD-741): Sandy Cleveland, a reunion coordinator for veterans of this ship; USS *Ellyson* (DD-454/DMS-19): Mona E. Donnewald, daughter of crewman Dwight Donnewald; USS *Hall* (DD-583): Patricia Horn, daughter of crewman Henry Cattoretti; USS *Haraden* (DD-585): George Zay, nephew of crewman Clyde Lewis, Jr.; USS *Hull* (DD-350): Liz Strannigan, niece of Robert Wilson, a crewman lost at sea; USS *Mississinewa*

(AO-59): Mike Mair, son of crewman John A. Mair; National Association of USS LCS(L) 1–130: Ginny Rooney, wife of John Rooney, LCS(L)-82 crewman; and USS Spence (DD-512): Roy Cope, Jeannette S. Marshbanks.

Personal Writings

Limited Editions, Memoirs, Monographs, and Compilations

Baldwin, Jack L. The Days of War as Remembered by J. L. Baldwin.

Beto, Richard. Frank Beto and the Mighty Chase.

Blanton, Earl. Boston to Jacksonville (41,000 Miles by Sea) USS LCS(L)(3)-118.

Cartier, Giles E. A Life.

Creighton, James A. No More War Stories.

Dunn, Charles L. Memories of a Tin Can Sailor.

Gebhardt, Joseph. A Brief History of the LCS(L)-51.

Hawk, Edgar A. This Is Our Story 50 Years Later, U.S.S. Melvin DD680.

Herod, Jack, Lt. (jg), ed. The Gangway: A Pictorial History of the USS Randolph's First Year at Sea, October 9, 1944 to October 9, 1945.

Malcolm, Ian. The Battle of Surigao Strait Revisited.

Million, C. R., and S. E. Whicher, ed. Tarawa to Tokyo, 1943–1946: Published by the Officers and Men of the USS Lexington as a Permanent Record of the Ship's Activities in World War II.

Moynahan, John H. A Ship and a War, USS Ammen DD-527, 1944–1945.

Nilson, Roy. Memoirs of Roy Nilson.

Novotny, Ray. In the Wake of the Jelly Bean.

Rice, James Chauncey. Diary of the Stanly and Its Actions.

Rooney, John. Sailor (interview with Julian Becton, Commanding Officer of the USS Laffey)

Stewart, James M. 90-Day Naval Wonder, 2003.

Stone, Raymond T. My Ship! USS Intrepid.

The Story of the Bennion. Compiled, printed, and distributed by the officers and crew of the USS Bennion (DD-662), 1947.

Strand, R. A. *Naval History of the USS* Spence (compiled).

Surrels, Ron. *DD522: Diary of a Destroyer.* Plymouth, NH: Valley Graphics, 1996.

Tydeman, William A. *USS J. William Ditter (DM-31): Recollections of Thirty Years Ago.*

Diaries, Journals, Letters, E-mails and Action Summaries

USS *Bunker Hill* (CV-17): Arthur L. Hage, Al Turnbull.

USS *Bush* (DD-529): Albert Sidney Blakely, Robert R. Carney, Ralph L. Carver, Edward D. Cregut, Frank Grigsby, S. R. (Ray) Mayhugh, Tom Owen, Bob Shirey, Gilmer Haydon Thomas

USS *Callaghan* (DD-792): Bill Benton, Samuel T. Elrod

USS *Cooper* (DD-695): Marvin H. Davis

USS *Dashiell* (DD-659): Fred M. Wright

USS *Ellyson* (DD-454/DMS-19): Dwight Dean Donnewald

USS *Foote* (DD-511): Wilbur V. Rogers

USS *Hall* (DD-583): Henry Cattoretti

USS *Hull* (DD-350): Kent J. May

USS *Hyman* (DD-732): John Warren Jones

USS *Kitkun Bay* (CVE-71): Alfred Porter White

LCS(L)-118: Randall Lathrop

USS *Lexington* (CV-16): Robert R. Davis

USS *Liddle* (APD-60): Harold S. Deal

USS *Mannert L. Abele* (DD-733): Richard (Dick) Aukerman

USS *Spence* (DD-512): Roy Louis Merritt

USS *Twiggs* (DD-591): Donald R. Witmer

USS *Wilson* (DD-408): Richard Ryman

Books

Adamson, Hans, and George Kosco. *Halsey's Typhoons.* New York: Crown Publishers, 1967.

Appleman, Roy E., James M. Burns, Russell A. Gugeler, and John Stevens. *Okinawa: The Last Battle.* Rutland, VT: Charles E. Tuttle, 1960.

Beschloss, Michael. *The Conquerors: Roosevelt, Truman and the Destruction of Hitler's Germany.* New York: Simon and Schuster, 2002.

Bryan, J., and Philip Reed. *Mission Beyond Darkness.* New York: Duell, Sloan and Pearce, 1945.

Cutler, Thomas J. *The Battle of Leyte Gulf: 23–26 October 1944.* Annapolis, MD: Naval Institute Press, 1994.

Davis, Martin. *Destroyer Escorts of World War II.* Missoula, MT: Pictorial Histories Publishing, 1987.

Dower, John W. *Embracing Defeat: Japan in the Wake of World War II.* New York: Norton/New Press, 1999.

Drury, Bob, and Tom Clavin. *Halsey's Typhoon: The True Story of a Fighting Admiral, an Epic Storm, and an Untold Rescue.* New York: Atlantic Monthly Press, 2007.

Fahey, James J. *Pacific War Diary: 1942–1945.* Boston: Houghton Mifflin, 1963.

Feifer, Gregory. *Tennozan: The Battle of Okinawa and the Atomic Bomb.* New York: Ticknor & Fields, 1992.

Foster, Barry J. *The Last Destroyer.* Infinity, 2002.

Friedman, Norman. *U.S. Destroyers: An Illustrated Design History.* Annapolis, MD: United States Naval Institute, 1982.

Graves, Richard W. *Men of Poseidon: Life at Sea Aboard the USS Rall.* Nevada City, CA: Willow Valley, 1998.

Halsey, William F., and J. Bryan III. *Admiral Halsey's Story.* New York: McGraw-Hill, 1947.

Hara, Tameichi. *Japanese Destroyer Captain.* New York: Ballantine Books, 1961.

Hoyt, Edwin P. *The Battle of Leyte Gulf: The Death Knell of the Japanese Fleet.* New York: Weybright and Talley, 1972.

———. *Japan's War: The Great Pacific Conflict.* New York: Cooper Square Press, 2001.

———. *The Kamikazes.* New York: Arbor House, 1983.

Jones, Ken. *Destroyer Squadron 23: Combat Exploits of Arleigh Burke's Gallant Force.* Annapolis, MD: Naval Institute Press, 1997.

Lamont-Brown, Raymond. *Kamikaze: Japan's Suicide Samurai.* London: Arms and Armour Press, 1997.

Leckie, Robert. *Okinawa: The Last Battle of World War II*. New York: Viking, 1995.

Lott, Arnold S. *Brave Ship, Brave Men*. New York: Bobbs-Merrill, 1964.

Mair, Michael. *Oil, Fire and Fate: The Sinking of the USS Mississinewa (AO-59) in WWII by Japan's Secret Weapon*. Santa Ana, CA: Seven Locks Press, 2008 (forthcoming).

Manchester, William. *American Caesar, Douglas MacArthur 1880–1964*. New York: Random House, 1978.

———. *Goodbye, Darkness: A Memoir of the Pacific War*. Boston: Little, Brown, 1979.

Morison, Samuel Eliot. *History of United States Naval Operations in World War II*. Vol. 4, *Coral Sea, Midway and Submarine Actions, May 1942–August 1942*. Chicago: University of Illinois Press, 2001.

———. *History of United States Naval Operations in World War II*. Vol. 8, *New Guinea and the Marianas, March 1944–August 1944*. Boston: Little, Brown, 1975.

———. *History of United States Naval Operations in World War II*. Vol. 12, *Leyte, June 1944–January 1945*. Boston: Little, Brown, 1975.

———. *History of United States Naval Operations in World War II*. Vol. 13, *The Liberation of the Philippines—Luzon, Mindanao, the Visayas, 1944–1945*. Chicago: University of Illinois Press, 2002.

———. *History of United States Naval Operations in World War II*, Vol. 14, *Victory in the Pacific, 1945*. Chicago: University of Illinois Press, 2002.

Nagatsuka, Ryuji. *I Was a Kamikaze*. New York: Macmillan, 1974.

Naito, Hatsuho. *Thunder Gods: The Kamikaze Pilots Tell Their Story*. New York: Kodansha International/Harper and Row, 1989.

9/11 Commission Report: Final Report of the National Commission on Terrorist Attacks upon the United States. New York: W.W. Norton, 2004.

Parkin, Robert Sinclair. *Blood on the Sea: American Destroyers Lost in World War II*. New York: Sarpedon, 1996.

Prang, Gordon W., Donald M. Goldstein, and Katherine V. Dillon. *At

Dawn We Slept: The Untold Story of Pearl Harbor. New York: Penguin Books, 1982.

Raines, James Orvill. *Good Night Officially: The Pacific War Letters of a Destroyer Sailor.* Edited with introduction by William M. McBride. Boulder, CO: Westview Press, 1994.

Rielly, Robin L. *Mighty Midgets at War: The Saga of the LCS(L) Ships from Iwo Jima to Vietnam.* Central Point, OR: Hellgate Press, 2000.

Rooney, John. *Mighty Midget U.S.S. LCS 82.* Phoenixville, PA: J. A. Rooney, 1990.

Sears, David. *The Last Epic Naval Battle: Voices from Leyte Gulf.* Westport, CT: Praeger, 2005.

Sheftall, M. G. *Blossoms in the Wind: Human Legacies of the Kamikaze.* New York: New American Library, 2005.

Sherrod, Robert. *On to Westward: The Battles of Saipan and Iwo Jima.* Baltimore, MD: Nautical and Aviation Publishing, 1990.

Sledge, E. B. *With the Old Breed at Peleliu and Okinawa.* New York: Ballantine Books, 2007.

Spector, Ronald H. *Eagle Against the Sun: The American War with Japan.* New York: Vintage Books, 1985.

Stafford, Edward P. *Little Ship, Big War: The Saga of DE343.* New York: William Morrow, 1984.

Staton, Michael. *The Fighting Bob: A Wartime History of the USS Robley D. Evans (DD-552).* Bennington, VT: Merriam Press, 2001.

Thompson, Robert Smith. *Empires on the Pacific: World War II and the Struggle for the Mastery of Asia.* New York: Basic Books, 2001.

Toland, John. *The Rising Sun: The Decline and Fall of the Japanese Empire, 1936–1945.* New York: The Modern Library, 1987.

Warner, Denis Ashton, and Peggy Warner. *The Sacred Warriors: Japan's Suicide Legions.* Van Nostrand Reinhold, 1982.

Wooldridge, E. T. (ed.). *Carrier Warfare in the Pacific: An Oral History Collection.* Washington, DC: Smithsonian Institution, 1993.

Wouk, Herman. *The Caine Mutiny:* A Novel. Garden City, NY: Doubleday, 1951.

———. *War and Remembrance.* Boston: Little, Brown, 1978.

Magazine and Newspaper Articles

Adams, Nathan M. "The Ship That Outsailed Time." *Readers Digest,* September, 1989.

Ahlstrom, John D. "Leyte Gulf Remembered." Naval Institute *Proceedings,* August, 1984.

Baldwin, Hanson W. "Greatest Sea-Air Battle." *New York Times Magazine,* April 1950.

Boyd, Thomas M. "My Father's Band of Brothers." *Washington Post,* June 17, 2007; Page B08.

Bradlee, Ben. "A Return." *New Yorker,* October 2, 2006, 52–57.

Burns, John F. "A Maimed Destroyer *Cole* Starts for Home." *New York Times,* October 30, 2000.

Camden Courier-Post, "Camden Man's Life Saved by Shipmate," August 30, 1945.

Davis, James Martin. "An Invasion Not Found in the History Books." *Omaha World Herald,* November 1987.

Freeman, Gregory A. "Don't Shoot, We're Republicans!" *World War II,* December 2005.

Gault, Owen. "The Mighty Midgets of Mindanao." *Sea Classics,* August 1993, 16–23.

Guttman, Robert. "Fleet Battered by Typhoon." *World War II,* January 1945.

Harper, Dale P. "USS *Laffey*'s Pacific Ordeal." www.thehistorynet. com.

Kennedy, David M. "Victory at Sea." *Atlantic Monthly,* May 1999, 51–76.

Lardner, John. "A Reporter on Okinawa." *New Yorker,* May 19, 1945, 32–40 and May 26, 1945, 46–57.

Newell, George. "Bunker Hill 9; Yamato 0!" *The Monument (Bunker Hill* Newsletter).

Nolte, Carl. "Doing His Duty: Vet's Grandson Gives Personal Effects Back to Kamikaze Pilot's Family." *San Francisco Chronicle,* March 29, 2001.

Philadelphia Inquirer, "New Bridge for Blasted Warship," August 31, 1945.

Roberge, Walter. "An Okinawa Story: The Last Great Battle for Destroyer-Escorts." *DESA News,* November/December 2005.

Seattle Times, "Saw Wife and Five Children Killed by Jap Balloon Bomb," June 1, 1945.

Tanglen, Larry. "Terror Floated over Montana." *Montana: The Magazine of Western History,* Winter 2002.

Wallace, Bruce. "Fate Spared 'Kamikaze Survivors.' " *Seattle Times,* October 03, 2004.

Yoshida, Mitsuru. "The End of *Yamato.*" *Proceedings,* February 1952.

Official Documents

Action Report, Commander Task Unit 77.4.32 (Commander Carrier Division 26). Serial 015, 18 November 1944, Office of Naval Records and Library.

Anti-aircraft Action Report for Action of 29 July 1945: Loss of U.S.S. Callaghan (DD792).

The Battle for Leyte Gulf, Strategic and Tactical Analysis. Vol. 5, *Battle of Surigao Strait,* October 24–25th, U.S. Naval War College, 1958.

Calling All Destroyers: "Kamikaze": The Officers and Men of the USS *Wadsworth* (DD-516).

Naval Ordnance and Gunnery, Vol. 1, Naval Ordnance, Department of Ordnance and Gunnery, United States Naval Academy, 1957.

USS *Abner Read* Action Report.

USS *Claxton* War Diary, 1 November 1944.

USS *Lindsey* (DM-32), *Battle Damage, 12 April 1945.*

USS *Sigsbee* (DD-502), *Action Report, 14 April 1945.*

★ Citations ★

Medals, ribbons, and commendations seem little to show for the dangers, efforts, and sacrifices that airmen, sailors, and soldiers display in battle. Often the words in the written citations that accompany them seem scripted, and none can fully convey the surrounding horror and confusion. Moreover, recipients often feel the words call undue attention to them as individuals in situations that inspired collective achievements and sacrifices.

That said, the citations remain poignant tributes to the selfless actions and sacrifices of men and women in war. Included here are brief excerpts from just a small sample of citations accompanying awards received by airmen and sailors during the long months at war with the wind.

20 April 1944: Lieutenant Commander Robert Morris Morgenthau, USNR, USS *Lansdale* (DD-426). Bronze Star Medal* Citation, in part: "Morgenthau was instrumental in enabling the LANSDALE to engage effectively the attacking enemy torpedo planes and prevent serious damage to a valuable merchant convoy. . . . Disregarding his own safety after abandoning ship, he rendered valiant service for over two hours in administering aid to men in the water until finally rescued."

---

*The Bronze Star Medal is a U.S. Armed Forces individual military decoration that may be awarded for bravery, acts of merit, or meritorious service. When awarded for bravery, it is the fourth highest combat award of the U.S. Armed Forces and the 9th highest military award (including both combat and noncombat awards) in the order of precedence of U.S. military decorations.

12 December 1944: Lieutenant Junior Grade Frank Melvin Cratsley, USNR, USS *Caldwell* (DD-605). Bronze Star Medal Citation (in part): "During the re-conquest of the Philippine Islands on December 12, 1944, Lieutenant (jg) Cratsley at the risk of his own life, entered burning compartments, littered with unexploded shells and dense chemical fumes in order to extricate shipmates. In addition, he was extremely courageous and skillful in fighting the numerous fires which threatened the ship."

26 March 1945: Lieutenant James Edward Gilbert, USNR, USS *PC-1128* Silver Star Medal* Citation (in part): "Skillfully maneuvering his ship through enemy mined waters to the side of a mined vessel, Lieutenant Gilbert facilitated the removal of all living personnel and rescued other survivors from the water, although air attack was probable and there was danger the other vessel might explode. Remaining in mined waters until long after darkness, he effected the rescue of all survivors."

1 April 1945: Ensign Charles Daughtry Towers, USNR, *LCS(L)-118.* Silver Star Citation (in part): "When a nearby friendly vessel was struck by an enemy suicide plane, resulting in severe damage and raging fires, he bravely and voluntarily led a fire and rescue party aboard the blazing ship. Despite the intense heat and frequent explosions on the stricken vessel he supervised the fire fighting in a truly heroic manner and personally led a group of men into a flaming compartment amidst exploding ammunition in order to effectively fight the fire below decks."

6 April 1945: J. M. Cross, Fire Controlman Third Class, USNR, USS *Bush* (DD-529). Posthumous Silver Star Medal Citation (in part): "After his ship had been initially seriously damaged, he remained aboard during successive crash dives rendering assistance to wounded and assisting in damage control measures. When it be-

*The Silver Star is awarded for gallantry in action against an enemy of the United States. It may be awarded to any person who, while serving in any capacity with the U.S. Armed Forces, distinguishes him or herself by extraordinary heroism.

came necessary to abandon ship he gave his life jacket to a wounded shipmate. While in the water, he supported a seriously wounded man until he himself lacked strength to remain afloat."

6 April 1945: Ensign Robert Malcolm Fortson, USN, USS *Leutze* (DD-481). Bronze Star Medal Citation (in part): "During fanatical Japanese suicide air attacks, Ensign Fortson directed the guns under his control in destroying two hostile planes and assisting in the destruction of at least two others. When one of the attacking planes crashed his ship during her attempt to assist a friendly destroyer in distress, he maintained rigid control of his battery despite numerous casualties and coolly directed the control of damage."

6 April 1945: Lieutenant Junior Grade Willis Everett Hardy, USN, USS *Hornet* (CV-12), VF-17. Navy Cross* Medal Citation (in part): "Participating in the interception of a large force of Japanese aircraft, Lieutenant, Junior Grade, Hardy attacked an enemy fighter plane, causing it to crash into the sea. Sighting two hostile dive bombers, he shot down both in quick succession. Centering his fire upon a third dive-bomber, he skillfully exploded it in midair after which he set off in relentless pursuit of another Japanese dive-bomber, which crashed into the sea, exploding with terrific force upon impact."

6 April 1945: Wesley G. Northey, Boatswain's Mate First Class, USN, USS *Bush* (DD-529). Silver Star Medal Citation (in part): "During repeated strafing and suicide attacks by enemy aircraft when loss of his ship became imminent, Northey volunteered to man one of the 40-mm guns still in operation and, together with other volunteers, maintained rapid fire against enemy planes. Although it was evident that the third suicide plane coming from the port side

*The Navy Cross is the second highest medal that can be awarded by the Department of the Navy and the second highest award given for valor. The Navy Cross may be awarded to any member of the armed forces while serving with the Marine Corps, Navy, or Coast Guard (in time of war only) that distinguishes himself in action by extraordinary heroism not justifying an award of the Medal of Honor. To earn a Navy Cross, the act to be commended must be performed in the presence of great danger or at great personal risk and must be performed in such a manner as to render the individual highly conspicuous among others of equal grade, rate, experience, or position of responsibility.

would crash on or near his mount, he remained steadfast at his post, keeping the Japanese plane under fire until it crashed approximately ten feet from him. Later succumbing as a result of wounds received, Northey by his valor and devotion to duty upheld the highest traditions of the United States Naval Service."

7 April 1945: Thomas Francis Kelly, Aviation Radioman Third Class, USNR, Torpedo Bombing Squadron Eighty-Four attached to USS Bunker Hill (CV-17). Distinguished Flying Cross* Citation (in part): "Despite intense antiaircraft fire of all caliber from the battleship and the surrounding screen which damaged his plane, Kelly materially aided his pilot during the attack in which at least nine torpedo hits were scored on the warship and contributed greatly to the success of the operation."

12 April 1945: Nick John Korompilas, Pharmacist's Mate Third Class, USNR, USS Mannert L. Abele (DD-733). Navy and Marine Corps Medal† Citation (in part): "After reaching the main deck to abandon ship with the others from the forward battle dressing station in the wardroom, Korompilas courageously returned aft through the wardroom to the galley to rescue the chief commissary steward and, although the vessel was in immediate danger of submerging, led the severely burned and dazed man to safety."

12 April 1945: Lieutenant Harold Murdock Scott, Jr., USNR, USS Bennion (DD-662). Posthumous Silver Star Medal Citation (in part): "With his ship under concentrated attack by eight to ten planes on the afternoon of April 12, Lieutenant Scott courageously took four targets under fire with the heavy antiaircraft battery within a period of three minutes. During many attacks by enemy suicide planes while his ship was acting as a radar picket, he directed the guns in

---

*The Distinguished Flying Cross is a medal awarded to any officer or enlisted member of the United States armed forces who distinguishes himself or herself in combat in support of operations by "heroism or extraordinary achievement while participating in an aerial flight."
†The Navy and Marine Corps Medal is the second highest noncombatant medal awarded by the United States Department of the Navy to members of the U.S. Navy and the U.S. Marine Corps. The medal may be awarded to service members who, while serving in any capacity with the Navy or Marine Corps, distinguish themselves by heroism not involving actual conflict with an enemy. Typically, it is awarded for actions involving the risk of one's own life.

destroying twelve Japanese aircraft and in assisting in the destruction of four others."

12 April 1945: Lieutenant James Malcolm Stewart, USNR, *LSM (R)-189.* Silver Star Medal Citation (in part): "Although his ship sustained damage when a Japanese suicide plane crashed onboard, Lieutenant Stewart continued to fight his ship against additional air attacks and, bringing accurate fire to bear on the attackers, succeeded in shooting down three hostile planes."

14 April 1945: Lieutenant Fred Milton Wright, USNR, USS *Dashiell* (DD-659). Bronze Star Medal Citation (in part): "Following a near miss by a bomb, which caused serious damage in the forward engine room, Lieutenant Wright skillfully directed repairs that enabled his department to resume normal operations during an extremely critical period."

16 April 1945: Bonnie Lee Cathcart, Seaman, USS *Intrepid* (CV-11). Bronze Star Medal Citation, in part: "After his ship was struck by an enemy airplane and bomb, during heavy air attack, in enemy waters, which caused large fires, he calmly and courageously entered a burning and smoke-filled compartment and assisted in removing three badly injured men, thereby saving them from certain death. Although wounded at the time himself, he continued to search for casualties and later joined the firefighting parties until all fires were extinguished or brought under control."

16 April 1945: Lieutenant Alvin Lloyd Gallin, USN, USS *Bryant* (DD-665). Bronze Star Medal Citation (in part): "When his ship was subjected to a coordinated attack by six Japanese planes, he coolly and capably assisted in conning the ship so that the entire main battery was able to bear on the selected targets."

16 April 1945: Ross Epworth Peterson, Electrician's Mate First Class, USN, USS *Laffey* (DD-724). Posthumous Bronze Star Medal Citation (in part): "With the attacks continuing unabated, he directed personnel on electrical switchboards in the prompt securing of damaged electrical circuits, thereby averting electrical fires and overloads and assisting in the maintenance of power supplied over vital, nondamaged circuits. Fatally struck down when another bomber crashed his station."

16 April 1945: Lewis Philips Reed, Gunners Mate Third Class, USN, *LCS(L)-116.* Silver Star Medal Citation (in part): "After a suicide plane crashed into his ship and killed and wounded many of the crew, Reed manned a machine gun and, despite his painful wounds, succeeded in delivering accurate fire against another attacking suicide plane that caused the pilot to lose control and crash into the sea."

22 April 1945: Luciano J. Filadoro, Boatswain's Mate Second Class USNR, USS *Isherwood* (DD-520). Bronze Star Medal Citation (in part): "Quick to act as dangerous fires broke out in various parts of the ship following the crash of the enemy plane, Filadoro voluntarily left the security of his station. . . . Acutely aware of the imminence of a disastrous explosion, he fought the raging flame with indomitable energy until the blazing charge ultimately detonated despite all efforts of the crew to prevent the disaster. Although instantly killed in the explosion, Filadoro had rendered valiant assistance in the emergency."

28 April 1945: Clifford Leroy Baldwin, Sonarman Second Class, USNR, USS *Daly* (DD-519). Silver Star Medal Citation (in part): "During a highly coordinated and savage Japanese suicide attack his ship was severely damaged and he, himself, seriously wounded. Despite his injuries, and in the face of continuing attacks, he remained steadfast at his battle station and continued to furnish accurate and vital information to machine-gun control."

4 May 1945: Lieutenant James William Kelley, USN, *LCS(L)-61.* Silver Star Medal Citation (in part): "When a nearby friendly escort aircraft carrier was struck and severely damaged by an enemy suicide plane, he, with outstanding bravery and initiative, placed his ship alongside the damaged vessel and capably supervised his crew in effectively fighting the fires raging aboard the carrier."

13 May 1945: Edgar Bergeron, Motor Machinist's Mate Third Class, USNR, USS *Bache* (DD-470). Commendation Ribbon* Citation (in part): "After his ship had been struck by an enemy suicide plane and serious damage ensued, he displayed exceptional skill and courage in extinguishing fires and repairing damage."

13 May 1945: John Isaac Vaught, Fireman First Class, USNR, USS *Bache* (DD-470) Bronze Star Medal Citation (in part): "Although severely wounded when his ship was struck by an enemy suicide plane, Vaught continued to man his gun in local control and aided in repelling another attacking plane, thereby contributing materially to saving his ship from further damage."

11 June 1945: Lieutenant Richard Miles McCool, USN, Commanding Officer, *LCS (L)-122*. Medal of Honor† Citation (in part): "When his own craft was attacked simultaneously by two of the enemy's suicide squadron early in the evening of June 11, he instantly hurled the full power of his gun batteries against the plunging aircraft, shooting down the first and damaging the second before it crashed his station in the conning tower and engulfed the area in a mass of flames. Although suffering from shrapnel wounds and painful burns, he rallied his concussion-shocked crew and initiated vigorous firefighting measures and then proceeded to the rescue of several men trapped in a blazing compartment, subsequently carrying one man to safety despite the excruciating pain of additional severe burns."

*Authorized on 11 January 1944. Originally created as a ribbon called the Navy Commendation Ribbon, it was the first of the commendation awards. Awarded to members of the Navy and Marine Corps or to other members of the Armed Forces serving with these branches, who distinguish themselves by heroism, outstanding achievement, or meritorious service. This is a personal decoration, which has often been awarded for Life Saving, in place of the medals originally created for that purpose.

†The Medal of Honor is awarded by the President, in the name of Congress, to a person who, while a member of the U.S. Armed Services, distinguishes himself or herself conspicuously by gallantry and intrepidity at the risk of his or her life above and beyond the call of duty while engaged in action against an opposing armed force in which the United States is not a belligerent party. The deed performed must have been one of personal bravery or self-sacrifice so conspicuous as to clearly distinguish the individual above his or her comrades and must have involved risk of life. Incontestable proof of the performance of the service will be exacted and each recommendation for the award of this decoration will be considered on the standard of extraordinary merit.

16 June 1945: Guy E. Legate, Boiler Maker Second Class, USS *Hall* (DD-583). Commendation Ribbon Citation (in part): "For meritorious conduct in the performance of his duties as a member of the whaleboat's crew on the night of 16 June 1945, when a United States destroyer exploded and sank. Under conditions of great personal danger from burning oil on the surface of the water and from flying debris from the exploding ship and with complete disregard for his own personal safety, he assisted other members of the boat's crew in rescuing a total of eight men who could not otherwise have survived."

27 June 1945: Captain Neill Phillips, USN, Commander *LCS(L) Flotilla Four*. Bronze Star Medal Citation (in part): "Demonstrating outstanding skill and courage in the face of repeated enemy air attacks, Captain Phillips efficiently coordinated the activities of ships under his command."

★ Roll Call ★

The following is a listing (organized by ship and ship type) of U.S. sailors, airmen, and Marines whose units participated in battle engagements against *kamikaze* attackers. Roll Call has been compiled based on direct contacts with veterans of these attacks as well as family members of veterans both living and deceased.

Roll Call is a list filled with meaning and work. For each Roll Call name, a veteran (or family member) specifically authorized the inclusion.* In the case of surviving veterans, Roll Call authorizations became the database for hundreds of personal interviews. In the case of both families and veterans, Roll Call authorizations were accompanied by a bounty of photographs, documents, letters, diaries, and other mementos. Digital images of many of these have been posted—and continue to be posted—on a book Internet site (www.dlsearsbooks.com).

Roll Call includes the names of only a small fraction of the men who served in this arena at this momentous time. Still, it is by no means an insignificant list, and it resounds with collaborative effort—and conscious memory. Many veterans I interviewed (more than a few with awards for conspicuous heroism) were quick to say what they did was not so much. They were not heroes—though they served in a ship (or squadron or unit) of heroes. They insist the real (and too often forgotten) heroes never returned and instead were buried or sent to the bottom of distant seas. Dozens of these particular heroes are remembered

*This explains why, in some cases, names that appear in the text do not appear in Roll Call.

in Roll Call—designated either "KIA" (killed in action) or "LAS" (lost at sea for reasons other than combat).

Roll Call's "unnamed" heroes are the family members (spouses, siblings, children, nieces, nephews, grand- and great-grandchildren) who strive to preserve loved ones' legacies. Their quiet persistence in "remembering" speaks volumes about human respect, appreciation, and age-defying love. This dedication is especially meaningful and poignant for families of sailors, airmen, and marines who made the ultimate sacrifice more than sixty years ago.

Roll Call attempts to expand the circle of recognition beyond the relative handful of people and events that could be included in this book. The constraints of researching, writing, and producing this book inevitably curtailed efforts to add even more names to Roll Call. For those whose loved ones' names are not included here, my hope is that by naming these veterans we honor them all.

The following is a key to the codes used throughout the Roll Call:

★—Battle Stars: Battle star information is for ships, not individuals. It is for World War II operations only and is based on information listed in the *Dictionary of American Naval Fighting Ships*, a publication of the Naval Historical Center.

♥—Purple Heart Award recipient: Award for "being wounded or killed in any action against an enemy of the United States or as a result of an act of any such enemy or opposing armed forces." Listings here are based on information obtained from individual veterans or from family members.

—Ship sunk or scuttled (date) as a result of enemy action or event of nature such as a storm.

PUC—Presidential Unit Citation awarded to ship or unit

NUC—Navy Unit Commendation awarded to ship or unit

KIA—killed in action

LAS—lost at sea

CO—Ship commanding officer

XO—Ship executive officer

AO—Auxiliary Oilers

USS *Mississinewa* (AO-59)
★★★★

20 November 1944

Fernando Cuevas
Herb Daitch
John A. Mair
Charles Scott
Winston Whitten

APA—Attack Transports

USS *Henrico* (APA-45)
★★★

John Brooks
Calvin Carl
Robert G. (Duke) DeLuca
Glenn Grant
Leonard D. Howell
Joseph J. Javaruski
Raymond J. LePage
Tom Love
Gradus L. Shoemaker
Joseph Zenzius

USS *St. Mary's* (APA-126)
★

Joe Crain

APD—High-Speed Transports

USS *Chase* (DE-158/APD-54)
★★

Frank Beto
Lawrence Rothstein ♥

USS *Dickerson* (DD-157/ADP-21)
★★★★★★
Henry Cueba
Boyton (Bud) Huxtable ♥
Joseph E. Kreutzer ♥
Wallace M. Sjoquist
Edward J. Young ♥ (KIA)

4 April
1945

ATF—Fleet Ocean Tug

USS *Arikara* (ATF-98)
★★★
Albert Krasson

USS *Pakana* (ATF-108)
★
Donald Edward Berg
George E. Davis

BB—Battleship

USS *New Mexico* (BB-40)
★★★★★★
John Ray Leach

CA—Heavy Cruiser / CL—Light Cruiser

USS *Nashville* (CL-43)
★★★★★★★★★★
Ben Limbaugh ♥
Rufus B. Thompson, Jr.

USS *New Orleans* (CA-32)
★★★★★★★★★★★★★★★★★
James Montgomery

CV—Aircraft Carriers, Air Groups (VB, VF, VT—Bombing, Fighter, Torpedo Aviation Squadrons)

USS *Bunker Hill* (CV-17)—*PUC*
★★★★★★★★★★★★
Robert Schock ♥

VT-84
Edward Duffy
Thomas F. Kelly ♥
Al Turnbull

USS *Franklin* (CV-13)
★★★★
Bill Albrecht
Jesse Arthur Bond, Jr. ♥ (KIA)
Louis Casserino

USS *Hornet* (CV-12)
PUC
★★★★★★★

VF-17
Ted Crosby
Willis E. (Bill) Hardy

USS *Intrepid* (CV-11)
★★★★★
Robert E. Bernard
J. Arthur Bohn
Bonnie Lee Cathcart, Jr. ♥
Warren Edward Click
Edward T. Coyne
Raymond D. Dow (USMC)
George B. DuBois
Warren J. Fegely
Edgar Foltz, Jr.
Lee Galbraith
John F. (Jack) Gamble
Charles D. Harper
Burke J. Landry
Donald A. Lorimer
Salvatore Maschio
William C. McCreery, Jr.

Robert F. Patton*
Enoch N. Peterson
Broaddus W. Robertson
Ben J. Tate, Sr.
Daniel W. (Dan) Watkins
Norman L. Weckter

Air Group 18 (aboard *Intrepid*)
VT-18
Wallace Russell

USS *Lexington* (CV-16)
PUC
★★★★★★★★★★★★
Robert R. Davis
Raymond E. Dora
John R. Edenfield
Richard J. Fullam
Rudolph Gonzalez
James T. Harper
Morris R. King
Charles F. Ryberg
Ralph Truax

VF-16
Arthur P. Whiteway

VF-19
Bruce Williams

VT-16
Selbie Greenhalgh ♥
Warren E. McLellan ♥

---

*Also served aboard USS *Mannert L. Abele* (DD-733).

USS *Randolph* (CV-15)
★★★
Alan J. Sanderson

CVE–Escort Aircraft Carriers, Air Groups (VC-Composite
Aviation Squadrons)

USS *Gambier Bay* (CVE-73)
★★★★

25 October
1944

VC-10
Burt Bassett
Joseph D. McGraw
Richard W. Roby*
Gene Seitz

USS *Kitkun Bay* (CVE-71)
PUC
★★★★★★
Ronald Vaughn
Alfred Porter White

Ommaney Bay (CVE-79)
★★
Clifford Grant

USS *St. Lo* (CVE-63)
PUC
★★★★

25 October   Larry Collins
1944   Evan H. Crawforth ♥
               Joseph A. Lehans
               Bill Pumphrey
               Winston Brock Short ♥

*Brother of Alfred J. Roby, Jr., USS *Melvin* (DD-680).

VC-65
Thomas B. Van Brunt

USS *Sangamon* (CVE-26)
PUC
★★★★★★★★
Donald T. Schroeder

VC-43
Thomas H. Hogan

USS *Suwannee* (CVE-27)
★★★★★★★★★★★★★★
Charles P. Casello
Paul K. (Cactus) Walters

USS *White Plains* (CVE-66)
★★★★★
PUC
Lloyd E. Grayson
Thomas T. Welsh

DD—Destroyers

USS *Abner Read* (DD-526)
★★★★
Lee P. Chase

1 November
1944

Paul (Sam) McQueen
Roy O'Neal Smith
Emil N. Rossi
John Claude Swartout

USS *Ammen* (DD-527)
NUC
★★★★★★★★
James Baca
Leon Darrow Carver
Giles N. Chancellor, Jr.

Charles Francis Corgiat
Donald Costelow
Rolland Floch
Herbert James Garcia
William Earl Hart
Harvey L. Haysler
Hubert Hunzeker
Ernest L. Johnson
Joseph Isaac Masters
John Henry Moynahan
Warren E. Sandidge
Peter Wagner

USS *Anthony* (DD-515)
NUC
★★★★★★★
Bob Lee George
Daniel M. Nolan II

USS *Aulick* (DD-569)
PUC (Destroyer Squadron 23)
★★★★★
Godwin Aguillard
J. R. Croker ·
Brian Masterson
Arthur Rhodes
Robert L. Skinner
Horace Wright

USS *Bache* (DD-470)
★★★★★★★★
Edgar Bergeron
Hugo Cipriani
Kittridge G. Hall
William F. Jeffries ♥
Roland M. O'Dette ♥
John I. Vaught ♥
Wade T. Winstead

USS *Bennett* (DD-473)
NUC
★★★★★★★★★
John H. Austin ♥ (KIA)
Robert N. Boyd
Michael A. Capuano
Lawrence C. Finn
Raymond Gindle
Charlie Greco
Edwin Hamilton
Frank Hanratty
Roland G. Laliberte
Joseph Mulholland
Donald Reese
Don Sheridan ♥
John E. Syrek
Stanton J. Taylor
Orin G. Wood

USS *Bennion* (DD-662)
PUC
★★★★★★★★★
A. Louis Canut
W. Frank Cobb, Jr.
Joseph DiNardo
Clyde A. Fawcett
Joe Fonte
Richard Jack Foy ♥
Jesse C. Frazier
Mahlon Fulton
John B. Gregg, Sr.
Virgil M. Harter
William F. McDowell
Gordon Meyer
Bernard J. Pace
Charles (Chuck) Pike
Robert (Bob) Pitts
Johnnie Hope Qualls

Charles A. Sandy
Harold M. Scott, Jr.
Victor J. Sepe
Paul D. Shaffer
Leon J. Sims
Louie G. Smith
Alton V. Titcomb
John W. True
George M. Yandek

USS *Black* (DD-666)
★★★★★★

Maurice (Mike) Couwenhoven
Carl C. (Rusty) DeLoach
Fred Muth

USS *Borie* (DD-704)
★★★

Charles A. Besse
William F. Cain
Jerome Harvey
Robert V. Kenyon
Edward P. McGinley
Robert E. White
Stuart K. White, Sr.

USS *Boyd* (DD-544)
★★★★★★★★★★★

Edward Shaffer
Julius Warzybok

USS *Braine* (DD-630)
★★★★★★★★★

George Cintron
Walter Gaddis
Louis S. Hall, Jr.

USS *Bryant* (DD-665)—*NUC*
★★★★★★★

Daniel J. DeRoch
Alvin L. Gallin ♥
Dale B. Hanson ♥
Jack Taylor

USS *Bullard* (DD-660)
★★★★★★★★★

Arthur R. Brown
Thomas Cutarelli
Christ Karos
Frank J. Viggiano

USS *Bush* (DD529)
★★★★★★★

6 April
1945

Robert M. Aguilar
Miller West Beals ♥ (KIA)
Edmond B. Bennett
Albert Sidney Blakely
Albert Dasha Brody ♥ (KIA)
Franklin Coit Butler
Robert R. Carney ♥
George Carofino
Ralph L. Carver
James A. Collinson
Robert Melvin Cowherd ♥
Edward D. Cregut
J. M. Cross ♥ (KIA)
Stanton L. Gallaher
Frank Grigsby
George Scot Hay ♥ (KIA)
Virgil E. Holderness, Sr.
Moses G. Hubbard
John E. Lavelle
P. A. (Tony) Lilly, XO ♥
Hilliard L. Lubin ♥
Duard Martin

S. R. (Ray) Mayhugh
Robert F. (Bob) McGrath
O. R. (Mac) McKinney
Wesley G. Northey ♥ (KIA)
Paul O. Pedersen
Robert C. Peterson
Mario F. Petroni ♥
Narvis Robinson
John Sandt
Edwin Earl Sechrist, Jr.
Bob Sharp
Bob Shirey
Gilmer Haydon Thomas
Robert W. Thompson
Paul P. Trella ♥ (KIA)
Rollin E. (Westy) Westholm, CO ♥
Robert F. Wise, Sr.

USS *Caldwell* (DD-605)
★★★★★★★★
Vaughn Adjemian ♥
Mel Cratsley
Richard Blair Hodgman
Jerome Raymond Hould
Wesley F. Wadsworth
Lawrence J. Welch ♥ (KIA)
George Wendelburg (CO) ♥

USS *Callaghan* (DD-792)
★★★★★★★★

28 July
1945

William Benton
Samuel T. Elrod ♥ (KIA)
Marland Moreau
Wayne N. Pressler
Joe Sprouse
Burton R. Williams
E. C. (Woody) Woodward ♥
Daniel G. Wyatt

USS *Cassin Young* (DD-793)
NUC
★★★★
Wallace M. Dickerman ♥ (2)
Millard Horton ♥
Charles E. Serey

USS *Charles Ausburne* (DD-570)
PUC (Destroyer Squadron 23)
★★★★★★★★★★★
Donald L. Vick

USS *Claxton* (DD-571)
PUC (Destroyer Squadron 23)
★★★★★★★★★
Tom Clyce
William E. Monfort
Robert W. Proudfoot
Charles Wilke

USS *Coghlan* (DD-606)
★★★★★★★★★
Gail Pifer

USS *Colhoun* (DD-801)
★

6 April
1945

John Glascott ♥ (KIA)
Salvador Gonzales
Edward E. Mueller
Joseph F. Orabona
Joseph Charles Osseck ♥ (KIA)
James Monroe Pollock, Jr.
Thomas MacMillan Rorrison ♥ (KIA)

USS *Converse* (DD-509)
PUC
★★★★★★★★★★★★
Pat Collins
Larry Dixon
Francis Martin Duffy
Clifford E. Tullis

USS *Cooper* (DD-695)
★

2 December 1944

Clarence Brinker
Glenn Wesley Brown ♥
Raymond M. Corsetto
B. H. Davis ♥ (KIA)
Marvin H. Davis
Thomas J. Hogan ♥
Carlton S. Howe ♥ (KIA)
Harvey K. Huff ♥
Harvey Amiel McGinnis, Jr. ♥ (KIA)
Giacinto (Sonny) Miele ♥
Earl Taylor
James W. Villiers
James (Bo) Walters

USS *Cowell* (DD-547)
PUC
★★★★★★★★★★★★
Donald E. Roller
Dean E. Scully
Chester Trojanowski

USS *Daly* (DD-519)
★★★★★★★★
C. L. (Skip) Baldwin ♥
Charles L. Dunn
James E. Kelly
Adrian D. Shultz ♥
William J. Wyatt

USS *Dashiell* (DD-659)
★★★★★★★★★★★
Carl F. Croneberger
Lawrence Forde
Houston W. (Pete) Honeycutt
Paul H. Johnston
Fred M. Wright

USS *Dewey* (DD-349)
★★★★★★★★★★★★★
Lorin J. Nelson

USS *Douglas H. Fox* (DD-779)
★

Eddie (Chick) Elliot
Charles Hansen
Alex Makar
Stan Rosenberg

USS *Drayton* (DD-366)
★★★★★★★★★★★★
Marvin Gabrielse

USS *Drexler* (DD-741)
★

28 May
1945

Robert L. Anteau
Eugene Brick
Richard Dale Campbell
Joseph J. Curgino ♥
Dudley Gallup
Fred W. Mitchell ♥
Ashley (Pop) Walton

USS *Edwards* (DD-619)
★★★★★★★★★★★★★★★
Wallace (Wally) Paulson

USS *Evans* (DD-552)—*PUC*
★★★★★
Martin M. Fleisher
James E. Staton
Clem Trytko

USS *Foote* (DD-511)—*PUC* (Destroyer Squadron 23)
★★★★
Philip Blistein ♥
Wilbur V. Rogers
Angelo J. Vergona

USS *Frank E. Evans* (DD-754)
★
Lex Taylor

USS *Gainard* (DD-706)—*NUC*
★
Robert E. Garst, Sr.
Milton Mlynarski
Richard E. Odell
William Williams
Paul N. Wilson

USS *Gregory* (DD-802)
★★
Richard Jackson (Holly) Hollenbeck
Eugene W. Leganza
Howard Tomlin

USS *Haggard* (DD-555)
★★★
Fred Schnorr
H. W. (Bud) Weigand

USS *Hall* (DD-583)
★★★★★★★★
Thomas J. Ahern, Jr.
Henry Cattoretti
Martin Fitzgerald

USS *Hall* (*cont.*)
Mel Gelfand
Louis J. Layman
Guy E. Legate
Bernard Wezner

USS *Halligan* (DD-584)
★★★★★★

26 March
1945

John Franklin Brown ♥
Harvey D. Conrad ♥ (KIA)
John Poremba ♥
Gerald (Jerry) Porter
Stanley P. Sheffer ♥ (KIA)

USS *Halsey Powell* (DD-686)
★★★★★★★

Jack Barrett
Kenneth F. Courteau
Casey Kraft

USS *Hank* (DD-702)
★★★★

Herman C. Martin
Gerald Moore
Henry S. Smith
Clyde Oden (Shorty) Taylor
Theron (Ted) Teagle

USS *Haraden* (DD-585)
★★★★★

Urban W. (Bill) Bloom
Alfred J. Comeau
Thomas Cunningham
Peter DiBara ♥
John B. DiBella ♥
Timothy P. Donohue
Frank (Red) Doyle

Thomas Joseph Inman
John Kaye
Clyde Lewis, Jr.
Robert Dale Mead
Thomas (Tommy) Robertson
William L. Smith
Carl D. Spiron
Alfred P. Zaluski

USS *Haynsworth* (DD-700)
★★★
John Friel
James Lee Goodman
Norman Long, Jr.
Martin M. Maloney

USS *Hazelwood* (DD-531)
★★★★★★★★★★
Thomas Craigo
Edward Czajka ♥
Frank Diveny
John Hankinson
Howell Hedrick
Raymond Heinrich
Carl Robert Mull
Robert E. Noble
Donald C. Petrie
Gene Thomas
Ray F. Williams
Otis Wolfe
Richard Zimmerman

USS *Heywood L. Edwards* (DD-663)
NUC
★★★★★★★
Edward J. Bailey, Sr.
Maxie Eual Bennett
Nevin L. Blasser

USS *Heywood L. Edwards* (*cont.*)
Robert H. Chantler
James Wesley Garrett
Daniel Pick

USS *Howorth* (DD-592)
★★★★★
Oscar Blank
Russell A. Bramble ♥
Curtis O. Branson
Richard Chaney
Jay V. Grimm
Henry Hamner
A.R. Kephart
William F. Lamp'l, Jr.
Robert B. Lyons ♥
Adrian Keith Matchett
John A. McCoy
James Leon McNairy, Sr.
Larry Nelson
Robert D. (Don) Peterson
Orvill Raines ♥ (KIA)
Osmand (Ozzie) Schwiesow
Milan (Smiley) Smilinich ♥
Collie C. Stigall, Jr.
Harold B. Sutherland
Ed C. Wilkins

USS *Hugh W. Hadley* (DD-774)—*PUC*
★
Elmer W. Allen ♥
Calvin A. Borror ♥
L.B. (Pete) Boyd ♥
Robert I. Eaton, Jr. ♥
Ernest (Ernie) Horton ♥
Charles D. Nelson
Alvin Safranek

USS *Hughes* (DD-410)
★★★★★★★★★★★★★★
Chester Bradley

Oliver Jones
Lloyd J. O'Brien
Cyril Namur Peat
Ellis Rittenhouse
Gordon Sayner
Anthony J. Skic
N. R. (Nick) Smith

USS *Hull* (DD-350)
★★★★★★★★★★

18 December
1944*

Patrick H. Douhan
Kenneth L. Drummond
Ray McDonald Guthrie (LAS)
Fredrick Clark Sloane (LAS)
George Louis Stipetich (LAS)
Austin Hamilton Travis (LAS)
Robert (Scotty) Wilson (LAS)

USS *Hutchins* (DD-476)
★★★★★★

John F. Doyle ♥
Bobby Lee Judd
Bob [Ole] Olston
Donald G. Seville

USS *Hyman* (DD-732)
★★

R. J. Acheson
DeVon Andersen
Paul Hommel
John Warren Jones, Jr.
William C. Knoll
Donald N. Milbrandt
Robert F. Moldenhauer
Raymond Novotny
Mike Padavic
Kenneth Poelker

*Sunk during typhoon.

USS *Ingraham* (DD-694)—*NUC*
★★★★
Edelbert (John) Potempa
Oscar Yates

USS *Irwin* (DD-794)—*NUC*
★★★★★★
John (Obie) O'Bannon
William Herman Smith

USS *Isherwood* (DD-520)
★★★★★
T. D. (Tex) Austin
Forst Blankenship
Jesse R. Campbell ♥ (KIA)
Bill Fetters
Luciano J. Filadoro ♥ (KIA)
Clyde E. Griffith
Elvan M. Hall ♥
James B. Lenihan
Attilio Santangelo ♥ (KIA)
Richard K. Watson ♥ (2)
Melborn Eugene Wilson ♥ (KIA)

USS *Killen* (DD-593)
★★
Raymond E. Cloud
Charles Conlee
Donice Copeland
Harold R. Johnson

USS *Kimberly* (DD-521)
★★★★★
Wayland M. Boren
Louis Boyett
James Dalton
Henry LeRoy DeWitt
Henry W. Fuller

Robert Gacke
James E. Gibson, Jr.
Arthur McArthur
Curtis O. McDougle
Richard Young

USS *La Vallette* (DD-448)
★★★★★★★★★
Robert E. Lynch
Joe Winstead
Eustace Warren Wood

USS *Laffey* (DD-724)
★★★★★
Lawrence R. Delewski
Lloyd N. Hull
Ross Epworth Peterson ♥ (KIA)
Aristides S. Phoutrides
O. Glen Radder
S. D. (Bob) Robertson
Edward Samp, Jr. ♥
Oliver J. Spriggs

USS *Lamson* (DD-367)
★★★★★
John R. Carter
Lawrence Gean Christiansen ♥ (KIA)
Hank Pericle ♥

USS *Leutze* (DD-481)
★★★★★
Eugene Balinski
Ted O. Barkley
Lewis W. Campbell, Jr.
Malcolm Fortson, Jr.
DeVal Gillette
John R. Goff ♥

Clarence (Doc) Koepke
James Thomas Merideth
John Perkins
Dennis Roche
Walter J. Summ

USS *Little* (DD-803)
★★

3 May
1945

Walton Carter Brock
Alfred A. Piazza
Franklyn A. Whall

USS *Longshaw* (DD-559)
★★★★★★★★★

18 May
1945

Omer L. Bacon ♥
Frank C. Clark
William L. Davidson ♥
Henry H. Deane ♥
Harry Leonard
James R. Macomber ♥
Joseph G. Schneider ♥

USS *Lowry* (DD-770)
NUC
★★★★

Earl R. Bishop
William Kelton Holder ♥
Claude Woodring (Woody) Pearson

USS *Luce* (DD-522)
★★★★★

4 May
1945

Ashton O. (Sonny) Jones
Charles B. Robinson ♥ (KIA)
John R. (Jack) Wickens ♥ (KIA)

USS *Mahan* (DD-364)
★★★★★

7 December
1944

Paul Hendricks
George Pendergast

USS *Mannert L. Abele* (DD-733)
★★

12 April
1945

Richard (Dick) Aukerman
William R. Bays ♥
Gordon E. Chambers
Robert Frederick Delap ♥
Alfred M. Garcia
Jack Gordon Hendrix ♥ (KIA)
Marvin Keith Jacobs
Donald Kemlein ♥
Nick Korompilas
Anthony (Wes) La Bua ♥ (KIA)
Jim Morris
Robert F. Patton*
James Daryl Rano ♥ (KIA)
Jack E. Utterback ♥ (KIA)

USS *Melvin* (DD-680)
★★★★★★★★★

Paul O. Avery
William R. Campbell, Jr.
Edgar A. (Ed) Hawk
Curtiss Houghton, Jr.
William A. Robie
Alfred J. Roby, Jr.†

USS *Monssen* (DD-798)
★★★★★★★★

Ralph J. Bennett
Harry J. Gaitley
Zygmunt (Ziggy) Doroba
Virgil Melvin

*Also served aboard USS *Intrepid* (CV-11).
†Brother of Richard W. Roby, USS *Gambier Bay* (CVE-73), VC-10.

USS *Morris* (DD-417)
★★★★★★★★★★★★★★★★
David M. Aronsohn
Robert T. Foley ♥ (KIA)
Joe A. Gallegos
Don W. Greenwalt
Leo E. Labaj ♥ (KIA)
Harold Joseph Pettick Peters
Otis L. Pierce

USS *Mugford* (DD-389)
★★★★★★★
James R. Cofer
George R. Garmon, Jr.

USS *Mullany* (DD-528)
★★★★★★★
Henry Lee (Slim) Caulder
Matt Caulfield
Homer (Rocky) Jacobsen ♥
Harlan Johnson
Gerald Lundgren
Elmore N. Scott
Harmon C. Thompson, Jr.
John C. Wiessler

USS *Murray* (DD-576)
★★★★★★★★★★★
Gilbert L. Ericson
Glendon O. Flora
George S. Mabee
Joseph R. Morris
Howard Emmitt Turner

USS *Mustin* (DD-413)
★★★★★★★★★★★★★★
Benjamin Paul (Speedy) Brannon
Horace E. Buck
Dale Payne

Albert J. Reale
James E. Robinson
John C. Taylor
Natale J. Tigano
Dale Woodruff

USS *Newcomb* (DD-586)
★★★★★★★ *NUC*
Theodore E. (Ted) Baker
John Bennard ♥
Harold L. Haynes
Raymond (Hoffer) Hoffman
Royce W. Holyfield
Joseph LaValle ♥
Stewart F. Powers
Robert Reid ♥ (2)
William R. (Bill) Smith
Victor John Souza ♥
Richard Spencer
Alfred Tiboldo ♥ (KIA)

USS *O'Brien* (DD-725)
★★★★★★
Avon R. Blevins
Edward Daley Cosden
Thomas Roger Joseph
Paul Norris
Sydney (Syd) Schafman ♥ (2)
Ray Woods

USS *Paul Hamilton* (DD-590)
★★★★★★★
Cecil L. Gray
Martin Luther Long
Paul Tausend

USS *Picking* (DD-685)
★★★★★
Edward (Ed) Gavin
William Ruprecht
Robert Wichmann

USS *Preston* (DD-795)
★★★★★★
Henry Geldersma ♥
Claude R. Kinder
Fred D. Underwood

USS *Pringle* (DD-477)
★★★★★★★★★★★
16 April
1945

Jacob Bagby
Logan Bond
Warren H. Chapple ♥ (KIA)
Robert J. Cunningham
Mathew A. Dymek ♥
Mike Goettina
Henderson Hemphill
William L. Herman ♥ (2)
Joseph Hoffer ♥ (KIA)
Milton Mapou ♥ (2)
Sylvester Sandelier ♥
Elmer Ray Scarbrough ♥
Basil Sweet

USS *Purdy* (DD-734)—*NUC*
★
Weldon (Web) Boley
John (Jack) Curran ♥
Samuel Humphreys Davis III ♥
Robert F. Grose
Elbert (Curtis) Henson
H. Jack Krome
Dale R. Snyder
John Tiffany
Kenneth E. Vogel

USS *Putnam* (DD-757)
★★★
Bill Banton

Robert K. Cravens
George Hansen
William Harrison
Vernon Keith Leonard
John Anthony Ortelle
Otis Henry Payne, Sr.
Pete Visalli

USS *Ralph Talbot* (DD-390)
★★★★★★★★★★★★
Orville J. Docktor

USS *Reid* (DD-369)
★★★★★★
Leonard L. Olson

11 December   Jesse N. Pickeral
1944

USS *Richard P. Leary* (DD-664)
★★★★★★★★
Roy Crawford
Lee Dawdy
John J. Di Palma
Merle W. Dumdei
Robert J. (Bob) Durand
Francis E. Gauthier
Nicholas Hoyda
A. Robert Read
L. William Seidman
Jack M. Threatt
John Ben Wicker
Clifton C. Williams
Leon Wolper
William H. Young

USS *Saufley* (DD-465)
★★★★★★★★★★★★★★★★★
Gordie Domico

USS *Sigsbee* (DD-502)
★★★★★★★★★★★
Clyde Gordon Ferguson

USS *Spence* (DD-512)
PUC (Destroyer Squadron 23)
★★★★★★★★
18 December
1944*
Robert E. Cope (LAS)
Roy Louis Merritt (LAS)
Harold Anthony Monnig (LAS)
Albert Rosley
Alexander Sepanski (LAS)
Dean C. Strahm
Robert L. Strand (LAS)

USS *Sproston* (DD-577)
★★★★★
Claud Hefner
Max D. Shiley
C. L. (Ledge) Ward

USS *Stanly* (DD-478)
PUC (Destroyer Squadron 23)
★★★★★★★★★★
Irvin D. Brewer
Sylvester (Hilly) Hillesheim
John C. Lott, Jr.
James Chauncey Rice

USS *Sterett* (DD-407)
★★★★★★★★★★★★★
Gerald E. Taafe

*Sunk during typhoon.

USS *Stormes* (DD-780)
★
John J. Canty ♥
James D. Crull
Edwin D. Gilbert
Harry E. Halvorson
Roy H. Lanes
Robert Edward Mitchell
Harlan S. Nice
James L. Schrock

USS *Trathen* (DD-530)
★★★★★★★★
Clifford D. Cline
Gilbert F. Jarrell
John (Kutsagoitz) Kaye
William (Bill) Powell

16 June
1945

USS *Twiggs* (DD-591)
★★★★
Alfred O. (Bud) Emig III
Vincent Grella ♥ (KIA)
Charles W. Knittel
Joe McDonough ♥
Robert Melville
George Minni ♥ (KIA)
Leo L. Preston ♥
Joseph L. Sanchez
Donald R. Witmer ♥

USS *Wadsworth* (DD-516)—*PUC*
★★★★★★★
Tito Aquinaga
W. V. (Tuck) Blankinship ♥
William B. Boa
Harvey Bloom
Don Bullock
John E. Dodge
Melvin J. (Mel) Fortney

Paul A. Herman
Richard M. Lowe
Bob C. Matheny
William D. Miskill
George P. Pollock

USS *Walke* (DD-723)
★★★★★★

John D. Caldwell
George P. Ducousso ♥ (KIA)
Benjamin Edward Hall, Jr.
Warren Kenneth Mathews ♥
William (Bill) Rugh ♥

USS *Wickes* (DD-578)
★★★★★

Charles (Chuck) Ehlinger
Jack Fassino
Richard C. Holt

USS *William D. Porter* (DD-579)
★★★★

Thomas L. Selby

10 June
1945

USS *Wilson* (DD-408)
★★★★★★★★★★★

Ray Holder
Darrol Ottow
Richard Ryman

USS *Zellars* (DD-777)
★

Broadus (Bill) Bailey
John R. Mohr ♥ (KIA)
T. C. (Ted) Slugocki
William E. (Wes) Smith

DE–Destroyer Escorts

USS *Bowers* (DE-637)
★★★★
Robert Graves
Frank Martinez
Anthony Natale
Henry J. Seeba

USS *Bright* (DE-747)
★
Andrew Chester Mushensky
Donald Winslow Randall

USS *John C. Butler* (DE-339)
★★★★★
Paul J. Stuhlreyer

USS *O'Neill* (DE-188)
★★
Harry S. Brewer
James Creighton

USS *Rall* (DE-304)—*NUC*
★★★
Richard W. Graves

USS *Stafford* (DE-411)
★★
Ben J. Bryant

DM–Destroyer Minelayers

USS *Aaron Ward* (DD-773/DM-34)—*PUC*
★
Charles Chester Jewett, Jr.
John J. Morgan ♥ (KIA)
Bruce M. Muirhead
Carl Schroeter ♥ (KIA)
Raymond A. Smith

USS *Adams* (DD-739/DM-27)—*NUC*

★

Richard (Dick) Fye

USS *Gwin* (DD-772/DM-33)—*NUC*

★★★★

Garth F. Braithwaite

Richard J. Hausman

Francis R. Torrey

USS *Harry F. Bauer* (DD-738/DM-26)—*PUC*

★★★★

Fred H. Bell ♥

Wilfred Morgan

Robert M. Morgenthau (XO)

John J. (Jack) Wild

USS *Henry A. Wiley* (DD-749/DM-29)—*PUC*

★★★

Elton J. Benton

Harvey S. Jacobs

Donald J. DeSoller

William R. Horner

William E. Tucker

USS *J. William Ditter* (DD-751/DM-31)—*NUC*

★

Wayne Barker, M.D.

Bertram D. Bekemeyer

William I. Bradley

George H. Cambria ♥

James Verdun Creasman

Roland A. Du Sault

Keith Albert Emerson

Edward C. Faytak

James E. Fleenor
Dudley V. Frye ♥
Oscar James Jarvis
August J. Larney
Eugene A. Reese

USS *Lindsey* (DD-771/DM-32)
★★
Walter L. Gau
Robert V. Halabi ♥ (KIA)
Olen Eugene Jewett ♥ (KIA)
Paul (P. D.) LaRochelle ♥
David D. Lingard
Leonard (Pete) Petersen ♥
Elden Reed Van Wagoner
Harold A. Voss
James Robert E. Wilson ♥
Dean (Buster) Wiseman ♥ (KIA)

USS *Shea* (DD-750/DM-30)—*NUC*
★
George Lyman Barker (KIA)
Edward T. Horak
Claude C. Slusher, Jr.

DMS–Destroyer Minesweepers

USS *Ellyson* (DD-454/DMS-19)
★★★★★★★
Dwight Donnewald

USS *Hobson* (DD-464/DMS-26)—*PUC*
★★★★★★
Arthur LaFlamme

USS *Macomb* (DD-458/DMS-23)
★★★★★
James R. Tankersley
Robert J. Wynn

USS *Rodman* (DD-456/DMS-21)
★★★★★
Richard Van Zandt
Hampton Lee Warner

LCS(L)–Landing Craft Support, Large

LCS Flotilla Four
Joseph Allen Dodson, Jr.
Neill Phillips (CO)

LCS(L)-7
★★
David Demeter

16 February
1945

LCS(L)-12
★
William Hurney

LCS(L)-19
★
Daryl Babler

LCS(L)-27
★★★
Harry G. Meister

LCS(L)-31
PUC
★★
Robert A. Wells

LCS(L)-32—NUC
★★
Connell C. Medley
Joseph I. Wiskotoni

LCS(L)-34
★★
Edward V. Hathaway (XO) ♥

LCS(L)-35
★★★
Henry E. Henke
Vernon Kolen

LCS(L)-37
★
G. T. Molstein

LCS(L)-38
★
Edward J. Anderson

LCS(L)-44
★★
Clayton J. Burden
Nisi Ligor Dionis
James D. Phillips

LCS(L)-47
★★
Lawrence S. Moore

16 February
1945

LCS(L)-49
★★
Robert E. Alexander ♥
Edward G. Steenbergen
William Earl Travers ♥ (KIA)

LCS(L)-51
PUC
★★
Virgil C. Branch

LCS(L)-52
★★
Charles Lawrence Cullen
Nick Stoia
Virgil Thill

LCS(L)-54
★★★
Harold Tolmasky

LCS(L)-55
★★
Louis V. Plant

LCS(L)-57
★
C. A. Philippe Von Hemert
Harry L. Smith (CO)

LCS(L)-61
★
A. P. (Pete) Jensen
James W. Kelley (CO)
Mark V. Sellis (XO)

LCS(L)-64
★
John E. Littleton (XO)
Joseph C. McLendon

LCS(L)-65
★
Lloyd O. Daniels

LCS(L)-66
★
Robert P. Grimes

LCS(L)-74
★★
Donald A. Wiegele

LCS(L)-82
NUC
★
John A. Rooney

LCS(L)-86
NUC
★
Oscar L. Russell
William John Mason

LCS(L)-87
★
Rosse V. Long

LCS(L)-89
★
Ralph H. Magoon

LCS(L)-99
★
O. Landon Miles (CO)
Dorris M. Phelps

LCS(L)-102
★
J. Raymond Weddell

LCS(L)-109
★
George Gottridge
Eugene M. Labor
Frank J. Pugel
Martin L. Smith (CO)
Joseph Steinberg

LCS(L)-114
★
Gerald Mefferd (CO)
Arthur L. Reeves
James D. Shofestall

16 April
1945

LCS(L)-116
★
Ray B. Davis
Lewis P. Reed

LCS(L)-118
NUC
★
Earl H. Blanton
Charles D. Towers

LCS(L)-119
★
Daniel R. Friday
Lewis J. Shioleno, Sr.

LCS(L)-122
NUC
★
Richard M. McCool (CO) ♥

LCS(L)-125
★
Herman R. (Buzz) Stewart

LSM (R)–Landing Ship, Medium, Rocket

LSM (R)-189
★
NUC
James M. Stewart (CO)

LST–Landing Ship, Tank

LST-538
★
Harry W. Jarrett, Jr.

Patrol Craft

PC-1128
★★
James E. Gilbert (CO)
Norman E. Smith

★ Index ★